D1413283

Michael Brown

MARKED
TO DIE

SIMON AND SCHUSTER   NEW YORK

Published by Simon and Schuster
A Division of Simon & Schuster, Inc.
Simon & Schuster Building
Rockefeller Center
1230 Avenue of the Americas
New York, New York 10020
SIMON AND SCHUSTER and colophon are registered trademarks
of Simon & Schuster, Inc.
Designed by Eve Kirch
Manufactured in the United States of America

10   9   8   7   6   5   4   3   2   1

Library of Congress Cataloging in Publication Data
Brown, Michael Harold, date.
    Marked to die.
    1. Festa, Gerard.   2. Italian American criminals—
Biography.   3. Organized crime—United States—Case
studies.   I. Title.
HV6248.F34B76 1984   364.1′092′4 [B]   83–20274
ISBN 0–671–45090–5

For Kathy

Facilis est descensus Averni.

PROLOGUE

For some reason the noises bothered me. Throughout the months I had
spent at the "hideout" there had been moments of minor edginess—an
unfamiliar car with plates from another state, or a van parked for an
inordinate length of time on the country road that curved past the small
gray clapboard house—but those had turned out to be false alarms.
The sounds I now heard behind the home of mobster Jerry Festa
sounded suspiciously like human footsteps. And because of the isolated
location of his house, and the late hour, I knew it was unlikely that
someone would simply be happening by. The nearest gathering place
was a social club operated by a veterans' organization miles to the
north.

The noises stopped. I decided it must have been some forest animal,
and headed for the road where my car was parked. I had been to Newark recently and Festa was afraid I might be trailed back to him. I
never parked directly in front of his house.

A year before, when I first met Festa, there had been a similarly
unnerving experience. That spring a television news director from
Pennsylvania had approached me to interview the hoodlum, who had
got in touch with the station through two intermediaries. I learned that
Festa was a local product who had moved to Newark and wound up
in the midst of a murder—and a covey of unusually violent criminals.
He had testified against those criminals and, with his large family, had

7

been placed in the Witness Protection Program. Festa was eager now to speak out against a government program which he charged had not adequately helped him and his family adjust to society after their identities had been changed.

At first I declined the task of questioning him, wary of another mob story and uninterested in the program itself. But the news director, Nick Lawler, was keen on the possible scandals Festa could unearth in the Scranton area, and he finally persuaded me to conduct the clandestine interviews for his station.

When the day came to meet Festa, I did so in a small motel—a Red Roof Inn—near Harrisburg, Pennsylvania. He was accompanied by a former state policeman carrying a shotgun; I was surrounded by a television crew and equipment. Everyone seemed suspicious of everyone else, and Festa was working a black piece of cloth over his head with small holes cut for his mouth, nose, and eyes to prevent his being recognized by his current neighbors. The room was muggy and full of tension, and outside a July thunderstorm was drenching the highway. As Festa began telling me his story, asserting that his former cronies still meant to have their revenge, there was a sudden loud noise from the hall, and everybody in the room jumped. But a maid's mop had simply banged against our door.

I spent the next several days interviewing Festa and his second security guard—his eldest daughter, known as Janet—and became intrigued with what had happened to his family: his wife, four other children, and a cousin. Though Festa provided a fascinating glimpse into the low levels of organized crime, I was still reluctant to pursue his story. But I gave him my phone number, and occasionally I would hear from him. A few weeks later I was able to make my first trip to his new home, which was in remote farm country.

Inside were two teenage daughters and two preteen sons. They said virtually nothing and kept out of sight in the kitchen, throwing only an occasional furtive glance at me. They also spent some time tossing a football in the yard, to which their parents restricted them. Festa's wife, Rose, was a ravaged woman, tranquilized, traumatized, and hopeless. She was wracked both by the illnesses which had attacked her body and by haunting images from the criminal past, which had been psychologically devastating. As Rose and I talked, Festa's cousin Marie, a woman in her sixties, flitted into view on several occasions, only to disappear into the rear rooms or the back yard, where she tended the dogs and hung out the laundry. Unaccustomed to visitors but quite hospitable when they did arrive, the Festas placed before me a hearty Italian meal that Marie had cooked.

The children still said very little at dinner. Afterward I thanked Marie for the delicious meal and was struck by how very shy she was. In seven years of living as a fugitive she had rarely talked with any strangers. I was also impressed at how grateful she was for my compliments, and how tired and beaten she appeared. Not at all the criminal type, she was a maternal woman who now found herself in a house where a shotgun was always at the ready, the curtains were drawn, and a metal pole was fitted behind the front door as a barricade. Until I met her and Rose I was not inclined to write about this fugitive family. But that visit changed my mind.

Shortly after my first journey there I began staying with the family for protracted periods of time. Although neither I nor the law enforcement agents I talked with felt there was currently any massive search for Festa by "the mob," he was constantly terrified of retribution, and perhaps I became susceptible to these grim apprehensions. Also, my research was beginning to substantiate many of the wilder stories Festa had told me, and though I'd been in situations far riskier than staying at his hideout, I had nonetheless become sensitized to any movements near his house.

And that night I again heard the rustling. It approached from the woodland near the house, then moved up into the back yard. Too loud for a rabbit or muskrat. A deer? Or maybe some kids sneaking back there to drink beer or smoke pot? I crouched down, trying to identify the cadence of the noises. Then came a welcome silence which lasted a full minute. Again I started toward my car.

The footsteps returned. Raised in the city, I was not skillful at deciphering the sounds of the forest. But what I did know was that the motions were now of longer duration and were heading directly for Festa's back porch. Sure he was still just inside the front door, I quietly let him know what was happening. "Jerry," I said. "Take a look out your back window. I heard something outside."

He sounded greatly flustered. "What?" he barked.

"Just take a look out back," I said. "It sounds like an animal back there, but I want to make sure."

Festa dashed across the living room to grab his shotgun from under the couch. Then he marched out the front door to the western side of the house. Before I caught up with him two loud explosions echoed through the overgrown gullies. He was standing behind a corner of the building pointing the shotgun toward the back yard.

"Hold it," I said. "Somebody down the road's going to hear this. It's probably a deer!"

I heard a noise on the second floor of the house and looked up to see Janet observing the scene from a bedroom window. She was a restless sleeper. And she kept a gun near her bed.

Again I urged that we go back inside. Festa ignored me. He unleashed another shotgun blast as a warning and fell back behind the corner of the house, listening intently. "Never the fuck mind," he finally said angrily. He stared into the darkness. "If it's Johnny Quartuccio sneaking back there, then that motherfucker's gone."

BOOK ONE

THE MIST AND THE DARKNESS

I am Newark, forger of men,
Forger of men, forger of men—
Here at a smithy God wrought, and flung
Earthward, down to this rolling shore,
God's mighty hammer I have swung,
With crushing blows that thunder and
Roar . . .
    —Clement Wood, "The Smith of Gold"

I. A Sound of Sirens

THE CITY OF NEWARK stands at the still backwaters of the Atlantic Ocean, a center of regional industry and the locus for despair. On clearer days, when a hard northwesterly rinses the plains, the glass of new office buildings reflects the decaying brownstone shell. More often the city's features are cloaked in a lemon haze of shimmering oxides; towering vats of oil and the stanchions of an antique liftbridge are phantoms in an evening's smog. To the south and east, elevated highways rise from the bulrush swamp like the spiny remains of ancient reptiles, and course past heaps of desolate landfill.

On the central streets, litter rolls on the walks like wind-blown thistle; bridges and monuments are scarred, scorched. In the swelter of an August noon, youngsters call in rousing Spanish from under the spray of a fire hydrant that is rusted and gnarled. But their relief is short-lived, and not a block away, welfare lines are long. At dusk, near tarpaper tenements, gangs of youth gather to set old storefronts and drums of trash afire. The inferno is enlivened by the mars bubbles on cruisers belonging to Newark's city police, for as they hurry by rubbled lots, their pulsing red lights turn shattered glass into glowing embers.

Though in the state of New Jersey, Newark seems more an obscure borough of New York City than a metropolis in its own right. As in other blighted sectors of the nation's largest city, nine miles to the east, Newark's older residents (retired barbers, bakers, masons, firemen,

13

contractors, and longshoremen) venture forth only in the day. It is then that the commuters, three hundred thousand strong, stretch the twenty-four-square-mile town to its seams. Chemicals, textiles, electrical parts, and sides of beef, and a multitude of other products, move in truck caravans along the New Jersey Turnpike to converge with the main line of the Penn Central Railroad, the Newark International Airport, and the expansive seaports near Ellis Island, where foreigners, many of them of Italian and German origin, were once graciously waved ashore.

In the light of day too are seen statistics born of the night. Though it was not quite as large a crime colony as Houston, and was behind Miami in the drug trade and by a handful of homicides, Newark in 1981 generated a higher robbery index than any other city, and substantially more arsons than Dallas, Atlanta, Philadelphia, *and* Miami combined. With a murder and assault rate twice that of New York City, and registration of 76,865 offenses by authorities in Essex County, of which Newark is a part, this netherworld had become the core of violence for all the Middle Atlantic states. Here, in broad daylight, at the very busiest corner, a policeman directing traffic was assaulted by a psychopath who planted an axe in his back.

Leaders of cities and towns in this area have fallen like dominoes, in some instances charged outright with working for recognized figures in organized crime. In northern New Jersey, during recent times, indictments have been handed up against a United States senator, a couple of state senators, an assemblyman, two superior court judges, several prosecutors, a leader of the New Jersey Senate, three police chiefs, the president of a state health care association, a newspaper publisher, a school board president, a former president of the state bar, a county Democratic chairman, a lawyer accused of selling babies, an array of prominent bankers and businessmen, and even a Baptist minister said to have taken a bribe—-to name a few. Though not all the charges have led to conviction, Newark has observed an impressive parade of elected officials in its courtrooms, including its last two mayors. The city has also seen a school principal assassinated for wronging some local mob associates. And in nearby Passaic an elderly man was mugged so often police offered him a walkie-talkie to carry along with his cane.

When the hoodlums of nearby port cities are considered—the auto thieves of Elizabeth and the burglars of Bayonne—and when its position as the hub of illicit lottery, racial violence, and gangland murder is taken into account—the Newark area, over the course of the past two decades, has transcended ranking on a mere regional scale. Instead it has become a strong contender for the title of America's capital of crime.

Up in the North Ward, Marie Festa had seen the beginning signs of this distress, in the 1960s, from the rackety interior of the Number 13 bus that took her to work in a pork slaughterhouse each day. Past spires and parks and Borden's Ice Cream, and beyond the department stores of downtown Broad Street, busted tires and mattresses were abandoned at curbside in long ugly heaps. The boulevards seemed worn to the cobblestone. Her plant was in a neighborhood of clamorous warehouses: Wood planks were set on dank concrete, and on wet days rancid fumes wafted in from the smokehouse. For twelve hours at a time she stood at the end of a wiener stuffer, surrounded by hardened lard.

But now it was Sunday, and there was relief in knowing the saints, prime among them her favorite, Saint Anthony, would subtly speak to her this day. Up at eight-thirty, the squat, middle-aged woman walked up the block to Our Lady of Good Counsel Church, diligently accepted the communion host, and, across the way, bought the *Daily News* and a breakfast bagel. A meat loaf was prepared for dinner and, having never married, she would eat it alone. She napped with the television on and before bed that night read more of a mystery novel. This was what Sunday was for: casual tasks and repose, which helped her to forget that the city she had adopted twenty-two years before, and had grown to love, was in unchanging and apparently unchangeable decline.

Eighty-six miles to the northwest, in Scranton, Pennsylvania, Marie's younger cousin, Gerard, a career thief and con man, spent his weekend frantically avoiding a search squad. He was in his thirties, an imposing man reaching the wiry height of six-five, and he had a brilliantined shock of wavy black hair and a voice deep and barbarous— characteristics that never made it easy to hide. Yet when the need arose he could move with impressive speed and grace; he had demonstrated this the Friday afternoon before, when his seven-year-old daughter interrupted a conversation he was having with his estranged wife, calling, "Daddy! Daddy! There's a bunch of men here looking at your truck."

Festa had sprung to the kitchen window and peered through the flimsy curtains. In a cortege coming up the front steps were three police officers and Lee Mecka, a muscular detective in a fedora. With a few giant strides, Festa made it through the apartment's back door onto the fire escape, jarring loose the stubborn ladder and making a dash, just in front of the search party, over a headland and into the autumnal trees.

Jerry emerged an hour or two later. The sky was turning narrow and oppressive; it was nearly dusk. He made his way to his girl friend's apartment on the south side, where Rose, a shapely woman of twenty-six with dark blond hair, greeted him with gentle, weary eyes. She was accustomed to his being in trouble. By Rose's side was her daughter Janet, whose father had never been determined for sure. "We'll bring the kid with us," Festa offered huskily. "Come on. We gotta blow out of here."

From there they walked to the apartment of Rose's alcoholic uncle, where Festa, an eye to the windows, paced through the night thinking of the parole he had violated and the latest charge against him: fraud. He had bilked a dentist's wife for several thousand dollars in phony home repairs, a manner of larceny that supported his drinking and gambling but for which he had spent nearly five of the past six years in prison. (His prey was the elderly, or lonely recluses; homes with a window bedecked in lace curtains, or a yard overrun by uncut grass, were signs to him that a mark, a "meatball," might be awaiting his artistry. Wearing a businesslike green uniform and a caring smile, he assumed the role of an ambitious young helper who had happened to notice a chimney needing insulation or box gutters that were awry.)

Rose slept fitfully with her child. She had been through comparable upheavals before, with violent boy friends who kept her on edge. She had no home. Her mother was mentally ill, her father had disowned her, and she could not stay with her stepparents any more. For years Rose and her daughter had wandered haplessly around Scranton, and she had decided to take her chances with Jerry, who was more reliable than her other paramours and was finally getting a divorce.

At eleven the next morning the cops somehow found him again, and once more he escaped through the back, this time jumping from a second-story window. Bounding a fence, he pretended to the next-door neighbor that he was reading the utility meters. He slipped into the basement and watched the detectives climb the stairs to the uncle's apartment, make a peevish search, and leave.

He then went back to the apartment, where he and Rose spent the rest of the day fixed to the windows, moving only when night came.

Along with young Janet, they stole through the quiet streets and alleyways to a gas station, where they hitched a ride to the country and the home of Jeanie, a distant relative about Festa's age.

The travelers had worked their way past a huge junk yard and a shoe-shaped reservoir, safely circumventing the center of town. A small, leafy version of Newark, to which its rails and roadways are intimately linked, Scranton is also a concoction of warehouses and truck interstates once sustained by the heaviest of industry, iron and steel. But the populace here, a hundred and four thousand, at the time, and growing old, came chiefly to mine the anthracite—hard, clean-burning coal, which was soon depleted; around the city were blackened waste banks and the fathomless shanks of forsaken mines. In the distant valley, where the shops and department stores were, the silhouette of an old train station stood in smoke-gray stone.

The trio had headed into a shoulder of the Pocono Mountains and the hamlet of Elmhurst, where Jeanie lived in a neat two-story house with horse stables and a big, overgrown pasture. Throughout the vicinity were springs and ponds obscured by misty mountains and fallow farms where deer could hide.

Jeanie was not at home but they had been admitted to the house by her sweet and senile mother, who cordially led them into the living room. She did not wait up for her daughter, a party-loving alcoholic who would surely be home late.

When Jeanie sailed in on a day's worth of beer and a scotch called "Ten-High," she was with yet another new boy friend. "What in hell youse doing here?" she asked, casting a fond eye on Jerry, with whom she had once had a brief affair.

"My car broke down about a mile from here," Festa lied. "Figured we'd drop in and spend the night."

Jeanie gave Rose a dirty look and stumbled to the bedroom, but she soon returned wearing only panties, a bra and a sexy expression. Festa urged her back into the bedroom but Jeanie persisted, returning once again to the living room, this time in the raw.

Despite Rose's embarrassed presence, Jeanie sat in front of them obscenely resting a leg up on a coffee table and nuzzling closer. She wanted to talk to Jerry about the time they had gone riding together. "You remember the stables?" she asked pointedly. There was mischief in her eyes.

"Lookit, Jeanie, I got no time to fool around," he finally said. "I got a problem, a big problem. The law's after me and this cop named Mecka's really pushing it."

Jeanie stammered that she just happened to know the detective. She had met him in one of the bars, and she could go and talk to him the next morning.

"Christ no, forget it!" he said. "I don't want you talking to nobody. It's a bum fucking rap."

When Jeanie tried to guide his hand to her body, Festa swooped her up and carried the drunken woman into her bedroom, telling her boy friend, "Chrissakes, keep her here!"

In the morning Jeanie seemed to have forgotten her indiscretions of the preceding night. She put a chicken in the oven for her three guests and left with her boy friend for more ale. But her friendliness this early Sunday carried with it a suspicious ring, and twice she phoned back to the house to talk to her mother, emphatically instructing her to make sure Jerry stayed for dinner. "They'll be right back," her mother said absently to Jerry, hanging up after the second call. "They're just looking for some strawberries. She said, don't worry if some cars come around. It's just friends." The old woman shook her head in resignation. "I swear I don't understand that girl half the time. I hope it don't mean another one of her crazy parties."

At this Festa threw an alarmed look at Rose. "Cars?" he said. His neck was tingling. "Nah, I don't dig that." They prepared to leave, hurriedly collecting their clothes, which Rose had washed that morning, and putting them on, still damp. As they did so the phone rang a third time. Now, for some reason, Jeanie wanted Jerry's voice on the phone. Festa suspected a cop was standing right next to her somewhere nearby.

As the fugitives left the house and started out the driveway, they suddenly heard car wheels hitting hard against the gravel at a turn-off down the road. Jerry grabbed Janet, who had been hopscotching near the front yard, and they made a break for the pasture. Crawling in the bushes near a stable, they watched as six vehicles, including Jeanie's truck, rolled up the driveway and rocked to a halt. Out of one of them strode Detective Lee Mecka.

Janet held her mother tightly. She was a frail girl of seven with fine blond hair and a wan, thin face. Low in the mountain laurel, motionless as a cataleptic, the young girl could hear a police squawk box above the soothing rustle of leaves. The house itself had by now been surrounded by men with shotguns, and two patrol cars were driving back and forth on an old, overgrown bridle path a hairsbreadth away. Rose and Jerry whispered in Janet's ears to keep her from talking. When the patrols headed back toward the house for instructions and coffee, Festa led his companions to some heavier brush. There they flattened on their bellies.

To Rose the tension was suffocating, and at each sound of distant footsteps she trembled. Panic caught in her craw as it had when she was a child hiding in a coalbin from her abusive stepfather. Behind the rushes of emotion was the vague certainty that for better or worse her life would never be the same. She whispered hoarsely, "Maybe me and Janet should walk down the road, just leave. Tell them you took off somewhere."

Festa scowled. "Just stay down," he ordered. "They'll never fucking believe that." He watched the house with eyes that were chestnut in color, the irises rimmed with an odd band of gray. But this dull coloration belied his phenomenal acuity of vision, an ability to identify faces and cars at a quarter of a mile and to take mental snapshots of people and scenery that would be permanently on file.

When the cars stopped their circling Festa moved further back, to a clump of huckleberry bushes at the edge of the woodland. On the forest floor the leaf mold was thick and dry, and the sawtoothed weeds pinched like large mosquitoes. The afternoon sun, still strong enough to keep the air in the sixties despite a brisk breeze, glinted through the tree canopy onto sweet ferns and witch hazel.

A persistent bee flew near Rose and her child, but Janet was oblivious to most of these discomforts. She had learned long before to live in transient and spartan environments: as an infant she slept in a dresser drawer, and when Rose could finally afford a bed, it was in an attic flat across from a hardscrabble tavern.

Still, the little girl was bored and restless, and she kept saying in her piping voice, "Mommy, I'm hungry." Jerry solved this by making a game of it, breaking off a twig and pretending to eat it. He told Janet, "Mmm, good celery." She giggled and they played a little game of hide-and-seek.

Finally Detective Mecka walked out of the house with Jeanie, and from the distance they could hear a motor start. The cops were leaving. "Stay here for now," Festa told Rose. "And Chrissakes don't make any moves till you see me. They're gonna be back. We gotta find a better place." He crawled into the brush until the seedlings and brambles thickened. Then he got to his feet, crouched low, and was gone.

When she was alone with the child, Rose's mind raced between hazy thoughts and worst-case scenes. If she fled now, while he was gone, he would surely disappear from her life again, leaving her broke and alone. And she knew she loved him: his confident, tough way. Yet in her mind she saw shotguns, felt their searing blasts. And she knew from the hunters who hung out in the Scranton taverns that black bears lived here among the berry bushes. She mouthed the word to an entreaty: *"Our Father who art in Heaven . . . pray for us sinners . . ."* She heard a rabbit scampering and almost screamed.

Jerry hiked over a hilly grove and discovered a small ravine. The forest there was dense with stands of oak, maple, gum, white ash, and black cherry. He made his way back to Rose and Janet and led them to the gully, which they cleared of branches and moist leaves. Around them the forest still held its green, with only modest infusions of bronze and yellow. But within three weeks the timber would rival the splendid fall foliage of New England, a flaring mosaic of gold, scarlet, crimson, magenta.

"That filthy no-good cunt," Festa muttered at the thought of Jeanie. Rose cupped her hands near her mouth like a yodeler and lit a cigarette, blowing the smoke toward the ground. All the while there was the faint yelping of dogs in the distance.

"Where are them dogs coming from?" Rose asked.

Festa stared silently at the ground, rubbing his sweaty forehead. "I dunno," he replied. "Christ, I just hope that motherfuck ain't making a run at us with bloodhounds."

As the sun lowered, Rose said, "We'll never find our way out of here." She was whimpering, ready to give up, and he answered her with silence.

After a while he left them again and moved back toward the house. Jeanie's truck was still in the driveway and inside the lights were on. Before he could head back to the woods, a car pulled up. It was Mecka again. Now Festa himself was flustered: he was stranded here with no assurance the detective wouldn't extend the search into the night with floodlights, and Rose might panic and try to run away.

Not long afterward, however, Mecka reappeared on Jeanie's porch bidding a grateful good-bye. As Festa watched from the undergrowth, Jeanie's boy friend walked to the truck and carried back a case of beer.

Returning to the bivouac, Festa found Rose holding the sleeping child and sobbing. He stopped her talk of surrender by insisting that they leave the area and move in together somewhere out of state. For all they knew, he reminded her, Janet could be his child.

Long before, Festa had decided he and his first wife Dottie were beyond reconciliation. She had once had him arrested for aggravated assault, and though it was only one of twenty-two entries on his local rap sheet, and the charge was later dismissed, the incident remained an acute embarrassment to his family. And years before, when he was in the reformatory at Elmira, New York, for the swindle of another old lady, Dottie had sent him a cool divorce letter that arrived on December 10, which for him had always been a dismal and ominous day. (It was the same day that he had been accused of the Elmira crime to begin with, and on this date the woman who raised him, Marie's mother, his aunt, would die.) After receiving his wife's note he was disturbed enough to break a jail clerk's jaw, which landed him in solitary for thirty days. Consumed by the steel-gray infinitude and the bare routines (cocoa in the morning only, and nothing to read), he pounded on the walls until the pain welled up to his elbows. One night he dreamed about his dead mother, a lame Irishwoman; had she been alive—and they on speaking terms, for she had disowned him in the end—she would have told him to find someone else, to let Dottie go . . . With such ephemeral images came now, in the woods, memories less mundane: the inmate found hanging in a cell, and the rape victims. There was no chance of his going back to Dottie, any more than there was of surrendering to Mecka and heading for another cell.

He decided they should move toward the barking dogs, since there might be another house nearby. They came upon a clearing and a ramshackle farm. The dogs were there in a pen. Nearby was a dirt road on which they walked for four miles until it joined a two-lane highway.

Festa bent down beside the road and rubbed mud on his face, the guise of a man with car trouble. Soon a car pulled over and Festa told its driver he had broken his drive shaft. The man gave them a ride.

They were dropped off near a junk yard on the outskirts of town. They called an old friend named Pete, who had been Rose's steadiest customer when she worked the streets. He gave them an emergency ride to Newark, where Festa figured his cousin Marie would take them in for the time being. Surely Marie wouldn't mind. She had known him since he was an infant, and they were like sister and brother; he was as close as anyone she had. But Rose thought, "I don't even know her. How's she gonna take to living with a couple of tramps from Scranton?" Nevertheless, Rose once more went with the tide.

Climbing into the trunk of Pete's car, Festa said, "I don't wanna see no daylight till we hit Jersey."

Outside of Scranton the car ascended into the foothills, where the dense foliage deepened and a foreboding dark reached up from the hollows.

Rose was a nervous woman, already crushed in many ways. Old men had paid for her services since she was a teenager, and now she had a chance to break away from it with a man she had loved for years. And Janet—she did not want the girl to miss school while they were evading the law, and if the girl came with them the police would track them down through school registries. She decided to send her back to Scranton temporarily, to stay with her friend Fran.

They connected with the Pennsylvania Turnpike and made their way past the sedate frame houses of Wilkes-Barre on a discreet out-of-the-way course that took them arching through Hickory Run State Park and a game preserve. Past the airport at Allentown, just north of Philadelphia, they suddenly swept northeast across the pebbly, braided shallows of the Delaware River, skirting Trenton and the Brunswicks. Then they headed straight north.

Festa climbed out of the trunk at a rest stop, numbed by hours of cramped solitude, dizzy with the smell of tires. As they entered Essex County, alongside Newark Bay, the highways, even at so late an hour, burgeoned with trucks rolling shoulder to shoulder near the bracken inlet. At the thick-silt backwaters, waterfowl and muskrats had been rudely displaced by huge white-lit refineries, pipelines, and cylinders that climbed like vines in a sterile futuristic city. From the vents and stacks came rotten-egg vapors rolling forth like fog, and unsightly lots were jammed with old truck carriages, backhoes, sea crates, pallets, diesel pumps, and cranes. A huge petroleum tank was painted in red, white, and blue letters: GO NAVY.

At the center of the county was Newark's cream-and-buff skyline, constituted mainly by insurance firms, churches, and a multitude of old-vault banks. Confused by the crisscrossing boulevards, which fused together several congested parts of town, they wandered on Broad Street until they got their bearings and headed for the North Ward and the main drag of its Italian section, Bloomfield Avenue. Now and again in the twilight came the high, haunting whine of police sirens.

Each time he heard the sounds Festa's stomach grew tight. But the cruisers turned off before reaching them, or merely passed them by on the way to more urgent police matters. They made it to Lincoln Avenue, a quieter side street where, a half-dozen blocks down, on a corner, was a modest red-brick apartment building and Marie Festa's lonely basement flat. Set for another work week at the pork factory, she was getting what sleep she could before her rising time at five. Nowhere in the day just past, a September Sunday in 1964, had there been a clue that it would place her on an endless course that would alter her life, and the lives of those around her, in an unimaginable way.

Marie stirred and climbed from her bed as the buzzer sounded, followed by loud thuds at her thin front door. Alarmed, she grabbed a housecoat and ran her hands through her straight black hair. She approached the threshold and the tawny crucifix hanging over it.

"Oh, Jesus, what now? Overcharging again? Fleecing? Fighting?"

"They're trying to frame me," he snorted. "I got run out of town."

Marie pursed her lips and scowled but allowed her cousin in without hesitation. She had deep-set eyes and a pleasant, plump face. "Well, bring her in," she said when Festa told her his girl friend was waiting outside. "She can't very well stay in a car all night."

Rose told Pete to take Janet back to Scranton, where Fran, who lived in her apartment building, would look after the child. "Don't worry, babe," she said, turning to her daughter. "We'll send for you."

It was four in the morning, the beginning of a slow, winding way. Years would pass before she realized it, but for Marie, the spirit of innocence had vanished forever. Though she herself would commit no crimes, and would remain faithful to her Church oblations, she would find herself surrounded by a gang of professional criminals—fifty or so of them—who would strip her of her home, her belongings, her history. They would reduce her to a flesh-and-blood ghost, and rob her of her very name.

II. Cowboys of the Night

THE BASEMENT APARTMENT on Lincoln Avenue was at once turned into a shadowy fortress. The only sign of life inside was an occasional billowing of the shades as Festa peered out to check on the street traffic. He attached a sturdy new bolt to the door and answered the phone only if he knew beforehand who would be calling. To enter her own home after work Marie pressed a code on the buzzer.

Though with no more ingenuity than before, Lee Mecka expanded his hapless pursuit into Newark, alerting the Essex County authorities. But the detective never thought to approach Marie's apartment, and so Jerry would stay the remainder of the year there, grinding Pall Malls into an overflowing tray and playing cards with an older neighbor named Nanny. He ventured to the parking lot from time to time, but mostly he watched the soap operas.

When he materialized that early Monday morning, Marie had been not so much surprised as disappointed. Her cousin's whole life had consisted of hiding and escape of some sort, it seemed to her. From the age of four he had begun running away from home to be with his father, and there had been an embarrassing newspaper article about how his mother had to get a court order to retrieve him from her former husband. He was an emotional child with certain phobic fears: He had run from parades because of the drum rolls.

24

His father was Marie's closest uncle. She called him "Poppy." Between marriages he often lived in the same home as Marie, her sister, and her mother, whose husband had also left his family. Poppy held a variety of jobs—painter, wallpaperer, coal miner—and he had worked in a laundromat and later as a maintenance man in a state mental hospital. He had four sons by two other marriages, but none like Jerry, "The Big Fellow." That son had never accepted his parents' divorce and he showed it by being the great troublemaker in school, skipping classes and teasing the nuns as they swiped at him with chalkboard pointers. He also had been caught lifting a wallet from the five-and-dime store downtown, but that too he had gotten away with. While the clerk was calling for the police, he slipped down a back stairwell and through an alley.

He was certainly a mischievous child, looking up girls' skirts with a mirror as he did, but Marie, nine years his senior and herself a model of good behavior as a youngster, had always hoped he would grow out of it. Instead he ended up in a reformatory near Philadelphia. Marie's mother often visited him there and became an adopted parent of his. When he got out at the age of sixteen he went right to their place, a three-floor structure at Lee Court, where his father was also staying.

So he had been every bit as transient as Rose, and resentful of the instabilities in his own family. Though his cousin Marie had moved to New Jersey during his teenage years, she kept track of his exploits and his tendency toward trouble and accidents. On one occasion, as military police were taking him back to Fort Dix after he had gone AWOL, the paddywagon was hit by a truck and turned over. Another time, while he was assisting a disabled car on the highway, a passing car veered off the road and pinned him between two automobiles. But his good luck was just as noteworthy, and in the Army he was hot enough at craps to buy a new flight jacket and jump boots. He left the military to take up with his first wife, but they seemed always to have problems between them, and his gambling addiction carried over to the backroom clubs in downtown Scranton. There was hardly a bar there where Jerry had not gotten into a fight over some girl or won a memorable pot of money.

Jerry had a manner about him that was irresistibly appealing. No one could keep track of all the friends he made, except to note them as an unwholesome lot. With them he drank to oblivion, provoked more brutal barroom brawls, and learned about thievery. Something in his conscience had run amuck. He would later rob the doctor who gave him his marital blood test, cured a serious illness when he was two years old, and indeed had delivered him at Mercy Hospital. He started work as a home repairman and had quite an aptitude for carpentry, but naturally he grew bored with the legitimate end of it. He grossly overcharged his customers with the help of an assistant named Hank Ellis, or he conned people outright by playing on their sympathy.

About Rose, Marie knew almost nothing. But it was apparent the young woman had a hard life and was trying to escape it. Marie was impressed at how Rose, like herself, was humble, quiet, willing to work. Not long after their arrival Rose took a job in a greasy spoon to shore up the finances. It would last only a few weeks. Sensing that something was bothering her, Festa snuck into the diner one night and caught the manager trying to rub her buttocks. He stormed over and tore her apron off and knocked the guy over the counter. When Marie's plant wages were depleted, and even cigarette money was unavailable, Festa sold a pint of his blood at a seedy downtown clinic.

Rose had about given up on their being together. He seemed more loyal than most men she knew, and she realized he already had two daughters by Dottie. She did not believe he would leave his wife. Time and circumstances had finally worked in her favor, however, and she was happy they were living under the same roof. She was also somewhat fearful. Jerry's wide, leaden fists had functioned with gruesome effect in the Scranton beer gardens, where, as she knew, his fighting had antagonized half the city and had made him a legend to the other half. She had watched him charge clubs and knives during these fracases, and he could box a draw with a prizefighter named Brady. She may have seen him lose badly once or twice, but even then it was another paddywagon and not an ambulance that stopped him. Jukeboxes were overturned during his rampages, chairs turned to sticks, plate-glass windows shattered.

Festa's head was huge. His eyes were set in a raccoon's mask, the puffy dark tissue of an insomniac, and the left one was drowsy and askew, a souvenir from a huge black man called Big Sam. (They had squabbled over a pool table at Cooper's tavern, and though Festa managed to crack Sam's cheekbones with a cue ball, leaving him out cold, he had not done so before the eye was popped from the socket by Sam's desperately groping fingers.) His nose was long and bulbous at the end, running past high cheekbones, and though the wide nostrils and perpetual frown advertised a sour disposition, this he could dispel magically with a beaming grin. His thin Celtic lips were one of his mother's few legacies. Another was the Irish ostentation, a flamboyant showman-ship. When he played the guitar and sang his melancholy dirges—"A Certain Smile," or "Danny Boy"—the words were surprisingly soft and pained despite his gravelly, movie-gangster's voice.

Yet for Rose these intimidating characteristics were also a source of security and affection. So were his confident gait and modish clothes. Sometimes it seemed to Rose as if he could move heaven and earth if he wanted, and except for just now, his pockets were always stuffed with money. Just as she had seen him bust somebody's teeth, relocate a nose, she had also witnessed his peculiar moods of sentimentality and generosity. Often he bought the whole bar round after round of drinks, or paid an old wino's rent. Robin Hood, she teased.

Jerry and Rose had led the fast low life in the underbelly of Scran-ton, a world where unwanted babies were left at a hospital's front steps or near a supermarket. Their circle of acquaintances had included pill poppers, purse snatchers, burglars, welfare pimps, and crooked con-tractors like himself: Jerry attracted them like a magnet. He was the shining star of their clique, the brains and brawn, and it was his name that appeared in the headlines ("Festa Pays $25 Fine for Disturbance Role," "Festa Jailed Indefinitely for Swindle"). The most notorious case was that of a childless widow, Cecelia Meyers, who saw twenty-six thousand dollars disappear from her family inheritance. There was also an old man who inexplicably wrote him check after check for do-ing virtually no work. "The gift of gab," Rose called his bedeviling charisma.

On December 10 Festa's lawyer back home arranged a reparation of eight hundred dollars to the victim of his most recent swindle, Ethel Davis of Dunmore. No longer was he a fugitive from the law. He im-mediately borrowed a Cadillac from his best friend, Robert Martin, a short, muscular bookmaker who, before he also moved to New Jersey, in West Orange, had been Festa's partner in the Scranton brouhahas. Martin was pretty good at pinochle, too. Tense and temperamental, he had tattoos on his arms (a showgirl kicking out from a champagne glass was the most obvious), and when he wasn't on roofing jobs or in bars with Jerry, he drove tractor-trailer trucks, taxicabs, and construction equipment, moving back and forth from Pennsylvania to New Jersey depending on where the action was. They had played touch football when Jerry—four years his junior—was in the fifth grade, and from then on there were few things the duo had not done together.

In Martin's car Festa set out posing again as a roof repairman. He spotted a neighborhood at the northernmost boundary of Newark above Branch Brook Park where there was an old cramped two-family house with a neglected front yard. It looked musty enough to belong to a spinster, and in fact it did. He was met at the door by a woman in her eighties who was obviously senile. To bolster her chimney, he told her, she needed new flues and a crown.

When the woman retired back to the parlor, where she spent the rest of the day in a rocking chair, Festa took a tire iron from the automobile and descended into the basement. He pounded it against a water pipe to simulate the sounds of workmanship. Then he snuck away to a bar for four hours. Late in the afternoon, when it seemed prudent to do so, he returned to announce the job's successful completion. As she prepared to write him a check, he was startled to hear the front door open and footsteps approaching.

He had thought the woman was living there alone. In walked a matronly lady in her sixties. She carried herself like a schoolteacher and had a face that put him in mind of a bulldog. Her clothes were woolly and worn and she had on thick coats of rouge. She was the old lady's niece, and she too lived there. Her name was Dolly.

"What a handsome young man we have here," Dolly said fawningly. "And who might he be?" Instead of making a run for the door, preventing another fraud arrest, he stood in wonderment at the sight before him. "Oh," she said, touching his cheeks. "You could be a movie star!" From her cackly voice he could tell she was nearly as eccentric as her aunt. And she was unmarried, a perfect "meatball."

He put on his best bashful look, sending her the vibes of a suitor. They smiled warmly at each other. Dolly spotted her aunt tearing out the check. "Here," she said. "Let me see, auntie. Don't bother. I'll type it." She smiled at him. "I hope you did a good job," she giggled. He followed her to an office alcove, where she fell into his arms before he had a chance to expect it. They were immediately infatuated with each other. He left with twenty-three hundred dollars not half an hour later.

As he had so many times previously, Festa found it remarkably easy to gain the confidence of a person whose despairing need was that of companionship, and he instilled in Dolly, and other meatballs he was soon to discover, the unmistakable impression that he cared about every detail of their lives, what new events were transpiring among their relatives, what was diagnosed on their latest trip to the doctor, or how their neighbors were treating them. He did this with everyone he knew, and there was a degree of sincerity to it. He was an inquisitive man. He found every new acquaintance a curiosity. In place of work, he sat and gossiped over coffee with these people, or volunteered to paint their hallway. In short order he had them believing they were his soulmates, and if that failed to generate the requisite gifts of money, he would surreptitiously spray a canister of lighter fluid between the furnace and the chimney. In the course of conversation he would then suggest as a matter of good housekeeping that he check around for any possible gas leaks. As he struck a match along the joints, a blue flame would materialize before their startled eyes, dancing, wiggling the length of a cellar ceiling. "Oh, my God!" was how he remembered their response. "Please fix it." They were grateful when he or Hank gave them a "discount," charging only a thousand dollars for the vital repair work.

As Festa had known since his early twenties, when he first began working the trade, there was a bewildering number of people out there who, though they dressed like paupers, had inherited substantial wealth in the form of stocks, bonds, and insurance investments from their husbands or parents. They usually did not withdraw these funds, allowing an impressive compounding of interest over the decades. Especially in northern New Jersey, where the money was old and concentrated, the meatballs seemed both unusually prevalent and vulnerable. They were wealthy people disheartened that no one was with them to share their abundance, and Festa could instantly identify their most pressing needs. Better, he exuded the promise of fulfillment.

Jerry let hardly a day pass without phoning Dolly to see how she was, or to complain about some new financial problem he had. Inspired by the hope that a prospective husband had finally been found, she fed his voracious need for gambling and drinking funds, unhesitantly opening her checkbook. Rose had always recognized Festa's resourcefulness, but Dolly was an astonishment to her: Jerry would return from her house with five thousand to buy Christmas gifts, three grand to pay a poker debt, a large check for a fabricated divorce (with Martin posing as his demanding attorney). The woman also gave him the use of her own car, a 1958 Pontiac, and bought him a truck for his roofing firm. In a flight of girlish romanticism she named it "Starway Roofing."

Marie was baffled at his sudden wealth but had seen it all before. "Oh, no," she said. "Not roofing again."

"I'm just hot," he said, explaining that it was "gambling winnings."

In the spring, when the rain stopped freezing, Festa called Hank

Ellis to help with this new meatball named Dolly. She was a "major score," he told his Scranton friend. Ellis responded quickly. A carpenter by trade, he was a quiet and clumsy man who followed Festa's every dictate. In his ten years of servitude to Jerry, Ellis's loyalty had been rewarded with cars, spending money, and, as was now the case, a place to stay while he was working. He moved into Lincoln Avenue, sleeping on the floor in the living room.

Hank was charged with carrying out what Festa advertised as a complete "overhaul" of Dolly's house, a permanent refurbishment which would enhance its durability and value. Though he made it sound like a major undertaking (as if the foundation would be fortified, the wiring redone, new insulation installed), in reality Hank put a few new shingles on the roof, painted the outside, and replaced the gutters. Festa asked for and got from Dolly twenty-five thousand for the house job. She had been a legal secretary, a career she had somehow survived with no common sense.

Careful not to take outlandish sums with no excuse at all, Festa next pulled at her heartstrings, telling Dolly he desperately needed open-heart surgery. Three weeks after this "operation," which was done out of state, presumably in Pennsylvania—and cost her seven thousand dollars—he phoned her from a bar in West Orange with more bad news, pretending that he was in the train station. "Complications" had set in. His doctor was ordering more intensive care and a convalescence in the Adirondack Mountains. Of course, he said, he would never be able to afford it.

She told him she would be right over to his apartment to meet him. He rushed home and wrapped himself in tape, dishcloth bandages, and gauze. Rose was stunned at the lunacy of the idea, but she did as she was told and hid in a closet.

"My!" Dolly said upon her arrival at his sickbed. "I didn't realize it was this bad. Oh, my poor darling baby."

Festa moaned as he lay on the bed. "Oh," he stammered. "Excuse me if I sound tired, darling. It's the medication." Dolly sniffed at the air in the room, which was ripe with the alcohol he had been drinking. He quickly explained that "the doctor says for me to drink lots of brandy." In the closet Rose strained to subdue her laughter as Festa groaned again, closing his eyelids. "Do you have the money, darling?" he mumbled, painfully rubbing at his chest. He began fading into a fitful sleep as Dolly looked at him mournfully. Quietly the meatball walked from the room. But before she did, another few thousand in crisp bank bills was left for her ailing sweetheart.

* *

They took the money and bought their first home. Cousin Marie went in on it with them. Since she was now forty-four, her prospects of finding a husband were dim, and she did not look forward to any further aloneness. She put up some savings for the down payment and took the mortgage on her own credit. Despite their disparate backgrounds, she and Rose, in the time together at Lincoln Avenue, had grown as close as sisters. Rose had become pregnant by Jerry and was sick most of the time. She needed Marie's assistance.

They chose a house at 566 Ridge Street, in the Forest Hills area. A district that had remained stable amid the proliferating ghettos, it consisted of old wood-shingle-and-brick houses which had served New-ark's professional stock before the exodus to the suburbs. For the most part those who lived there were quiet, respectable blue-collar workers, store owners, civic employees who had graduated here from apartments, and a few doctors. Branches of thick-bark maple reached overhead like gesturing arms.

A two-story frame dwelling in the Colonial revival style, the house had eight rooms, a basement, and an attic. A columned porch ran the width of the front and sidled along the southern wall under flared gables and bay windows. The rooms were built with sound craftsmanship: layers of rock-hard plaster, parquet floors, and oak pillars in the foyer. A wide wood-railed stairway led to a loveseat on the first landing and tall, stained-glass windows. There were cathedral ceilings and a stone fireplace.

The price was $28,500. They put down a third of it. "I'm gonna make this your dream house," Festa vowed to Rose.

His roofing ventures were quickly expanding, and the routine of it suited him fine. He would knock on a few doors to drum up business, drop off Hank and a few other itinerant laborers to do the actual repairs, and hit the bars, playing pool, talking with the bookmakers. At quitting time he would collect for the day's work and survey the homes for any loose cash or jewels. If the owner looked like a meatball, he would stay and visit into the evening.

Hank came with them to Ridge Street, and rotated between an attic bedroom and a couch in the basement. On weekends he took the truck into Scranton to visit his wife, but otherwise Hank, dutiful Hank, had become a fixture. Festa had first met Ellis while Hank was tending to some boarding houses owned by an older aunt who had raised him, and he too had been caught in the same home-repair fraud that had sent Festa to Elmira. He was only four years younger than Jerry but looked up to him as a big brother, nearly a father. He drove the car for Festa, brought him coffee, and mounted the roofs when actual carpentry had to be done. He uncomplainingly followed his boss's orders and withstood his scoldings.

Marie got a charge out of Hank, the way he impassively accepted life—any comings, any goings—and the way he kept himself. She hated to say it, but his hygiene was that of a hobo. While he sat watching television, an ash would grow to a precarious length from his cigarette, collapsing onto his pants and shirt. He gave it no mind. They were dirty anyhow. His teeth were gray, his pudgy face unwashed. And his socks, they joked, could stand up by themselves. They smelled as strong as Limburger. He coated his shoes with roofing sealant instead of polishing them, and once in the restroom of a bar the toilet paper clung to the sticky boots so that, in front of the whole place, he came out dragging a roll of it the length of the dance floor.

But Hank's sense of direction made him a most valuable chauffeur, and he was good at the roofing jobs. He could eye a surface and figure to the foot how much material they would need, and while Festa was below, chatting with the owner, Hank would swab concoctions of diluted plastic cement around the crevices. (They might get a thousand for nothing more than making the metal glisten, but that had always been Festa's strategy. In East Orange, once, there was a woman who declined to let Festa and another roofer cap her deteriorating chimney. They snuck back that night in a heavy rainstorm and, with a truck and lasso, pulled the smokestack to the earth, forcing the issue.)

At a bar in Orange, Festa heard about a good roofing prospect down the street at 17 Windsor place, a house whose porch was in a state of collapse (perhaps under the weight of a cardboard box which served as a home to a pack of stray cats) and whose yard was a veritable jungle of chest-high weeds and falling branches. The owner was Minnah Booth, a retired piano teacher.

He knocked on the door and encountered an obese woman in a soiled sweater, cotton house dress, and navy blue ski cap. She looked about eighty years old and as eccentric as anyone he had met. But she opened the door only a crack. As far as her chimney went, she wasn't interested.

Michael Brown 32

That evening at suppertime he decided to call her. He knew Minnah owned apartment buildings in Brooklyn and other real estate in New Jersey, which meant there very well might be cash around. "I hear you're a wonderful piano teacher," he told her on the phone. "Could I please come by just to hear you play?" This she found agreeable. He went there promptly and inside discovered an atmosphere of unsparing squalor. The rooms and hallways were a mound of yellow newspapers, bags, boxes, food scraps, junk mail, dirty clothes, cat-food cans—so much trash there was literally a path through it on the way to the studio.

She lived alone and was afflicted by elephantiasis, which prevented her from going upstairs, she mentioned. She told him she had not been up there in ten years, since the death of her mother. When she was young, she said, she and her mother had traveled around the world. She had studied music in France and had a refined accent to prove a cultured upbringing.

Music was her only passion. In addition to the piano in the studio, there was an upright in the dining area and three more pianos, including a baby grand, in a second unused studio. She burst into a concertino of double-octave chords. He did not know the names of any composers, but if necessary he would learn them. "You're wonderful," he said. "Can you please teach me? I've always wanted to play."

He knew right off that for Minnah to order any home repairs, her piano would have to be in jeopardy. Before his first lesson the next day he was watching a rainstorm and thinking about Minnah. He remembered the chimney he had pulled down, and a brainstorm struck him. He would leave her front door slightly ajar when he went back, and while she was teaching him the rudimentary chords, Hank could sneak to a room above the studio. There he would drill a small hole through the floor.

Festa ordered Hank to fill up a gallon jug with water and get a hand drill. "Don't drill till you hear the piano," he told Ellis as they pulled in front of the house.

He scaled the debris and began his lesson. Soon he heard a noise at the other end of the room. Hank was drilling in the wrong place. "Oh, *wrong* key," said Jerry as he sat there with Minnah. "Wrong finger. I got it *wrong*." He was nearly shouting. Hank got the message and began drilling directly above them, causing plaster chips to scatter on the piano top. "Just right," Festa said loudly, another message to his assistant, who was making the hole much too big. A moment later a large chunk of plaster fell near the teacher and her pupil. They were doused with water.

Festa sprang from his seat and moved the instrument away from the deluge. As he did so he noticed that behind the piano were several old grocery bags. One of them was ripped, and he could see it was filled with money. He took two of the smaller bags when she wasn't looking. "Now don't worry," he said. "I'll be here first thing in the morning." From the bags he would count out eleven hundred dollars.

They returned before eight o'clock the next day. Minnah was relieved and grateful to see them. As Hank patched the ceiling above the piano, Jerry snuck among the clutter looking for more cash. The woman kept many years' worth of lesson fees in different bags, according to their denomination. She had also collected Social Security payments, and stacked the envelopes pyramidlike in the pantry. Because of their height they were beginning to spill onto the floor. In the dining area and living room were boxes from Robert Hall containing brand-new dresses, nightgowns, and sweaters. None had ever been worn. They were dusty, moth-eaten. There were also small boxes of what appeared to be costume jewelry strewn on the floor, but closer inspection revealed that the pieces were real gold and platinum set with rubies and diamonds. Upstairs were pocketbooks filled with rent payments. A bag was crammed with silver dollars and quarters.

Pleased with their emergency aid, Miss Booth decided to have them get to the root of the problem, which, Festa sadly informed her, would entail replacement of her aging copper roof. Though the material they used would cost only seven hundred dollars, he told Minnah he needed four thousand just to start the job. She agreed unhesitatingly.

Thus commenced a year-long mockery which would exceed any of his previous scams. A big score in Scranton had been eleven grand, but out of Minnah he cleared more than ten times that amount. She sat all day in a rocking chair next to a potbellied stove in the kitchen and Festa noticed that she ate from a flat tin can, which he at first assumed was tuna fish. It turned out to be cat food.

Bags were carried out at every opportunity: there were five thousand in cash hidden in two upstairs bedrooms and four more in the basement. There also was a large laundry bag of silver coins, and a pile of 1941 bonds under a mattress. Had Minnah observed the thefts, she might not have cared. On Festa's thirty-seventh birthday, which was September 19, she gave him a hundred and ninety-six shares of AT&T. "There's plenty more," she mumbled nonchalantly.

While Marie was too preoccupied with her job to watch her cousin's antics, Rose fully understood Jerry's methods by now. She felt sorry for Miss Booth, as she called her, and brought her hot meals and Thanksgiving dinner. In turn Minnah let Rose take some of her jewelry. "That's no good," she would say, waving off a ring. "That's old." Rose began feeling increasingly less guilty. If they didn't take it, she rationalized, "some lawyer would get it."

With this money they decorated and improved their house—Rose's palace, her great sanctum. Hank and others in the roofing crew brought up the wood and paneled the cellar. White aluminum siding was slapped over the cream-colored exterior, and the inside walls, which furnace soot had turned to jailhouse gray, were quickly repainted a more cheering color. So were the dining room and foyer.

They were not married yet, but the house was the cement of their relationship. To think she had once lived in an attic! On August 2, 1965, they had their first baby together, a hairless eight-pound-thirteen-ounce girl, Alicia. Just thirteen months later, a second daughter, Sophia, was born. The scene at the hospital was at once joyous and comical. Jerry had panicked when Rose began labor and, shouting for a nurse, pushed her bed into the corridor. By the time Sophia was delivered he was so thoroughly soused that he stood admiring the wrong baby. Theirs he thought to be one with curly black hair. But Sophia was much like Alicia before her: less hair on her head than fuzz on her chin.

They dressed the girls in the kind of clothes Rose had seen the classy people buy, and surrounded them with decorous mementos of their infancy: studio photographs, bronzed baby shoes, silver cups with their names engraved. Once they got their footing, Janet rejoined her mother at the strange new place. She was bitter at first at how long she had been away, and jealous of the attention lavished upon her stepsisters. But this animosity soon wore down and she accepted them as her own. Marie became her aunt, Festa her father.

Rose often thought of how long it had taken for her and Jerry to build a family together. Over the course of twelve years she and Jerry had woven in and out of each other's lives with great unpredictability. She had been walking by Cooper's rathskeller when he first saw her. He had been inside drinking with Martin. He was in his twenties, she only fifteen, and he packed a slushy snowball and hit her jeans-clad bottom. "What an ass!" he called. She had an eye for him then, this strapping man in a new hunting shirt and spotless boots, but he had ended up with her cousin, Tootsie. She dated Robert Martin.

Rose had just run away from home then. She loved her stepmother, a hard-working cleaning woman who was actually her aunt, but her stepfather always complained about how much food she ate, how much her clothes cost, and when he was drunk and mad he threw chairs and lamps at her. He was the one who, in a tirade of complaints about having her there, let her know she was an adopted child.

When she was eleven, this man, a coal miner, began raping her. Always it was when her stepmother was not yet home and he was in his cups. Holding both her hands with one of his, he was like a beast grunting on top of her. She struggled at first. Eventually she gave up. She was too stunned to scream. But always it was disgusting. Here she thought he was supposed to be her daddy.

She bled when it was over that first time, and cleaned herself in the bathroom with a sponge. She threw her nightgown in a garbage pail and put on different clothing. That did not remove the scent of beer and sweat from her nose, however, or what plagued her ears. She could hear him from the hall, contentedly snoring.

Unsure who her real parents were, Rose had left that home (in the section of town known as Providence) and taken refuge with a woman who did bathroom abortions and some street hookers who taught her the trade. The Christmas after meeting Jerry she had ended up in a house of detention, and a pimp named Lou claimed legal guardianship of her. He bought the teenager a fur, high-heeled shoes, and new ruffled blouses from New York, and she also was given a bank account and all the hamburgers she could eat in his gaudy Italian restaurant. Men came to get a look at her as she sat all dressed up in the anteroom, businessmen who enjoyed innocence and youthfulness. Usually she did three a night. Lou rented the motel room.

She had naturally preferred the company of her friends Tootsie, Bob, and Jerry. She liked to drink Cokes in a booth with them at Cooper's. Lou had forbidden her hanging out with such "scum," and one evening, after she had tried to leave his harem, he burst into the bar with a husky goon to help drag her out. "Hold it. She ain't going nowhere she don't wanna," Festa said.

"I'm her legal guardian," snapped Lou. "This girl's underage."

Festa rose from the booth. "Yeah," he said. "She just told us how she makes her room and board." He went over to the jukebox and dropped in a nickel. Then he pulled Rose away from Lou and draped his long arms around her, dancing. As Lou stood glowering, Festa whirled around toward the pimp and swiped off his awkward black toupee. He dropped it on the floor. "C'mon, Lou," he taunted. "Let your hair down." Rose made it to the ladies' room before the first punches were thrown. When she peeked out, a few minutes later, Lou was gone. The bouncer was on the floor, bleeding.

More than a year later Rose and Jerry had crossed paths again as she was stepping off a Greyhound bus from Newport News, Virginia. She had gone there to try and make it legitimately, as a hostess, but it hadn't worked out. She was homeless and broke again, and afraid she was pregnant. As she descended the station steps, she heard a car horn honk and an unmistakable booming voice: "Hey, Rose!" Across the street was Jerry in a steely blue Buick.

He had just left a Sunday dice game when he spotted her. She was wearing a blue-and-white dress, and she had been crying. He took her to a bar where Bob Martin came in and got deep into Rolling Rock. Bob grew jealous and abusive and they had a fist fight in the parking lot, where Festa knocked Bob groggy with a roundhouse punch to the forehead and hung him on a parking meter. Festa found Rose a room in a highway motel. There they talked all night and made love for the first time.

But from then on it hadn't proceeded at all smoothly. Jerry had his wife and two or three women on the side and at one point it seemed as if all of them were pregnant. He was arrested soon afterward and Rose gave birth to Janet. She was seventeen then, and the child was born in a charity ward—April 6, 1957. No one was there to witness the event, but Rose felt such a flood of love that it took the edge off the grief. "I won't ever allow you to be alone like me," she said to the infant. "We're in it together." She stared out from the hospital at one in the morning, bitter at the world, tears flattening on her cheeks. Festa came to visit before she left the hospital (and just before his jail term began), and so the child would not have a "father unknown," they decided to put Martin, who was unmarried at the time, on the birth certificate. It upset Rose every time she looked at the girl. Janet was not a healthy child and she only had Goodwill clothes to wear. She was as tiny and scraggly as a newborn chicken.

Rose stayed with her stepmother and older stepsister for a while. They wanted her to put the baby up for adoption, but Rose was opposed. She got a job as a seamstress and told everyone the father was in the service. But her stepfather, who had been in the hospital for tuberculosis, soon returned home and she and the child left for the attic flat near Cooper's tavern. They had only a bed and chair for furnishings and mice roamed near where Janet slept. Rose improved their lot by going back to a few old customers and taking handouts from the flunky men she had "dated." One of them, a burglar named Bochak, broke her jaw and knocked her senseless. She got back with Jerry after his prison time was up. In light of the other options, it had not been so bad, escaping with him through that forest.

Marie did not approve of Rose's unspeakable past, but she could see that Rose was, like herself, a harmless retiring type. And Marie was happy to be part of a family. Her own mother and sister had remained in Scranton, and she had been alone in Newark since May of 1942. She was grateful now to be in the company of relatives, especially the two wonderful new babies. It had been her love of children that made her fond of Jerry in the first place: She remembered him from the time he was an infant and his mother, Mary Gallagher, had to massage his head with warm oil because a forceps delivery had bruised his skull. But he outgrew that in a hurry, and became a robust little boy whom Marie could take to parks and vaudeville shows when she was free, and soon he became the neighborhood basketball star. He was like the little brother she had always wanted.

He sure was a big boy now, and just like when he was a kid, he was not about to listen to her. He had held only a few legitimate jobs in his life—in a pocketbook factory, a body shop, on a construction site driving a belly-dump—and then only for the shortest durations. Authority had been anathema to him from the start, and more so since the reform school in Phoenixville, Pennsylvania, where a disciplinarian they called "Brother Knockout" would come in dancing like a boxer and slam him on the side of the head. From then on, when he was in a fight, Jerry would fix in his mind the image of the sadistic Brother if he really wanted to hurt somebody.

Even when he was in the Army he could not stay still. He was seventeen when he enlisted (on a forged birth certificate) and there were the several times he went AWOL. When he got out of the service he and Dottie moved for a few months to West 109th Street in Manhattan, where his friends were holdup men who shot heroin. His mother also moved to New York. She was a seamstress who was chronically depressed, lamenting the divorce which had come before Jerry was two, and the attack of polio which had made her legs drag. She felt devastated by Jerry's constant running away and she died in quiet destitution from a combination of pills and alcoholism.

Festa's Uncle Louis was his hero. Uncle Louis wore camel coats, ties, and a white Stetson: a sharp-looking guy, and not the prissy type. Some said he owned a cathouse, and there was a story about his being shot at once. He gave Jerry rides in his new Oldsmobile and took him to see professional boxing bouts, and Jerry was impressed by how cool he was. Once Jerry ran off with a couple of crates of turkeys while his uncle kept the poultry clerk busy.

Uncle Louis soon turned out to be tame compared to his nephew, who got caught in a stolen automobile and hung out near the bars playing blackjack. But now, at Ridge Street, he was beginning to look like that cagey uncle of his. Rose could not get over how he was wearing new suits, having his nails manicured, and toning down his temper. Soon there were two Cadillacs and an Oldsmobile in their driveway, and thirty-five thousand cash in a secret bedroom wall safe. The new friends he was making in the night spots of Orange and West Orange were exciting to him: the bookies he gambled with into the morning, jewel thieves, fences. He was awed by the big money they carried ("This ain't Scranton, Rose. They blow their nose with a G-note.") and how wide open it was: the cops joked about bribery, and Festa often gambled with a local police chief. He felt an electrical intensity when a big mobster came in, guys who worked for local chieftains such as Ritchie Boiardo or Joe Paterno, and in return the wise guys noticed the big newcomer who was so respectful and polite. They also saw how he always had lots of money.

His favorite hangout became the Cabaret on Verona Avenue. He went there with some people he met through his old poker partner from Lincoln Avenue, Nanny. She was a toothless woman whose husband had owned some carnival concessions, and she worked the counter at a nearby fast-food franchise called Chicken Delight. Her sons began to help Festa and his roofing crew, and they told him about a guy at the Cabaret, Teddy Riviello, who bought and sold stolen merchandise in volume—suede coats, jewelry, and television sets. Teddy was like a silver fox: thick-rim glasses, a conservative suit, a mane of wavy white hair. Festa visited one of his warehouses to do some bargain shopping and they got to know each other better. Through these trips he also met Riviello's partner, Johnny Quartuccio, who was the antithesis of Teddy.

He wore green work pants and drove a battered car. But Festa immediately liked Johnny.

Festa bought an Alaskan seal coat with mink cuffs from Riviello and presented it to Rose.

"Jerry, what are you getting involved in?" she inquired.

"Nothing," he said.

"I know what's going on, Jerry. I don't like it."

He decided to tell her. "Teddy knows the right people. They're hijacking trucks. I can get whatever I want to. I know how to handle myself. They like me. One hand washes the other. I'm a roofing company. I make money."

She was somewhat upset by it, but the commodities he could suddenly afford were a wellspring of pride and dignity: the china, the leather swivel chairs, the hard-oak bedroom set. Her eyes feasted on a diamond necklace he bought her. She made a few attempts to slow his avarice, imploring that he "just stick to roofing," but at the same time she was intoxicated by what seemed like an elevated status to her. It was better than living, like an alley cat, in Scranton.

* *

Johnny Quartuccio took Jerry and Hank out on the porch. He was a thin, excitable man who bit his fingernails to the quick and fidgeted with the curls in his hair. He told them they were "laying on a million dollars" with the roofing schemes but, from now on, they should not waste time courting meatballs. "I work for the best, the best," Johnny advertised. "Believe me, nobody gets caught. Nobody. We've got the cops in our pocket, believe me. I'm telling you. We can't get hurt." Henceforth, if they found a stash of cash—or stocks, or a stamp collection—they would not bother with the façade of home repairs. They would go right in, he said.

Both Quartuccio and Riviello had been regaled with Festa's absurd roofing stories. Riviello had gone to see a meatball for himself and returned with a blank check on which they wrote in the amount of twenty thousand, payable to Hank Ellis, and forged the woman's signature. Hank cashed it through a bank president Riviello dealt with in Bloomfield. Johnny had heard about it and said, "How do you do something like that?"

"I'll prove something to ya right now," Festa had told him at the Cabaret. "All you gotta do is come with me and come off like you're a bookie I owe money to. Act like I'm in deep shit if I can't pay, that you'll hurt me." Then they had gone to Dolly's house. Festa said, "Dolly, this guy's nobody to fool around with." She looked over at Johnny, who had on a somber expression, and they left with five hundred dollars.

Such an uncanny faculty to find covert reserves of wealth dazzled Johnny. And Festa liked the idea of making money faster. He could go through a grand some nights, drinking and gambling. So the morning after their porch conference they headed for the residence of a roofing customer who wasn't home. Festa dropped Quartuccio off seven houses away so the car would not be seen, and circled the block. He watched for the return of the owners.

Johnny was gone only thirty minutes. He collected jewelry and cash from a safe and made it back unnoticed to the automobile. Though he had introduced himself to Festa as a carpenter, Johnny had been a professional burglar most of his life, learning the trade from an old hand named Alton Hughes. And Johnny had become one of the city's best second-story men. He could work marvels with a pair of screwdrivers or a steel punch. Applying just the right amount of pressure under a window, and sustaining it steadily for a long moment, he could cause the screws to rise slowly out of the lock as if they were mesmerized. And he worked the tools in a door frame like chopsticks. Some doors he could open with a metal card, or just a well-planted bump of his butt.

He liked Festa's speed at picking up on his knacks, so it was the beginning of a run of more than a hundred burglaries, with a cumulative take that would indeed reach about a million dollars. And Johnny Quartuccio replaced Martin as Jerry's closest friend.

Early in the game, Johnny came by and said, "I got another score for us. We gotta go down the Shore and see Nicky Boy."

Festa said, "Nicky Boy? Who's he?"

"I grew up with him," Quartuccio explained. He seemed a bit squirmy as he continued. "He's got the score, and he's with big 'people.' " Johnny pointed a finger to his own head. "He's a crazy bastard, but he's got it up here. Don't think he don't."

Then Johnny launched into a story about how Nicky Boy Valvano once caught a guy named Joe conniving at cards, leaped across the table at him, and bit off one of his ears. Almost everyone told stories like that, and Jerry was entering a domain where embellishment, if not outright lying, was of course a means of livelihood. But if a story was passed on three times, say, without growing more lurid, and maintained its insignificant details as well as the sensational ones, the odds were in favor of accuracy. There was usually a useful gauge in these anecdotes, even if they were hyped, and whatever the accuracy of the Valvano story, on the back of one federal mugshot of him was written the word "hitman." (So redoubtable was Nicky Boy that whatever he wanted from a lesser crook like Johnny he was almost certain to receive. Unexceptional as a burglar himself, he relied instead on his deep-seated meanness and his coordinative powers to scheme.)

They took Hank as the driver for the hour's ride to Lakewood, in Ocean County. All the way Quartuccio kept saying, "Nicky Boy don't take no shit off nobody, nobody. He's into bigger things, he don't just rob every day." When they reached their destination, a hotel with a restaurant, rather like a resort complex, Johnny said, "Hank, Nicky Boy's funny. You better wait outside." He turned to Festa and, using the nickname he had invented, said, "Coombs, Coombs, watch what you say!"

When Nicky came into the room he looked as if he had been sleeping. He was a thickset hoodlum with rectangular sideburns and a thin, acidulous mouth rather wider and higher on the right than left: he always looked as if he were whispering out of the corner of his lips. His eyes were murky and vague, and he was dark-jowled, nappy. After a brief introduction he got right down to business. "There's an old sea captain. Collects coins. A ton of 'em. We been trying to score him for a long time." He gave them the general address and directions and hurried off. Burglaries were good for daily fuel, but he had stocks and bonds on his mind.

It was cold out and the Jersey Shore, host in summertime to hordes of weekenders, was snowbound, desolate. They headed further south along the peninsulas and inlets where tiny islands looked like pieces of a jigsaw puzzle. When they arrived at the village they found a cluster of five cottages. On one, the windows were covered with plastic sheets. Festa spotted footprints coming from it, and something made him say, "That must be it." When no one answered the door, Johnny went to the left side and effortlessly pried open a window. He opened the front door for Jerry and they began anatomizing the place—the closets, the bedroom. The coins were in a large dresser; they filled five drawers. There was more silver in two heavy boxes. The two men rounded up all they could find and called Hank to help carry the swag back to the car, where it was dumped onto the back seat and in the trunk. The weight was such that the rear bumper nearly scraped the asphalt.

Johnny sat in the back on top of the coins. His head was bent against the ceiling. "Take your time, Hank, take your time," he kept repeating. He was all hyped up. "We'll get stopped in a minute. Take it slow. Watch the signs."

Johnny kept talking about Nicky Boy. He was part of a Newark crew that vastly surpassed anything in Festa's experience. They were Mafia footmen who crossed between robbery and murder with intimidating ease—utterly conscienceless, utterly unafraid. Under Valvano was an obscene and merciless contract murderer named Jerry "The Jew" Donnerstag. He killed for cheap, Johnny said, "at the drop of a dime." In association with them were two other mobsters who, in ingenuity and viciousness, transcended Donnerstag and Nicky Boy. One was Raymond Freda, a freelancer. The other was Frank Basto, known as "The Bear."

Hank drove up to Johnny's apartment in Belleville. When they got the stuff inside, Quartuccio could hardly contain his pleasure. He rubbed his palms together so fast Festa expected to see smoke rise from between. He gave Jerry a number to call—Valvano.

"Nicky?" Festa said gingerly. "This is Jerry. We got it."

"What?" Valvano exclaimed. "You got what?"

"We got the score."

"What? Already?"

Festa set down the phone and helped sort the coins, which were in bags and boxes all over the kitchen floor. Hank was sent to bring Rose to see this, and when she arrived, Johnny was so busy scanning and counting he didn't so much as bid her hello.

In one box Jerry found a little paper bag containing all manner of rings: diamond rings, gold insignia rings, Masonic rings, and one with a Nazi emblem. There were forty in all. Suddenly, Festa said, "Oh, hey, Johnny!" He took out two gold-plated derringers mounted in a velvet-lined display case. Quartuccio was an avid gun collector, but there was more to it than that. Near the pistols were glass-encased coins of mint-condition gold. Johnny rushed up to Festa. "Oh, Coombs!" he said. "Coombs!"

Valvano arrived with a stone-faced man who took from his briefcase some reference books, a coin-test kit, a jeweler's eye, and a penlight. *Maronna mia,*" Nicky remarked. "I don't believe this shit." Rose and Jerry were less impressed. To them a silver dollar was basically just that: worth a hundred cents. But then the guy with the scope picked one up and mumbled, "This here's worth a hundred fifty bucks." There was also a coin called "The Flying Eagle Penny" which, this prospector claimed, was worth an additional couple thousand dollars.

They stayed there all afternoon and into the evening. When Festa returned the next morning he could tell that Johnny had been counting all night: his beard had sprouted and his hair was an Afro. They took the loot to the back room of an old coin shop that had ostensibly gone out of business. There was a small smelter inside, operated by a friend of Valvano's. He gave Jerry and Johnny only seventeen thousand apiece, and there was twenty-five hundred for Hank. They knew they had been cheated. The jewels alone were worth more than that. But they were afraid to complain to Valvano. Not so long before, they knew, Freddie Spillman, another of Nicky Boy's thieves, had been murdered gangland style.

Marie saw these new friends coming to the house and was irritated. They treated her like she didn't exist. All they did was whisper. "Why don't you go carry a lunch pail," she scolded, "like everyone else?" Rose was apprehensive. Aside from so blatantly breaking the law, she felt her boy friend was not as much in control as he claimed. These men liked him but were not at all respectful of his greatest asset: physical size. Though he towered over them, they were leading *him* around.

He had gotten into an argument with Herky, owner of the Cabaret, recently, and she had never seen him so badly beaten up. Four henchmen had locked the front door, pinioned his arms, pistol-whipped his face, and planted kick after kick in his groin and stomach. When he arrived home he could hardly talk, and he had so many bumps and gashes his face was barely recognizable. "This ain't happening again," was all he would say. "It ain't like fucking around in Pennsylvania no more." He was in Jersey with the big boys and his fists, in the face of a gun, were impotent.

He needed "connections" with some powerful men like those Riviello and Quartuccio were affiliated with. Either that or he could expect to get shortchanged again on his scores, and beaten up again too. Instead of functioning on the periphery of organized crime, he began to nurture direct connections with those for whom Johnny expressed such respect. Which was how he moved his crew into the bigger pond— under the protective banner known, to the general public, as La Cosa Nostra.

*   *

"Don't get a paper asshole," he told Rose. "I'll hit something big and retire on it. I'll get out."

She was unaware of all the pertinent details, but what was going down was not hidden from her. She worried about Festa's getting caught. With roofing fraud it was difficult for the police to put together a compelling case. But Festa now favored the quick and more exciting break-and-entries ("b-and-e's"), and was leaving the daily chores of his home-repair business to Hank.

Rose would have needed a ledger to keep track of all the new characters who were treating her palace like their own flophouse. Every day a new face seemed to appear at the door (was it Joe or Paul, Billy, Pete?), and a number of them, including of course Hank Ellis and Bob Martin, and now Johnny Quartuccio, were actually allowed to live there while they were straightening out their finances or problems with their girl friends and wives. The same charisma that had endeared him to the meatballs began to enrapture those whose living was crime.

Through the afternoons, while Marie was at work, Festa openly treated the living room as his central office. He fielded a constant influx of calls from the fences and thieves moving in and out of his orbit, or, if he was ready for a score, he sat there in dark clothes and a turtleneck waiting for Quartuccio. "I ain't gonna get rid of crime all by myself," he replied to Rose's complaints. "If it ain't me doing it, it'll be somebody else." Then he and Johnny would leave with the punches and gloves and screwdrivers.

Through the vertiginous list of burglaries, certain features were the same. He or Johnny would hear about a house or business keeping a specified cache of valuables on its premises—the information would come from Riviello, or a building superintendent, or perhaps a hairdresser who heard the women talking in the shop—and would follow up these tips by riding to the address and casing it out. (When were the owners gone? What were the doors like? Was there a burglar alarm?) Then the two men would take two or three others along if the score promised to be big enough, and at least one person, often Hank, would remain as the lookout in a van or car, circling the vicinity. Once inside, Quartuccio and Festa would survey the premises for hidden alarms and, more to the point, for hidden drops and safes. Their key target was usually the master bedroom, but on the way they might flip up the couch cushions, rummage through a desk, or look behind books in a library, and feel above doorways or in closets for hidden compartments. After that they would carefully disassemble and reassemble the dresser drawers. Items of worth might be found pinned inside a pillow or buried under a rug. But much of the time they knew precisely what to expect (from their inside information), and when the score was complete—after, at the most, half an hour—and the merchandise had been rounded up and carried out in pillow cases and bags and their own pockets, Festa and Quartuccio would take the stuff to Herky at the Cabaret, or to Teddy Riviello, who had the connections to sell the stuff. Their haul was usually coin collections, stamp books, bonds, guns, cash, an occasional fur. And always the jewels. Upon the sale of these items they paid Hank and the other participants a small part of the transaction (perhaps a seventh or so of what they each collected); handed several hundred dollars to the person who had given them the information (or if it was a sizable hit, and that person powerful, several thousand). The rest was split down the middle between them.

It was a pattern that recurred twice a week or so. At the beginning Festa was content to organize the burglary case-outs and let Johnny go in on the actual theft, but Riviello warned him to accompany Quartuccio inside and watch him: he wore a girdle into which he would slip necklaces, tiaras, earrings, and gems—a manner of chiseling known as "zincing." As it turned out, his cheating was but one of Johnny Quartuccio's many idiosyncrasies. He was Festa's own age—both had been born in 1929, the year of the stock market crash—and he was by nature so energetic that he could rarely sit still for any length of time. He paced constantly. He would drive the entire night looking for places to hit, and sleep during the day. He had a pleasant, rather childish look, except for the white patches on his cheeks where he had had his wife try to pluck out his beard hair by hair, for he hated to shave. He had long shaggy sideburns, a pointed chin, and eyes of aquamarine.

None of these features prepared the onlooker for the truth of his quirky nature, however—a personality that, seemingly cute and comical, plummeted to the depths of obsession and mania. The wise guys told stories about his voracious sexual appetite, his ability to go through three or more prostitutes in a night without relieving himself to satisfaction, and they played on his unfulfillment by giving him the nickname "Johnny Relief." He also had that hobby of collecting weapons—snubnoses, Magnums, forty-fours, and scope-rifles, which were kept in boxes with oiled rags. He made his own silencers out of steel wool. In the afternoon, after awakening (and taking a drink of honey and hot-water, his first meal), Johnny would spend hours lubricating the weapons, cleaning every groove of a pistol, polishing the handles—in short, *nursing* them. Nobody called Johnny Relief a professional killer, but there was certainly an array of cautionary stories about his past, which had been spent, in large part, in a three-room flat with his parents at 29 Drift Street in Newark, an apartment so small the Maytag wringer was in the kitchen. Nicky Valvano, as it happened, lived across the street, one door down.

Back when Johnny was twenty-three, there on Drift Street, he got involved in a running gun battle with several black men who were flirting with Angelina, his girl friend at the time. After a flurry of shots from his twelve-gauge double-barreled shotgun (and a brief appearance by Valvano himself, who was wielding a club), the blacks ran from the Italian neighborhood in a hail of lead, except for Harold Grandy, whom Johnny fatally shot. (One of the detectives who took the murder statements was a well-known friend of the mob, and whether or not this had anything to do with it, the matter was treated as basically one of self-defense, with very little time in jail.)

Johnny's temperament was also apparent at the time he was breaking up with his wife, after Festa got to know him. He vented his frustrations by destroying his own apartment. He pulled the stuffing out of the couch, kicked the refrigerator until it bled insulation, tore the lid off the clothes dryer, smashed dishes, glasses, and pictures, and carved up the dining room set with a hunting knife. For final effect he perched himself in the window with a twenty-two rifle and, as it was sauntering down the street, picked off his wife's dog, a Pekingese.

It was after this strident marital separation that Johnny moved into Festa's house, taking the first room on the second floor. While Johnny slumbered through the mornings, Festa would set up Hank and the roofing crew on a job, visit with wise guys in the diners ("Gus's," "De-Marco's," or "Ed's"), and feed his insatiable passion for gambling: the horses, monte, poker, and craps. His crew, which by now was composed of six or seven steady burglars, hit homes in Newark and the Oranges with accelerating abandon, cutting phone wires before their entry and hauling the take away in the van.

Only through bribery and good fortune did they stay out of the penitentiary. In Montclair there was the case of an older coin collector whose wife had recently died, leaving him in a vulnerable state of mind. They watched as he left his house on an errand and made their entrance through his underground garage. But he returned before the job was completed, and, as they were escaping, they were seen by a couple of house painters across the way. To make matters worse, Hank had spotted a police cruiser and taken off, leaving them without a getaway car. They dumped everything out of their pockets, disposed of their gloves, and walked as casually as possible through the wealthy suburb looking for a cab. But a roadblock had been set up, preventing taxis from leaving the vicinity, so they headed for a bus stop, and there, awaiting them, were police officers. At the station house Johnny was so nervous he could hardly contain himself: he had five gold coins hidden in his mouth. The police photographer asked Festa how long he had known Johnny.

"Why?" Festa asked.

"Because I think," said the cop, "that he's ready for the funny farm."

But the following day Quartuccio came up with an attorney accustomed to handling such matters, and a thousand-dollar bribe was paid to a captain and a lieutenant. The arrest was declared one of mistaken identity. They were charged with failing to give a good account of themselves and released with a fifty-dollar fine.

From their association with Riviello, Festa and Quartuccio had become acquainted with a wise guy whom Teddy described as "a big man, nobody to fool around with." It was this fellow on whom Riviello's power, his all-important "backing," rested. He was with the Philadelphia family of Angelo Bruno, which had an interest in the Ironbound (or "Down Neck") section of Newark, near the ports. Festa had met him while running errands with Riviello a few times. His name was Dominick DiNorscia, but of course he had a mob alias, and an interesting one. They called him "Tommy Adams."

Why everyone needed a nickname is hard to say. Perhaps it was the atmosphere of camaraderie against the commonweal, or simply that these criminals lacked so much in maturity and sophistication that their whole world was based on the concept of a boyhood club. They had their own codes, their own dress, and their own language. They had standards of admittance, bullies, and cliques. No matter that their sodality was a deadly one, nor that their dues could have powered a rather large corporation—the mob was nonetheless a puerile sort of brotherhood based upon rivalries, initiation, and games.

The base of operation for Tommy Adams was the town of Irvington, the first community west of Newark. But most of his business was with mobsters in the Ironbound area (near Marie's workplace), where the scenery consisted of diesel stations, distribution warehouses, and clanging lathes. Tractor-trailer trucks rumbled over rail lines separating this region of Newark from the rest of the city, tracks belonging to the Pennsylvania Railroad and CRR of New Jersey. Not far from Irvington itself were the crumbling buildings where beer, pipes, valves, pumps, zippers, paint, and varnish were made or stored. Many of these south Newark factories were missing panes of glass, which had been replaced with plywood boards.

Adams owned the Casa de Irvington, a large family-style diner where he sat watching for undercover agents and eating steaming portions of *pasta fassulle,* or hot shrimp and scaloppine, dusted heartily with pepper and garlic. As he did so his sons Jackie and Ralphie came in and out, and a thin man named Morgan stood by him. In the kitchen were three hulks who looked like bouncers in a topless bar.

When Festa first met Adams at the diner, which was being remodeled at the time, Tommy had said hardly a word to him. This reserve was the product, for him and his predecessors, of an ancient conditioning: Like others who had chosen "the life," Adams carefully adhered to the tradition of *omertà*—silence to the outside world. *"Noi siamo fino la morte"*—those were the words spoken upon initiation. Above family and country, "we are one until death."

Though he was now fifty-six and his power was on the wane, Dominick "Tommy Adams" DiNorscia was nonetheless a force to reckon with. He had put in his time for the bosses, running loansharks, gambling, and the docks, and no one could ever take from him the fact that he was one of the few who had been formally initiated in the rituals of the Syndicate, deputed by the highest of orders—indeed, ordained. As an *amico nostro,* a "made-man," he had entered one of the classic meeting rooms in which a crowd of *amici* gathered around a long table, and on it, crossed one over the other, were a pistol and a dagger. *You live by the gun you die by the gun.* His sponsor pricked one of his stubby fingers until there appeared a bubble of blood, and he held in his hands a burning piece of paper, repeating, *"Si che vi dico le nostre secrete io brucio come questa carta"*—if he betrayed their secrets he would burn like the paper. Then he kissed all the men in the room.

Like other made-men (or "buttons"), Tommy had been required to "make his bones"—to commit a murder before he was officially accepted—and his first errand was in a woodland, where he helped to dig the grave. Once Tommy had been a lieutenant; now he had slipped to the level of *soldato*. But the ranking was not like that of the military: a soldier who was a made-man had a goodly number of thieves, apprentices, bookies, and hitmen under his command. Because in New Jersey the competition was so intense (mobsters were to Newark what actors are to Hollywood), the standards of formal admission, and formal power, were surprisingly strict. The premium was on loyalty, management, moneymaking, and murder. Probably there were only slightly more than a hundred made-men in the whole of New Jersey, the nation's most densely populated state, for this was not Milwaukee or Sacramento: the northern region joined Brooklyn as the national headquarters of mob enforcement, and a soldier (or perhaps subsoldier) from here or New York would have been a boss of some kind in a place such as Atlanta, Georgia.

Although Adams reported to the Bruno family, he, like others with a piece of the Jersey turf, worked at the pleasure of the New York City brotherhood. Adams had been weaned on the old-school traditions, and he had a typically long criminal record dating back to 1926. The accent had been on robbery, interstate theft, and atrocious assault. His pseudonym spoke directly of his violence. The "Tommy" came from his middle name and an alias ("Thomas Carro") he used, but the "Adams" was derived from his penchant for grabbing a rival's throat in a dispute, and legend had it that he once ripped out an adversary's Adam's apple. He was also called "Buck," "Cowboy," and "Fats," for he was a capricious Cro-Magnon weighing well in excess of two hundred pounds. His transactions were frequently with another Bruno man, Tony "Bananas" Caponigro, but he associated also with Ritchie "The Boot" Boiardo, who was an underling to New York's Vito Genovese, and with the Carlo Gambino clan (which included Joe Paterno and Frank Basto). According to his dossier, Adams's interests were scattered up and down the Jersey Shore: he had helped set up Nicky Valvano in Lakewood, and his close friend was the southern New Jersey boss, Sam "The Plumber" DeCavalcante.

If back in Pennsylvania the mob was more of a force than in most other parts of America (commanding influence over drug laboratories, judges, pizza parlors, restaurants, trucking firms, and a factory that manufactured metal parts for missiles and warheads), in Newark the *mafiosi* were more numerous, more forceful, more blatant: during the 1960s they had control of the mayor and police chief—acting as an invisible government at times—and the city was perhaps the most wide-open turf in the nation, providing a truly awesome number of experienced killers for other mobs (in California or Massachusetts) who needed them. No one agency of government could accurately chart all the hoods in the state.

A former boxer, Adams was the most imposing man Festa had ever met. He was short, with a chest like a barrel, and though he waddled when he walked, he did so with supreme authority. He sent messages and gave warnings with his furry arching eyebrows, and talked volumes with his hands. (If he waved just once at Festa, Jerry knew not to disturb him; but when he welcomed a conversation, wondering how Jerry was doing, he held his palms upward as if feeling for rain.) When he was thinking hard or was ready for weighty business, Adams's eyes widened like silver dollars and he slowly ground his teeth. Hardly anyone fazed Tommy. Indeed, he had once grabbed the neck of Tony Bananas, choking the higher-ranking made-man.

Festa's association with Adams had begun at both the diner and the race track. Adams was a compulsive gambler, and shortly after the sea captain score, Festa bumped into him near the box seats at Aqueduct Raceway in Queens, New York. They got lucky together. When Tommy asked what horse he liked, Festa gave him a seven-to-one shot that won by several lengths.

That had warmed Tommy's heart. So had Festa's reputation as a rather prodigious moneymaker—not just as a con man, gambler, and burglar, but also of late as a businessman: he and Rose had bought the food stand on Mount Prospect Avenue, Chicken Delight, where Nanny worked, and it was grossing several thousand a week. Up at the diner, Tommy listened greedily to Festa's stories about all the burglaries he and Johnny were pulling. When he asked Festa for money, Jerry gladly gave it to him.

Rose found Adams thoroughly crude and intimidating, a man who, more than the others, belched and cursed in front of her. He slicked back his hair and had a wide nose and wore a diamond on his pinkie finger which seemed as out of place as his diner's beautiful chandeliers. Granted, Tommy was protecting Jerry, in return for a cut of his scores—and, thought Rose, there was perhaps a small current of affection down there in the gravel of his heart. Sometimes he treated Festa like a son. But Tommy was the kind of guy who could smile and look like a retired construction laborer who spent his days meekly growing tomatoes; at other times he rose to the most malefic of moods. He was the type who could drink sociably with Jerry all evening, she figured, then blow out his buddy's brains.

Tommy did not ask for favors. He commanded them. He would tell any available woman to empty the ashtray, and he never asked for coffee when he was busy, just shoved his cup forward and barked, "Yeah." These traits, she noted, were rubbing off on Jerry.

On the other hand it was Tommy who told Rose about her own father—things that nobody else, even her stepmother, would talk about. This topic had arisen during a dinner together at Casa de Irvington. Rose was explaining her family background and how once, after she left the home of her stepparents, she hitchhiked to Old Forge looking for her real father. An older woman with a bun of gray hair answered the door. It was probably her grandmother. She wasn't sure. She had been only six months old when she was given up by the family. But the woman invited her in for a little while and led her to a piano where there was a photograph of a blond baby who resembled herself. "Rosina," the woman said, smiling sadly. "Rosina."

"I was only there tops twenty minutes," Rose told Adams. "Then I could tell she wants me to leave—you know, not come back. I couldn't understand her too good. She was talking Italian. She said she didn't know where my father was. She called him 'Gus.' She handed me twenty dollars and took me to the door. My stepmother, she told me he was with the mob, beat up my mother, used to lock her up in a closet if she didn't go with men for money. Drove my mother insane."

Tommy asked his name.

"Rizzo," replied Rose. "Rizzo's my maiden name."

She could not add much more. She was uncertain even of her birth date. But Tommy had heard enough. He leaned back, stiffening. "Rizzo?" he said gruffly. "I knew him, yeah. Owned some whores. Was from the ole country. A Mustache Pete."

She said she was still thinking of trying to look him up.

"Don't," Tommy thundered. He caught her eyes and kept them. "Don't go turning over no dirt. You don't go looking for no people like that. He's old-school. The Black Hand."

Tommy did not speak to her often after that, not because she said anything wrong, but because Tommy was not given to conversing with women. Money was what was constantly on his mind. He extorted it from legitimate businessmen and criminals alike, relying on his notoriety as a muscle man. He was also preoccupied with current legal threats. He, Riviello, and Quartuccio had taken a bust on theft and conspiracy charges, and Tommy was concerned that Riviello or someone else would open up to the Federal Bureau of Investigation in exchange for a lighter sentence. Adams had a conviction for which jail time awaited him, and he hoped to overturn it on appeal—a prospect which would vanish if someone like Teddy turned informer.

Tommy grilled Quartuccio and Festa to see if anyone was talking. Any such hint would mean, for Riviello, an instant and unpleasant death. They assured him that they had not. But Adams nonetheless began to distance himself from Riviello, soon replacing him with Jerry himself.

Festa had been generous to Adams, and entirely respectful. "I hear all good things about you," he told Festa after one meeting about Riviello. "All good things. You doing anything tomorrow? Track or anything? I wanna talk to ya."

They arranged to meet in the morning. Festa was nervous at first. Tommy was coming to his own house. He had never before been to Ridge Street. But really there had been nothing to worry about. Tommy simply had a statement to make. "From now on, anybody gives you headaches, a problem, you tell 'em you're with me," he said over coffee. "Law, or anyone else. You got a problem, you just tell 'em you're with Tommy Adams."

* *

To think she once had walked these streets at five-thirty in the morning, and spent evenings on Broad Street, strolling, window shopping. In the wake of the 1967 racial riots, which had damaged a thousand businesses and taken twenty-nine lives, reducing the vicinity to a zone of guerrilla warfare, Newark's central wards had fallen into a state of malign neglect. The brownstones were stripped of their paint, and laundry hung out the front windows. Along the curbs and town greens was a kaleidoscope of debris—soda cans, milk cartons, pizza napkins, candy wrappers, bricks, bottles, boxes, straws. Newspapers and wine flasks clung to playground fences, and on the main library's front entrance the word KILL had been spray-painted into the stone.

"Jesus," Marie would think on the bus. "What's happening here?"

At the plant itself, High Grade Meat Packing, the atmosphere was not like it had been when she first came. Back in the old days they had all felt a noble purpose to their labors, in spite of a starting wage of fifty-six cents an hour and no overtime pay. They were helping their country in wartime, fueling the booming industries, and in that memorable era of camaraderie, the men broke their backs carrying the shipment boxes, grinding the meat, while she and the other women measured and linked wieners or made liverwurst. Not that there wasn't dissension: the older Polish women tended to resent the younger Italian ones, and the Irish couldn't drink in certain bars. But now tensions were higher and the ethnic differences had, with the times, turned into nastier racial disagreements. Some of the black girls spoke of casting a hex on them.

In August of this year, 1968, she would finally retire from the plant's drudgery, devoting herself wholly to the loves of her life: Festa's baby children. Had she ever married, Marie was sure she would have had a dozen offspring—that had always been her dream. But these babies, Alicia, who was three, and two-year-old Sophia, had brought her fantasies close enough to reality, and like their father, they had the most mischievous, winsome ways. Alicia was a study in perpetual motion, stuffing shoes and an Omega watch in the toilet and climbing around so much that, as a younger child, a net had to be strung across her crib. And Sophia, as soon as she could, crept into Marie's bed at night to sleep with her. This was after all the woman who had often rocked them to sleep, given them their baths and bottles.

Marie's assistance in raising the children had been essential to Rose, who was busy at Chicken Delight (she was the manager), and who was susceptible to every virus and allergy. From eleven in the morning to eleven at night, Rose supervised the entire fast-food operation: the slicing and cleaning of whole chickens, the singeing of their pinfeathers; and of course the twenty-nine-minute deep-frying of the meat, coated with "secret" batter and placed fifteen to a tray. She was helped by Janet, who, though only eleven, was learning how to cook and clean as well as any adult. The girl was less resentful than when she first arrived, and had been fully integrated as a family member. She may have hated Jerry those first few days—it was he who, as far as she could determine, had taken her mother away—but now she looked upon him admiringly, impressed by his "tailor-made" pants, his variety boots (white, black, brown, blue, and gray), and his striking wool sweaters. The girls in the fifth grade at Ridge Street Elementary told her, "I wish my dad looked like that," or "Your father dresses real cool."

Through his associations in the bars and diners, Festa recruited wanderers, drug addicts, and recent reform school graduates for his burglary regiment, which, because of its size and efficiency, was attracting notice in the underworld. These were for the most part thieves much younger than himself—in their early twenties—and, in addition to their need for heroin money, they were youth disoriented by the broken homes which had spawned and then spurned them. They assembled around Festa searching for guidance—a foster parent—and they confided as if he were some priest.

Of all the itinerants seeking shelter with the Festas, none meant more to them, nor they to him, than a twenty-year-old junkie, Peter Abe Feldman. Rose looked upon him as a younger brother; Festa admired his audacity as a thief. Where other junkies were disheveled, Pete could present a neat appearance when he was not too high on heroin (sharkskin pants, tweed sport jackets), and he had a streak of shyness and sincerity, which showed in his sad brown eyes and did not fit his sprawling rap sheet. Since 1962 Feldman had been arrested for incorrigibility, purse snatching, larceny, malicious damage, breaking-and-entering, heroin and barbituate possession, and overconsumption of alcoholic beverages. Though he was often a gentle and considerate kid, quick to guard Rose from the abusive junkies near the Chicken Delight—where she had met him in the first place—Pete also had a side that caused him, if he felt threatened, to beat up the resident of a home during a robbery, and soon his criminal record would include armed robbery and possession of a knife. He would enter a house, go to the icebox, fry himself some eggs, casually try on clothes and shoes found in a closet, and then carry out box after box of stuff in broad daylight, as conspicuous as a moving van. At other times he would do what he could to comfort a bound-and-gagged victim, leaving the door ajar so a neighbor could come in quickly and untie him.

The eldest of the four children of Abraham Feldman, a concentration camp survivor, Pete had been slipped into America as a small child, first to Elizabeth, New Jersey, where his family subsisted on soup and potatoes, then on to Newark, where his father, a psychologically disturbed man who often showed utter disdain for his children, had worked in a leather plant and as a welder until he opened a lunch wagon with his wife, Inga. Though their fourth-floor apartment at 311 Mount Prospect Avenue was tidy and well appointed, and his father was eventually able to afford a Corvette car, Pete possessed only ragged shirts and two pairs of pants through most of his childhood. There were no toys at Christmastime, and when his parents did have money around, they seldom gave any to Pete or his two sisters and younger brother. Pete stole milk and cookies as a child, and later worked as a grocery delivery boy and an air-conditioner repairman. He dropped out of South Side High School in the ninth grade; soon afterward he was committed to the State Home for Boys in Jamesburgh, and next to the New Jersey Reformatory in Annandale. His first hit of dope came at age thirteen.

Like the other junkies, Pete hung out near a four-foot brick wall at the end of the small plaza on Mount Prospect which housed Chicken Delight. The avenue rode a plateau high above the Newark Basin, thrust upward within sight of Manhattan on silt and crustal blocks of sandstone and shale. Much of Mount Prospect was a study in inconsistencies: sweeping chestnuts and high-rise apartments amid fruit stands, medical offices, and delicatessens. Steep, sparse yards fronted the older brick homes staring across at a row of dilapidated tenements.

Though the riots had spared Mount Prospect Avenue—contained by National Guardsmen before they reached uptown—the street had many destitute Puerto Ricans, blacks, and whites from the inner wards, and at the point where Chicken Delight was, serious degeneracy had already begun. Street thugs roamed the avenue in search of a purse or heroin buy, and after their business was done they would stop at the restaurant for a special snack, which included, with the chicken, cranberry sauce, French fries, and a muffin for a dollar forty-nine; or they could have cole slaw with fish filets and tartar sauce, fried jumbo shrimp, or sweet-dipped loin ribs. ("No need for pots or dishes," Rose wrote on the flyers. "We deliver—to your home or business.") The kitchen had been refurbished, the walls paneled and repainted, and the Festas had purchased four delivery cars.

In the small plaza was a beauty salon and across the street a small triangular park with broken benches on which the addicts sat. Next to that was a Pathmark grocery store. But what the junkies liked were the stores immediately to the right of Chicken Delight: a cramped little corner pharmacy where uppers and downers could be gotten, and an equally small liquor shop. Festa despised most of the junkies—they were weak and vulgar, he thought—and he slapped a few of them around when they blocked the sidewalk in front of his fledgling business or made catcalls at Rose. He claimed to have an aversion to drug taking (dating back to what happened to his mother), and he remembered his own experiences with heroin those few months in New York, where he had vomited and lost consciousness the first time he tried it and was revived by somebody putting ice on his balls. What galled him further was how dirty these addicts were. Their arms had telltale track marks. They had bruises, blisters, and scabs.

Pete could be like that too—teetering and wasted—but he kept order on the avenue and abided by Rose's rules. When a junkie wrapped his arms around Rose because she had refused to serve him, it was Pete who came to the rescue, threatening her attacker with a shiv. She introduced him to Jerry as "the boy that helped me," and the favor was returned those times they sat with him nursing Pete with soup as he was going cold-turkey, or saved him from an overdose. He was allowed to stay at Ridge Street any time he needed to, employed as a delivery driver, roofer, and burglar. They gave him his first real home.

Pete's presence in the house added to its hotel-like ambience. Although Marie considered him and Hank "those poor souls," and found Johnny humorous even if it bothered her that at times his eyes would roll back "funny, like a lizard's," there were all too many suspicious bundles being snuck into the house, and too many stealthy conversations. There was also just too much cash around. The Chicken Delight wasn't doing *that* well, and it couldn't all be from gambling and meatballs, she knew. Nor was there any mention of church, work, or school. And she was sure Pete was hooked on junk. They brought him up to her own room to dry him out once, and he was completely perplexed by the religious articles in there: statues of Saint Anthony and the Blessed Mother, a picture of the Sacred Heart, a black crucifix, and jewelry from her grandmother—earrings in the shape of a cross, and crucifix rings. Pete had gotten scared when he spotted some pearly rosary beads which glowed in the dark. "Take them out!" he had yelled. "Take them out!"

"Pete," she assured him gently. "The Blessed Mother would never hurt you."

"Yeah, yeah," said the junkie, who feared he might be hallucinating. "But could ya please just take 'em out of the room. Please?"

Marie could find amusement in some of that. But she also felt her cousin was admitting to their home a new and more ominous class of characters, so she was beginning to act like a stowaway, always upstairs with the kids, or in the laundry room or the kitchen. She would see this gruff new friend named Tommy Adams coming in with his henchman Morgan and somebody called Blackie Napoli and would retire to her bedroom, avoiding them like the plague.

In this, the final year of her naïveté, Marie admonished Jerry to stop freeloading with a guy like Adams. They were always at the late-night crap games in a Down Neck warehouse putting their money on the caprices of dice. "Why do we have to have all these rumdums?" she complained. "Hey, I feel sorry for Pete and them, but look at some of these guys moping around on dope, and *stealing*. Chrissakes, it's not right to go on that way, Jerry. These guys don't have manners. They're slobs. And you, you got a brain. Go out there and stick with roofing. Do it honest for once. You're not Rockefeller's son. Go punch a time clock like I did. Like everybody else."

Those stern lectures, however, were becoming less frequent. Marie seemed worn down by the momentum, the inevitability of his actions; and the misgivings she had about his life in crime were repressed under the gratitude she felt for being made a part of his immediate family. "Right or wrong, blood is blood," the closest person in her life, her mother, had said. (To her great grief, her mother had died two years before.)

To accommodate the steady parade of guests at Ridge Street, Adams brought the Festas a large stainless-steel coffee urn. The visitors had come to include not only the Mafia wise guys but also Tommy DeMarco and Steve George, two local cops. Janet would hear a knock on the door and a hurried voice. "I got a hot horse," George would say. "Where's your father? Where's your father?" Or Detective DeMarco would be there smiling as Festa talked about some score. DeMarco was soft-spoken, friendly; he would play with the kids and ask Janet about school. On the porch, in quiet tones, he and Jerry talked about potential burglaries the detective had spotted in the course of his investigations, and the cop told Jerry about recent burglaries, letting him know what was left behind. Festa also learned from DeMarco who was "hot" (ready to be busted) and where the stakeouts were, or what federal agents were in town. In return for these leads, the Festas gave DeMarco coins, an electric guitar, a gold watch, a swivel cocktail ring with diamond chips, and other gifts of precious metals and stones.

Johnny, who was still staying at the house, had of late begun straying away from Festa. Adams made Quartuccio nervous, and he did not approve of the others Jerry was meeting, dangerous guys like the Campisis of South Orange Avenue, who were known to pour black pepper in the graves of their victims as a way of discouraging snooping dogs. "Coombs, Coombs," Quartuccio said. "We could get killed for nothing, Coombs. And nobody'll know it." It was upsetting to Johnny that Adams had become so close to his partner; he resented the orders they had to take from him and the money Tommy commanded.

Festa in turn was growing wary of Quartuccio, who, when a score didn't pan out, would storm around the house ripping, cutting, and urinating on the floor in retribution. But they were still scoring together successfully, and growing bolder by the day. They robbed a homosexual businessman of cat's eyes and opals in Festa's own neighborhood, and from a pharmacist's house directly behind his own they took a wristwatch and silver. On one of the scores, which was given to Johnny by Donnerstag, Festa ordered Rose to come along as a decoy, and she sat in the truck as if she were a girl friend of Hank's. Boxes of coins from this robbery were then taken to Jay Weisman, a Scranton fence Festa knew, and while Jay and Johnny were sifting through the booty, Festa took Hank on another score: a secretary who worked for the United States Attorney and was known to keep her savings in cash. That was worth an additional eighteen thousand.

Around this time came a turning point in their greed and ruthlessness. They went into Pennsylvania and robbed Hank's own relatives, two of his aunts. Several nights after hitting the home of one of them, Festa became embroiled in another heated argument at the Cabaret with Herky, who, Festa felt, was welching on what he ought to be paying. Johnny had tried to mediate the argument, but failing that he returned to Ridge Street, figuring the argument would last till the bar closed.

But Jerry too was tired, and he came home soon afterward. As he entered the foyer he heard a scuffling sound on the floor above him, and when he ran to the staircase he saw a shadow shoot across the hallway against the bathroom light. He ran into Janet's room, the source of the commotion.

Janet burst out crying as he questioned her. Johnny had been molesting her.

Festa ran down the hall screaming at the top of his lungs. Marie, Rose, and Hank were there asking what was wrong. They could hear Johnny yelling for help from his room: "Rose! Rose!"

Festa returned with a three-fifty-seven Magnum and aimed it directly at Johnny Relief. He pulled the trigger twice, but the gun clicked harmlessly. In his haste, Festa had forgotten to load it.

There were only three bullets left, and they were on the other side of the cylinder. Hank and Rose grabbed Jerry, restraining his swinging arms. In the bedlam, Johnny made it downstairs and out of the place. He would hide out the next nine months in Long Branch, and, fearful of a cop stopping him on his trips into Newark—but more afraid Festa might spot him on the road—Johnny took the most eccentric of precautions. To avoid being caught with firearms he dug a series of holes in wooded areas along the highway, planting, in each of them, a rag-wrapped gun.

*　　*

Through the night corridors of New Jersey, the monte games and the girls dancing in the Cabaret bar, Jerry "The Jew" Donnerstag moved with all the modesty of a television celebrity. Eager for recognition, he, like Adams, wore an oversized pinkie diamond, and a silk shirt wide open at the collar. Over that was a brown leather jacket, and he had on tinted glasses. His job was that of a contract killer, but he wanted everyone to think he was the boss.

Earlier in the evening he had called on one of his apprentices. "I wantcha to go someplace," he said. "Come on. Let's take a little ride." They had burst into an apartment in the Portuguese section of Newark and found their target, the "opponent," in bed. The man and his wife were jarred awake by the sound of wood ripping from the lock point of their door. Immediately the man knew that the forty thousand dollars he owed to a gangster who ran a trucking firm was the source of trouble. The man was a new immigrant trying to make quick American money, and had he been able, he would have made good on the loan. But as the immigrant hurried on a pair of trousers, Donnerstag decided to make a game of it: an example had to be set, he said.

The immigrant understood this. *"Por favor, meu Deus no céu dos santos, eu pago!"* From a dresser drawer he took out a stack of bills, not nearly the amount owed, but a sign of how hard he would try. *"Aqui, pago,* much of it, this. Tomorrow, more."

Donnerstag was amused but unimpressed. He was in one of his moods. Besides, he had not been hired to collect any money but simply to do his specialty, which he fully enjoyed.

He smiled coldly and pushed down at the man's face until the immigrant was on his knees. It was a pitiful sight, especially since the wife sat on the bed watching her husband beg. (*"O que tu queres. Nada! Por favor deixe-me de mão a minha vida!"*) Donnerstag chuckled and lifted his right shoe to the man's mouth until the immigrant understood what he must do next, and kissed it. Then he dutifully kissed the feet of Donnerstag's accomplice, a muscular black man with close-cropped hair and prominent, pointed teeth. He too chuckled. The man's wife looked on confused.

"Thank you, sir," said Donnerstag, taking the money and tucking it into his pocket. Then he extracted a pistol, a thirty-eight.

"Nao, senhor, por favor, eu rezo, não use arma!" the man whimpered. "God in heaven!"

His wife knew instinctively not to cry or scream. She sat there in shock as Donnerstag propelled three silenced bullets into her husband's skull. But soon she did begin to scream uncontrollably, and it excited him. He got on the bed and put a pillow over her head, and mounted her.

That was the routine, and it was similar to what had happened at least a dozen times. Some detectives estimated he had murdered only six people; others, including underworld sources who knew him and had killed with him, said it was more than twelve, perhaps twenty all told. A freelancer, Donnerstag worked for the Italians in the North Ward, the Jews in the trucking business, and the Greeks from Palisades Park and Fort Lee. ("You want it, you got it," he would tell them. "I just wanna be paid.") He carried a derringer in his vest, when a vest was what he was wearing, and his other killing machine was two pieces of hand-sized wood with a taut wire strung between. He worked for as little as five or ten thousand dollars, and he killed in what the mob called "cowboy style."

But Donnerstag could also be cool and calculating, obtaining a photograph of his mark and trailing him for several days until he had thoroughly learned the routines. Night was good, but he also worked in the day. He traveled to Chicago and Florida on hits, and he killed junkies, other gangsters, and a Hell's Angel who had bothered him. The corpses were left in the trunk of a stolen car or at the base of a large landfill in Kearny, there to be bulldozed into municipal rubbish. Or they were cremated in Elizabeth, Newark, or Linden, where there were friendly funeral homes and efficient trash incinerators. In Jersey City the remains were stuffed into barrels of acid and then, it was said, sunk into one of the many tidal creeks that crisscross the cord grass.

Donnerstag too had come from a broken home. His original surname was Cohen, but his father, who was born in New York City, left his mother, a saleswoman and later an office worker in a hospital, when

Gerald was only two. The mother remarried a Russian immigrant by the name of Donnerstag, and in 1956 Jerry suddenly switched his surname to his stepfather's. That same year he married Harriet Schecter in a proper Hebrew ceremony in Irvington, where he worked as a store clerk and on a construction site. Soon he fathered three daughters with Harriet. He had gotten his start in the rackets through narcotics and numbers, but unlike so many of the others in those trades, he had a diploma—from Irvington High—and had spent two years as a fireman in the Navy. He belonged to the Bloomfield Avenue American Legion.

In 1961 Donnerstag had been arrested for assault and a homicide, but assault was considered a petty charge and the murder was declared "self-defense." He had done time the year before, but it was only a three-month term in the county lockup. The charge under which he was detained, however, was revealing: the sale of grossly obscene material. That was the kinky part of him, his most powerful side, and his carnality was mixed inextricably with brutality. Something in him wanted to mete out constant humiliations, of which death was the final draw. Perhaps the word "vile" was inadequate to describe this man who made girls lie in his bathtub and receive his excrement, or had them suck on the cold metal barrel of one of his pistols. Or who, before he felt relief, sometimes had to kneel by a corpse and punch hard at the lifeless body.

Certainly he was known to boast of these acts to his young assistants, instilling respect and fear. After a "job" was done he would have one of these naïve aides, often a black, Puerto Rican, or Italian, drive with him and an accompanying call girl to the night spots in Newark, where he celebrated with cocaine (which he snorted right from the bag) and Cutty Sark, his favorite scotch. Later he might take them to the Copacabana in Manhattan. They were groomed in his image: hot-combed hair, monogrammed shirts, shoes brilliantly shined. But in the end, after such errands, he discarded these protégés somewhat like used tissue. Quite a number of them disappeared.

Of late Donnerstag had been working several blocks from Festa's house, on that central street of the Italian neighborhood, Bloomfield Avenue. There the small shops were wedged hard by each other in one huge uneven mass: travel agencies, hamburger stands, cappuccino cafes, soda shops, funeral parlors, union halls, social clubs, real estate offices, and pasta factories. Across from DeMarco's, a corner diner where gambling stakes were held, was a small store selling statues and other religious charms—El Ojo Magico—with a sign decorated by a gypsy's bewitching eye. It was near this point that Bloomfield Avenue, heading in a northwesterly direction, connected with Mount Prospect Avenue and Ridge Street.

Much of this turf was controlled by the New Jersey branch of the Carlo Gambino crime group, which, in addition to Frank "The Bear" Basto (once a Genovese man), had recently accepted the services of Raymond Freda. Basto and Freda had been partners since their youth—Valvano had introduced them to each other—and their rap sheets, had they been taped end to end, would have run five feet and eight inches long—precisely Frank Basto's height. They too had been "cowboys" in their younger days, barging through jewelry store doors, jumping over bank counters with shopping bags, shooting at security guards, pistol-whipping a cop. Once they lost a pursuing patrol car by spinning their getaway car around on a highway and jumping the median.

Basto had toned down these more foolish antics, grooming himself for a climb in the Mafia hierarchy, where his rank was comparable to that of his friend Tommy Adams. Freda, however, ignored any and all mob strictures whenever they got in the way of making money, and eventually he could list among his deeds purse snatching, car theft, armed robbery, house burglaries, vault robberies, fraud, fencing stolen property, shylocking, bookmaking, extortion, bribery, prostitution, selling illegitimate babies (these from the hookers), counterfeiting, heroin and cocaine distribution, assault, kidnaping, prison escape, perjury and stolen bonds. Though it was not his only vocation, Freda robbed fifteen banks—more than Willie Sutton—and burned down a stable with twenty-seven horses inside. Freda and Basto were reputed mob enforcers—hitmen—and in their arsenal were M-14 rifles, strychnine, time bombs, and grenades, which they got from Jerry Donnerstag. Recently Basto had purchased from a Florida hand, Rickie Mahoney, a machine gun fitted with a silencer. "You never know when this will come in handy," he told Freda.

Donnerstag's ruthless attributes had made him an asset to the Basto-Freda-Valvano crew, if not a particularly respected one. The main problem with Donnerstag, as they saw it, was his mouth. He liked to brag. But Freda appreciated his "heart," his "balls of steel," as he puts it; "He'd kill you quick as look at you, one of the baddest Jews I ever seen." Donnerstag would tell Freda, "I'm just a dumb Jew, but if you want someone killed, I'll kill him." And he meant what he said.

However, Freda and Basto seemed to need little assistance in this regard. People who had associated with them also found themselves on the lists of the missing. There was the New York bank burglar Georgie the Torch: he was said to have been burned in an incinerator. There was also the burglar Freddie Spillman, who was rumored to be informing to the FBI and the Essex County prosecutor and was shot to death on September 18, 1962. And the thief Alton Hughes, whom Quartuccio had tried to emulate, met the same fate.

Hughes had been involved with Ray Freda in 1969, when Freda, who had just been released from the federal penitentiary in Lewisburg, Pennsylvania—where he served four years for a string of bank robberies—was still working with Basto, Valvano, and, now, Donnerstag.

"Bear was hanging around with Hughes," Freda remembers. "They had been making pretty good money. At that time they were going to banks and getting quarters by telling the bank they had laundromats and they were melting the quarters down. You would get one dollar and sixty cents for every four quarters, as the price of silver was high. I guess you remember when they put a big piece in the paper that people were hoarding silver and there was a change shortage. Well, it was us. It wasn't big money but it sure beat working eight hours a day for nothing."

Freda nonetheless needed much more money to pay back his boss, Joe Paterno, from whom he had borrowed twenty-five thousand to bribe a judge who had designed the very writ on which Raymond had been released. Paterno was the chieftain of a supercrew that controlled Bloomfield Avenue, and he served as Carlo Gambino's *caporegime* in New Jersey. One of the few quiet and dignified Newark hoodlums, Joe looked, in his horn-rim glasses and dark-blue suits (fashionably matched, often, with a red patterned silk tie), like a Wall Street broker or a senior banking officer. To generate the revenue owed to Paterno, Freda opened a gambling club on Tenth Street with Bear Basto, and at Paterno's request, they also went about devising a major jewel heist.

The mark was Lucien Piccard, a factory that made custom jewelry. In conjunction with some employees of a burglar alarm company, which handled the factory's security, Basto, Freda, and Hughes (a tall, thin burglar) were to enter the plant after the alarm men inserted a dead tube in the signal box, killing any alert to the main office or police station. One of the insiders was to leave a side door open, and they would go through the vault with a burning-bar. For backup they brought in Jerry the Jew Donnerstag.

Hughes stole a station wagon for the score and they bided their time at their club the night of the burglary. While they were waiting there, Rickie Mahoney stopped by to sell the machine gun. Basto gave Mahoney five hundred and hid the weapon in the back of the club.

Not long afterward Paterno called: it was time for them to leave. Freda stayed with the station wagon as The Bear, Donnerstag, and Hughes entered. Soon they waved Raymond over to the side to pick up two duffel bags bulging with watches, stones, and gold bracelets. They drove to an apartment Donnerstag rented on Elmwood Avenue for his bookie operations, and then they ditched the vehicle in East Orange.

The next night Basto went to Freda's home upset. "Everyone's hot as hell. There's a fucking bag of diamonds missing."

"You know I ain't got it," Freda said.

"Yeah, I know who I give it to—Al. Hughes was the only one left with a bag of the stuff alone, know what I mean?" Basto said Joe Paterno was seething.

Having exhausted his own share from the score to settle his debts, Raymond was more concerned with making money than immediately assuaging Paterno's anger. He teamed up with Hughes for another burglary, this time a safe job, in Mountainside. But the cops caught them inside. Freda offered the police brass ten thousand to say he was outside the building at the time of arrest, informing the cop he was a close friend of the Mountainside underboss, Gyp DeCarlo, who operated a restaurant known as the Barn. But the FBI had been monitoring the Barn for years and intercepted the call from the police, who told the agents about Freda's offer. Raymond was thus tagged with a second charge.

In the meantime, while Freda waited at home on bail, fretting over a return to prison, Rickie Mahoney stopped by to talk about a score he had for them. He never did make it home. Why or how will never be known, but he was shot in his car—something of a Freda trademark. Freda went to the funeral and the cops watching the ceremony gave him some very quizzical looks. He only smiled.

In the Byzantine flurry of activity—and these operations were typical of the Bloomfield crew—there was another meeting about the missing bag of diamonds. And there was an even more urgent discussion about rumors that Hughes was considering turning informer. He had been spotted talking at Branch Brook Park with two men who looked like federal agents, and Freda and Donnerstag were apprehensive. "He even said himself he ain't doing no more time," Donnerstag said of Hughes. "He's informing. He's gotta go."

It was said not in the tone of an order but as an anxious suggestion, for Freda carried much more authority, more "weight," on the streets. Still, Freda listened carefully, agreeing with Donnerstag despite the opposition of Basto, who considered Hughes a close friend.

Jerry Donnerstag continued to fill Freda's ears with dark scenarios and rumors, and Freda—already a parole violator—could bear no more indictments. What if Hughes opened up, Donnerstag reminded him, on Lucien Piccard?

Freda called Alton and told him to meet him downstate in a restaurant. "I got a score in Long Branch," he lied.

Hughes went to the small Jersey Shore community, which is in Monmouth County, a mob stronghold where the chief of detectives had recently committed suicide under suspicious circumstances. While awaiting Freda's arrival, Hughes stopped at Basto's summer cottage there and took a walk on the boardwalk, where he bought The Bear's children stuffed animals and candy. He also happened onto Johnny Quartuccio, who was still hiding there from Festa. "I'm down just for the day," he told Johnny. "We got something."

Hughes's corpse was discovered sprawled along the side of a road the next morning. It was stripped of all identification; even the monograms had been cut out of his shirt. There was a bullet hole in the back of his head. ("There wasn't much heat around where we lived," Freda remembers. "The cops felt it was just one less crook around. In Newark you never had too much to worry about. Those cops would take a hot stove.") Pressed on the Mountainside charge, Freda arranged for a meeting with a friend of DeCarlo's, a Union County judge. For ten thousand a suspended sentence was arranged, and to raise the slush fund Freda and Basto robbed a post office in Paramus. According to Freda, when their getaway was spotted they simply paid a few more cops.

It was in this vicious and frenetic cycle of activity that Jerry the Jew Donnerstag got his schooling, and Jerry Festa would soon join in. For Festa and Donnerstag had become acquainted with each other through the Cabaret, the diners, and through a problem that had arisen between Donnerstag's numbers lottery and one of its patrons. Nanny, now the cook at Chicken Delight, had a winning slip good for two hundred and fifty dollars, but Donnerstag refused to pay her, accusing her and her friend Barbara, who took the bets for Donnerstag, of cheating. Festa was irate over the matter, and though Donnerstag at first ignored him, a meeting was set up when Jerry the Jew learned that the Chicken Delight owner was with Tommy Adams.

They met at a shoeshine shop, where Donnerstag was carefully tending to his patent leather. He was with Freda's brother-in-law, Austin Castiglione. "Look, I'm gonna pay," said Donnerstag. "But I think the number got slipped in. If I find out, I'm gonna break somebody's ass."

But on the whole the conversation was surprisingly cordial, and soon Festa began to see a lot of Donnerstag, getting prospective scores from both him and Barbara. In return, Festa allowed Jerry the Jew to rent his basement for the gambling phones.

Donnerstag was impressed by Festa's agility and powers of observation—the way his eyes could sweep a block, recognizing faces there, recording the entire layout of a house, and spotting any strange car or license plate. And Festa, in comparison with the addicts Donnerstag usually dealt with, was quick-minded. Donnerstag greatly enjoyed a story about how Festa had, on Park Avenue in South Orange, foiled a sure capture by the police during one of his and Johnny's burglaries. As it happened, Festa was robbing the apartment of a renegade bookie when suddenly Quartuccio, who was the lookout, gave him the three-beep horn warning from the car. As the cops arrived, Festa rolled up his pants, mussed up his hair, took a robe from the closet, put his shoes under his arms, shoved his feet in a pair of slippers, and walked down the stars acting as if *he* were the victim. The cops said, "Please get downstairs and out of the way," and as they entered the apartment, Festa escaped in the cops' own car. Donnerstag told Basto and Freda about him. "That sucker can get in and out of anywhere," Jerry the Jew said.

That summer, on July 27, Donnerstag took Festa along on the theft of a 1784 painting by the British artist John Opie. It hung in the castle-like home of Dr. Earl LeRoy Wood on Ballantine Parkway. Back on July 7, Festa had broken in there looking for coins, but he had tripped an alarm and had to make a quick departure. Safely hidden, he had watched curiously as the police arrived with a local councilman who ran an anticrime vigilante group and often turned up at the scene of a crime. Two weeks later, Donnerstag told Festa he had talked with the councilman, who told him about the painting there, called "The School Mistress," which, he said, was worth six hundred thousand dollars and was protected by its own alarm. It was then that Donnerstag took Festa back to the house, stopping on the way at a club the councilman owned to double-check the final details.

After a ten-minute conference they went on to Ballantine Parkway.

Festa quickly opened the French doors and ripped the alarm wire away from the painting, knowing now just how long it would take the cops to respond. They took the picture back to Festa's house, where it was photographed with a Polaroid camera and bundled in rags and blankets.

Donnerstag had originally claimed the painting was going to be sold in Florida, but instead it was taken to Ray Freda for a West Virginia sale. Festa had seen Freda only a few times, and hardly knew Basto, except to have met him at the Democratic Club; and though Basto seemed a jovial man, Festa was leary of Freda, who had glazed, bulging eyes. His apprehension was altogether warranted: Freda gave them the paltry sum of five thousand for the score, and again, as had been the case with Valvano, nobody complained. Anyway, Freda was not around much longer. The day after this score he was remanded, on his parole violation, to the Federal Detention Headquarters on New York's West Street before being shipped back to Lewisburg, where he would spend the next year—a particularly eventful one for his friends Donnerstag and Festa—behind prison walls.

*   *

In transit between points of detention, Raymond Freda crossed the path of Riviello, who had just begun his own prison term. Riviello appeared drawn and edgy, and Freda sent back word to the streets that perhaps Teddy, in exchange for leniency, or out of frustration, was indeed going to talk.

Though in fact such was not the case, Festa heard the rumor and shared it with Rose, who was already reeling with tension and confusion. The apparent molestation of Janet had caused a long, deep funk, and she was always exhausted: there was Chicken Delight to run, and on February 22, 1969, she had given birth to another child, Allan, the son they had long wanted. Rose needed tranquilizers to endure Jerry's newest cohorts, especially the intimidating presence of the brutal-sounding hooligan who called himself The Jew. Donnerstag enjoyed telling her his bloodiest stories.

Rose was easily scared, and when she was scared she became paralyzed and acquiescent. Her whole life had been like that, just drifting with the nearest, strongest currents. Although she was accustomed to living outside the law, she felt uncomfortable around the gangsters gravitating to Jerry. What made it more disturbing was her own involvement. She had come to be a conspirator on some of the thefts, and was sometimes ordered to be a lookout on the robberies, which terrified her. A few times she thought of leaving, but she was bound by the children and by her own inertia—compounded by a dedication to Jerry that had increased since, in February of 1967, he had officially become her husband in a civil ceremony.

The food shop might as well have been a criminal nerve center. While Rose tried to keep a balanced budget, wise guys and cops kept coming in charging this and charging that, and Festa was always calling to tell her to send food and money over to the crap games. He was still out all hours with Tommy Adams, and when his luck ran bad he was borrowing shylock sums that stunned her. On the rare occasions when she had the nerve to complain, he would reassure her that he would get out of debt once he hit the "big score." Or he might have a temper tantrum and knock over the dining-room table.

At 8:30 P.M. on June 17, 1969, Rose was admitted to Room 210 of Saint James Hospital. Her stomach ached and burned, and the radiologist confirmed that she had an ulcer the size of a quarter. Surgeons removed a portion of her stomach.

Soon Festa too was afflicted. Within forty-eight hours of his wife's diagnosis he suddenly felt as if someone had grasped him in a bear hug; a pencil dropped from his fingers; his arms were numb. He was rushed to a room across from Rose's ward and told he had probably suffered a slight heart attack. All he could hear was a machine going *blip-blip* and then suddenly a gruff voice in the hall. It was Tommy. He had forced his way past the nurses and appeared at Festa's sickbed. He was alarmed. "I treat you like a son," he said. "The doctors—don't worry. We get the best!"

But Festa could not bear hospitals and checked himself out the next day. He could stand the pain, and he was not going to change his ways now. At the end of June, when Rose was released, they all celebrated at the race track in Monmouth, where Jerry hit for eight thousand dollars. That made Tommy happy, since he was given half. Festa felt fully recovered.

In early autumn Detective George, who hung out a block away from Chicken Delight, came in the eatery looking for Festa. It was an incident that would cap Jerry's entrance into the name-laden, dizzying world of *mafiosi,* and demonstrate the stark dangers. The cop had been with a bunko squad, and in one investigation he had come across an eighty-one-year-old woman in Irvington who looked as if she kept large quantities of cash around. He gave Festa her name, address, and phone number.

"What's the best way of going about it?" Festa asked. "You know, uh, go up and see about a roofing job, or what? Just break in?"

Festa wanted to know her patterns, and George was most obliging. "Usually on weekends she goes to visit a friend. Then she goes to church and Sunday dinner."

That Saturday Festa began calling the woman's home. No one answered. Sunday he called again and still there was no response. At five-thirty he, Hank, and their decoy, Rose, set out on the job. After parking their car, Hank and Jerry surveyed the premises, and the best entry appeared to be the wood hatch doors at the rear that led into the basement. They broke through them and, with a screwdriver, snapped a latch on a door inside, coming up through the kitchen. The house was cold and dark. They proceeded past the phone stand in a small passageway and up the stairs across a landing. Hurriedly they surveyed the second floor. Only one of the rooms looked lived in. They went right to a closet and in it found a big bread box with a padlock. Festa bent the tin and saw it was filled with strongboxes. They took them and left.

On the ride home Festa forced open one of the boxes; it was filled with tens and twenties. Once they got up to his bedroom they pried the rest of them open, and Jerry spotted among the bills some jewelry store receipts. He said, "Hey. There's more up there."

He and Hank returned to the house, cruising around twice before again making an entry. They crawled on the floor so their flashlights would not reflect out of the building. "Jerry!" Hank summoned. "Look at this." He had found a purse full of money. He pushed it under the bed and toward Festa, who was on the other side, and as he did so his light happened across a cash-filled shoebox.

Back at Ridge Street, Jerry began counting the take—twenty-three thousand dollars—and instructed Hank to discard the strongboxes. Hank was leaving with the empty strongboxes when Adams happened by. "What? What?" said Tommy. "You got a score?"

Festa was sheepish, since he was obligated to report such matters to Adams ahead of time. "Yeah," he answered. But he told Adams it had not amounted to much. "We didn't get no chance for really searching the whole house."

Tommy insisted that they go back yet another time for a fuller surveillance. He drove Festa up to the place in his own car, a white Cadillac, but ordered Festa to go in without him. "I'm a fuckin' button-man," said Adams. "I can't get hung on no fuckin' burglary."

Festa quickly scanned the lifeless home and returned to the car saying he didn't see much more of consequence. Back at the house, he gave Tommy a thousand in twenties.

The next day Adams phoned, saying, "I need money quick. Got some problems at my restaurant. Sending Ralphie down. Give him a G-note."

"I dunno, Tommy. Um, shit, I ain't got too much. I'd have to take it out of the store receipts."

Tommy was unconcerned about how he got it. "Don't worry," he said. "Don't worry about it."

Jerry and Rose were planning a trip to Scranton that Monday, but before they left, Tommy's son Ralphie caught them unawares by coming in through the back door of the house while they were tallying Chicken Delight receipts and some of the burgled money on the dining-room table. The way the cash was spread out—all in small bills—must have made it look like a million dollars. Ralphie caught a glimpse of it before taking the thousand for his father and departing.

They were in Scranton for three days visiting friends and relatives. On their return Marie announced, "There've been a few calls from that Adams fellow."

At seven that night the phone rang again—Tommy. He said, "I want you up here *right away*."

Festa had never heard his voice at such a commanding pitch. "What's a matter, Tommy, got problems?"

"Get up here right away and I want you alone."

"You got problems, or what?"

"Well, just get your fuckin' ass up now. Come in the front way. I'll be waiting for ya."

Festa got off the phone, shaken. He told his wife, "Something's wrong, awful wrong. Tommy—he don't sound right. He wants me there—ah—all alone and he wants me now. I don't like the smell of it."

Rose too was concerned. "You want me to go up with you?"

"No. I just got through telling ya, I have to come alone."

"Where you going?" she asked.

"Up the house, and the funny part is, he told me to come in the front way. I always go through the back."

"What do you think's the matter?"

"I don't know, Ro, I don't know."

Festa's mind raced during the twenty-minute drive. *Did I say something wrong when I was drunk? Nah, I ain't been drinking here. Rivi-*

ello? No, what the fuck, Tommy's got the same rap anyhows, knows he's gonna see some jail. Couldn't be something I said about him, I ain't been throwing his name on the street. Did Hank do something stupid again?

Tommy lived west of Newark in a duplex structure with a small trim yard. Jerry rode by the house once before coming to a halt, trying to see if there was anything suspicious. Oddly, Tommy's wife did not seem to be home, as she always was. The entire premises were wrapped in darkness.

Instead of entering from the back, where he would come past the bedroom and through the kitchen to the dining room and parlor, he did as instructed, going in through the front door. One look at Tommy and he knew the situation was indeed extreme. As Adams opened the door his face was as hard as stone, the skin stretched back, his teeth slowly grinding. The white poodle was not there barking, as it normally was, and instead of saying hello, Tommy shook him down, looking for a concealed weapon.

"Tommy, what's wrong?" he said.

Adams barked back at him. "Get in."

As they entered the living room, Tommy pointed for him to sit in a chair which had been placed, for some reason, between that room and the passageway to the dining room. Adams himself sat on the couch to Festa's right, next to the sole source of illumination in the house, the night light at the bottom of an end-table lamp. The tiny light nonetheless showed Adams's eyes, which were big ovals. The rest of his face was in a shadow.

"Jerry. I treat you good?"

"Yeah, Tommy, why?"

"Never mind. I ever fuck you?"

"No, Tommy."

"I give you my name?"

"Yeah, Tommy."

"Nobody fuck with you? Law, wise guys, nobody? You with me?"

"Yeah."

Tommy's voice dropped precipitously. "Then why you fuck me?" he growled.

Festa squirmed in the chair. He had the feeling someone was in the darkness behind him. "Tommy," he pleaded. "What'd I do?"

"You know what you, what the fuck you did. Ya beat me out of

Michael Brown 72

money. You know—I didn't like you, you'd be dead right now, before we talk."

Festa's voice grew tight and higher. "Tommy, what're you *talkin'* about?"

Adams shouted. "That fuckin' score, motherfucker. Suppose they get my license up there? My car was on the scene. You know what'm talking about, you cocksucker. Right now I'm gonna kill ya." He was nearly screaming.

At any moment Festa expected a quick and final, fatal motion. But Tommy still sat there, yelling, "My kid, he lie?"

"Whatcha mean, Tommy?"

"He seen the fuckin' table loaded with the fuckin' money, cocksucker. You give me a G-note and then you give me another G when I send down. You make a hundred twenty-three thou!"

"What are you talking about, Tommy? You're crazy, Tommy."

"You told Morgan."

"What'd I tell Morgan?"

"You told Morgan you made a hundred twenty thousand, you fuck. My kid seen it on the table."

"Tommy, I told Morgan there *could* have been a hundred twenty in the house. I didn't have no shot for searching it. There could've been a hundred twenty."

"What about my kid—Ralphie lie?"

"Tommy, it was the Chicken Delight receipts."

Adams seemed about to explode. "What, you make that much? I'll buy you out tomorrow. Fuck, I'll take the store, you make that much."

"Tommy, I don't even know what you're *talking* about. The biggest bill's twenty dollars. From the store. A bunch of ones. What did Ralphie tell ya?"

"The whole motherfuckin' table was loaded."

"Ah, c'mon, Tommy. No way."

"You motherfucker, my kid lie? I'll kill ya now!"

"Tommy, I ain't fucking nobody. You believe that?"

"Morgan tells. Ralphie tells. Who the fuck are you! Ya fuck, you come from nowhere anyway. Who the fuck you been with? Who're you?"

"Tommy, what can I tell ya. I'm saying, no way; no way, shape, or form."

"Cocksucker, I'm gonna find out. You think you make a jerkoff out of somebody? Nah, nah. I want the money!"

"Tommy, what do you want?"

Adams let out his biggest burst. "I want money!"

Festa's voice came as close as it could to that of a lamb. "How much you need, Tommy?"

"Send me thirty thou."

"Tommy," he begged, "I haven't got no thirty thousand dollars!"

"Give a fuck where you get it. Rob a bank. I want thirty thousand."

"Tommy, there's no way, shape, or form."

"You get me thirty thousand or you're fuckin' dead."

"Phew, Tommy, huh, ya know what I got, ya know what I'm doin'. I mean, if I hit it you got it."

Now he screamed, "I want it right now, cocksucker. You got it."

"Tommy, I *don't* got it."

With this Adams pushed his wide body up from the couch. Festa distinctly heard a movement behind his chair, as if someone—such as Tommy's henchman, Morgan?—had moved from the kitchen into the dining room just behind him. He decided they were preparing to garrote him.

Adams seemed to be glancing just behind Festa. He walked to the couch, then back again, as if he were deep in thought. Festa figured this was it. He theorized that Morgan was awaiting the signal.

Tommy began ranting again. "You know I got a wife. You know I'm goin' to jail, cocksucker." His voice was a maddened baritone like none Festa had ever encountered. "You do this to me, Tommy Adams?"

"I didn't do nothing. How'm I gonna get thirty thousand? You wanna kill, what the fuck, what can I do? What can I say, Tommy?"

He barked, "How much you give me?"

"Tommy, I don't know. I don't even know what's in the bank. I gotta coupla Gs, maybe."

"Okay. Fifteen Gs, tomorrow."

"Tommy, I don't know. I'll do what I can."

"I don't give a shit what you gotta do. I'm gonna tell you one thing now. You go home, you pray. You pray you're lucky to walk out alive, you motherfucker. But I'm gonna find out and I'm telling you now, if I find out, you're dead. Dead!"

"Okay, Tommy."

"Tomorrow."

"I'll do everything I can," he said meekly, looking down. "Can I go now?"

"Yeah, motherfucker. Get the fuck outta here."

As Festa walked to his car his legs were shaking. All the way home he studied his rear-view mirror. Had he not been such a moneymaker for Adams, he was certain he would be dead. These were not like the mob guys in Scranton; there he even had fist fights with wise guys, he wasn't afraid of them. They would kill back home only as a last resort, and when a hit occurred, it was big newspaper news. Here it was hardly reported.

When he got home Rose was waiting up, and Marie got out of bed. She was naïve enough to say, "Who's he think he is? He's got a lot of nerve. You don't have to give him money from the store." But when Marie saw his face, she too was shaken.

The next day Festa took Hank and Rose around to several banks, where they changed tens and twenties from the score into hundred-dollar bills, so Tommy wouldn't become suspicious. He immediately sent fifteen grand up to Casa de Irvington.

Marie and Rose were more upset than ever before. First Johnny, now Adams. They seemed as vicious as they were untrustworthy. Some friend, this Adams, thought Marie.

But this was not Scranton any more. Festa was no longer the king of the bars. The champ. A man to fear. This wasn't Scranton any more; it wasn't a part of the same planet.

III. Foxfire

O N DECEMBER 16, 1969, the Newark underworld was beset by what the FBI director, J. Edgar Hoover, described as "the largest series of federal gambling arrests ever conducted in the area." In conjunction with Attorney General John Mitchell, Hoover announced a midnight raid in which fifty-five persons had been apprehended as members of a betting syndicate reaching into Upstate New York. Among them was Tommy Adams's close associate, Sam DeCavalcante.

The bust came on the heels of another major triumph for law enforcement, the conviction, in Superior Court, before Judge Ralph Fusco, of eighteen other gamblers and the old *caporegime* Ritchie Boiardo. Boiardo had ruled the First Ward of Newark since the bootleg days of Abe Zwillman, and his powers were attested to by statues he had erected of himself and his family on his twenty-nine-acre estate in Livingston. Most of the arrests, however, were minor ones: sitters who tended a bookie's phone, or those who collected numbers slips, the runners. Through the local and federal net slipped many criminals who ran gambling enterprises as a sideline to far more egregious acts, and among these was "The Super Jew," as he was known, Gerald Cohen Donnerstag.

In the wake of Adams's frightening diatribe, Festa, again in search of a powerful associate, gravitated ever closer to the rapacious gangster. Though Donnerstag was not a made-man in La Cosa Nostra (prevented from formal induction on the basis of his ethnicity alone, he claimed), the ease with which he murdered had endeared him to certain factions of the Boiardo group, and he was allowed to operate on Bloomfield Avenue under the auspices of Andy Gerard, an up-and-coming Boiardo lieutenant.

In reality, though, Donnerstag remained fearlessly independent, a swashbuckling type who listened to his own musings and traveled where he wanted to. Balding, he wore a hairpiece to shield his high forehead and combed the remaining hair over the topmost gaps. He had brown eyes that showed little of the coolness underneath, and his face, not at all a pleasant one, was red with hypertension. When Festa first saw him at the Cabaret, he was taken with Donnerstag's outrageous self-assurance, the thick gold chain around his neck and his pumping, chesty swagger. Donnerstag was trying to make time with a topless dancer there, and, after several rebuffs, he left suddenly and went out to his automobile. He returned with a white mink coat from a recent robbery and plopped it before the stripper. Then he squatted to the floor and took out a crisp wad of hundreds, peeling one off and dropping it to the floor with each few back steps toward the exit. ("Come on, I know I'm a sonofabitching ugly Jew, but my money talks," he said. She followed him out. He grabbed back the fur after intercourse. He also shat on her stomach.)

Donnerstag kept three apartments in the Newark area. His common-law wife, Shirley (whom he took up with after a divorce from his first wife in 1967), maintained the one in Belleville, at 375 Joralemon Avenue. They had three children. The other flats were for his numbers operations and his mistresses. In one of them had been a girl named Lynne, who died from what was recorded as pneumonia and a fit of choking, asphyxiation. Rumors began to circulate that Donnerstag had drowned her in a bathtub, and he did not go out of his way to squelch them. "You know, we all gotta go sometime," he snickered.

Festa and Donnerstag merged their crews and declared themselves partners. But burglaries would no longer be their mainstay. They turned instead to stickups. Their first major hit was a downtown jewelry shop. They sent in three of their steadiest holdup men, including Donnerstag's daily gofer, a bespectacled junkie named Wally Lombardo. Festa monitored a police scanner as the masked bandits emptied the safe and showcase. It was in the middle of the day, and a busy street, but The

Jew stood casually at the store's very entrance, smoking an unfiltered cigarette. Supposedly he was a lookout.

This was April 16, 1970, and a dozen armed robberies would follow. They took off a payroll delivery, a funeral parlor, and some of the wealthier suburban homes. In case a police cruiser pulled up, Hank Ellis was stationed in a second vehicle, the "crash car," which, if necessary, could be plowed into the cops' path; and Pete Feldman, the young addict staying at Festa's house, was also called to service. Knocking on a door, he would flash a detective's badge to the residents, show them mugshots of fugitives he was supposedly seeking, and display a false identification card as they let him in. These paraphernalia were provided by a real-life cop, Sergeant Raymond Grill, who also gave them handcuffs and walkie-talkies. Recently suspended from the city force, Grill worked in a Livingston gas station.

The victims were herded at gunpoint to a bedroom or bathroom. There they were handcuffed or otherwise bound to a shower stall or a piece of furniture. As Lombardo went in, accompanied by an interchangeable cast of accomplices, Donnerstag and Festa cruised the area, again as lookouts. Lombardo was from the Ironbound section. He was roughly Feldman's age, and as reliant on dope, but more obsequious, a follower. And he was treated on a lesser scale than two of Donnerstag's other regulars, Joe Zelinski and Joey Bontempo, who were crueler in style than Lombardo.

At night, after the day's work was done, Donnerstag led Festa down new byways of the brotherhood and into a veritable supermart of Runyonesque names. At a guarded loft in Lower Manhattan, where they hocked a ring once owned by the actress Tallulah Bankhead, Festa met a swarthy fence named "Billy the Chink." In the Newark clubs were also "Red Light," "Charlie the Blade," "Cabert," and "Nicky Skins." It was through Donnerstag that he met Frank Basto, but not knowing Festa well, Basto, who was providing them with fake identification documents used to cash stolen traveler's checks, said little to Jerry, a reticence that would radically change in the coming year.

The same was not true of Nicky Skins. He and Festa talked frequently at Jimo's, a restaurant on Fourth Avenue. There they plotted the heist of precious metals at Englehardt Industries, from which they were to extract four one-hundred-and-twenty-three-pound silver bars. Though he wore collegiate sweaters, and looked more like a fashionable bartender than a hoodlum, Skins (real name: Nicholas Stefanelli) was as much a leg breaker as Donnerstag, and it was he who, every Wednesday, collected the shylock money (or "shy") which Festa owed. Rose doled out the weekly interest of 30 percent from her restaurant coffers, and when she complained that the payments seemed never-ending, Skins showed no diplomacy whatever. "Talk to your husband," he said. "Talk about it with him before you fucking open your trap."

Donnerstag was a bridge between the established executioners of New Jersey and those who, like Festa, were working their way up the bottom rungs. Jerry was still new on the block and as such was excluded from certain discussions at the hangouts. He had not made his bones as a killer, he lacked "heart." But he was a good moneymaker, of course, and he had what The Jew called a "golden gut." By this Donnerstag meant his keen and constant intuition, the way warnings would seemingly come to Jerry in the form of his stomach turning taut as a board and a prickly sensation moving from his spine to his neck. Jerry the Jew first fully appreciated these signs during a holdup in Jersey City. Beforehand, Festa had said he did not "feel good" about it, and indeed they quite unexpectedly ran into a sheriff's deputy. A gun fight ensued, and during a frantic getaway, Lombardo got shot, though not fatally.

Still, they were scoring big together in Scranton, Belleville, Newark, and East Orange. Occasionally Festa went inside himself during a holdup, but more often he let the flunkies do the dirty work. On July 22, 1970, however, while Donnerstag was mourning the death of his stepfather (and duly practicing the Hebrew rituals of Shiva, staying at home for a week), Festa took Hank on a good old burglary score. It was at 545 North Seventh Street in Newark, and he felt the juices flowing again: going in a house to search for hidden treasures was a rush to him not unlike the anticipation of sex. But his intuition was off this time, and they were caught inside when a neighbor was alerted, finding themselves in the Second Precinct. A pay-off had to be made to a court clerk, John DelMauro, and two detectives, Joseph S. Costa and John Cuff, who fixed their records so no previous arrests would be noticed by the judge. In September the sentence (sixty days) was suspended and they left the courthouse with another fifty-dollar penalty.

Though never again would their relationship be a close one, Festa missed Tommy Adams. The older gangster had not been so lucky with his own legal hassles, and by this time he was in the federal corrections system with Johnny Quartuccio. But before Adams left, they had smoothed over their differences, and Festa had attended Tommy's going-away party, a fund-raiser in the same house where, not a year before, he had faced what he thought was certain death. He told Tommy how his life had changed with Donnerstag, and how well the robberies had gone.

Adams was pleased. His former apprentice was getting tougher and bolder, wiser to the streets. He took Jerry aside, into his bedroom, and shocked Festa by affectionately throwing his arms around him, hugging him good-bye. Tommy sounded woefully slow, but perhaps he too had a sound intuition. "Watch the Jew," Adams said. "He's got the big fuckin' mouth." For some reason, tears came to the aging gangster's eyes.

* *

Hanging out at the intersection of Mount Prospect and Second Avenue, near the Chicken Delight, Peter Feldman's kid brother, Jed, was back to playing games as the corner clown and street bully. He threw eggs at passing traffic and tried to pick fights with guys younger than he. Since Rudy, his very best friend, was away in the service, he spent the summer with his old grammar school pal, Hugo. He told vulgar jokes to the girls, and snuck up to the other junkies with a Pathmark grocery bag over his head. He liked to scare the hell out of them.

Jed, like his brother, had been staying with the Festas and working as a delivery boy. But he'd been fired and evicted from the house when he was found selling amphetamines from the back room of the food shop. Festa was still mad at him, and Jed told Hugo he was afraid Jerry would beat him up. When he saw his former boss coming by he would walk down the street to a shadowy stoop and hide there until Festa had passed him.

His biggest preoccupation, however, was his own family—especially his father. The Festas had taken him in because he was abused at home, but lately he had taken to hitting his old man back, discovering that such retaliation stopped the beatings. "If I knew when I was a kid what I know now," he told Hugo, "there wouldn't been no trouble." He didn't get along well with his oldest sister, Anja, or "Angie," either. She was often in the company of Gerald Donnerstag, someone Jed looked up to as a role model. But Jed's sister hardly spoke to him. Jed was the black sheep. He hit Angie's car with an egg. Everyone on the corner roared. Angie didn't think he was funny.

Jed had just turned twenty. He wore wrinkled khaki pants, scruffy loafers, and white T-shirts which were always clean. They were sleeveless, too, to show his arms. He had a build like a boxer (which he aspired to be) and a cherubic, hillbilly look about his face, which was surrounded by curly blond hair. Below these angelic tufts, and above the bright blue eyes, clusters of acne were burgeoning as a consequence of his drug use, and on August 27, 1970, had come problems with the law. Driving through Forest Hills with Hugo in his beat-up old Mercury, Jed was stopped by a patrolman who, searching under the front seat, came up with eight capsules of heroin. At the Second Precinct station house, Hugo had been filled with fury: he was not a user himself, yet Jed was declining the blame. Fortunately another cop came by. "He's the one," he said. "There's the troublemaker." The cop pointed right at Jed Feldman.

Somehow Jed had gotten through Sumner Street Grammar School without learning to read. But he had been good at math, and a good fighter in the schoolyard. Until he dropped out in the ninth grade. Back then, he and Rudy had been quite a team. They stole cases of soda from a delivery truck near Catholic High School, started up cranes on the construction sites every Saturday, shoplifted at S. Klein's department store, threw compressed gas cylinders in the Passaic River to watch the bubbles rise, and hung around the freight yards. Once Jed hopped a train and had to beg his way back from Trenton on a bus. He had not been able to jump off as the train left Newark.

Their home life had been more a burden on Jed than on Pete, because their father doubted that Jed was really his own child. Jed was thus accorded even less in the way of guidance, or clothes. He and Pete had nasty fist fights over his wearing Pete's new iridescent pants without permission. When Jed worked at a Shop-Rite, or in the family's lunch wagon, or shoveling snow, whatever money he made was immediately confiscated by his father. He was always penniless, and bruised from his father's whippings.

Their father was obsessed with his own past. His parents had died in a concentration camp under Hitler—turned into lampshades, Mr. Feldman figured—and the only time he spoke to his sons was to reminisce about how he had worked, or so he said, for the Russian underground, and what it was like waiting for the Gestapo to kill you in those death camps. These recollections had a profound effect on Pete, who, though basically shy and warmhearted, was consumed with bitterness. "I never got a break in my life," he would say later. "In my younger days when I was at school, there were a lot of people didn't like Jews. My father told me, if they hit you, turn the other cheek. I did, when I was a kid. I turned the other cheek, and got smacked on the other one, you know? I didn't turn it no more. That was it. I fought back." Pete had tried his hand at odd jobs—Festa's roofing, cleaning out pipes, and working in a gas station—but his struggling spirit was never properly routed. He "fought back" by robbing people who he felt were luckier.

The Feldmans lived in a five-story yellow tenement fronted by a small dingy courtyard only a two-minute walk from the Festas' chicken business. Jed had followed his brother's path to the campuslike reformatory at Jamesburg, where he ate bean and baloney sandwiches and thickened his biceps by bailing hay. He never did follow the Jamesburg motto: "Go placidly amid the noise and haste . . ." He surfaced from there on July 14, 1967, and started "dip-and-dabbing" heroin. He smoked good Colombian ("sure-enough stuff"), popped uppers and downers, or, on special occasions, such as New Year's Eve, he did orange-sunshine acid.

Rose had often spotted him with the other addicts on the corner, drinking Southern Comfort, getting into fights, always shoving people. They were introduced by Nanny, and Rose hadn't liked his attitude at first. Too cocky. But Rose grew to like him too. He helped sweep the walk and was growing more respectful. He started to look upon her almost as a mother, and she would watch his parents walk by, saddened that they would not even say hello to him. Nor would they help him when trouble came. In January he had been arrested for breaking a kid's nose over a football game. Jerry sent him a carton of cigarettes and went to court vouching for the boy's character.

But Jed was not the type to listen. If the Festas scolded him, he laughed in their faces, and each evening he appeared with the other junkies swarming near an old coffee shop where, in the basement of one building, they could press in their syringes without interruption. Then they would gather like cockroaches in the small park across the street, chasing out the old people who liked to feed the pigeons. Occasionally one of them would overdose, and instead of helping, the others would run away. Precisely such an accident happened to a baker's daughter whom Jed considered his girl friend. She died before he got back with some ice from the Chicken Delight, but at least he tried to revive her.

Michael Brown 82

Most of the time Jed scared girls away. He was too used to arguing with them, as he did with Angie, who called him "Mr. Pillhead." So he and Rudy would go to Seaside Heights on the Shore looking for women, or Jed would sell hot televisions or ratchet sets and go to Times Square looking to buy a whore.

Jed told Rose he was never meant to be born. He claimed his mother jumped off a windowsill when she was pregnant and did a belly-flop on the floor, trying to abort him. He also told Rose about his fights at home. He had come in bloody and crying one evening, saying his father had thrown him down a flight of steps. "Well, come sit by the desk," said Rose. "I'm gonna call Jerry up."

Festa told her to bring him home. They said he could stay as long as there were no drugs. (Hitmen were okay, but *that* they didn't want near the four children.)

"Yeah, yeah, okay," Jed had promised. "I just don't wanna go back to the apartment." He was given a room on the attic floor and the job of delivering chicken. He ballooned in weight because he was pilfering from the deliveries. He also did some roofing, but the store was his main chore. His sister Angie was working at Chicken Delight, and there was some friction. Instead of a uniform, Angie came to work in hot pants, and Rose did not like her seeing so much of Jerry the Jew.

Rose just could not take to Donnerstag. Never had she met a more insolent man, nor one so cruel. He called his own wife "Olive Oyl" (she was thin, gangly), and sometimes when Donnerstag was mad at her, he would mutter, "Olive Oyl's gonna get found in the bathtub one of these days."

"What's with you and this bathtub?" Marie, hearing this, would scold. "How can you say such things?" But she didn't really believe him, not when it came to murder. Marie figured he was just "rude and crude"—"appalling," really. By now, though, she could not have any illusions that Jerry was simply gambling and roofing. It was wide-open: The jewelry sat right on the dining table. But she too was getting caught up in what she would later call a "whirlwind." At first she had cried to Rose about the wrongdoing in their household, and yelled some more at Jerry, but her cousin wasn't even slowing down. It was getting faster. She felt punishment was in store. She had prayed at first that he would halt his criminality. Then she had reoriented her prayers. Now she prayed he wouldn't get *caught*. In the everyday presence of criminals, she had begun to consider them normal. Unfortunate though it was, they happened to come along as a sort of package with her new family.

So her loyalties were now on that side of the law. That was where "her" children were. She began to view police as the enemy at times—it might break up the family, if Jerry got busted—and no matter how she tried to put down such feelings, well, if her cousin was happy (and scores made him happy), she was happy too. Except for that eccentric shyness—which prevented her from even working at the store—she had no trait more pronounced than that of loyalty.

Marie made an effort to be nice to Donnerstag, who was constantly in the house, but she also couldn't stand him. She preferred the lowlier, nicer "down-and-outers" who were brought in: besides Hank and Jed, a Scranton kid named Carmen Malavenda was staying there. Maybe her cousin "never could pick his friends," as she so kindly put it, but if so, she felt, it was more a matter of being overhospitable, generous, than anything bad. When he was a kid he had always been this way, bringing those "hobos" and any other strays he could find home for Sunday supper. Now there was Carmen Malavenda, a pleasant enough guy, eager to please, grateful, and no dope addict. But his surname gave Marie the twitches, superstitious as she was. It sounded like a Neapolitan idiom her mother always used. Malavenda—*en maleventa*. That meant a bad wind was coming.

She felt sorriest for Jed. He was not quite as dedicated as Pete (who watched over Rose with the affection of a brother or a boy friend), but important changes were germinating in Jed too. He worked hard cutting grass, or painting around the house, and in return Festa let the kid drive yet another car he'd bought, a new Toronado.

At other times, however, they were at odds: Festa couldn't stand the way Jed ate cold soup from a can, or how, occasionally, he snuck into Jerry's recliner. "The poor guy's never had a chance," Marie would tell Festa. "So how could he be any better?" She worried about how high he looked when he came in sometimes, and was dismayed at such antics as his going to a Catholic church once and, despite his Jewishness, receiving the host at the altar. (Her sensibility was further affronted by Pete, who stole a gold chalice from a church.) Yet Jed could be so innocent and dear, going shopping with Marie, and carrying in all the groceries.

Jed was popular with the children, especially Janet, whose mind was the equal of his even if she was only fifteen. They sat for hours in front of her stereo listening to "Roses Are Red" and "Momma Told Me Not to Come," and the Rolling Stones were among their favorite

AM groups. (They wouldn't have been caught dead listening to Barbra Streisand.) Janet knew he was into drugs, but he told her, "Some day I'm gonna be clean." He warned her not to try narcotics or she would "get like me" and "not care if you live or die." He would pretend to be helping her with her homework, but, of course, he couldn't spell; so instead they watched Porky Pig cartoons and ate pepperoni pizza.

The younger girls, who were entering grammar school, also had crushes on Pete and Jed. The Feldman brothers would give Alicia and Sophia bubble-gum rings as a gift of "engagement," and when they played house the little girls always made Pete his "tea." They would wrestle with him and Jed on the floor (unlike Johnny, the boys didn't touch them in funny places), play hide-and-seek, and at night Pete would carry them upstairs. But even so young, these girls realized Jed's mind was not quite right; he would try to help with their coloring books and not be able to keep the crayon between the lines. He gulped down Marie's sandwiches and told her how he hoped to join the Army, like his friend Rudy—or perhaps the Marines.

While Pete was in and out of jail, or back at his parents', Jed grew closer to the Festas, and this made Pete uncomfortable. He did not trust his brother. "He's gonna hurt ya," Pete said. And the younger brother often had differences with Hank Ellis, who, though he was seventeen years Jed's senior, felt in competition with him. They argued over the recliner, over who had to do what errand, or whose turn it was to decide what they would watch on television (Hank's favorite was "The Addams Family"). Hank complained about Jed's "irresponsibility," the way he stumbled off on some of his deliveries high. But when it came down to it, Hank was afraid of a fist fight with the muscular kid, and so he generally put up with Jed's sarcasm and tauntings ("Hey, Hank, when the hell you gonna take a bath?").

Aside from a warm feeling that they were doing them good, Marie and Rose found the Feldman brothers a source of unmitigated—and unintentional—comedy. There was the day Pete dressed up as a woman for a payroll score around Halloween (he was the decoy) and looked so strange that Marie's dog, the ever lovable, ever fierce Pinkie, bit his leg above the high heels. Or Marie taking Jed to the Marine recruiting center, where he dismally failed the application, unable to spell the word "sister" when it asked for "next of kin."

What Jed wanted most now was to be a wise guy like Festa and Donnerstag, and already he had some experience with junkie robberies.

He showed up once with a cabin cruiser on a trailer, and another time a dune buggy. He would ask Jerry if he could go on a score with them. "I don't know what the hell you're talking about," Festa replied, afraid the kid had too big a mouth.

But such attempts at camouflage, in a house filled with theft, were clumsy and pointless. "I ain't dumb," Jed told Rose when she lectured him on going back to school. "Jerry and The Jew ain't got no education, and youse are doing fine." At the store, when Festa stopped to pick up Hank for a score, Jed was resentful, snappy. He began to talk to Donnerstag, trying to get on The Jew's good side after his eviction from the house, and Donnerstag began to respond to him. (Jed's departure, meanwhile, left Janet in the doldrums. The night he left, in the middle of Festa's tirade, they had no chance to say good-bye, and since she wasn't allowed to hang out on the street, there was little opportunity to talk with him again.)

On the corner, where Jed sat on the stubby stone wall, he enviously watched the Festas' comings and goings. Jerry seemed always to be with a new face, or one that hadn't been around in a while—Paul Brady, or Bob Martin. Jed looked on Donnerstag as the in-charge type of guy, a natty dresser in big cars. And Donnerstag was beginning to sell dope to the addicts, so he was friendly. "What's up, Jed?" he would say.

Below the surface, however, Donnerstag detested addicts. "They're put on this earth to use," he told Rose. If you needed to get rid of one, you overdosed him with heroin, gave him a "hot shot."

Throughout September, Festa and Donnerstag had been preparing for the robbery of a home in Glen Ridge, but it had been postponed when they became embroiled in a heated argument over Donnerstag's desire to let Jed in on the score. He was looking to break in a new junkie, and the kid would come cheap, accepting any small share.

Festa neither liked nor trusted Jed by now. "You can't put that kid on no stickup," he said. "I don't fucking think he knows what's the end of a gun. We ain't even had him on a burglary." The kid was on too much dope, too unreliable, he said.

But Donnerstag was insistent, and the quarrel ended up in the bedroom. From downstairs Rose could hear her husband shouting, "No way. No fucking way." At one point Festa jumped from the bed and challenged Donnerstag with his fists. But there was no fight. Donnerstag dropped the argument for the time being, letting the dust settle, and

Festa recovered his composure too. Once his mood leveled it had scared him that he had provoked The Jew even as much as he had. With Adams gone, he had no more backing.

Despite their estrangement, Rose still considered Jed a "good boy." There was mischief in his eyes, but she had never seen a more beautiful smile. At first he had avoided going back into the store, sending in a friend instead for his Coke and French fries, but soon he was again seeking Rose's comfort and advice, which she still gave him.

Back at Ridge Street, in the home where, like everywhere else he had been, acceptance had in the end eluded Jed, the activity resembled that of a small bus station. While Marie hovered about with a dust cloth, Donnerstag and Festa talked on the porch, analyzing jewelry or barking out orders to Hank and Carmen and Wally. This was a milieu of men who were castoffs from the normal world, who bled society like so many leeches, and then acted as if society were to blame—irrational men with the most elemental viewpoints and urges. Though she sensed a tragedy in the making, Marie had come to view their household and friends as "us against them," as if they were at battle with civility. When Donnerstag made lewd remarks, or talked about chopping off some-body's fingers, she and Rose sloughed it off, and mechanically con-tinued down the alley.

Hugo could tell that Jed was restless. He kept walking from the corner to the stoop of his parents' place and back. He was increasingly reliant on sure-enough dope, and suddenly, one memorable day, Hugo was shocked to see him flashing some heavy bills, buying everyone gifts, telling everybody he was "Jerry the Jew's man." After that, Jed never returned to the corner.

* *

On September 23, the same week he bribed his way out of the burglary sentence, Festa prepared for the robbery of the house in Glen Ridge, an ornate suburb to the north of Newark. A beautician who had been a dinner guest at the house sent word, through Nanny's son, Joey Cicala, that there was a concealed elevator in the master bedroom which descended to a basement vault. There, said the hairdresser, a small treasure in jewels could be found.

They had been casing the house for weeks, of course. Surrounded by two sun porches and an expanse of yard, the brick residence held court over a busy corner of Ridgewood Avenue. Its alarm, the two men noted, was wired directly to the police station. The job would have to be done as a stickup. Burglary would be too precarious, he and Donnerstag agreed.

Late in the morning final details were put in order. They had decided two of their crew members would masquerade as gardeners while approaching the house. One of them would be Wally Lombardo; the second had not yet been decided upon. In his twenties, Lombardo was rather an intelligent equivalent of Hank Ellis, slavish and slovenly. But Donnerstag, who supplied Wally's dope, had been dressing Lombardo to fit the role of a wise guy, and at night, as they made their bar rounds in New Jersey before heading over to the Copacabana, Lombardo wore silk shirts, a leather belt, and Gucci shoes.

Festa and Donnerstag went to Belleville for a pair of gardener's outfits. Then Donnerstag went to gather the crew members.

He returned with both Wally and Jed Feldman.

Festa was exasperated. He took Donnerstag into the dining room. "I thought I told ya, no Jed. No way. He's a fucking junkie."

"Don't worry about it. So's Wally," said Donnerstag. "I can control him. The kid wants to go. He ain't afraid." Donnerstag was in no mood for a debate. He would be the boss today. That was just like him. One day he would listen to Festa, appease him, flatter him; the next he would push him around. And get away with it. At times Festa was fearless; at others he was "deathly afraid." When Donnerstag made up his mind about something, was fully intent on a particular course of action, Festa always backed down in the end. Though more powerful physically, he was that much weaker of "heart." Like the lion in *The Wizard of Oz,* he had a sentimental side. His main concern was Jed's unreliability, but—well, the kid had stayed in their house for a long time. He was being dragged into something which was over his head. There was some grudging compassion down there.

Jed knew enough to avoid Festa. He busied himself with Wally and they got into their uniforms. Rose was also upset. She had never seen her husband so fidgety before a score. He was pacing, and when he sat in his chair he kept pumping his right leg up and down. Every now and then he would mutter a curse at Donnerstag, or snap at him. But Jerry the Jew could not have cared less. He said, "Rose, Jed's pants are too long. Get over here and hem them."

They waited for the hour when the home's regular gardeners usually quit work. Donnerstag briefed the crew about the entrances to the house, and while he did this, J. B. DeVingo, the next-door neighbor, happened by. He raised his eyebrows when he saw Wally and Jed in the peculiar outfits. DeVingo was a streetwise man, and it was he who was closest to Detective DeMarco, a friend of twenty-two years. DeVingo was a bailbondsman, and his own brother, Anthony, was a made-man with Andy Gerard. Though DeVingo had been privy to a few of Festa's lesser scores, he knew he was not welcome to stay in the living room today, so he went to have coffee with Marie, who, as always, was obliviously doing chores in the kitchen.

The arrangement was for Hank to circle as a lookout in the van while Festa and Donnerstag monitored the area in a Cadillac. Jed and Wally would go up the driveway in a stolen car borrowed from Nicky Skins, who kept it on hand for just such purposes. When they arrived at Ridgewood Avenue they would park around the corner for final instructions, and when Festa and Donnerstag saw that the real gardeners had left, they would signal Jed and Wally to go in.

The two robbers entered through the rear door. They aimed a small-caliber handgun at Mrs. Theresa Raffaldini, the woman of the house, and went for the bedroom elevator, which, to their confusion, had not one but *three* buttons. Wally decided against trying any of them, fearful he might activate the alarm. And he was anxious to get it over with as soon as possible: Jed was nervous as all hell. His voice was faltering, his hands quaking visibly as he held the gun. "Son, please take it easy," said Mrs. Raffaldini. "Please, take what you want and leave. My daughter will be home from school any minute."

Outside, Donnerstag and Festa glided down Ridgewood Avenue and made a U-turn, noticing that the car was still in the driveway, which ran near a long brick walk. They headed a short distance in the westward direction, crossing paths with Hank.

Wally searched the first floor and took the woman's jewelry, and they bound and gagged her. Before leaving, Jed paused with Lombardo to gently loosen the knot around her feet.

On their next orbit, Donnerstag saw that the car was gone. "That's it," he announced. "They're out."

They bolted back to Ridge Street, where Wally and Jed dumped their take on the dining-room table. There were mostly rings and earrings. But there were also two beautiful watches, one of them gold, the other platinum with diamonds. The latter had an iridescent blue face and was clearly more expensive. But Donnerstag gave it to Festa and took the gold timepiece for himself—a generosity which immediately made Festa angrier. If Donnerstag was being so kind, it meant that he was hiding something, as far as Festa was concerned. Wally had probably slipped several of the most valuable pieces to Donnerstag without Jed's seeing them. That was probably why Donnerstag had wanted such an inexperienced kid on the score, Jerry thought.

Followed by Jed and Wally, Hank took the stolen vehicle back to its garage. In the meantime Festa went with Donnerstag to sell the wares at Martin and Son Jewelers on Broad Street, in the central part of town. They were paid sixty-eight hundred dollars for the merchandise and proceeded back to the Chicken Delight, where Hank was handed four hundred dollars for his role as a lookout and Jed twice that amount. "Thanks for letting me come with youse," Jed said excitedly.

"I didn't take ya," Festa said coldly. "Donnerstag took ya."

"Did I do as good as Pete?"

Festa was irritated. "You got the score, didn't you?" he said sarcastically.

Despite the rebuff, Jed's feet were a yard above the sidewalk as he walked out of the store. It was time to celebrate, get high. He walked briskly past the corner dinette, a small barbershop, and a dry cleaner's on the way home.

Donnerstag tried to smooth things over with his partner by asking Festa if he wanted to join him and Wally in New York that night. They were heading to the 21 Club. They would have their pictures taken as souvenirs. "Smile," he said. "We got the score."

Festa only grumbled. He still felt that in taking such a chance with Jed, Donnerstag had overstepped his bounds.

Pete stopped by the house later, as Festa was heating a pot of meatballs and spaghetti for supper. "Gee, Jerry, why didn't you tell me?" he said. "God, you know I would of gone with youse."

Jerry pretended he did not know what Pete was referring to.

"Well, why don't you take my brother, for instance," Pete said. "He's down giving bags and money out down on the corner. He's telling everybody, 'I'm with The Jew now.' Me, I keep my fucking mouth shut."

Jed was also pumping his veins with dope. Rose had never seen him so happy. He was buying food for all his buddies, loads of chicken and ribs, order upon order of French fries. The next day he would proudly walk into the Howard Savings Bank on Bloomfield Avenue and open his first account with the money he had left: two hundred and fifty dollars.

Festa worried all night and into the next morning. He had already put it in Donnerstag's mind that Jed was untrustworthy, and Wally had compounded that, telling Donnerstag how Jed's hands shook. "I know what ya mean," said Rose. "But, Jerry, it's over and done with."

"Nah, shit no," he responded. "This ain't over with yet." He told his wife to prepare for a "commotion." He planned to leave Donnerstag. Jerry the Jew was too bossy, and taking too many risks. Adams might have been brutal, but at least there was a consistency in his methods. Donnerstag was unpredictable, and just as tough. But in leaving him Festa knew he could expect resistance. They made too much money together, and Donnerstag would be afraid of how much Festa knew about him.

At eleven the next morning Festa stopped by the restaurant, which Rose was just opening. He said hardly a word. She could tell he was psyching himself up for a confrontation, trying to build up courage. He went off by himself in the car.

Donnerstag also stopped by for a moment and noticed Rose's somber mood. "What's with you?" he asked.

"Jed's too young a boy," she said. "He'll get in trouble."

"Christ," Donnerstag joshed. "You're a crepe-hanger."

Festa wandered aimlessly around Newark, chatting with a few wise guys at the Quick-Stop Diner, taking a slow ride to Aqueduct to catch the fourth race. His thoughts were once more consumed by how he needed protection, someone who could hold his own against Donnerstag, should there be a violent dispute.

Rose had gone to the store early to prepare a special order. In the afternoon she returned home to change her clothes. The phone rang. It was J. B.'s wife, Josephine DeVingo, who asked Rose to stop next door for a cup of coffee. There was nothing strange about this. A coffee break with the DeVingos was an almost daily routine.

At the front door she was greeted by J. B. He appeared cordial despite his craggy face, which was as tough as barbershop leather. As she slid into the kitchen booth, Rose noticed immediately that the *Star-Ledger,* neatly folded to an inside page, was lying conspicuously on the table. Though the day had been filled with more major news (the conspiracy trial of DeCavalcante, and the issuance of a subpoena to Angelo Bruno), these items did not appear to be what J. B. was studying over his coffee. He had pointedly shaped the paper so that it displayed an article on page thirty-six next to the panty-hose ads. The headline, which he obviously intended her to see, made Rose swallow hard. "Robbers bind, gag woman," it read.

Aware that DeVingo was studying her reactions, Rose tried to ignore the news story and gossiped with Josephine. Finally J. B. grew impatient. "Didn't you read this?" he asked.

"What is it?" she said.

"A big score some guys pulled off." He was being coy. "Look at this." He shoved it over closer to her. She took the newspaper and read the last paragraphs with alarm. "One [of the robbers] was described as dark, with long sideburns, bushy hair, wearing black-rimmed glasses and a baseball cap." That was Lombardo. "The second holdupman was described as medium height, with curly blond hair, long sideburns, and wearing a long-sleeved dark-blue shirt and dark gray gloves." That was Jed.

It was apparent that J. B., having seen them the day before, had put it all together. But he was still being cute about it. "Look," he said. "These guys must have been professionals. They even used uniforms." He could see Rose was getting nervous. Usually droopy and lethargic (for she still took tranquilizers), she was now fully alert, her eyes darting back and forth. She excused herself after a hasty second cup of coffee.

Festa got home at about five-thirty in a surly mood. He watched television but was hardly interested in the program. He was still psyching himself up. Hank came in, acting chipper. Stupid motherfucker, thought Festa. If I told him the world was ending tomorrow, he'd fucking say, "Oh, yeah?"

At the store, the news clip went around in Rose's head like the neon sign in Times Square. She worried that DeVingo would try to somehow shake them down. He and DeMarco were known for that.

Jed came in. He was not high, as he had been the day before, but there was a big change in him. He was back to being as cocky as when they first met. "You see Jerry the Jew, tell him I gotta talk to him," he said. He acted like he owned the store.

He aggravated her. If he'd gone to school like she always told him, he had the potential to be somebody, she thought. "You want something to eat, get it, go to the wall with it, or take it home and eat it," snapped Rose.

Festa called her and said he was sending Hank to drive her home. He needed to talk.

"It's in the paper," she told him.

"I know," he said angrily. "I seen it."

She also told him about DeVingo's curious behavior. After he hung up, Festa walked next door feeling for any vibes. Nothing suspicious was said, but when he returned to the house there was a message from Detective DeMarco. Five minutes later the cop called again. "Jerry, where's The Jew?" DeMarco asked.

It sounded urgent. "Why? What's the matter?" Festa asked.

"Well, got to talk to him. Now. Very important."

Festa called Donnerstag and he came right over. He was dressed up and had on a strong musky cologne. Soon the detective pulled up front in his big black automobile. Donnerstag got into the car with him and they talked for several minutes. Watching from the window, Festa noted as Donnerstag walked back that his gait was not at all carefree. His neck was somewhat bent below his shoulders, yet his head was oddly upright, stiff, pushed forward. There seemed to be no wrinkles on his face; it was as hard as marble. And he was throwing arrows with his eyes.

They went into the seclusion of the dining room. Donnerstag was in the most determined of moods. "Got a problem," he said in a low voice.

"What?" Festa said. "What?" All the psyching he had done immediately evaporated. Something made him fear for his own life.

"Jed got made on the score," explained Donnerstag. "The whole schmeer. He's gonna talk."

"How could he have been made?" asked Jerry. His voice got high. "What the hell you talking about?"

"Some cop put together the description. They sent his mugshot up to Glen Ridge. They're busting him tomorrow."

"How in Christ's name could that happen? They sure?"

Donnerstag ignored the queries. He was excited in a mute sort of way. He reeked not of any odor—not of the musk oil—but of some intangible and awful gravity. "Jed's been made," he said. "The kid's gotta go."

*   *

Through much of his life, Gerard Festa had pillaged the households of those who worked honestly and diligently, participated in terrorizing holdups, and gambled away tens of thousands of other people's money. He had sired a number of illegitimate children, and some of his own peers accused him of fairly shocking depravities. He cheated hapless old people and assaulted those who were weaker physically.

These were acts of sociopathy and decadence, to be sure. But none of them carried life imprisonment as a penalty. In his long history of criminality, he had somehow managed to avoid a direct involvement in murder—and with it the prospect of spending the remainder of his years in jail. Which petrified him. Now Donnerstag was telling him to get ready for his first homicide.

Rose heard them arguing from the kitchen. She hoped her husband was making his break from Donnerstag as he had vowed he would. She went into the dining room to see if they wanted coffee; really she wanted to know what the wrangling was all about.

Donnerstag was baneful. "Rose," he ordered. "Leave the room."

Rose made some sounds on the first steps of the stairs as if she were ascending them. Silently she detoured back into the kitchen and hid in the butler's pantry adjacent to the dining room. From there she could hear her husband saying, "You're talking about murdering this fucking kid over something we ain't even sure of."

Donnerstag maintained that the subject was unworthy of further deliberation. "He's gotta go. The cops are informed. They know." He tried to call Wally Lombardo, who could be ordered to administer Jed a "hot shot," but Wally—probably passed out in bed, next to a needle—was nowhere to be found. "Okay," Donnerstag firmly announced. "They're busting him tomorrow and for all we know they may even go hold him tonight. We do it ourselves."

The blood left Festa's face. He fought to contain his emotions but his words were coming out staccato. "You're fucking—murder a nothing kid? Christ, send him away someplace. Do something . . ."

Donnerstag peered at Festa over the top of his rimless glasses. A cigarette was balanced on his lower lip. "Hey, hey, Jerry," he said with restraint. "There's no alternative. Wanna get locked away for twenty years for robbery? You know we ain't got a handle on the Glen Ridge cops up there. The kid's a fucking rat anyway. You were afraid yourself he'd talk."

"You get a hold of Wally," Festa said. "Do it your way. Give him a hot shot. Do whatever you fucking want. I don't want no involvement. What the fuck. Fuck the robbery. Nobody got hurt."

Hank meekly sauntered into the room. His face was deadpan, driveling. "Sit down, Hank," said Jerry the Jew. "We got a problem. Jed's going. Gotta whack him. We gotta move now."

Though frightened, Ellis never changed his expression. That was Hank: living in the oddest, most incomprehensible daze. He would have said about anything to please Donnerstag. That was why, when Donnerstag talked about finding a place for the murder, he thoughtlessly blurted, "Well, my brother-in-law in Pennsylvania. He's got a bottomless pond."

"Where?" asked Donnerstag.

"In Pennsylvania, in the Poconos. Up by Tompkinsville."

"That's where it's gonna go," Donnerstag decided. He told Hank they needed something to sink Jed's body, a weight. They chewed on that a few moments until Donnerstag said to Ellis, "Go to the garage and get the lawn roller and some wire. Put it in Jerry's trunk."

Festa complained about the idea of a relative's pond. Both men were from Pennsylvania. There was too great a chance that they'd be traced, he said.

"That's where we go," Donnerstag retorted. He rose from his seat and looked hard again at Jerry. "You and I have to do it. You're in it. It's unfinished business. You go by the rules."

Donnerstag left for his apartment on Joralemon Avenue in Belleville, a ten-minute drive. He made his way past the commonplace houses that populate most of the town, the neat bakeries, specialty shops, and golf course. He needed to change his clothes and pick up his artillery.

Rose walked into the dining room. Her husband's face was sallow. "He's gonna hit Jed," he told her unbelievingly. They conferred a few minutes and devised a ploy. After Donnerstag returned, she would call Festa's father in Scranton from a phone upstairs, out of earshot, and have his father call back pretending to be ill. Jerry would say he had to tend to him.

Then Festa walked out to the garage where Hank was absently fumbling for some wire and the roller. "You know what the fuck you're doing?" Festa screamed. He tried to blame Hank for their predicament. "You got us in it good now, you dumbest of fucks. Why'd you mention Pennsylvania?"

"I, I didn't know what to say," Hank mumbled.

"I'm from Pennsylvania. You're from Pennsylvania. And this pond!

Why don't ya just fucking write our names on a piece of paper and leave it there!"

"What'm I gonna do?" Hank asked quietly.

"You work for me," Festa bellowed. "Understand? So you do one motherfucking thing, you motherfucker. You get your ass lost. Don't find no fucking pond. We can't just break out of this, cause you're dead, I'm dead. So just don't find it. Hear?"

Donnerstag returned dressed in fatigues. He had two pistols wrapped in cloth, a thirty-two-caliber handgun and a hammerless Ivor Johnson, the rubber-handled thirty-eight he would use. He put the weapons on the table and began cleaning them with alcohol, rubbing the bullets with steel wool. He handed Festa the thirty-two, which Jerry put into his pocket. Donnerstag was calm. His hands were steady.

The phone finally rang. Jerry's old man was on the line. Festa told Donnerstag Poppy was sick. "I'm gonna have to go to him."

Donnerstag was no meatball. "This comes first," he said.

Donnerstag cleared the table and again scrutinized his partner over the top of his glasses. It was a look that said, "What, no balls?" Festa pretended he was not afraid, that killing did not really bother him. But still they argued. Finally Donnerstag lost his patience. "This is a sanctioned hit," he lied. "I spoke to Andy Gerard. There's no way out of that, and you're as deep as me. We go by the rules."

Rose had wandered to the front porch distractedly. She saw Jed's face in her mind. He was just an aimless, harmless urchin, and he had that innocent smile, so charming despite a chipped front tooth. She said to herself, "No, nothing'll come down. Jerry's gonna do something. He always gets out of things." She saw Jed's face again. "Him they're gonna slaughter like some cow?"

She heard a noise up the short, uneven driveway to the right of the porch. Hank was pushing the roller to Festa's car. He looked nonchalant, that stolid look she was so accustomed to seeing. "What're you doing, Hank?" she whispered.

"Oh," he said. "Nothing."

Hank shuffled back into the house, where Donnerstag gave him another order: "Go see where Jed's at." Ellis left in a chicken delivery car. It was a short drive and he spotted the kid immediately, sitting bare-chested on a crate at the corner of Mount Prospect and Second Avenue, near the rundown coffee shop. It was 9:00 P.M. The Thursday night action had not yet started. Jed was alone.

Hank wiped beads of sweat from his brow. The temperature had been in the upper eighties much of the day and the air was sticky with humidity. Back at the house, he informed Jerry the Jew of Jed's whereabouts. Donnerstag went with Festa in another car to the corner, where Jed was still sitting idly. He called to the boy and Jed hurried to the car.

"Lookit," Donnerstag said. "We gotta helluva score. We'll be traveling for a while. It's a big one. Keep your mouth shut. Go get your dark clothes, get your gloves. Don't tell nobody nothing, that you seen us or nothing. You're going out with the girls."

"Okay," he said excitedly. "Okay."

"Meet us at the house in twenty minutes."

On their return to Ridge Street, Festa saw that Hank had pulled his black Oldsmobile 98 from the driveway. They drove Donnerstag's car in. They would use Festa's vehicle on the "score," Donnerstag said. "Soon as he comes, we go."

Jed came up the sidewalk jauntily, walking with a small hop. Festa went inside and found Rose in their room looking out of the window blankly. "Rose . . ." She turned around. He could tell she was crying. She had seen Jed arrive. She knew they were actually going.

She caught her breath. There was a look of panic on her face. "I'm going down there, Jerry. I'm not afraid."

"You don't know this guy," he murmured sternly. "You don't know what The Jew's really like. No way."

She said, "I'll just go down there and let him know I know."

"You can't," he stressed. "Look: I told Hank, get lost. We won't find the place."

She turned away from him and went back to looking outside. He heard more sobbing.

Ellis got behind the steering wheel and Festa took the front passenger's seat. Jed climbed in behind Hank, Donnerstag behind Jerry. They cut a quarter of the way through Branch Brook Park and over an idyllic stone bridge. Outside this park the avenue was a bustling business zone resembling Bloomfield Avenue. They stopped at a Hess station for gas, and as they did, Jed slouched down in the back seat while the attendant filled the tank.

"What's a matter?" Donnerstag asked.

"That's the guy who thinks I ratted on him," Jed replied.

Donnerstag looked up, pointedly catching Festa's eyes. "Uh-huh," he thought.

They went to the end of Park Avenue and headed for the Watchung Mountains. Jed remarked, "I hope this is a good one. Where're we going?"

"Pennsylvania," Donnerstag muttered.

Jed swung his head to Festa. "Oh, Pennsylvania. You know the joint?"

"No, not really," Jerry said. He was morose, and it was getting hard to hide. Along the way would be a radio station, a country club—and a funeral home, a graveyard. They angled through East Orange (a somewhat cleaner and less populous extension of Newark), and the Edison National Historical Site in neighboring West Orange. As it headed northwest, into the Caldwells, the road curved and became hilly. Though now the urban atmosphere was slowly dissolving into spacious growths of pin oaks and sycamore, the commuter traffic was still heavy. There were fast-food stands, plazas, and small office buildings.

The last rays of a crimson sun refracted through the outer perimeter of the metropolitan smog. The sky was cloudless. Hank guided the car onto Route 46, moving along the Parsippany-Troy Hills, which overlooked the large catch-waters of Boonton and Denville—the Jersey Meadows. He switched to Route I-80, a new and wider set of westerly lanes.

Jed watched the interaction of tree shadows with the headlights. This was all there was to watch: the shadows looming high to the sky as the car approached, then instantaneously falling away. "So you think this'll be a good one?" the kid asked.

"Yeah," Donnerstag mumbled.

"I hope it's a big one," Jed said. He kept trying to make conversation, but Donnerstag was almost silent, preparing himself. Hank was the only one who kept up his end of the small talk. But Hank was preoccupied too. Festa had told him to get lost. But what would Donnerstag say about that? More to the point, what would he *do*? Usually he listened to every syllable out of Festa's mouth. Hadn't he gone from pounding on gutters to setting up meatballs to holding a gun on an armed robbery, just as he was told? He almost always did as instructed—Festa had been the key influence in his life. Before Jerry hired him after talking with him on his mother-in-law's porch in Scranton—where Jerry told him about all the box gutters and chimneys in Jersey and promised him thirty dollars a day—Hank had been a di-

Michael Brown 98

rectionless wayfarer, a fifth-grade dropout who hardly knew his own parents, raised as he was by relatives. Indeed, even the section of town he was born in—Minooka—had an awkward name. Minooka! He had gone from there to a place called Willow Grove, near Philadelphia, worked some carpentry for a guy named Grant Michaels, got married to a rotund woman named Gladdie. Nice woman. He visited her weekly, of course, and recently he had brought her to Newark, moving into an apartment at 20 Mount Prospect Place, near Chicken Delight. Near Jerry. Jerry was maybe closer to him than his two brothers. Jerry stuck by him when Quartuccio complained about having such a slob around, and when the wise guys called him "The Mongoloid Child." He knew he wasn't the swiftest guy in the North Ward, he knew he was clumsy—spilling tar all over himself—and sometimes a little lazy—sneaking off a roofing job, or just going downstairs and running the water, not washing, just running the water, when Jerry told him to take a bath. And he wasn't the type to fight back when people insulted him. He even trembled if Rose scolded him. But you couldn't say he wasn't loyal, and you couldn't say Festa wasn't kind of a hero to him. Festa was *mighty*. Things happened around him like in a storybook. Like on television. He actually *did* break chairs over guys' backs when he was mad, he actually *did* throw people over a counter, or across the bar, knocking the drinks over like bowling pins. *Strong.*

But get lost? Festa wasn't big enough today, tonight. Donnerstag was a killer.

Hank kept close note of the large green signs on the highway. The scenery was becoming unrecognizable, changing into a rural landscape that looked the same mile after mile, and it was getting so dark he could barely see the far side of the road, a mass of pines and hedges. Signs of civilization had been reduced to a few old water towers which looked like Fourth of July rockets, and on the other side of Lake Hopatcong the towns and hamlets were sprouting less frequently. Red lights blinked from an occasional radio antenna rising above the trees.

There in the back seat, his head upright as a cadet's, Donnerstag was mixing some important thoughts of his own. If they were going to be safe about the matter, certain there would be no "weak link" who might buckle under and talk later on, they would have to go one step beyond murdering Jed. Hank too would have to go.

Festa stared at the barns and silos and the highway gutters which were marked with white paint every tenth of a mile. They were getting near the Delaware Water Gap, and soon they would be in Pennsylvania.

He shifted in his seat, sneaking an occasional glance at Hank. Ellis seemed not to notice. Festa wondered what Donnerstag would do when he realized Hank was lost. Would he take Jed into a woods, waste him there, waste Hank too? Or maybe he would just postpone it till morning and have Wally give the kid a hot shot.

He was fainthearted. There had been times when he felt murder in his heart, like when he raised a broken bottle to a guy coming at him with a whip-chain, or when he found his girl friend at this guy's house near Scranton and barged in, throwing the man over a railing, knocking him over a couch. But all that bluster was gone. Those were uncontrollable emotions. Donnerstag was different, more calculating, more controlled.

Route I-80 rose and fell. Hank lightened on the accelerator as the road grew winding. The headlights ignited a sign: SCENIC OVERLOOK ONE MILE. The rock was steeply cut and stratified, and huge talus boulders along the pavement cast more shadows. In front of them was Mount Minsi and below them the narrow Delaware. They were at the river gap, and as the night cooled a white vapor curled up from the water and over the guard rails, as if from a caldron.

Ellis paid a toll and passed another sign: FOOD PHONE FUEL. There were exits for the Pocono resorts, and for Shell and Sunoco gas stations. With the evening's mugginess had come battalions of mosquitoes, which dashed themselves against the windshield and spotted it so that the glass refracted oncoming lights. Ellis slowed as they descended an especially long mountainside; this was where state cops would hide. There were orange road markers and roadside posts casting new shadows that looked like phantom hitchhikers. Except for an occasional truck or Greyhound bus, and the rumbling shock absorbers and swishing tires, which sounded like surf, the night was shorn of sound.

"How far now?" Jed asked.

"Altogether it's a two, three-hour ride," said Hank. "So we're not far."

"We got all the tools?" the kid wanted to know.

Donnerstag answered him. "They're in the trunk."

Now on Route 81, they approached the exit for Tompkinsville, about ten miles north of Scranton. Hank pulled off the highway and made a right, heading to the village of Clifford at the northernmost reach of Lackawanna County. There was a small cluster of houses with driveways and basketball nets. But some of the older places were abandoned and there were vast desolate fields marked, it seemed, only by broken telephone poles, huge tree stumps, and busted barbed wire. *Well, my brother-in-law in Pennsylvania . . .*

They made it by a blinking red light and an old Atlantic station. There were fewer fences, fewer homes. White weeds were all there were in the darkness of the land, but the sky remained clear and, though two days past its last quarter, the moon was bright.

They passed an old shanty—that's about all they could see on this part of Sickler Hollow Road. And pretty soon Hank navigated a small hill and pulled up a dirt road. Festa rustled. *Fuck yeah, he's lost.*

Then there was a gutted barn and a white farmhouse with a decrepit mailbox that said "Tardosky." Hank said, "There's my brother-in-law's place."

You stupidest of motherfuckers!

The car rolled on the narrow road over stones and gravel. Ellis slouched over the wheel, straining to see. *He wants a pond, he's got one.* A mist was rising from the water here too, vaguely enveloping the hilly humpback terrain. By sunrise it would be a rolling fog. Donnerstag said, "Come on, Jerry. Let's look it over. You guys wait here."

The car scraped against some wild cherry trees. The road was only twelve feet wide. Donnerstag and Festa walked down a short path to a tiny clearing. They could hardly see the lay of the land, but in some spots the moon made the water glisten. They made their way through the fen and down to the reeds. They were at a point where the pond branched around an islet just off shore, and from their restricted vantage point they could see only this one outreach of water, which looked like nothing more than a brook. (Actually the pond site was several more acres.)

"This ain't no lake. It's a creek," Festa said. "It don't even look deep."

Donnerstag tried to peer further out, but the moon was not bright enough. It was after midnight. "What the fuck," he said. "What's with this fucking Hank? He crazy? We travel all this way to a fucking creek?"

The pond was teeming with life. Frogs honked, croaked around them; muskrats stepped and scurried; perch and turtles leaped, splashed.

Festa was relieved. Donnerstag didn't like the place. Hank and Jed started walking down from the car. "Where is the place?" asked Jed. He stood at the water's edge, facing the reedy island and pulling on a pair of calfskin gloves. He had expected a house score.

"Oh, it's across way over there," Donnerstag said, pointing to the other side. "That's where the score is. We gotta find a way to get to it." He shifted his feet on the spongy peat and he, Hank, and Festa began to walk back toward the car.

Suddenly there was a swishing sound, cloth against cloth. Donnerstag's pants. He was rushing back to the pond. Ellis and Festa turned and saw three quick flashes of light, and heard a sound like firecrackers. They saw Donnerstag holding his thirty-eight with both hands not more than a foot from the back of Jed Feldman's head. Jed's body sank to the ground very slowly, and his head nearly touched the water.

Jerry and Hank ran over. Donnerstag stood near Jed's feet. They were horror-struck. The boy seemed to be visibly giving up the ghost, for there was a pale blue ring of luminosity around his head—an aureole, a halo. (This may have been moonlight on a patch of mist, as Festa speculated, but more likely it was caused by the fluorescent biochemistry of a fungus that grows on the peat and rotted twigs covering the surface here. The botanists call the phenomenon *armillaria mellea,* but to local folk it is known as foxfire.)

Two bullets remained in Donnerstag's chamber. He turned and pointed his gun squarely at Hank. Instinctively Festa drew his pistol on Jerry the Jew and shouted, "No, Jerry, no."

Donnerstag was taken aback. He kept his gun trained on Hank but stared at Festa quizzically. Festa had a determined look about him and his hands were not quivering at all.

The standoff lasted a moment or two but it could have been an hour. At last Donnerstag dropped his arm, shifted the pistol to his left hand, and turned away. Hank was motionless, bewildered. He watched as Donnerstag reached down, grabbed Jed by the collar, and dragged the body around so that the feet were now closest to the shoreline. He looked up at Festa and said, "Now, you."

Festa pumped a couple of shots toward the body.

"Give it to Hank now," Donnerstag said. Hank stumbled to the body and shot at it. "Give him back the gun," Donnerstag instructed. Festa took the thirty-two and Donnerstag said, "Shoot again."

There was not much in the way of rationality. Instead of getting the lawn roller from the car's trunk, Donnerstag collected both guns and rubbed off the fingerprints with his shirt and gloves. He heaved them to the right of the small island, one further than the other, both at least ten yards into the pond. He redirected his attention to the most important item of evidence: Jed's corpse.

Hank was charged with helping Donnerstag remove Jed's outer clothes. They stripped off his shirt and pants as Festa held a flashlight. The water creatures made their occasional noises, startling them each time. Hank and Donnerstag began to drag the body into the pond, toward the islet, a collection of floating bushes and reeds about ten feet high. The water reached up to their chests as they waded out, and Hank began to sink in the bog. "You won't sink," Donnerstag said. "Just keep walking."

Donnerstag dragged the body to a point fifty-six feet from shore, right beside the island. As Hank attempted to plow his way back, Donnerstag struggled to conceal the cadaver, which kept rising to the surface like a beach ball. Eventually he was able to entangle it below the surface, in the undergrowth, near an old rowboat.

Hank started to sink again. He screamed.

"Get him out of there," Donnerstag called to Festa. Jerry went in a ways and yanked Hank out. Ellis had muck up to his knees. Soon Donnerstag returned to shore. "We should get out of here," he said. "Somebody maybe heard us."

Festa's flashlight glanced across Donnerstag's face, which appeared to be covered with large gnats. "You got bugs all over your face," he told Donnerstag.

Donnerstag was slightly amused. "That ain't bugs," he said. "It's Jed's brains." He dipped his soiled eyeglasses in the water and rinsed them off. Then he took his T-shirt and wiped his face. They gathered Jed's belongings and put them on the floor in the back of the Oldsmobile.

Hank started the car. There was still the sough of nocturnal animals. They drove back down the bumpy dirt road, the headlights prudently extinguished. Except for the uneven musicale of bullfrogs, and the bats sweeping down to pick off insects above the pond, the silence of the road was overwhelming. Above, the early autumn constellations of Pegasus and Andromeda shone bright in the deep black sky between rolls of the incipient fog.

Not much more than half a mile away, Bill Cooper, a retired state trooper, had heard the shots but would never report them. He figured it was just a few hunters moonlighting in the pleasant air of earliest morning.

* *

Rose had few thoughts of sleep. She could still see Jed's smile. When at last she could no longer contain her grief, she went into Marie's room. As usual, Marie had not been privy to what had happened during Donnerstag's visit. She had been occupied with the four kids, making sure they brushed their teeth, dressing them for bed. When Donnerstag was there she made a point of not listening.

So it hit her like a ton of lead. "What is all this?" she shouted at Rose. "Armed robbery, then? Murder! Don't tell me this. No, don't tell me any such things, I don't want to know about it. My God, this destroys me. This destroys us all, the whole family . . . No, they'll be back. They won't do *that*. Don't tell me this. Christ, Jesus! Somebody involved in the mob getting murdered—*well*. But not that harmless boy!"

She knew all about her cousin being a thief: he had a great history of that. *Blood is blood, right or wrong.* And she had picked up enough conversation to know that it was house burglaries they were doing. *But armed robbery? Murder?*

Rose nodded. Marie shouted some more. Both of them cried. Vainly they attempted to convince themselves that it would not happen, that Donnerstag was bluffing. Neither of the women had believed he was truly the killer he liked everyone to think he was. He was a "blowgut." He was just psyching them.

Back in Marie's homeland of Pennsylvania, the excursionists had come out the same way they went in—on Township Route 511. After they were back on the paved road the threesome drove up to a stop sign and made a right-hand turn. Donnerstag, searching through Jed's pants, came up with a wallet. He tore the license and Social Security card into tiny pieces, which he would scatter out the window. He found six dollars in the billfold. "That's the cheapest hit I ever done," said Donnerstag. He let out sort of a hyena laugh.

The rock cuts just above the entrance to Route 81 southbound became almost a tunnel. The car went on just west of Carbondale, where, a century before, anthracite coal was transported on a gravity rail link between the hollows. (That was after the Munsee Indians gave up their stake to the land, and after the Scranton family, which had operated an iron furnace in Oxford, New Jersey, moved into the area to replicate their previous successes—much to the skepticism of native farmers and lumberjacks, who referred to these industrial attempts as "the Jerseymen's folly.")

They went by Clarks Summit (where Rose's real mother, Sophie, was confined to a mental ward) and swept along the northern boundaries of Scranton and through the town of Dunmore. The fairway turned into Route 380, passing the hamlet of Elmhurst, where six years previously Festa had evaded Lee Mecka in Jeanie's horse pasture. Donnerstag was in a cheerier mood, but still his mind worked in emotionless patterns, like clockwork.

Surely he remembered the first time he did it, nine years before. It hadn't bothered him then either. He was working at the Hi-Lite Tavern, his stepfather's bar on Tenth Avenue in Newark. He got mad at a drunken black kid named George Winston. Let go a few rounds into the guy. Right there behind the bar. The cops saw how cool he was about it and remarked that he seemed like a born killer. Nonetheless, he was let off. After the autopsy it looked as if the kid's heart had been ripped out of his chest.

He turned to Hank and said, "Remember, Hank. This never happened."

"Oh, I know, I know," said Ellis.

Donnerstag wanted to keep tabs on the pond. "How close're you to your brother-in-law?"

"I can have Gladdie do it," said Hank.

"Well, if it stays under until the cold weather, we got it made," Donnerstag said. "It'll freeze there and then they'll never be able to identify it." He kept drilling into them that, should anyone ask, they would all say Jed ran off with two girls from California.

Hank drove blankly onward. He knew he was in for a good yelling—maybe a beating—when he got back. But actually that was not the prime thing on Festa's mind right now. He was afraid that Donnerstag might try something else unexpected. Why else would he have ordered that they use Festa's car? On the trip up Jerry had sat sideways so he could monitor any sudden movements. But the guns were at least gone now, and Donnerstag seemed to be through for the night.

It all started when Jerry was in the sixth grade and along with his friends broke into a house and stole some lemon meringue pie. He had always heard the first murder was your worst, but he had not quite anticipated the negative feelings it unleashed. Snuffing out a boy's life.

Hell, he had his own baby son . . . And the whole thing had been nauseating. Grosser than when his first girl friend in Scranton had a miscarriage in the toilet bowl and the doctor said to bring it to his office in a jar and Festa picked it up with clothes pins and the fetus was the size of his hand, nearly, and the consistency of liver.

Before the Oldsmobile reappeared at the Delaware Water Gap, Hank pulled over to the shoulder so they could dump the rest of Jed's clothes, which were rolled into a ball. Festa climbed over a guardrail and down a small embankment, then threw the bundle into the isolated woodland.

Along the route Donnerstag noted a Howard Johnson's and The 76 Truck and Auto Restaurant. He mentioned stopping for breakfast. Nobody else was hungry. Instead they pushed into the agricultural zone of northern New Jersey, where peppers, blueberries, and tomatoes are grown. At about four they arrived at Ridge Street. The sky was still gray. "Remember, don't talk about this at all, not even among yourselves," Donnerstag warned them. He told them to strip off all their clothes, including their shoes and socks, and he took them away to destroy them in an incinerator. Hank changed into some work clothes and went home.

Upstairs Rose lay on her bed wrapped in a white blanket and smoking cigarettes one after the other. She heard the shuffling, the whispery tones. Marie had slipped back into bed to petition the Lord harder than ever, harder than at any time since her mother died: *Don't let this awful thing have happened.*

When Festa came up to the bedroom Rose knew from his haggard face that the worst had been done. "Jerry, nothing happened, did it? Right, Jerry?"

He said nothing. In place of words his head moved up and down. Tears were trying to sneak out. He went over to the crib and picked up seven-month-old Allan. Rose saw her husband's body heaving; he was breathing hard. He put the baby back down and stretched out on the bed, staring at the ceiling, which became his own private movie screen. On it he replayed the killing a hundred times. What he kept seeing was the way Jed's legs turned to rubber and the way they began slowly, slowly weaving to the ground.

Rose said little more, fearful of a violent argument. Her grief had turned to anger. *How could he have let Donnerstag do it? Why didn't he stop it? I seen him stand up to Donnerstag before. Why not now? Did I marry a coward?*

She went downstairs and made herself a cup of coffee and thought about how strong Festa had been when she first met him. No one pushed him around. He came into her life and sometimes it was like he had saved her. Before him there had been that guy Bochak, just before she ran away with Jerry. *Bochak had been a monster. Once he got her in his car and took her to an isolated spot called Snake Road and took all her clothes off and strapped her hands to the door handles and her feet to the bumper and went on a terrifying joy ride, scaring her to death just for kicks. Festa she felt at least loved her, wanted to protect her. But what happened tonight had switched on a different channel. This was the same Jerry? The same White Knight who, while wanton and brutal, could also be fearless, defending underdogs in a fight? This was Jerry? She didn't want to look at him.*

"Rose, believe me, I didn't kill the boy," he said when he got downstairs.

She was icy. "If you didn't kill him you won't go to jail. Let's call the police."

"You crazy?" he yelled. "Who's gonna take my word of how it come down? It doesn't matter. I was there. I'm just as much to blame. There ain't no way I can get out of it. I'll go to the chair. You want the father of your kids to burn?"

The father of my children is a murderer? Rose did not want to open the store. No way could she face Pete if he came by, nor Jed's other siblings, Ramona and Angie.

"You got to open it, Rose," he demanded. "You can't let The Jew know something's up. He'll be fucking looking for that. You can't never leave him know that I told ya."

Rose stayed home, letting Nanny open the Chicken Delight. Hank came by for work just before eleven. But first he sat on a chair in the living room, where Carmen Malavenda had somehow managed to sleep through most of the night. Festa stood over Hank glowering. "You stupid son of a bitch. I was backed into a corner," Festa screamed. "You see what happened? The Jew was gonna kill you too. You! That wasn't no fucking television show. That *happened*. Why the fuck you find the fucking pond, motherfucker? I told you, get lost, didn't I! Huh, cocksucker?"

Hank was meek. "You're right, Jerry. You're right." He was just relieved Festa was not belting him.

"What the fuck, time to grow up, you dumb shit. You're gonna have to suffer with me, now. This *happened*."

At eleven-thirty Donnerstag called. He had a possible score, he told Jerry. "Meet me at the store."

Donnerstag arrived at Chicken Delight just a few minutes after Festa got there. He was acting as if nothing had happened—humming, whistling—but in fact he had had second thoughts about the whole matter and had a new announcement. He said, "Hank's gotta go."

"Uh-uh, no way, shape, or form," Festa said. "Uh-uh. I'm telling ya. No way."

"It's gotta be done," Donnerstag answered. But this time Festa was unyielding. If Hank was killed, he knew, he would be the next to go.

"Okay, have it your way," said Jerry the Jew. "But remember. That was a registered hit, and I got to tell Andy Gerard. Hank's your responsibility now. You and Hank are married."

Donnerstag told him they had to go for a "meet" about the score, which supposedly involved a factory payroll robbery. But first they stopped at Festa's house to drop off a car. As they pulled up to the house Festa saw Hank puttering in the driveway. More important, a detective's car rolled by and dragged to a stop. Donnerstag got in and it cruised to the next block and halted there, idling. Festa told Hank to leave ("Screw!") and went inside to watch from the window. He saw Donnerstag standing in the middle of the street talking through the car window.

Donnerstag walked back to the house and said, "Everything's taken care of." DeMarco, he claimed, had "taken care of business." He told Festa he gave the detective five hundred dollars for the tip.

As soon as Donnerstag came in, Rose had hurried up to her room. He was immediately suspicious. "Where's Rose?" he inquired. "Where's your wife? Something the matter?"

Festa said, "Oh, she just ain't feeling so hot." Then Jerry went up to their bedroom and told her, "Rose, you gotta go down there. Act normal, like nothing happened. You know *nothing*."

"I know a lot," she said spitefully. "I wanna spit in his face. I can't face him."

"He's looking to get rid of Hank. I'm telling ya, he'd have no qualms getting rid of you. He'll be looking for every little thing. All of us could get it."

She wore a vacant look. "Maybe that would be better." But she went down and had coffee and pretty soon the men left.

They drove forty miles down the Garden State Parkway to a rest stop. Festa did not like the smell of this. Jerry Donnerstag was hardly speaking. The details of this "score" were much too scanty. They went to a picnic bench where Donnerstag spoke out of earshot with a sharp-looking guy who sported an open white shirt and sunglasses. Festa thought the guy was getting a look at him. Maybe they would hit him too.

Donnerstag came back and said, "Nah. We can't do that score. It's too big. We'd need too many guys." From there they went to the race track at Freehold. Festa was hardly betting. "What's wrong, you sick?" Donnerstag kept asking. "Maybe you should see a doctor." Referring to their first murder together, he said, "How'd it make you feel?"

"How's it supposed to feel?" Festa answered, trying to act unbothered. He knew Donnerstag was feeling him out.

Once home, Festa sent for Hank and told him he had to have "eyes in the back of your head," because Donnerstag might have Wally or someone else shiv him on a chicken delivery. "You sonofabitch, I'm gonna tell you now, The Jew said you gotta go. I told him, no way. Now he tells me I'm responsible. I gotta know where you are at all times." Hank looked dumbstruck, like finally he was getting the message.

A day or so later, Pete went up to Festa and asked him if he knew where his brother was. Festa said he heard Jed had taken off with two girls in a car that had California plates.

Pete stared at him skeptically. "Jerry the Jew did something, didn't he?"

"What are you getting at Pete?"

"Uh-uh, no, uh-uh, Jed went on that score with that son of a bitch, uh-uh. That fucker killed my brother, didn't he?"

"Pete, you're ten million miles off base."

In his moments alone, Festa tried to make sense out of the irrational chain of events. It seemed to him that this whole matter had indeed been a shakedown. He decided the cops had found out about the score from that next-door neighbor of his, and had concocted a story about Jed being an informer just to make a tip. Apparently he was right. No one ever did go to Jed's place to arrest him. Probably the detective had wrongly assumed he could come by and clear up the matter—pretend a fix had been put in—before Donnerstag took any action. It was all senseless, a huge mistake. And he could spend the rest of his life in some dank jail cell for it. He kept seeing the wisps of fog and the gunpowder flashes and Jed going down. Maybe it was more like a loud cap pistol than firecrackers. It went *pap, pap, pap*.

* *

"I'm in no mood for a birthday cake," said Marie. "None whatsoever. I don't want any. It's just another day. Birthdays are for kids. To me, I'm just a year older, that's all."

Donnerstag was insistent. "Oh, no, you've got to have a cake." He turned to the others, suspicious. "How come you're not having a birthday for Marie? Everybody else has one, why not Marie?"

She was trying her best to act normally despite the nausea churning in her stomach. She could not look at this man. It was unfortunate that his nickname was "The Jew." Jewish people were not like him. He destroyed. They built. And they worked hard for a living, were doctors, lawyers, went for long years to school, went by the rules, knew pain, suffering, morality. Donnerstag had no standard except self-gratification. She detested him, and those other brutes her cousin was so fond of. A priest once said in his sermon that you should never hate, but you could *detest*. So she detested him.

It was all she could do to smile and pretend that she knew nothing of the murder six days before; the thought of celebration—especially with him—was so revolting. "I'm fat enough," she said. "Cake is for kids."

Donnerstag would hear none of it. He gallantly picked himself up and marched off to Kielb's Bakery to pick up an ice cream cake for her fiftieth birthday. He returned with his common-law wife, Shirley, and they presented Marie with a nightgown and perfume. Their next door neighbors, the DeVingos, were also there.

The cake was frozen, hard as a rock. Donnerstag placed it on the dining-room table and called into the kitchen for a sturdy knife. As he strenuously pressed down to cut her a piece, Marie recoiled in silent horror. She thought, "He's gutting the cake. This is how it must have been with Jed. Those are the same hands that did it." Yet she forced herself to grin.

With Rose it was no better. In the weeks following the execution it seemed that Donnerstag was at Chicken Delight every day, asking how she felt, looking her over carefully, trying to rattle her. Apparently he had instructed his wife to keep close tabs on Rose at home, for whenever she went upstairs, Shirley was sure to follow, asking if there was anything wrong. Rose's nerves were shot. She had weird, repetitive

Michael Brown   110

thoughts: *Jed's cold. Jed's cold.* She had stayed away from the store for three days after the murder, and when she went back she felt like everyone knew what had happened. Nanny kept telling her how bad she looked, and Angie, still working there, said, "I wonder where the hell my brother went." Rose hoped she was imagining it, but they all seemed to be asking leading questions.

The most difficult task was facing Pete. "You look like you lost twenty pounds," he told her. "What happened?"

"Nothing, Pete, I'm just tired," she droned.

Pete was waiting for her to say something, throwing her more skeptical looks, wondering out loud where his brother was. She did her best to keep him at a distance, waving him away when he came to help behind the counter or in the back room when she lifted the supply crates. "This ain't you," he complained. "You're not talking. You're avoiding me."

There was no place for her to hide, and it was crazy how everything looked so dark. No matter how clear the sky, how direct the noon rays of autumn, it appeared to her as if everything had a long, obscuring shadow to it—murky, black. Gloom had materialized as thick as her cigarette smoke; she swore she could see it. When it *was* an overcast day, with intermittent rain, she would stare out the window and think of Jed in that pond, wrapped up in wet leaves like those collecting in the Ridge Street gutters. Soggy. And chilly, as winter came. "Jed's cold," she thought.

Everywhere she turned she heard his name. "Is it true Jed went to California?" they'd ask at the store.

"I guess so," she muttered.

The junkies would come running in and say, "Did you see Jed?" or "Did you hear about Jed?" Any day she expected one of them to say, "Hey, they found him dead." A couple of them came in and told her they had spotted their old buddy going down Mount Prospect Avenue in a car. They were so sure of it that it twisted Rose's mind. Was it possible he was alive, that Donnerstag, Hank, and her husband had mistakenly left him for dead? Or, Christ!—was he back from the grave?

She even began to hallucinate, seeing his smile, hearing his laughter upstairs. Something woke her up one night and when she opened her eyes Jerry was snoring and next to the bed was bright red blood flowing from a pair of feet. She looked up and Jed was grinning at her.

"You sure you weren't dreaming?" Marie asked, for Rose had run into her room.

"No way," she panted. "I woke up. I seen him."

Maybe it was too much medication. She was also beginning to sleep for phenomenally long periods of time, so long that Marie or one of the kids would check to make sure she wasn't in a coma. Twenty straight hours she could sleep. She needed bennies to stay up, and twice-a-week shots of Valium for her anxiety attacks: Several times she was taken by ambulance to the hospital after her legs began trembling and the blood just drained out of her head. Voices sounded like they were at a great distance even if they were in the same room. She feared a heart attack was on the way.

Eventually she climbed out of it, but not before terrifying thoughts that she might go insane, inherit the same fate as her biological mother. A few months earlier her mother—Sophie Rizzo, wife of the fierce Black Hander Augustine who, it was claimed, had beaten her, abandoned her—had suffered a diabetic coma, and though Rose really did not know this woman, she had gone to visit her at Clarks Summit State Hospital. Rose had seen her mother only a few times as a youngster, and hadn't known for the longest time who the woman actually was. She would stop at Rose's stepmother's house for food (she lived quite like a bag lady) and would hardly look at Rose. She was an obese woman and occasionally someone would find her in a catatonic state sitting on steps somewhere, oblivious to the world. So they had taken her to the asylum for shock treatments. She was only forty then and had grown worse with the years.

Rose's visit with her had been frightening. She had gone past the cubicles into a green room and a bunch of lunatics with bowl haircuts came up to Rose and tried to touch her. Her mother looked just like they did and had on shabby clothes. She was confined to a single room and was totally out of it. When Rose was introduced as her daughter, the woman said, "No. Not Rose, not Rosina. Rose is dead." Then her mother took a few slices of bread out of her bra, where she had hidden them, and began searching under a cot, calling, "Rosina? Rosina?" Rose just wanted to get out of there.

Her stepmother was a concerned woman who had kept in regular contact with Rose (despite what had happened between Rose and her husband). She would visit Ridge Street, see the coffee urn, see all the men trooping in and out, and say, "What's Jerry doing, Rose? I don't like the idea of all these men in the house. It's none of my business, but I think that's three-quarters of your illness. Jerry's treading on dangerous ground."

"Rose, straighten up," Marie would add. "We can't undo what's done."

But the anxieties built one on another. Lonesome for his old friend Johnny Quartuccio, Festa went to visit him in Danbury, Connecticut, where he was doing a nine-month sentence. There Festa discovered that Johnny already knew what had gone down. "Coombs," he said. "What did you do, Jerry? God, how? How did it happen? You better watch The Jew. He hears anything, he kills spur of the moment, Coombs."

Though she would never have thought it possible, Rose now found Donnerstag more despicable than Johnny. It was nearly the last straw when Donnerstag announced that he was formally marrying Shirley and asked Rose to be maid of honor, Festa his best man. "I'm leaving," said Rose. "I'm taking the kids. I can't go through with it." She was getting so she didn't want her own husband touching their own baby. But in the end she gave in and on November 4 they participated in the wedding ceremony as if nothing were wrong.

Janet was more forthright than her parents. She hated it when Donnerstag would call in Keith, his eight-year-old stepson, and, as a demonstration of how tough he was making this child, punch the boy in the face repeatedly, sending the boy reeling, daring him to cry. "Leave him alone," Janet would protest. Donnerstag would give her his frigid gaze. But she was scornful. "That's a man? You're a man?" She also stood up to him one night when he was driving her home from baby-sitting his kids and tried to get her to have sex.

She didn't say anything about it, just buried herself in work, cooking, cleaning, answering the phones at Chicken Delight—picking up where Rose left off. She had a quiet ambition in life, medicine. She wanted to be a nurse or a doctor. She smiled when she thought of her old pal Jed. She too wanted to go where the sun blazed and the surf was high: Perhaps she would visit him some day in California.

Donnerstag was getting more irrational, wining and dining Angie Feldman like nothing had happened, and at the same time antagonizing her brother Pete. He drove alongside Pete on Bloomfield Avenue one day and drew a gun on him: "Where's your brother?" He was always looking for hints of who knew what, and trying to intimidate Pete.

"What do you want him for?" Pete asked. "And what you gonna do with the gun? Shoot me? Go ahead, shoot." From under his car seat Pete pulled out a gun of his own. Donnerstag drove off, but Pete caught up with him later. He said, "I find out you hurt my brother, Jerry, I'm gonna kill you." But soon Pete was again behind bars.

Worries about the homicide had cut Festa's activities in half. He was preoccupied and peevish, snapping all the while at Hank. He wouldn't use his Oldsmobile for the longest time, and when he did—on Christmas Eve—he hit an ice patch and smashed it. Instead of cooling it, Donnerstag was initiating ever more violent holdups, for which, if they continued at such a pace, they would all surely go to prison. On March 16, in an armed robbery in the East Mountain section of Scranton, Festa backed off the score at the last moment when Donnerstag brought in an especially unruly young guy named James Condit. He did not like the feel of the score, nor did Martin and Quartuccio, who had rejoined the crew. (Condit and Lombardo were energetic that day; they handcuffed an older lady, Elsie Schneider, to a railing and pistol whipped her when she went to press an alarm. Three weeks later, at the Community Medical Center, Mrs. Schneider, traumatized and afflicted with a weak heart, died.)

Festa sought friendship at the mob hangouts, where, compared to Donnerstag, the hoods possessed poise and equanimity. At Ed's Diner and the Democratic Club he began to talk more with Frank Basto, straying from Donnerstag, letting their partnership fade. Jerry the Jew was selling dope supplied by Raymond Freda, and wearing bigger diamonds, buying new cars. He had a new associate named Tony Garcia, who, along with Lombardo, helped him push his drugs. But Garcia did not last long in the partnership. Within a year he too would become a bullet-riddled body.

* *

The winter in Newark had been the standard fare, days of biting cold or icy rain with intervals of nearly balmy winds, followed by fronts of snow. In the mountains of northern Pennsylvania, before winter set in, three teenagers had paddled along the shore of Tardosky's pond setting muskrat traps. Philip and his friend Michael kidded Philip's younger sister, Linda, about a curious object they sighted at some distance across the water, telling her it must be a dead body. "We're gonna go out to it," said Philip, teasing her into a fright. "We'll go in right by that guy." Instead they had gone home and mentioned to their parents what they really thought: that it was a prank arranged by some local kids, a Halloween dummy.

In the spring, on April 17, 1971, two weeks after Elsie Schneider died in Scranton, Robert Tardosky, a nephew of the farming couple on whose property Jed had been killed, also saw the object while he was up at the pond, but he thought it was an inordinately large turtle, belly-up. His father had unsuccessfully attempted to cast out to it, so that day, with the ice gone, Robert thought it might be interesting to take a boat out there and bring the shell back for his children.

It was a chilly Saturday morning. At eleven o'clock he caught up with his old buddy Eugene Telep, who was coming out of a sporting goods store. Telep, an employee of the state's Department of the Auditor General, in Harrisburg, was up in Greenfield Township visiting his parents for the holiday weekend, Russian Easter. Tardosky told him about the turtle and that the water near it was now fully navigable. "Let's go out and take a look," he suggested.

They traveled the four miles to a small hill just before Clifford and cut onto Township Route 511. The owner of the property, Jack Tardosky, who normally would have been keen on investigating such an oddity, remained inside; he suffered from arthritis and had to use a walker. He was an old miner who allowed the local residents—dairy farmers, many of them—to fish the pond for a dollar fee or (better) a six-pack of beer. It was quite a bargain, considering the abundant bass and pickerel there. Tardosky's farm, once a cornucopia of corn and potatoes, which thrived in the rich wet-loam-and-red-shale soil, had grown back to brush, neglected and fallow. Neighbors frequently arrived for rabbit hunting or to pick the blueberries which grew at the shoreline amid the "hardhack" brushwood; others brought rowboats and canoes to scout the spring-fed pond. They were intrigued by the notion that the small lake was "bottomless"; Jack was said to have lowered a hundred feet of clothesline without hitting the bottom, while another local farmer, Philip Edwards, whose son first spotted the object, had tried the same experiment, lowering a hundred and fifty feet of line at the pond's center and touching nothing at all solid. In reality, some theorized, the water was probably no more than thirty-five feet at its deepest; they argued that the bottom consisted of a deceptive layer of thick, consuming sediment: quicksand.

Telep and Robert Tardosky went seven-tenths of a mile up the dirt road to the only point of accessibility on the southern shore: a small downward clearing. From their vantage point it appeared to Telep that his friend was correct. "Sure does look like a turtle," he commented. It was light-colored with a pattern resembling polka dots, but to confirm their suspicions, Telep concluded he should indeed go out there in a boat. He said that after lunch he would be back with his cousin's canoe.

He dropped Tardosky off and went to eat. While Telep was at lunch, as it turned out, Tardosky, his curiosity rising, wandered back to the pond with field glasses to determine if it was a turtle or an old mattress. He was with his children as he looked through the field glasses. He took the kids back, and when they were out of hearing range he excitedly called up Telep with a new perspective. "I think what's floating there," he said, "is a man."

Telep rendezvoused once again with his friend, bringing along a set of stronger, ten-power binoculars. Reconnoitering the densely vegetated islet, he observed, "I can make out a body. Yep. Sure looks like the head's under water. The legs too. Guy's rear end's up in the air. Got polka-dot boxer shorts on." Then they called a friend who had been a cop. They were told the State Police barracks probably would not send up an investigator until it was confirmed that the object was in fact a body.

A methodical and not overexcitable man, Telep decided to run some holiday errands seven miles away in Carbondale before heading out to the body in a boat. "It sure isn't going anywhere," he remarked. "It'll be there when I come back with the canoe."

He returned to the pond at three o'clock and was met by Jack's wife, Betty. She and another neighbor helped Telep unload the boat and he paddled the short distance to the reeds. He stopped about five feet from the target and, with a paddle, poked at the soggy corpse, lifting up a leg with it. There certainly were no lingering doubts about what it was. The body's head—facing the vegetation about eight feet from the island—was submerged in decayed lily-pads and reeds. Telep quickly returned to shore, frightened by the implications of the discovery and repelled by the odors of decay.

A state trooper, Sergeant Edward C. Gunster, was summoned to the scene. He called the "R" Barracks in Dunmore for a member of the Bureau of Records Identification. In the meantime a small crowd had assembled near the path, relatives and friends and Robert Tardosky himself. Sergeant Gunster made sure no one tampered with the evidence, a routine rein on the onlookers known as "preserving the scene," and the barracks sent up Trooper Francis E. Zanin to collect the official evidence. Gunster indicated where the body was and Zanin took photographs of the islet, shooting first from the road's shoulder, then moving closer through the brush. Next he turned to Telep and asked to borrow the boat.

When Zanin got out there he could see that the aquatic plants held most of the body under but that otherwise it was a classic example of what medical examiners call a "spring special": The season's warmer air had caused bacteria to germinate in the intestines, producing methane gas which made Jed's body rise. The cadaver was in a most advanced state of decomposition, its skin excoriated and blistered and the face bloated beyond recognition. The eyes were sunken, colorless, shriveled like raisins, and the scalp had shed most of its hair. It was clothed only in a white T-shirt pulled up to the neck, a brown sock on the left foot, a dark leatherlike glove, and the boxer shorts (which had been purchased at Pathmark and had small sword bits as a design). On the land itself was a ragged pair of dungarees (apparently not Jed's, as his had been ditched the night of the murder) and, under those, a right-hand glove matching that on the body: leather webbing interspread with the cloth.

Telep had consented to official use of the canoe, but when Zanin asked if he would help drag in the body, he said, "No way." He was feeling squeamish enough. Tardosky volunteered his services. They set out again and attached a rope to the head and one foot, which made for a most unpleasant sight. As they tugged it back to land, the foot looked as if it were coming loose from the leg, and water spurted from the bullet holes in the head. Zanin could tell that the water near the island was not anywhere near as deep as the rest of the pond— only two or three feet near the shore. He watched as the corpse's skin flaked off and floated downward, settling on the bottom. Tardosky got sick to his stomach.

As they proceeded back, Zanin noticed a gold ring on the little finger of the right hand. It was slipping off. If it reached the muck it might be lost forever. He quickly reached down and took it off, noting that it was a signet ring, well-worn, and naturally soiled. The initials on the face appeared to be "JT," in fancy English script.

The body was stuffed into a rubber zipper bag and taken to McGranaghan's Funeral Home in Carbondale, where an autopsy would be performed the next morning. Though the coroner, Dr. Anthony Cummings, would have preferred to conduct such an examination with the use of X-rays, no local hospital would accept the corpse, fearing bacterial contamination. At ten-thirty a Scranton pathologist named Dr. Edward Skovira arrived at the funeral home along with a handful of observers and Trooper Zanin. The body was placed in a garage—the doors left open—and the grisly task began.

Because of the state of degeneration, the autopsy was an abbreviated one, lasting only an hour. Dr. Skovira hurriedly established that the remains were those of a white male, five foot ten and one hundred sixty-nine pounds. From the mouth he extracted a partial upper plate and stemming from it was a single denture. This led Dr. Skovira to estimate the subject to be thirty-five years old, "give or take ten years." An inspection of the skin revealed a puncture wound on the right side below the rib cage, another in the "post-auricular region"—behind the heart—and one in the head behind the right ear. An incision was made into the scalp itself, and upon closer examination it appeared there was not just one bullet hole there but three. They were perfectly round and closely clustered, and inside one were metal fragments. An inch above them was a fourth hole shaped like a teardrop. Next, Dr. Skovira had little choice but to initiate the especially unpalatable chore of removing the brain, which had liquefied into a gelatin-like matter. From the cranial cavity (which showed multiple fractures too, on the opposite side) four more bullet fragments were recovered. An incision was also made into the abdomen, but the search for more bullets stopped before any more were located: the intestines had turned to mush.

Throughout that Sunday curiosity seekers wandered along Township Route 511, expounding dark theories, feeding each other's fears. A police helicopter whirred three hundred feet above, taking photographs and rippling the surface of the pond. Reporters converged on the scene but did not see Eugene Telep there. Afraid his discovery would somehow lead to retribution, he had retired to the security of his parents' home.

Closer to downtown Scranton, in a bar called the Nativity Club, Jerry Festa had stopped the night before to drink screwdrivers with Bob Martin and sit in on a game of poker. He had been returning to Scranton with increasing frequency, casing out burglaries and taking breathers from Newark's hectic pace.

He heard the news from a television set over the bar. "Police say the body . . ." He sent a shocked look over to Martin, then excused himself from the game for a closer look at the news report, walking casually by a pool table and toward the restroom. He listened to the rest of the story, went into the toilet, threw some water on his face, and vomited.

He played several more hands of poker so as not to arouse suspicions at the table. Then he picked up a Saturday edition of the *Scranton Times,* which had not yet had time to print the story. He headed back to the hilly interstate and New Jersey.

* *

"Rose, they found Jed. I seen it on TV. That's it. I'm done now."

She tried to plant some hope. "Now don't jump to conclusions. Don't jump to no conclusions yet. Maybe it's somebody else."

Since Feldman's death, Festa had had a mail subscription to the *Scranton Times,* so he could watch for any item about the pond. When the April 19 issue arrived in the middle of the next week, he noticed a photograph of the pond on an inside page with a headline that declared, "Signet Ring Main Clue to Dead Man's Identity." At first he had drawn some comfort from the state trooper's mistaken impression of the ring's initials, but it had since been taken to a jeweler in Dickson City who washed it with acidic solutions, polished it, and examined it under a microscope. As the news item recounted, the ring bore the initials "JF," not "JT." Festa tossed the paper on the kitchen table. "Ah, shit," he said.

Hank, Pete, and Jerry the Jew came into the house to talk about doing a score that day. As Pete went into the living room to watch television, Festa nodded for Donnerstag to meet him in the kitchen. "The paper's in there," he whispered. "Read it."

Wally Lombardo came in while Donnerstag and Ellis stood looking at the newspaper. Festa gave Donnerstag an alarmed look—no one else was supposed to know about the killing—but Jerry the Jew said, "No. It's okay. He's all right. He's all right."

At first Donnerstag chuckled when he saw the story, but he got upset about the ring. "What the fuck's this? And what's this about a fucking glove?" He turned to Hank, who had been charged with stripping the upper portion of the body. "I thought I fucking told you to take everything off," he said angrily.

"Oh, I did," said Hank, "I did."

"Well how's the ring there?"

Hank slouched and lowered his head, mumbling, "It must've been on the hand that was underneath his body."

Festa at first tried to mollify Donnerstag, emphasizing the most important point: that the body had not been identified. He also underlined the confusion over the initials, doubting they could be traced back to Feldman. "Jed may've got that ring on some score."

Donnerstag's mood brightened. "Read this," he said, shoving the paper over to Lombardo.

Wally looked at it hastily. He said, "So what?"

"There's Jed," Donnerstag said, pointing to the photograph of the island. Lombardo let out a small laugh.

Now Donnerstag was the optimist. "Look at the age," he said. "You're talking a twenty-year difference. It's decomposed. His own family wouldn't bother to go up there and identify him. We're making a fucking mountain out of a mole hill."

Rose had gone into the living room to keep Pete occupied and also because she was still not supposed to know. When she came back to the kitchen, Donnerstag pushed the newspaper over to her and gave her an analytical look over his glasses. Festa's lips began to tremble. If Jerry the Jew found out she was aware of the murder, his wife might be executed. He immediately called Donnerstag out to the porch for a confrontation. "Hey, what the fuck you doing?" he shouted at Donnerstag.

"What's a matter?" The Jew asked.

"What the fuck, why—hey, you know, we ain't playing no more games."

"Does Rose know?" Donnerstag asked.

"Well, does Shirley know?"

"Course not," said Donnerstag. "You crazy?"

"Well, then, are you fucking crazy?" He thought about attacking Donnerstag, stabbing him—and Lombardo too. "Why does that fucking douche bag Wally gotta know for?"

"He's with me."

Festa was on the verge of going after Donnerstag. "Fuck you," he said. "Look: I ain't trusting nobody. That fucking junkie kid shouldn't know nothing!"

Donnerstag did not have a gun on him, and he was quite aware of Festa's size. "Don't forget," he said calmly, "he was on that too."

Festa exploded. "He wasn't on nothing. He was on the fucking frigging robbery—that's it. We're talking a whole new ballgame. I'm telling you now, you're going too far. Wally ain't got a piece of the murder."

"Calm down, calm down," Donnerstag said diplomatically. "They're never gonna identify the body. You said it yourself. Right now they're gonna put it in a steel box, leave it there a coupla months, and that's it. It goes in the ground."

Donnerstag and Lombardo left. Rose went over to Jerry, trying again to be of comfort. "Maybe it wasn't Jed," she told her husband. "Don't be so sure."

But he was certain. The matter was not over. There was the ring, there was the glove, and those feelings he so relied on were sending out alarm signals. His stomach was taut as a board. His face felt stretched, his nose cold, and a prickly sensation ran right up to his neck. It came from the base of his spine.

BOOK TWO

GHOSTS OF
FLESH AND BLOOD

The Fates are just, they give us but our own.
Nemesis ripens what our hands have sown.
                    —John Greenleaf Whittier,
            Letters to a Southern Statesman

I. All The Bear's Friends

WHILE FESTA INCORPORATED was redistributing the county's jewelry supply, such transgressions paled in comparison with those of Frank "The Bear" Basto and Raymond Freda—they of the high-stakes crew on Bloomfield Avenue, which had little time for simple burglary. During 1971 their meditative moments were spent designing new means of breaking into banks.

As mob moneymakers, both had earned their stripes in a style no less bold than that of an old-fashioned train robbery. But bankers had outsmarted them of late, keeping less cash in the teller drawers and installing newer alarms, newer customer counters, and television monitoring systems. Most frustrating were the "bait packages" they mixed with the other money, trick bundles of bills which, upon getaway, would explode into a cloud of tear gas and indelible red dye, making it easier for police to track them.

Returning to Newark on October 8, 1970 after a five-year term in the federal penitentiary at Lewisburg, Pennsylvania (where he was joined by his friend "Pops," better known as Carmine "Lilo" Galante), Freda learned that Basto, his closest pal in more youthful days (he was now thirty-eight and Basto thirty-four), had devised a wholly new, seemingly ludicrous technique of bank-busting. Basto would steal a four-drive Bronco wagon and attach a sturdy steel cable to its rear. At the end of the cable was a hook. The hook was latched under the inside slot of a bank's night drop, where deposits are made after regular hours, and the drop yanked from the wall by a quick, forceful surge of the jeep. Having removed this façade (which would have greatly inhibited maneuverability inside the vault, because of the inner slot), Basto would next lower into the chute a three-foot length of hose with twenty lines at the end of it, each with a heavy-gauge fish hook at the end. He shook the hose around until one of the hooks snagged a moneybag, then pulled it out through the now-widened drop.

Despite the risks of such blatant theft—which was carried out late at night with the standard lookouts, getaway cars, and, often, police protection—Freda was fascinated by the improvisation and chose to take it a step further. He decided to manufacture an imitation night-deposit box that could be clamped over the real one, causing deposits to collect in his own contraption, which could then be unhooked and hauled away. As Freda would later explain in a letter to a journalist, "I went out and found me a convenient bank that had a Diebold night-drop. It was on Route 53, in Mount Tabor, New Jersey. I took a lot of pictures of the night-drop, then I measured it with a steel tape I had with me. After doing all that, I took a small sledge and knocked the handle off the night-drop's door. I took the handle away with me.

"Me and [another burglar named Dave] made a trip to New York for aluminum to build the thing with. After a few days it was looking real good. The more we worked on it, the more it resembled the pictures I'd made. The only big difference was that our drop would stick out seven inches from a bank's wall. It would fit over and around a bank's drop, and would lay flush against the wall. A hanger on the back of our drop would fit down through the handle of the one on the bank; and by reaching through the open door of our drop and tightening the wing-nut (in the upper portion, out of sight), the drop would be snugged firmly against the bank's wall. A trap door in the drop's bottom could be opened to remove the bags deposited in our vault. Any Yale night-deposit key would open the drop's regular door, since we had removed all the lock's tumblers. We tried hanging it on a fake handle we had built, and it worked fine."

After a month of work on the device, which included engraving an official-looking symbol on the metal, which was pounded into shape at a warehouse he rented, Freda went out at eight o'clock one night and clamped it over the drive-by deposit box at the People's Bank of Denville, in Morris County, eighteen miles northwest of Bloomfield

Avenue. It appeared to be working all right, but then, at ten o'clock, when the supermarket receipts arrived, six cars suddenly lined up all at once, a volume that, without the benefit of time to empty it, caused Freda's invention to jam. There were too many bags and envelopes inside; it was immediately discovered and confiscated by the authorities.

Another unsuccessful idea of Freda's was to replace Basto's hook-lines with a live monkey, which he purchased on Newark's Perry Street and spent long days trying to train in his simulated night-drop vault inside his warehouse. "I went out and got a couple of bank-bags and bought some bananas and nuts for him. But I knew I would have to keep him kinda hungry while I was training him.

"I would wait till everything was quiet and nobody was around, then I'd let him out of the cage. The monkey was the meanest bastard I ever seen! I can't tell you how many times he bit me . . . I let him watch me put some peanuts in a bank-bag and poke it through the night-drop door. Then I got the monkey and put him in the drop, too. Right away he starts fooling with the bag. After a while I opened the night-drop's door. The monkey kept foolin' with the bag but he wouldn't jump up with it. I had named him Chico. I called him, but he paid me no mind."

(Though Freda would later deny it, he told detectives in 1975 that he had shot the monkey in the head. "Fuck the monkey," he was quoted as saying. "There's a million monkeys all over the place." Nor was this the only time Freda was rumored to have used animals in his heists. Though details are scanty, and Freda again denies it, investigators in the confidential squad of the Essex County Prosecutor's Office say that on one occasion Freda held an executive hostage during a robbery and, when the businessman refused to tell him where the stash was hidden, stripped this man in a basement, tied him up, and sent his assistants to a pet store for some white rats, which he unleashed onto the hostage's bare body after rubbing him down with provolone cheese.)

Freda was to find higher profitability in the more conventional trades of counterfeit and drugs. Soon after his release from Lewisburg, at a regular print shop in Stamford, Connecticut, he manufactured four million dollars in bogus bills of three denominations—hundreds, fifties, and twenties, two hundred and fifty dollars to a sheet. At first the printer used too much ink (Ulysses Grant needed a shave, Freda joked), but soon the quality was such that buyers arrived from New York and Las Vegas. To rid himself of the counterfeit, which brought from federal agents of the Treasury Department forceful and immediate "heat," he sold each hundred dollars' worth of it for only four actual bucks, nonetheless clearing one hundred and sixty thousand. While several of those who were passing around the counterfeit on the street level were apprehended, and Freda was followed by Treasury agents everywhere he went, he managed—through impressive talents at diplomacy, and a prodigious cunning—to himself escape another prison term: In return for abandoning his trail, Freda told the agents where the printing plant was, and they busted it. With his proceeds he bought a laundromat.

After that, Freda immediately transformed himself from a counterfeiter to a narcotics distributor. Indeed, he was soon to become the major source of cocaine, then heroin, for the black dealers in Newark, and by virtue of that standing was considered a major trafficker for the state's northern region. His connections were from New York, Colombia, France, and Southeast Asia—importers he had met at Lewisburg.

While Frank Bear Basto remained in the field of armed robbery (and also hijacking, paying particular attention to precious-metals shipments), Freda violated Mafia strictures which, at least in the Carlo Gambino family, during the early 1970s, prohibited any involvement with dope. He also raised the wrath of Newark Detective Joseph Martino, who Freda was later to decide was one of the few honest cops he had ever known. Himself a product of Newark's meaner streets, having been raised on the corner of Mount Prospect and Bloomfield Avenue, Martino had taken up where the Treasury agents left off, trailing Freda every waking moment in hopes of finding him with a kilo of cocaine. He was frustrated in these attempts by what the detective describes as Raymond's "sixth sense." Freda had little trouble spotting an unmarked car, especially those operated by federal agents, who drove vehicles with black-wall tires (wise guys preferred white-walls), kept their collars tightly buttoned, and carried their money not in thick wads, but neatly in their wallets. Coming out of a diner or social club (where his favorite was craps), Freda would roll down his window, start his car, then quickly turn the motor off. If he heard a car starting up behind him, it was Martino or perhaps a few FBI agents—whom he would then take on a wild-goose chase: long drives out to the country, or wrong-way journeys up a one-way street. When the heat was especially intense Freda would pull up to a tavern and exit through the back, where he had a second automobile waiting. (Had they stopped him while Freda was transporting any significant narcotics shipment, there would have been little chance of finding anything in the car. He had devised a compartment cut into the vehicle's floorboard which, by lever, would have spilled the contents onto the road.)

The margin of profit in narcotics astonished him. Freda could buy a kilo (2.2 pounds) of "pure" cocaine for eleven thousand dollars back then, and pay fourteen thousand five hundred for the same quantity of heroin; he could sell these drugs on a wholesale basis for up to twenty thousand dollars per kilo—a profit amounting to more than thirty thousand (on the average six kilos he sold) each week. He trafficked the dope not only in New Jersey but also to an attorney in the Pittsburgh–West Virginia area and to the "country-boy crews" of North and South Carolina. ("When it comes to money," he would say, "ain't nothing like 'junk.' ")

Freda was proud of how quickly he had cornered the market, providing drugs not only to the black and Puerto Rican dealers but also to the "outlaw" Campisi clan of South Orange Avenue, the renegade faction of the Genovese group. He had learned effortlessly how to "read" pure smack, how to cut his drugs with quinine, which increased the volume, how to spice them with less expensive drugs to enhance the "rush," how to turn cocaine flakes into rocklike form. Ever alert to a good flimflam, he observed that the rage of the streets was a powerful Mexican heroin which was brown in tincture, and so he began mixing his white heroin with Nestlé's Quick Chocolate powder to give it the Mexican appearance, adding a stimulant called Procaine for an extra edge. This raised the price per ounce by three hundred dollars.

Of those he dealt with, the most troublesome turned out to be a black bookmaker who owned a tavern called Betty's Lounge. His name was Alvin Little. At the time Freda was purchasing his dope from an importer off Third Avenue in Manhattan and reserving a bulk amount for Little, a tall, bald man who dressed meticulously and had ready access to large cisterns of cash. Before selling the heroin to Little, Freda would dilute each pound of dope with a pound and two ounces of lactose, mix it in a plastic garbage bag, mash it on his pool table, and, for the day, make as much as twenty-six thousand. When Little and his financier, a hood known as Roe, requested two more kilos, Freda purchased these from a Jewish distributor in New York who was procuring it from a detective stealing the dope from the police evidence rooms, where heroin confiscated in the notorious "French Connection" case (approximately a hundred and sixteen pounds), as well as many more pounds acquired in other New York raids, was quietly disappearing.

Freda picked up the dope in the parking lot of a sleazy Manhattan hotel, and by the time he "stepped on it," doubling the volume with lactose, he made some fifty-two thousand on the deal. With these funds he bought a ranch home in Denville (where the night-deposit caper was soon to take place) and lavish furnishings, including a gold-plated sink for the bathroom and a twenty-four-carat toilet seat, which strikingly complemented a carbon-black bathtub. He was a man who very much enjoyed the trappings of wealth: expensive gew-gaws for his young daughter, a maid to help his wife, Delores, and, for his Doberman Pinschers, butcher-delivered meat.

The drug transactions spawned extreme forms of violence, and though he readily smiled and joked—he too had an amiable demeanor—below the surface Freda was certainly a nasty sort. (As a child he had cruelly beaten up another boy for a couple of dollars, and broke a junkyard dealer's leg and arm with an iron pipe in an argument that began over a faulty alternator.) Soon those around him met torturous deaths. Little's friend Roe was kidnaped for a ransom of cocaine (and not released before a torch was put to his feet) and Louie Mileto, one of Freda's contacts in New York, was hardened in a freezer and hacksawed into small pieces in a Brooklyn basement. Whether Freda was involved is not known. But Little himself was found dead of two bullet wounds in the head after being lured out of Betty's Lounge on August 29, 1971, at 9:30 P.M., by two white males in a mint-green Chevrolet who, posing as detectives (in rain hats and beige and blue trenchcoats), shoved him into the car with, "Get your ass in there." According to underworld sources, the murder was accomplished by Freda, his brother-in-law Austin Castiglione (a quiet type who was also close to Basto), and perhaps another of Freda's associates—Jerry Donnerstag. Be that as it may, the motive was obvious: Little owed Freda eighty-seven thousand and was reneging on the payment, complaining that the dope had been diluted beyond salability. ("That black bastard!" Freda was later quoted as saying to another gangster, Ira Pecznick, who was buying an M-14 rifle from him. "He tried to burn me. I don't care if he told me, 'Look, I don't have the money. I'll pay you a little at a time.' I could take that. The guy's a good customer. But instead he tried to burn me. These niggers are so dumb. I ain't taking that shit.") At Little's wake, Freda brazenly appeared among the mourners near the casket and yelled, "You still owe me eighty thousand, ya fuck."

Bothered by agents now from the Federal Drug Enforcement Administration—who on a search warrant had dug up his entire back yard—Freda, the owner also of a small construction firm in Bloomfield, moved his family to Boonton Township. He put a pool, two barbecue pits, and a gazebo in the yard, not to mention the Italian tile imported for their hallways and kitchen. He rented a store in which he built a clandestine money drop in a false light fixture as a precaution, and paid off some bank loans he had fraudulently secured, because the FBI, he learned, was ready to indict him.

In the course of operating his home-repair company, which employed six men, Freda crossed paths with a printer from Hackensack who badly wanted his basement finished but was lacking in funds. In return for remodeling the basement, Freda persuaded the man to print another four million in offset counterfeit. His men went to work, in the meantime, paneling the cellar and installing a stolen wall-to-wall rug. The counterfeit was packaged in the same denominations as the previous run, and alternated with a hundred serial numbers, so that the authorities had a harder time tracking it down. He then took the "money" in five suitcases fitted under a pile of plywood in the back of a company truck and delivered it to another associate of his, Donald Serito, and to Joe Adonis, Jr., son of a prominent gangster who, during Prohibition, was of the stature of Meyer Lansky, Lucky Luciano, and Frank Costello. Once more the Treasury Department put on the heat, and once more Freda bargained with the agents. This print shop also was raided, and the misguided printer and his son—neither anywhere near Freda's league—were busted. Raymond, of course, went free.

Such treachery and wiliness guided Raymond Carl Freda through a career impossible to communicate in a simple mob nickname, and so Freda had gone these years without one. How was one to fit his complex image into a single sobriquet? Instead, federal and county law enforcement officials would in moments of rapture judge him as one of the most incorrigibly and ingeniously criminal minds in the United States, and perhaps the most devious one in the Garden State.

Ray Freda and The Bear Basto were like college classmates who end up in business together, and Valvano had been close to Freda since Freda was about nineteen. Nicky Boy was in fact married to Freda's sister Dottie, and when Ray was in jail, Nicky Boy always took care of the warden or guards, ensuring that Freda had good liquor, cigarettes, and his favorite meal, mushrooms smothering a thick roundhouse steak. In the Hudson County Jail, Freda would be put in the "Blue Room," living quarters on the top floor where whores could be had.

Raymond had begun an active association with The Bear at the age of twenty-seven or so, when Freda was hijacking truckloads of meat, robbing car dealerships and banks, and growing tight with Demus Covello, a made-man (indeed, a lieutenant) for the Gambino unit run by Joe Paterno. Basto had started his own Mafia career with Ritchie Boiardo's soldiers, but gravitated to Gambino affiliates such as those with whom Freda was tied. He also had in common with Freda the reputation of an "enforcer"—a *ponteadore*—as well as an inventive mind. Together they hired a chemist to concoct a bogus perfume, "Chanel Number Five," which was packaged in counterfeit boxes and sold (for five dollars a bottle, where normally it cost about thirty-five) under the pretense that they had stolen it. The "Chanel" had a pleasant enough aroma in the bottle that quickly dissipated when exposed to the air.

The Bear was a heavy, jolly man. Though just under average height, he weighed more than two hundred pounds. His place of birth seemed muddled—some records said Glen Ridge, another Montclair— but all of them listed "ironworker" as his occupation, and indeed he *had* worked with steel: his specialty was cracking safes. He had been a professional burglar at least from the age of seventeen, and he had a proclivity—as all of them did—for stealing cars. He also dealt in stolen stocks and bonds, which, of late, he had helped smuggle into Europe.

Basto, like Tommy Adams before him, was a respectful student of the mob's old school, and just before teaming up with Freda, the source of his income was the most traditional trade—that of bootlegger, manufacturing alcohol for perfume companies that bought his unregistered spirits so they could fudge their production volumes to the Internal Revenue Service. One of Basto's stills, in Rockaway, was half the size of a courtroom, and his moonshine bungalows looked like the laboratory of a cottage scientist: labyrinthine pipes, copper columns, gas canisters, shiny galvanized tanks, oil burners, and hydrometers to gauge the proof. These traits of an inventor caused a body of lore to pile up around him, among which was a story about a car antenna he supposedly had rigged to an umbrella, with small prongs at the end, so it could be unfolded from the umbrella and, wedged between the corner plate joints of a jewelry store window, grasp the smaller rings, necklaces and charms. (It was used by two older women he purportedly hired to work it on rainy days.) However apocryphal such accounts, it is a fact that Basto had a facile mind for electronics; he was adept at short-circuiting or circumventing alarms with alligator clips, needles, or, so one story went, with carefully positioned mirrors that diverted— without breaking any connections—the photoelectric beams.

Both The Bear and Freda had been profoundly influenced by the unrelenting corruption in the Newark area, watching, as children, the cops who would stop dice games every two hours for a pay-off, let them drive without a license for a two-dollar bribe, fudge mugshots for the wise guys, and who drank in the after-hour clubs that occupied so many of the storefronts in the First Ward and near North Sixth Street, where Freda grew up. Once two cops caught Raymond stealing tires off a car, and all the youngster had to do was invoke the name of his Uncle Jimmy, a Genovese button-man. The policemen took him not to the precinct house but to his uncle's favorite social club, where they chatted for a moment, accepted money from Uncle Jimmy, then politely drove young Freda back to the scene of the crime and helped him start his car—the battery was weak. ("If you're gonna steal, kid," said one of the cops, "steal big.")

It was the wise guys whom Freda and Basto looked up to: they had the girls and the clothes and the cars, and they, not the police, controlled the Newark pavement. When no one had much cooking sugar in the dreary 1930s, Uncle Jimmy could get all the family needed; when Raymond complained about getting slapped around at a parental home, where he was confined and from which he would soon escape, Uncle Jimmy had a pointed conversation with the authorities and, upon Raymond's return, the beatings were stopped and the boy was given extra allowances of milk. His own father was a grave digger and as such lacked a similar forcefulness. "Them button-guys," Ray had stressed to his mother, "they can do anything."

Surrounded by an environment where stereotypes were of prime importance—Italian gang lords, Irish police—Freda and Basto had misinterpreted their Italian heritage as a calling to crime, and fully resented the North Europeans who, they felt, looked down on them. At the turn of the century immigrants from Naples and the Sicilian provinces of Messina and Palermo had begun arriving to Newark in significant numbers, to the extent that the 1930s alone would see 30,578 of them register through the port—an especially heavy concentration in a city that at the time had 442,337 residents. They were greeted not by streets paved with gold, but with jobs as sewer excavators and waiters. Few of their offspring attended college, and they felt alienated from Newark's most powerful ethnic groups, the Irish and Germans. Parochialism became deeply entrenched in the struggling Italian populace as, unable to muster political power on a city-wide scale, they formed, instead, neighborhood societies—many of them religious in nature, like the Società Teresa and the Società Vallatese. These societies, fighting against Irish conceptions that cast the Italians as despoilers of the Catholic Church's patrimony, organized barefoot, candle-carrying religious processions on the Italian feast days to advertise their devotion. From their homeland too were imported intense notions of family honor and personal vengeance, which was often accomplished with stilettos at the behest of organized crime. Perhaps it was no coincidence, then, that in 1935 the bootlegger Dutch Schultz was assassinated at Newark's Palace Chop House on orders from Luciano, Albert Anastasia, and the rising young aide named Carlo Gambino, all gangsters with vowels at the end of their names.

Which is not to say that either ancestral miseries or the preponderance of corruption could account for Raymond Freda's bizarre psyche. Unlike many of the button-men he sought to emulate, Freda was true to no one organization, and certainly not to any code. He would inform on virtually anybody to keep from going back to Lewisburg—or any of the other state, county, and city jails which had known his presence—and, though his friends did not know it, he had been a federal informant for a good many years. He would counterfeit bills while cooperating with the Treasury Department, or sell drugs while he was meeting with agents of the Drug Enforcement Administration.

Yet there was a near-comic rascality about his character that could draw laughter from those who heard of his eccentric schemes, and he was filled with bountiful confidence and optimism, revealing his wide white piano-key teeth when he smiled. He was of normal size (five foot ten) with long, arching eyebrows, low, lopping ears. Deep wrinkles ran down his face like guy wires, to the ridge of his nose. His clothes were as incongruous as they were cheerful and bright: pointed shoes, the busiest of shirt patterns, and red plaid pants. When he was excited or tired, his hair, pushed up at the middle, became a tangle of impish curls.

His most impressive features, however, were his extraordinary blue eyes, which were gelid, large, protruding. They projected a cold intensity so unnerving that anyone upon whom they glared would automatically turn away. His scrutiny was at once vacant and all-knowing, as if controlled by an inhuman intelligence.

His criminality was typical from a historical perspective. As a kid he played hooky and stole cakes, candy, motorcycle parts, musical equipment, car licenses and batteries. ("So many new crooks moved on the block," he is fond of saying, "it was getting hard to steal.") He played dice and served a juvenile term at Annandale and was obsessed with those automobiles: first a Buick, next a 1939 LaSalle club coupe, finally a shiny white Fleetwood with a motor that ran smooth as the Italian silk spread inside. Freda! Between routine terms in jail, he honed his natural skills at armed robbery and burglary so effectively that soon it seemed every car dealer had moved his safe to better view in the front window. Equipped with good crowbars, chisels, and a sturdy sledge, he could pop a safe's rivets and peel the steel in less than thirty minutes, even if it was reinforced with concrete. He was sixteen when he gained his first intimate knowledge of murder.

Basto was another jack-of-all-trades. In 1962, a year before he was sent to Lewisburg (where Freda was to join him later on), they had pulled themselves together for one of The Bear's final bank jobs, on Main Street in East Orange. A week before St. Patrick's Day, Freda simply walked up to a night watchman who was tossing rock salt on the sidewalk and began a cordial talk about the weather and how cold he was, pretending he had just missed his bus. The watchman invited him in for a warming cup of coffee and Freda noted a round-door safe near the boiler. More important, the man unknowingly revealed the only time the bank went unwatched—on the guard's one week day off, St. Paddy's Day. They waited for the Irish holiday (perhaps with particular relish), broke through a barred window, and escaped with one hundred and forty-eight thousand dollars.

On most of their bank burglaries Basto and Freda employed the torchman Georgie—their accomplice who later disappeared. While Nicky Valvano or another crew member was cruising as the lookout, they would jimmy a window, haul in a duffel bag of tools, burn a small hole at the top of the safe (in which a hose was inserted so that water could be poured inside to prevent the money from burning); and set to work cutting through the metal. They used a wide variety of cutting tips on the torches and, for added pressure, had an oxygen-fuel tank filled several hundred pounds beyond its recommended capacity. In a hail of sparks from the back blast, the nonferrous inner layers were melted, the plug cut, and the soggy cash was theirs. They dried the money in a clothes dryer or, as Freda once did, in a pot stove, stirring it like green macaroni.

At other times they did not bother with such a burdensome means of entry. Instead, with two or three others grotesquely disguised in full plastic costume masks (which did not quite draw the same immediate attention as the even more startling stocking masks), Freda and his men forced their way in through traditional stickups—and on one occasion made their escape in a delivery truck from a florist shop Freda had purchased, covering themselves with flowers. Beginning in 1963, Freda embarked on a spree that would include banks in Nutley, Belleville, Maplewood, Clifton, Garfield, and Fort Lee. If he was apprehended for the crimes—and sometimes there were as many as three cases against him—Freda, to pay his bondsman, attorneys, and the bribes, would commit yet another armed robbery or burglary, and, to leave behind a war chest, do one last job just before going off to jail.

To supplement his income from counterfeiting, banks, and narcotics, Freda also ran a still (until one winter the mash backed up in a sewer and turned the snow green); directed a small string of hookers in West Orange; burned down businesses for insurance money; and owned an Italian food-import store. He also lent out shylock funds and ran a crap game; and when he was concentrating on burglaries, he somehow managed to get a job where the information was easiest: at an alarm company. It was surprising, then, that despite such dexterity both he and Basto would be best known not as master criminals but as mob hitmen.

This reputation came about not because they were contract killers, like Jerry Donnerstag, but because they swiftly and ruthlessly eliminated those who were a hindrance to their own enterprises, or who were sanctioned for execution by the higher echelons of La Cosa Nostra (which, contrary to popular myth, rarely hired out killings). Freda, Basto, and Valvano had all been queried as material witnesses for the murder of Freddie Spillman. ("Make sure you know who I am," Basto yelled at a woman who said she saw him. "Make sure you know who I am!") Freddie Spillman, desperate to avoid pending prison time, had begun sending letters on March 5, 1962, to Prosecutor Brendan Byrne, promising to provide information on loansharking, gambling, robbery and burglaries. By summertime of that year word had leaked out, and at eight o'clock on September 18, as Freddie was walking out of his boarding house on the Heller Parkway, en route to his car, another automobile pulled alongside and disgorged several men in dark trench coats who emptied five shots into the burglar. Spillman fell against a parked automobile and slumped to the ground moaning, "I'm shot, I'm shot," as he clung to the bumper. He died on the way to the hospital of wounds in the back, neck, and chest. Within hours the city's homicide squad detained the three men, but they were not exceptionally worried about it. Though they would spend the next couple of days in jail, one of the detectives told them how to act in the lineup and what to expect from witnesses' testimony. ("I gave him three hundred and told him I knew nothing," says Freda, adding that one cop admonished them for causing him paperwork, suggesting that, in the future, "you fucking guys drop your bodies in another county.")

Now, in 1971, he and Basto were beginning to travel their separate ways, and Raymond was angry at The Bear. Basto, he thought, had told Paterno he was dealing in drugs, and so he opened a construction office in distant Rockaway, R and F Inc., which was a front for brokering stolen goods (and handling coin collections brought to him by Johnny Relief Quartuccio). Freda also continued to help Jerry the Jew with his own narcotics trade while Basto was busy with Jerry Festa, who had sought out The Bear for protection as he broke away from Donnerstag.

*   *

Where Freda and Donnerstag were temperamental, acting with hardly a moment's thought, Frank Basto was a patient hood, gracious, discerning, and avuncular. As a youth he too had gone slamming in with two-shooters, but Frankie Bear, in his thirties, had grown staid and poised. He was a planner, a man who painstakingly waited before he acted. That made him more powerful than his cohorts, and thus more dangerous.

Festa and Basto had become friends when The Bear moved into a sizable barn-shaped house on the corner of Delavan and Clifton avenues, the next block over from Ridge Street. Frank had sent word through Austin Castiglione that he wanted to talk with Festa, and he asked Jerry if his men could convert part of his huge garage into living quarters. Hank and Carmen had immediately begun the task, and every morning, after Festa had given them the day's instructions, he and The Bear had coffee together, discussing the local crap games or perhaps the swimming pool Basto also wanted built. Though Frank mentioned hardly anything about his own endeavors, Festa freely told him about some of his burglaries: the suitcase of guns they'd got recently from one b-and-e, the telephone company van used as a disguise on scores, and the hits back in Lackawanna County, where, with Quartuccio or Bob Martin, an estimated thirty-eight burglaries and robberies were, or soon would be, committed (leading to a special six-man police detail trying to track the mysterious outbreak). Festa also told Basto the details of a March 20, 1970, rip-off at the house of Dr. Edward Swartz of Scranton, which had been done with Hank, Johnny, and Tommy Adams. They had gotten a shopping bag full of jewels just before Adams was sent up the river.

"Tell me," Basto said probingly, "why are you doing these things when you got the chicken, you got the roofing?"

"Frank," said Jerry, "I know no other life."

That satisfied Basto. "Well," he said. "I may have something for you."

In those first few months, however, their relationship was purely social. They drank together, and gambled, and soon they were seeing each other on a daily basis. Festa became Basto's driver, and together they would go to the garment center in New York on some mob business, visit a jewelry store or two, then on to the racetrack in Queens. In the clubhouse at Aqueduct, Basto "made meets" with trainers who needed his advice, or with a crew that specialized in safe-deposit boxes on the East Side of Manhattan. But the central mission was always gambling, and this Basto did addictively-though with a strategy. He might protect his wager by putting money on win, place, and show, but it was long shots he bet, and two grand would be placed on each of the categories. If there were times his bank was up to eighty thousand in winnings, so too there were times when, heading home, they had to jump the bridge tolls.

So many days had gone that way: racetrack in the afternoons, crap and monte games at night. Festa would arrive at his house at eight in the morning and The Bear would come down in his pajamas and bathrobe, their conversation forever interrupted by the jangling phone. ("Yeah, I know that. Uh-huh. Okay. We'll make the meet at two.") Hank might drop in to ask a question, but he was not allowed to stay, and Quartuccio could not even come up the sidewalk. Basto did not trust him. If another made-man happened by, Basto would take him into the dining room to talk while Festa remained at the kitchen table with The Bear's tall, lean wife, Camille. Basto was a very private man. But soon he called Festa into some of the conferences, and they had confidential talks themselves. These were in the sun parlor, if the matter was particularly weighty, or up in Basto's bedroom, where there was a round canopy bed with a hanging headboard, Tiffany lamps, and a wood-burning fireplace. There was also a library full of books upstairs, and, in a hollowed-out portion of one closet door, a small crypt of diamonds.

This was no simple partnership. Though they were such different sorts, Frank took to Jerry quickly and deeply. He grew closer to Festa than either Martin or Quartuccio had, becoming Festa's boss, friend, and counselor all at once. But on his part Jerry was more timid underneath it all than he had been with either Adams or Donnerstag; he admitted to being "deathly afraid" of The Bear.

Rose too took refuge in the Bastos. Compared to the other "rumdums," The Bear had "intelligence" and "class." He wore subdued dress slacks and a London Fog coat, and Rose was impressed by his soft-spoken good manners. He never cursed in front of her, and each time Rose visited he hugged her and smiled warmly. ("You know, you remind me of my mother," he said.) He stole lawn furniture for her and took from the rich suburban homes anything else he could fit in his car: bushes, trees, statuary. He had an affectionate sense of humor; knowing she was half Polish, he sent her the latest jokes in the mail or phoned her with them. And when she and Jerry were quarreling, it was to Basto she went for comfort.

But for Rose the truly special relationship was with his wife. She and Camille spent whole afternoons sipping coffee together, talking about each new *mafioso* they met, or consoling each other over their husbands' reckless gambling. Day or night, Camille always looked to Rose as if she had just come back from a beauty salon: her blond hair shone against her brown eyes and olive complexion. These were the mob's sophisticated people, its version of the jet set, she determined.

She and Camille chatted long hours about their children. The Bastos had two daughters, one Janet's age, another who was younger.

There was no son in the house, and Basto naturally wanted one. He compensated for it by forming a close bond with Allan, Rose's three-year-old. The boy was presented with rings, watches, a bike, and a racing set, and once Basto's pool was built, Allan also had his own life jacket. If Rose and Jerry ever split up, Basto said, he would adopt the boy, and he seemed to mean it. Sometimes the boy was at their house as much as his own, and it was Basto who registered him in the prekindergarten classes he felt were necessary for such an intelligent child. It was also The Bear who spoke to the teacher and brought the boy home afternoons, he who gave Allan his snacks. When Allan saw him his face lighted up and he ran into Basto's big arms for a spin in the air. He called him "Uncle Frank."

Though Festa was older than The Bear, in his mind Basto grew to legendary proportions, the mentor whose every word was "brilliant," every action "right on the money," a man who was "the best at everything." Despite the exaggeration of such affections, there was no denying Basto's skillfulness at psychological manipulation, nor his adroitness as a crook. Fact was, Basto never missed an opportunity to make money, and could turn just about any situation his way. When Basto's Marquis sedan was repossessed because of delinquent payments, Festa admired the way The Bear went at night to the dealership, cut off the padlocks, and then, after taking back the vehicle, called the Lincoln-Mercury office to say he now had his payments in order and wanted the car returned. The dealer sheepishly said the car had been stolen and, after a visit by a cop Basto sent there, agreed to replace the "stolen" vehicle with a new one and settle up for the missing car's contents (which, Basto claimed, included a fur coat). The Bear thus came out of the game with cash and two automobiles. Another time, when Festa contracted botulism from a bakery, Basto had him send over to his house a sample of his feces so he too could put in a legal claim, and for more serious business Basto had chloroform to knock out night watchmen, and mixed strychnine with hamburger in case they encountered dogs. He also used a gray van equipped with police radios, walkie-talkies, a peephole for a telescopic scope, and a duffel bag of entry tools (punches, loops, keys, screwdrivers, crowbars). And he had a device that looked like a car pump jack, with an unfolding arm that knocked off locks by pushing up from under the door. Though he was careful never to divulge the most pertinent details, Basto alluded to a major jewel theft from Bamberger's Department Store in Paramus and would later be indicted for hijacking a truckload of prescription drugs and precious liquids around this time. When he had such business to tend to he dressed in black trousers and a dark turtleneck and told Jerry he would be "busy" that night. If Festa was himself stepping out on a score, Frank would say, "Okay. Good luck. Be careful now. Watch yourself."

Basto taught Festa the higher arts of this lowliest of trades. He was wrong, said Frank, to rely on a single fence for the sale of hot merchandise. He brought Jerry around to a number of illicit merchants and showed him how to make them all bid. He also took Jerry and Bob Martin to case out a millionaire's house Basto planned to enter with employees of the crooked alarm company. (Martin was told to go up to the house and jam a toothpick in the alarm switch so the residents would have to call the company for the "repair.") Soon Basto and Festa were cracking a couple safes together, or transporting jewels, and when gambling funds were low The Bear even monitored the police scanners during Festa's burglaries. They robbed the Dairylea Company in Scranton—with the help of a foreman there named Eddie Powell—and stole a safe from an old gambler named Harry the Hat.

They liked to cruise Belleville and Jersey City during the day, then get into the all-night crap game near the Quick-Stop diner on Bloomfield Avenue. Basto called Jerry "the luckiest guy I know," and it was true that Festa had once broken the house for seventy thousand. But they collectively lost nearly two hundred grand another night. This was paid with wrinkled bills hidden in a spare tire.

If the gambling had got out of hand, this did not mean Basto hadn't in other ways improved Festa's character. Jerry was also developing patience and "polish"; there was less cursing, less belching around Rose, and no more junkies. He warned Jerry to stay clear of gangsters such as Raymond Freda (who, he said, was so impulsive he once shot the wrong guy in the neck). "Look, Jerry, let me tell you something," he lectured. "You're no hitman. It ain't your *schtick*. You got involved in something you shouldn't of. I know about you, Hank, and The Jew. I know all about it. It's gotta be done right." Jed, he said, had been "a shoemaker's job."

All Marie knew about men such as Bear Basto was what she had seen on television, or at the movie house on Broad Street long ago. And whatever it was he did, his emergence had lifted the recent blackness which had enshrouded them. He was a "perfect gentleman" who steered her cousin away from the "muckety-mucks"; and the children—of whom there were now five—were all fond of him. (The new child, Joseph, was born in February of 1972, and the pregnancy, as a consequence of the pressure over Jed, had been especially difficult for Rose. She had a heart murmur, and the infant was delivered by Caesarian and brought home to a family distraught over the death of the other boy who once had lived there.)

Donnerstag was still stopping by, and Marie had to baby-sit his children. But Jerry the Jew always left when he saw Basto there, and for that she was endlessly grateful. Both Donnerstag and Nicky Boy were "Satan's prey," and her constant prayer was that Jerry not be tied to Jed's murder. As Marie lay sleepless in bed she hoped to herself that they wouldn't be able to identify the poor boy, which nearly made her feel a part of the crime. But the stress of those guilty nights was partly dispelled by Marie's much-loved pets: two German shepherds (Candy and Thunder) and the toy terrier Pinkie. She had always had a special affinity for animals, whether angel fish or singing canaries, but Pinkie was special. The dog was devoted to her, and only to her; he would follow Marie to the laundry room and bathroom and up the stairs when it was time for bed. She couldn't sit a minute without his jumping up in her lap, and they would sit for hours in an overstuffed chair on the porch while she blew up balloons for Pinkie to pop with his claws. She called him "my son" as she sat there talking to him.

It was some chore trying to keep this family of hers cohesive in the midst of all the turbulence, but who had time to dwell on it, with the two young boys and the cute pair of grammar-school girls who needed constant watching over? They were always digging up the yard, or walking too far down the street, or mischievously trying on Rose's fancier dresses and jewelry. They locked themselves in a cedar chest, and climbed all over the love seat, and loudly—embarrassingly—complained about Hank and how his boots smelled. Nor did they much care for most of the other men who were around, not for Johnny, who did funny things with their pajama buttons when their father was in the other room, or for Donnerstag, a "bossy" guy who always chased them away, telling them to go play in the cellar. Alicia snuck out of her room and saw all these cursing men looking with an eyeglass at a jewelry box one evening, and after Rose shooed her back upstairs, she said, "I know what you're doing. I know dad's stealing things."

At the age of seven, Alicia was often kept at home because of her frail health (bouts of both rheumatic fever and encephalitis), but she was still the most energetic, the scrappiest of the bunch, chasing after Sophia, or after Allan, who they pretended was Ringo Starr. The boy would get mad as a hornet at times and seek shelter with Uncle Frank so he wouldn't get spanked; once he threw a shoe at his sisters and it went through the china cabinet. Alicia's greatest love was horses, an affection developed on trips to the track with her father and Uncle Frank, and she was crazy about the Bastos' pool parties. Daddy and Uncle Frank would grab at the children's toes like sea monsters pulling them under, and it was neat the way The Bear would roll into the water and push a tidal wave over the side. He bought them real telephones for their room, and was like Santa Claus at Christmas.

All of which ran contrary to the larger side of Basto, a ruthlessness that had made him as feared a soldier as Newark had. This was no mean feat in a city which was controlled not by one major crime family (as most large cities are), or even five (as in the nation's Mafia center, New York), but by seven. These included branches of all the New York City groups along with soldiers from Philadelphia's Bruno organization and southern New Jersey's DeCavalcante. Of these cabals the one with the most local manpower was operated by Boiardo (and assistant Andy Gerard), but overall, in a national perspective, the most powerful family with a stake in New Jersey was that of Carlo Gambino. His *capo*, Joe Paterno, was Basto's immediate boss.

The Bear's reputation had been built not on killing junkies or small-time thieves but as an official enforcer whose threats were made sparingly but seldom went unfulfilled. The shouting in crap games turned to a murmur in his presence, and if some problem demanded his appearance at a construction site, work stopped immediately. The reason for such dramatic reactions was that he so carefully and quietly went about his work of killing at the personal behest of Paterno, or so it was said. Although information of this sort is difficult to establish— and when it does exist is likely to be embellished—the most reliable intelligence agents in the state listed The Bear as a "strongarm" who also protected the interests of Peter LaPlaca, Angelo "Gyp" DeCarlo, and Anthony "Little Pussy" Russo (members of the Genovese family); Harold Koningsberg (a front for Carmine Galante); and "Bayonne Joe" Zicarelli (an old Bonanno hand). These assessments were muddled by the almost certain fact that each of these bosses had their own regular enforcers, and, as with a myriad of other names that could be offered, Basto was in all probability simply an associate of theirs. Yet they showed how diverse his range of business was, and one state report grandiosely described him as "one of the most powerful figures in organized crime." In point of fact Basto was basically a highly trusted soldier, or perhaps a lieutenant, the next rung up. But his reputation for murder was extremely strong in mob circles, and he had been linked fairly or unfairly with half a dozen hits. As with Donnerstag, federal and local detectives differed in their estimates of how many—if indeed any, for he had not been convicted—Frank Basto had killed: some guessed a handful, some went as high as thirty. And according to knowledgeable underworld sources—among them Vincent Teresa, a Boston hoodlum who turned state's witness in 1971—Basto and another Paterno protégé, Butch Miceli, operated an execution squad so effective that it rented its services to other mobs in Boston and New Orleans, and had an involvement in New York's "Gallo War." These sources have stated that the Basto-Miceli squad was a force for any mob on the East Coast to reckon with—men who thought clearly and quickly and were of course absolutely silent. If, as it has been reported, the Basto crew did indeed have an arsenal at its disposal—nitroglycerin, time bombs, jelly dynamite, and machine guns—and if, as seems likely, Basto journeyed out of Newark and out of state to do his "work," then simply calling him a "hitman" is too weak a term. Frank the Bear was a professional assassin.

Festa first saw his quietly efficient deadliness in a bar where they were drinking one night. A drunk was making noise as Basto tried to talk with Nicky Skins. The man kept bumping The Bear and cursing, a habit Frank disliked. He asked the man to be quiet several times, but he was thoroughly intoxicated and only laughed at The Bear. In a movement that was barely perceptible, Basto took out an Army shiv he carried and stabbed the drunk, who fell off his bar stool clutching at his side. Basto went to the end of the bar and finished his discussion.

If Basto had an out-of-town job, he often traveled under cover of darkness. Federal agents who trailed him watched as he left his home in the small hours of the morning dressed in a trench coat. But he was a difficult man to follow, since he used cars registered under false names yet verifiable if a call was made to the Motor Vehicle Department (the mob had someone there on the pad); and he was fully aware of those who watched either him or Paterno. Basto's wife noted a strange car in the neighborhood that was only around on weekdays, and he discovered it was the FBI, surveying the neighborhood from a base in a boarding house at Clifton Avenue. He burgled the room during the next weekend and, so the story goes, took a lens from a camera just to let the agents know he was there.

The Bear said virtually nothing about a crime like murder, for the statute of limitations on it never runs out. But Jerry and Rose had noted the importance of the trench coat—not just any of his coats, but an old navy-blue one that he kept for good luck. He didn't wear it on safe burglaries, or on thefts such as the Bamberger's score, and when he did take the coat, flinging it over or under an arm, Rose was left with the distinct impression that a particularly grave order of business was coming down. Instead of hugging Rose as he usually did when he left, he was brusque—a stern look on his face and his smile gone. Camille was not nervous during his robberies, Rose noticed, but leaving with that trench coat made his wife excitable and irritated; she would smoke, talk nervously, drink cup after cup of coffee. "Oh, God," she would sigh. "Bad trouble tonight." Camille would watch him from the kitchen as he boarded some car carrying an overnight bag.

Festa went with Basto to case a stolen car for use on one such trip, and watched the house for him while he was gone. And there was the time Vinnie Teresa had taken fifteen thousand from a Paterno man and, told to return it, was heard to say, "Fuck Paterno." Basto and Festa went on the shuttle to Boston, where Teresa had been told to attend a meeting in a motel. Festa opened the door when Vinnie knocked, and as soon as Teresa saw Basto standing there, he dropped halfway to his knees and turned alabaster, saying, "Please, Frank. Please don't hit me." Basto told him he had forty-five minutes to come up with twice the sum he actually owed, and when "Fat Vinnie" said he only had the fifteen grand, goes this account, Basto said, "I don't care you don't got it. Get it." Teresa returned with the penalty amount.

Because Basto, unlike most killers, did not boast of his crimes, his name was not especially well known outside the innermost chambers of the Mafia. Subtlety was the key to his shrewdness. But a further gauge of his ferocity was that the most cowboylike of the Jersey mob— the Campisi group, which was known to have tried to murder honest police officers—had itself employed Basto as an enforcer, and according to mob gossip, The Bear had once killed a wayward Campisi wife.

Though Festa could not measure up to that, The Bear was attracted to Jerry's earnings, his loyalty, and the fact that he could manage a legitimate business in the face of everything else. "Ya know, you're kinda like a big brother to me," Basto told him.

"Frank, that's impossible," Festa replied. "Because you're *my* big brother." And these words were closest to the truth. Any time Festa made a good score, Basto was simply given some of the money. But, then, The Bear offered to be helpful himself, saying that if Jerry wanted he would help him murder Johnny Quartuccio in retribution for what happened with Janet. "But it's gotta be done right," he said. And by that he meant a method of disposal called "tarping," in which a corpse was gutted, filled with lime, wrapped securely in a sheet of tarpaulin, weighted, and sunk in a river or pond. "They'll never identify it," The Bear explained.

Though Johnny was spared, Festa heard of an informant from Florida whose body they would need to discard somewhere, and he went with Valvano and Basto to search out a place. They traveled to the northern corner of the state over the Pennsylvania border, where the only population was an occasional farmer or sun-deck resort home. There, down a winding road along the Lackawaxen River, which rose and fell dramatically with the upstream sluices of a dam, and where the forest gave off the exquisite scent of pine, they went into a large, ramshackle Country-Western tavern, the Rowlands Inn, to pay court to Philip Cardinale, a Genovese associate. Because of his extraordinary obesity and dark skin, Cardinale had a nickname close to that of Basto: they called him "The Black Bear." At the summit of a nearby mountain, near Route 590 and accessible only to those who had memorized the vexatious dirt paths, was Cardinale's junk yard—a pile of scrap metal, metal drums of all shades of colors, and sundry other garbage. (According to the Pennsylvania State Crime Commission, forty-four stolen vehicles were found on the property in 1974, but, on what some have described as curious grounds, an indictment against Black Bear was dismissed the following year.) The junk yard had a burning grate ostensibly used to melt insulation off electrical wiring. Valvano told Festa that the yard was good for another purpose: there, he said, they incinerated bodies.

But that did not appear to be what Basto had in mind, for they went with Cardinale thirty miles away to another desolate spot: an overgrown swamp land next to a small, deteriorated cottage. Basto and The Black Bear walked down to the pond for a ten-minute conference. As Frank carefully studied the water, Valvano commented, "They'll tarp it and it'll never come up." But when The Bear returned he said only, "Whaddya think, Jerry? This will make a nice summer house for Camille and the kids." He gave Festa his cute little smile.

If murder was not a topic of their conversation, Festa, on other matters, was directly privy to Basto's criminal depths. Together they burned down a supermarket in Hoboken for a cut of the insurance, and that was followed by Festa's second arson, a diner. He was also at Basto's home the time a long black Cadillac pulled up the driveway and Camille came running from the kitchen, saying excitedly, "They're here." Out of the car climbed Joe Paterno and, flanked by two body-guards, a thin man with a hawkish nose who had on a tieless shirt, a rumpled blue overcoat, gray slacks, and a hat. "Look," said The Bear. "It's the old man."

As Carlo Gambino entered Frank's back door Festa left by the front. Filled with apprehension and awe, he plopped himself on his recliner at home and said, "Rose, you wouldn't believe who's over Frank's house: The old man, Gambino."

"Who the hell is Gambino?" Rose asked in all sincerity.

Of the twenty-three or so Cosa Nostra families in the United States and Canada, each headed by a don, Carlo Gambino, frumpy though he might appear, was indisputably the most powerful one. He was the *capo di tutti capi,* or "boss of bosses," for the entire New York region. By virtue of his seniority on the syndicate's national commission, Don Carlo was chairman of all the nation's Mafia.

Gambino's family was composed of an estimated five hundred members and four hundred permanent associates, as well as several hundred lesser apprentices and runners. All told, his family was larger than those of his peers Vito Genovese (recently deceased) and Joseph Bonanno combined. Gambino had so effectively consolidated his power that he controlled the families of both Bonanno (who was no longer considered a Mafia chieftain) and the New York boss Joseph Colombo, who recently had been shot. Gambino's power ran from western Connecticut into Atlantic City, commanding influence also in the Philadelphia suburbs, New Orleans, Las Vegas, Florida, and California. His legitimate businesses alone would have made him a somewhat prominent figure: meat packing, trucking, labor unions, waterfront interests, furniture, food imports, and computers. His labor-relations firm, S.G.S. Associates, Inc., of Manhattan, had as one of its clients Wellington Associates, owners of the stately Chrysler Building, according to the *New York Times.*

A quiet and courtly man who in youth looked like a high-school jock and president of the forensic society, Gambino had arrived in the United States in 1921 through Norfolk, Virginia, as a stowaway from Palermo. He and other youthful *banditti* (part of what was called "The Twenties Group," an elite formation of La Cosa Nostra's brightest and most disciplined soldiers) had had to flee the homeland after engineering—at the orders of a don named Vito Fero and another powerful boss, Salvatore Maranzano—a strong resistance of local police and, later, after Gambino's departure, the assassination of certain crime-busting officials appointed by the Fascist leader Benito Mussolini. It was a case of nearly open warfare between the gangsters and the government, and Gambino, as a part of that, had his roots implanted in the seedbed of modern organized crime. He was raised amid the very hillsides which sent into the New York–New Jersey ports (and also New Orleans) a terrorist cabal that would become known, because of its inclusion too of Spanish thieves, as *Mano Negra*—the "Black Hand."

If a true history of La Cosa Nostra were possible, in spite of the rigid secrecy which accompanied its birth and growth, it would most likely date back to 1417, when in Seville a brotherhood of thieves and card sharps called "Compañia de los Garduños" took an oath of secrecy forbidding any mention of a rising group of hoodlums who worked for *capatzes,* captains who sold their services as murderers, along with their stolen wares. As the writer Miguel de Cervantes Saavedra described them, they were "swaggering young ruffians with large mustaches, broad-brimmed hats, Walloon ruffs, colored stockings, and showy garters" who had done favors for the government during the early Inquisition and, in recompense, were free to murder, rob, and bribe. At this juncture of history Spanish kings ruled much of Italy and Sicily, and in Naples, on the Italian mainland, the "Garduños" begat the "Camorra," a Neapolitan version of the Spanish crime ring, and in its turn the Camorra, during the middle part of that century, begat the Camorristi of Palermo—hill bandits so bold they waged field battles with the Royal Italian Army. Upon the defeat of the Sicilian Camorra by the government in 1911, the organization was succeeded by a related group, the "Maffia," named, according to various speculation, either for an island near Tanzania called Maffia or because it stood for *Mazzini Autorizza Furti, Incendi, Avvelenamenti*—thefts, arsons, and poisoning at the command of the revolutionary leader Giuseppe Mazzini, who reportedly was assisted by the Camorra in an 1846 revolt. As the Black Hand was evolving independently and on a far less organized scale in the United States, it was joined by compatriots such as Gambino to form the American Mafia, and still later, when non-Sicilians were admitted, "The Combination"—"this thing of ours," *La Cosa Nostra.* So Spain, not Italy, was the cradle of the club!

With the arrival of village captains, the *caporegimi*, from Sicily, America's underworld became more tightly unified, and soon, among the powers in New York, a large group led by Joseph Masseria was operating in the sordid atmosphere of Tammany Hall. Masseria was thereafter murdered by Maranzano, and in the wake of his death, Gambino, a Masseria man, shifted over to Maranzano. But Maranzano was himself executed in 1931 at the hands of Lucky Luciano, who organized the New York Mafia into its five families. In the aftermath of *that* disturbance, Gambino aligned himself with the family run by Vincent Mangano and his underboss, Albert Anastasia, who, along with yet another boss, Louis Lepke, had convinced Luciano that the syndicate needed a formal enforcement arm, one that was to become known in the press as Murder Incorporated. In the nine years between 1931 and 1940 (when its activities were greatly curtailed by Brooklyn Prosecutor William O'Dwyer), Murder Incorporated—if published accounts can be believed—may have been responsible for well in excess of a couple of hundred assassinations. Its tentacles were strongest in Newark, Jersey City, Chicago, St. Louis, and Florida, as well as Brooklyn itself.

But on October 25, 1957, Anastasia, by this time a resident of Fort Lee, New Jersey, was murdered by two hitmen (one of them Joey Gallo) on orders said to have emanated from Carlo Gambino, who quietly assumed leadership of the family and its enforcement arm. Gambino acquired still more power when Vito Genovese—at one time the nation's most powerful don—was convicted of narcotics conspiracy in 1959, soon after the mob convention in Apalachin, New York. When the next leader in line, Thomas Lucchese, indicated he was not interested in succeeding Genovese (and Joe Bonanno, who was also vying for the throne, was kidnaped and stripped of his official power), Gambino, a discreet, cautious gangster who had spent a total of only twenty-three months in jail during his life, began to amass a wide base of support and finally attained the role of "boss of bosses."

Genovese had long maintained the strongest hand in northern New Jersey gangdom, and his death in 1969 left a power vacuum that was quickly filled by Joseph Paterno. Paterno's debonair manner and old-school upbringing had made him a trusted *capo* for Carlo Gambino, and he was an exceedingly unpretentious, polite man. His home, on Abington Avenue in Newark, was not far from Jerry Festa's house. Paterno's businesses included a lucrative oil-import holding, and real estate in the Hackensack Meadowlands, where a racetrack and sports complex would soon be built. But his capital base had been in counterfeiting wartime ration stamps and forging bonds. His time in prison was a full twenty-three years in his past, and since then he had built a low-key but powerful base in Nutley, Belleville, Bloomfield, and the Oranges, before discreetly assuming turf in Newark. As Gambino's power in the state increased—abetted by the 1970 imprisonment of Genovese's manager in New Jersey, Jerry Catena—many Genovese family members began to look to Paterno for guidance and protection, and his own closest aides, prime among them Butch Miceli and Frank Basto, inherited the enforcement duties. As "Don Carlo" Gambino rose in stature, so too did the importance of his enforcers, and they were charged not only with protecting Paterno's turf but also with helping other mobs. So Frank the Bear Basto, this man who was now so much a part of the Festas' lives—and whom Marie thought of as a gentle man (saying there was no comparison between him and a brute like Donnerstag)—was quite a bit more than just another gangster, one the children happened to like. Uncle Frank appeared to be a part of that old Anastasia branch known, once upon a time, as Murder Incorporated.

*   *

Through those corridors of crime west of New York, Donnerstag was moving about with a new Eldorado and a stunning Piaget watch. The dope business was treating him well, and he was grateful to Freda for showing him the ropes. "Ray," he said. "Why didn't you put me in this a long time ago?"

In a tenth-floor apartment in South Orange, Donnerstag surrounded himself with plastic bags, scales, and a pile of white powder, portioning the heroin with what looked like a crochet needle. In addition to what Freda gave him, Donnerstag was getting his bulk supplies from a distributor in Fort Lee, cutting it with quinine and sending it off to the street.

By August of 1972, though he still visited the Festa home, Donnerstag's relationship with Jerry was increasingly unfriendly, and when he telephoned, Rose told him her husband was not at home. There was a new tension in the Festa household: Hank Ellis had vanished—just picked up and run away. It had happened after a violent beating from Festa, who was irked because Hank had told his wife about Jed's murder and then had gone and broken up with her, taking up with a married woman who lived just around the corner from the Chicken Delight shop. Afraid Hank's wife, now back in Scranton, might talk, Festa had lost his temper and slapped Ellis all over the dining room, repeatedly knocking him to the floor. Hank had shown up at the store the next day as if nothing had happened, made the day's deliveries, and that night brought the receipts to Ridge Street. But then he borrowed some shy money, bought a car, piled his belongings on the roof of it, and headed south with his new girl friend, Lillian, a janitor in an apartment building.

And Festa was still furious with Donnerstag for telling Lombardo about the homicide. Though the Festas were more secure now that they had a relationship with The Bear, Rose was suffering anxiety attacks that knocked her breathless; sometimes she had to kneel in front of the air conditioner to breathe. They had learned for sure that Feldman indeed had *not* been an informer, and the thought of how Jed must have looked after a winter in the pond still nauseated Rose. "Don't worry," Camille Basto, who had apparently heard about Jed, tried to console her. "These things have a way of working out."

In Pennsylvania the murder trail was cold. The state police had circulated a flyer to sheriffs' departments and other agencies in seventeen states with a description of the dental plate, the fourteen-carat signet ring, and the body itself a month after the discovery. Investigators had fanned out to jewelers all around Lackawanna County hoping one would remember selling the ring. But none had, and no local dentists recognized the dental plate. Desperate for leads, the police had also published a description of Jed's false tooth in the June 1971 issue of the *Pennsylvania Dental Journal,* and reviewed descriptions of missing persons from mental wards and prisons in Pennsylvania, New Jersey, Connecticut, and Massachusetts.

Wally Lombardo had known about the murder since October 1970. He had asked Donnerstag if he would be doing any more holdups with Feldman, and Jerry the Jew had quite casually said, "No. He's gone away." The following February, bar-hopping at night, he told Lombardo it had been a senseless killing—a shakedown—and that he was afraid Festa's wife knew all about it. Then he had fallen back into his macho routine, telling the junkie, "I like the way you handle yourself. If you keep it up we can go far together. But if you ever fucking cross me," he added, "I'll do the same as I did with Jed."

In the course of their drug transactions Wally did indeed cross Donnerstag by stealing some of the heroin, and Jerry the Jew pistol-whipped his face. Afraid that was not the end of it, Lombardo went into hiding just north of Newark until June 26, 1973, when he was jailed for armed robbery.

Wally's role had been assumed by another heavy drug user, Joe Carbone. He had frequented the Chicken Delight for several years, dating Angie Feldman and doing scores for Festa when he was called upon. He had also been running guns. A thief since the age of twelve, when he broke through a screen at the Dairy Queen on Broadway, Carbone, now twenty-five, had much in common with Jed besides youth. Raised on Bloomfield Avenue by a grandmother who owned an apartment building where a crap game was run, Carbone too had been alienated by upheavals in his home life, and like Jed he had spent a goodly number of his teenage years—four to be exact—at the reformatory farm in Jamesburg. Carbone constantly found himself in police precinct houses for stealing and dope busts; eventually he did time in both Annandale and Bordentown, where the younger incorrigibles were sent.

It was during a stay at Caldwell Penitentiary that Joe had met a sickly old Boiardo button-man named Vic Pisauro. He helped the ailing wise guy shave and dress, and cranked up his bed for him when they were in sick bay. In 1968, when Carbone was released, the first day out he looked up the old *mafioso* at the First Ward Democratic Club and was repaid for his kindness with a job as a bartender there. Hanging out at DeMarco's diner, near where his grandmother had lived, he began running into Jerry Donnerstag, and they became closer when Joe graduated to a job at the Cabaret. Between stints in jail and his narcotics errands—making purchases in Spanish Harlem or transporting stolen shipments of tranquilizers for a pharmaceutical firm near Lake Hopatcong—Carbone had been another frequenter of Ridge Street, and an admired one. He was a cool talker, a good dancer, a sharp dresser, and Janet, now at the age where boys were becoming more interesting, had a crush on him. In his black dress pants and starched white shirt he was not at all like Wally or Hank. Rose said he should have been an actor.

His days with Festa were over (*they* had never liked each other), and the relationship with Angie Feldman in the past. Toward the end of 1972 his life began to revolve around Jerry the Jew. He thought Donnerstag was chic, a "wise guy's wise guy," and each day they met at the High Street Pleasure Club to discuss their heroin trade. Afterward Carbone would cut the dope, bag it, and deliver ten-dollar pouches to their street pushers. At first he was given only 25 percent of the profits, but later that was raised to seven thousand a week, an equal share. It got so that when Freda and his partner Austin Castiglione were short, Carbone even sent some bulk quantities over to them.

After the day's transactions were complete, Carbone accompanied The Jew on his nightly forays to the Democratic Club, to Don's 21 restaurant, in the center of Newark, and on to Jersey City and afterhour clubs in Manhattan. It was on these nocturnal excursions that Joe first recognized Donnerstag's almost sexual urge to commit violence. At a bar in the Ironbound section he watched as Donnerstag picked a fight with four burly guys at the bar, provoking a glass-smashing, chairsplintering brawl by throwing a bottle at one of them.

To Carbone, Donnerstag was at once intriguing and repulsive, an ambivalence symbolized perhaps by the way Joe viewed Donnerstag's style of dressing. Carbone noticed that he wore top-of-the-line watches, expensive shirts, and the best of suits, but that, like most wise guys, he could not match colors, and so in the end he looked gauche. Besides, his shirts weren't tucked in properly, his hair defied the comb, and his pants were always the wrong length. But the bar women came after him for his money, and he stressed to Carbone the intermarriage of romance and capitalism. ("Joe, you're smart, you're good-looking. Me, I know I'm ugly. I admit it. But I got an Eldorado, I got a pocket of money. You could be standing on a corner without a set of wheels, without two quarters to rub together, and you're not gonna get laid. I'll have all the cunt I want.")

He did in fact come up with a few attractive women. They partied together with a sixteen-year-old girl who did anything for a sniff of heroin, and Donnerstag might go through three hookers in a week's time. But he liked the idea of having his wife Shirley and a family at home (this almost certainly because all wise guys liked to pretend they were good to their families, when in fact their actions caused nothing but pain), and he apparently had second thoughts about Lynne, the woman he was rumored to have killed in the bathtub. Carbone accompanied him to her grave and was surprised to hear Donnerstag sobbing there. "I didn't mean it, baby. I'm sorry," he would say. He bought a stone marker for the grave and took away the temporary metal cross which had marked her final resting place. To Marie's consternation he stored the metal marker in the Festas' yard.

An unusually reflective man for a thief, Carbone would one day look back upon Donnerstag as "a guy locked into an unreal world," and "capable of anything." He was fascinated by how much Donnerstag resented his ethnic origins, saying that he wished he had been born Italian, and how instinctively leery of him most people were. Carbone was himself uncomfortable at how swiftly Donnerstag's moods could change from violence to guilt, and he gauged The Jew's outer shows of fearlessness as hiding a terrified insecurity. Many times Carbone suddenly became nervous as he sat with Donnerstag in the car. He could feel "evil" flowing all around Donnerstag—not in a mystical sense but in the way his actions, even small actions, had a subliminal effect. If Donnerstag hadn't been a contract hitman, Joe decided, he would still have been a murderer of some sort—probably a thrill-seeking strangler, Carbone figured.

Donnerstag began stopping by a field where his young stepson, just arriving at junior-high-school age, played middle guard on a football team coached by a young attorney named Joseph Falcone, who had recently been sworn in as an assistant county prosecutor. "Gotta be tough, gotta be tough," Jerry the Jew screamed at Keith from the sidelines. "You stink, kid! Get in there, get in there, you pansy fag. C'mon, or I'm gonna put a dress and panties on you tonight."

Falcone was angry. Keith was perhaps his most dedicated and talented player, and he considered both Donnerstag and Carbone to be suspicious characters. Donnerstag had on a full-length leather coat and introduced himself as a Florida businessman.

"Whoa, whoa," Falcone said, trying to stop Donnerstag's shouting. "Your kid's one of the best we got. I had ten more like him, we could play the high school team."

Donnerstag seemed not to listen. He went to a few more practices and games, always cursing at the youngster, and he promised to donate practice uniforms, which never came.

The two hoods cruised together down Mount Prospect Avenue, where Angie was wondering more and more about her brother Jed. From talking to Nanny at Chicken Delight, she had an odd feeling he had not simply run away, and she decided it might have something to do with Festa, whom she despised. Also, her friend Donnerstag had come into Don's 21 on McCarter Highway, where she was now working as a waitress, and, sitting at a booth with Carbone, asked, "Have you heard from Jackie?" using the name Jed was called at home.

"No," Angie replied. "I didn't hear from him. Why? You heard from him?"

"No," he answered. He turned to Carbone and chuckled.

Angie noticed that smirk, and her curiosity got to the point where she went to a gypsy fortuneteller working out of Down Neck. The card reader told her Jed had been killed and put somewhere wet. Angie began to think he indeed might have died.

Though Carbone had not been told about the murder directly, he had overheard discussions between Donnerstag and Festa and remembered their excitement over a Scranton news article Festa had received in 1971. Dated April 20, the story speculated that the mystery body might be that of a "bail jumper and alleged bunco artist who vanished from Scranton in March 1969" and had "a host of disenchanted friends here as a result of a reported diamond swindle." The man was muscular, like the body, and he was forty, about the age guessed for the corpse. To top it all his name fit the ring's initialing: James Flood.

During July of 1973, Carbone took a burglary bust and was packed off to Essex County Jail. In his wing he met Wally Lombardo. Learning that Carbone could get messages to his alienated partner, Donnerstag told Joe to mollify Wally so the junkie wouldn't talk. "Tell Wally bygones are bygones, and no one has any more bad feelings toward him," he instructed Joe. "Everybody's forgot what he done."

Carbone was released on August 1, and Donnerstag was there to take him home, eager for any news about Lombardo. "Wally tell you anything?" he asked.

"Well, ah, you know, he mentioned you guys had the junk operation and that," said Carbone.

"Did he talk to you about anything else?"

"Yeah," said Joe. "He did."

"Did he mention Jed Feldman to you?"

"Yeah. He did."

This greatly angered Donnerstag. Wally should never have mentioned that, he shouted. But Jerry the Jew said little more until one of their late runs to the Keyboard Lounge in Elizabeth two weeks or so after Labor Day, when he finally spelled out the details to Carbone. He described how he walked up to Jed and then "the others had target practice on the body."

Donnerstag began working for an asphalt company in South Brunswick which was operated by Austin's brother, Jimmy Castiglione. He had been given the front job of "materials clerk," signing in truckloads as they came, and it happened that at this same time another area contractor, Mario Sianni, owner of Aetna Trucking near New Brunswick, had refused to cooperate with Castiglione in a bid-rigging scheme. Donnerstag was given a ten-thousand-dollar contract to kill the businessman.

Jerry the Jew decided Carbone would handle the killing. "I got work to be performed," he told Joe. "It's time you broke your cherry, made your bones."

"Yeah, Jerry, I'll do it," said Joe.

He was given a shotgun and the addresses of Sianni's home, business, and current job site. "Follow him around a few days," Donnerstag schooled him. "Make sure everything's done right. Get out of the car, walk up to him, and hit him point-blank. Take the gun back with you."

Carbone had always wanted to be a wise guy, and doing a hit would greatly enhance his stature. But he also had that thoughtful mind. He was a reader. He knew about Ayn Rand and he talked about concepts such as the "power of volition." Now he thought a lot about how one's environment affects one's behavior, and about whether he should kill this man. For two weeks he followed Sianni around, trying to psych himself into it, and there were several good opportunities to make the move. But each time he was overcome by his feeling that it was a foolish, needless murder, over too small a matter. As he was to explain later, murder was not his "cup of tea."

Donnerstag became impatient. "What the fuck's taking so long?" Aware that if he waited much longer his own life would be endangered, Carbone called James Bradley, a DEA agent who had helped Joe get his parole reinstated the previous April after he had been thrown back into the slammer. The agent had done it in return for a promise that Carbone would help the agency pin a narcotics rap on Donnerstag. Joe had reneged on the deal, but ever the opportunist, and unabashed, he went back to Bradley in search of protection and told him about the planned execution. "I got the contract, and I'm not going to do it," he said to the agent. "Maybe you should get somebody to warn the guy his life's in danger. He didn't really do nothing." Bradley informed the New Jersey State Police, who picked up Jimmy Castiglione, took him to an isolated graveyard, and, since they could not formally charge him with anything, administered "stick therapy," warning the crook off with an old-fashioned beating.

Donnerstag heard about that and called Carbone that Friday. He told him to wait at home in Nutley for someone to come by and pick him up. He wanted to see him.

Carbone was naturally upset, but he did not feel his life was immediately on the line. Shirley drove up and took Joe to the Joralemon Avenue apartment in Belleville. It was a small apartment, with a kitchenette to the left of the entrance and a well-kept living room dominated by a velour sofa covered with a protective sheet of plastic. Crystal candy dishes decorated a long coffee table in front of it, and a sky-blue curtain formed a backdrop for garish figurines of Pantaloons, pixies, and a German figure in a dirndl dress. One of the figurines looked like the Prince of Siam. A miniature water fountain was also in the display.

Austin Castiglione was already there, and Donnerstag took Carbone down a short hall to his bedroom. "Did you tell anyone?" he asked.

Carbone shook his head nervously. Donnerstag didn't believe him. "Well, maybe you told some broad you were laying with—you know, bragged," said Jerry the Jew. He mentioned the graveyard beating.

Carbone fidgeted. "No way, Jerry. That's out of my character."

Donnerstag pressed on, saying he thought Carbone had "told the law." This time, however, he was not going to "act hasty" and make the same mistake he had with Feldman. "But if I found out, I'd put a bullet in you right now. I'll find out by Monday. Just remember, the same thing that happened to Jed could happen to you," he repeated.

In an attempt to reassure Carbone after frightening him, Donnerstag next smiled at him as if everything was all right after all. He was just checking him out, Donnerstag lied. "Listen, take the Eldorado for the weekend, enjoy yourself." Carbone's own car was in the shop for repairs. "Come back here Sunday night."

That was the only time he had ever offered Carbone use of his best automobile, and that bothered Joe too. But he drove off in the fancy Cadillac just the same. And after that, Carbone disappeared, like the other young dope users who got too close to Jerry the Jew.

*   *

Though Jerry Festa had more brains than the average street criminal (certainly enough to run a small business and a construction crew), he idolized mobsters in the way youngsters do sports stars, inspired by such movies as *The Godfather,* which, while providing high entertainment for most of the nation, made hoodlums noticeably proud. In the five years since he met Adams, his propensity for ingratiating himself with strangers had put him in touch with a dazzling array of mob associations. He collected shylock loans for Bruce Scrivo, who took him down to Boiardo's guarded estate in Livingston; he socialized with the Campisis, and with Joe Zarro and Vinnie Tursi. Nobody was tougher than these guys, or slicker than Andy Gerard, who took a personal liking to him. There were those whose nicknames, like Basto's, represented some kind of animal ("Petey Rabbit" and "Moose Marrone"), colors ("Blackie Napoli," "Whitey Miano," "Petey White," "Petey Black"), jauntiness ("Sporty," "Peppy," "Junior," "Sonny"), fruits ("Charlie Apples," "Tony Bananas"), gambling ("Charles Monte," "Blackjack Joe," "Johnny Rackets"), geographic locations ("Garden State John," "Hoboken Pete"), majesty ("The Count" and Billy Hong, the "mayor of Chinatown"), size ("Little Pussy," "Big Pussy"), and the sinister ("Pat Shadow"). There was another "Adams" (Tommy's son Jackie), another "Jerry the Jew" (Cohen), at least three Martins, and two Tommy DeMarcos (one a wise guy, one the cop); a number whose nicknames sounded non-Italian ("Jimmy Higgins"), or were short and snappy ("Demus" and "Ditty"), or of the more classic mold ("Newsboy Moriarty," "Harry The Hook," "Johnny Lobbs").

Though he was not close to all of these men, Festa was now a member of their club. He went with them to North Carolina, or Atlantic City, or Las Vegas, where he and The Bear stayed at the Sands. But recently he had slipped into the bad graces of Moose Marrone and Nicky Valvano, who were infuriated when he backed off a major antiques score in Wrightstown, New Jersey. ("If I gotta kill ya I gotta kill the whole family," Valvano warned him. The Bear and Freda stopped a hit that time, but not before Nicky Boy stormed into the house around midnight, screaming, "Get a motherfucking gun, you piece of shit, no-balls scumbag, because you're dead." Marie listened aghast to this and other tirades.)

Part of the reason Festa was spared in the Valvano incident was that The Bear had "claimed" him as one of his men. But just as important, Festa had also begun working for the irrepressible Freda, who was a force to contend with in the most vicious mob circles. Freda had known Festa since the "School Mistress" theft years before, but it was only now, in the winter and spring of 1973, that they grew close— despite the warnings from Basto.

An expert burglar was just what Freda needed. In recent months the FBI, DEA, and state police had all been haunting him, and he was shying away from his heavier transactions in counterfeit and dope. His phone had been tapped, his car was being trailed again, and he had failed a lie-detector test on a robbery in which the FBI suspected him of having held hostage the wife and children of a bank president.

So he and Festa now began conducting their business north of Newark, in the rich, largely untapped zones Raymond was so fond of: the suburbs. Though Newark itself had shrunk to 405,000 people, and had a skyline more on the order of Buffalo than Detroit, within a fifteen-mile radius of its downtown were approximately eighty-five contiguous hamlets and cities, with a population that could be up- wardly calculated at about 2.3 million—comparable at the time to a city such as Houston. If the city of Newark itself was one large ghetto— and more than half black—the outlying towns where New York execu- tives had migrated were as rich and white as parts of Chevy Chase or Malibu: huge hillside homes with porticoes and hand-carved window sashes. In short order Festa and Freda were to accomplish about twenty-five burglaries here and in Morris County, the region immedi- ately to the west.

Freda's notion of keeping a low profile was Festa's idea of taking— as The Bear warned he would—the most strenuous risks. It was not beyond Raymond to head back to a score just after the cops, on call, had swept through the area, or to walk off in broad daylight with suit- cases of jewels and cash. With Jerry's help he had set up the armed robbery of a house owned by the former mayor of Denville, whose visiting nephew was blindfolded and tied to a pole. Perhaps the most berserk example of Freda's audacity came when, through another hair- dresser informant, he had learned of an elder woman who wore a dazzling three-carat diamond ring. He had Festa drive him near the beauty salon until he spotted the woman departing from her regular appointment. Then Freda filled one hand with Pond's hand cream and staggered down the street, pretending he was drunk and bumping into the woman. As if in a clumsy gesture of apology, he grabbed her hand to shake it, tore off her ring during the confusion, and left her standing there in shock and pain with a handful of hand cream.

Freda! He would have been an endless source of amusement to

Rose if it hadn't been for the crawly feeling she had in his company. If Valvano had terrified her, barging into the house, screaming and red-faced, frothing at the mouth that night, Freda, despite his gremlin looks and geniality, made her more alert, more wary of him than any of the others. He arrived in his T-shirt and work pants like a tornado of energy, scrutinizing everything with those big glazed eyes. He was unable to sit still, standing as he drank his coffee, and if Jerry wasn't there—but was instead over with Frank—Freda spat fire. "Doesn't he want to fucking make money? This is bullshit! I got this thing I'm laying on. I want him here now!" Every day he wanted to do a score, and it was not beyond him to pull a robbery on the way home from another crime. He had such a maniacal look that she never wanted him walking behind her back.

Though Freda tried to lure him away from Basto, Festa stayed with The Bear and developed a relationship with Paterno himself. It was difficult for anyone in the house to believe the *capo* was in the same kingdom as the other hoods at Ridge Street; with his neatly combed black hair and conservative suits, Janet, for one, thought Paterno could have been a doctor or a lawyer. He never partied, and his few guests included a neighborhood priest. But Janet liked none of these men. She thought they were phony, and that Basto, despite his displays of affection for the children, was cold underneath. At Christmastime, when a basket of liquor came with Paterno's greetings, she had thought, "Oh-oh. This means we're really in it now."

Her mother was more impressed. The Paterno home was a brick structure at 76 Abington Avenue, and though it was no mansion—that was not his style—every inch of the house was in splendid taste, Rose thought: gold fixtures and marble tile. He had other residences in Sea Bright and Florida, where many of the Jersey mobsters were retiring or establishing new turf, and his discreet wealth was only occasionally referred to in the press—one of which, the *New Jersey Monthly,* listed him as a "runner-up" to the richest men in the state, with assets estimated to be in excess of ten million dollars. According to a *Newark Star-Ledger* story in 1972, Paterno, at the age of forty-nine, was "a rising New Jersey underworld boss who has managed little exposure"; he had "quietly been moving in on the world's richest territory—the Bergen County meadowlands." Indeed, along with his brother-in-law, Joseph Marino, a real estate dealer, Paterno and his firms—A.V.L. Realty and A&P Realty Co.—controlled, according to tax sheets, six acres directly on the site of the future sports complex (which the New

York Giants would soon call home), and three acres just outside the arena, in addition to 21.4 acres they owned individually and had been suspiciously trading among themselves and other associates at increasingly inflated prices since 1963.

Paterno's courtliness was greatly at variance with the crudity of most wise guys. When Rose visited his home, he immediately rose and offered her his chair. At first Festa was allowed to stay only long enough for a cup of coffee, then Basto would blink his eyes, smile, and look down, indicating it was time for Jerry to leave. But "Mr. Paterno" appreciated Jerry's manners, and soon Festa was visiting there more frequently and staying longer whiles. He went with Basto on business trips to New York for the *capo* (picking up packages of cash from a fur-coated woman in a chauffeured limousine), and when Paterno's car was stolen, Festa was charged with retrieving it and reporting the crime to the police. Paterno suspected the FBI had taken the automobile to plant a bug in it, and thus spoke neither in the vehicle nor—if it had to do with murder—in his own house.

Paterno was Basto's sponsor and mentor, and each Sunday at eleven in the morning he conferred with The Bear and two of his other lieutenants, Demus Covello (under whose wing Freda stayed) and James "Jimmy Higgins" Palmieri. At the slightest sign of surveillance in the neighborhood—or for that matter any strange cars at all—Basto and Festa would cruise the area as lookouts and bodyguards, a gun at rest on the car seat. Basto took his trench coat and went off on a trip during one period when someone was bothering his *capo,* and when he returned Paterno came by his house, hugged him, and led him to the sun parlor, saying "I told the sonuvabitch he shouldn't of done that."

As the summer of 1973 turned to autumn, Paterno's confidence in Festa had grown so deep that Jerry, in his fantasies, figured he too might one day become a made-man. He had helped Basto clandestinely deliver a package to Carlo Gambino in a hallway of the Empire State Building, and his behavior had grown more civilized. But Rose noted a menacing quality developing. Her husband seemed tired of the way guys like Skins and Donnerstag could intimidate him, and he despised the nickname they had given him—"Chicken Delight." Festa no longer turned squeamish at the thought of homicide, and at Paterno's house, when he got up to leave, the *capo* would say, "Jerry, where you going? Here. Come sit and stay." It was no longer "Mr. Paterno." Now Jerry simply called him Joe.

II. The Bust

J OE CARBONE was alive. Immediately after leaving Donnerstag's apartment that Friday, he had taken a room in a motel with a girl friend named Norma. There he had thought through Jerry the Jew's threats and decided they were real: Donnerstag would find out he had told the police about the murder contract and kill him.

It seemed irrational to him that anyone planning to murder someone would warn him first, but he hadn't been raised in a rational world, and Donnerstag was not a rational man.

I'll find out Monday. No doubt he would. Only four people knew about the planned hit, and none of the other three would go to the cops. The tide was clearly against him. On Monday morning Carbone headed directly to the Federal Building, in the heart of Newark's business district, and met with Jim Bradley at ten. Bradley told him the threat was sincere. He knew all about Donnerstag, and he was also familiar with Castiglione's close friend Freda.

"Up to you, Joe," Bradley said. "If you want we'll take you in custody right now. The shit's going to hit the fan."

Carbone agreed, and an agent went with him to his Nutley home to get his clothes and the shotgun Donnerstag had given him. Unsure just who would handle Carbone, since it was not yet a federal case, the DEA office got in touch with Martin Holleran at the State Commission of Investigation, which was interested in building its narcotics files. The commission had a flexible budget. It could afford the most immediate necessity: a secret hotel room. Carbone was introduced to Holleran on October 2, the following day, and at the SCI's offices on State Street, in downtown Trenton, a call went out to an SCI field investigator, Special Agent Cyril Jordan, a former New York detective. He was told to return to headquarters immediately, and on the way back to the state capital, coming down Route One, he spotted Holleran's car and stopped. "Get in," Holleran said. He was with Joe Rosamilia, who would also be put on the Carbone case. Rosamilia had been a Newark cop. He knew the turf. He had been raised in the First Ward among the likes of Quartuccio and Valvano.

"I want you guys to really work this kid," Holleran ordered. "Set this whole thing up right." The next morning they sat down with Carbone at the SCI offices. They were impressed. The kid dressed well, thought pretty logically, and was a real salesman, talking a mile a minute, not just about dope, or the threat on his life, but about jewel thefts and safe burglaries. There was a large robbery ring operated from a house on Ridge Street by a tall guy named Festa, he told them.

Jordan had spent twenty years with the New York Police Department. He had seen many situations involving organized crime and had known the informer Joseph Valachi since he was a patrolman in the Bronx. In his years as a detective Jordan had served subpoenas on the biggest names in the business: Mike Miranda, Genovese, Catena, and Gambino (who had graciously invited Jordan into his dining room while his wife screamed at the visitor, "What are you trying to do? You'll have him killed!"). The Manhattan detective force was widely considered the best in America, and the action there was higher-scale than anywhere else. They looked upon New Jersey as something of a bastard child of the city, and its gangsters as "greaseballs." But the Jersey hoods were as vicious as in New York—perhaps even wilder— and Jordan was immensely excited.

When Carbone mentioned a homicide, and even gave them the victim's name, Jordan said, "Okay, okay, Jed Feldman. But let me tell you, this is going to get heavy, and if I catch you in one lie, lying once, I'm going to the boss and I'm going to say, 'Fuck him.' "

Carbone nodded in acknowledgment and, amidst ever-larger stacks of legal pads and tape reels, talked continuously for the next several days.

In Newark, Donnerstag was perplexed. There was no question in his mind that Carbone had run off because of the murder contract, but he figured the kid would come back. He was just hiding like Wally had, he thought. As time dragged on, though, with no sign at all of his assistant, Jerry the Jew worried. Festa noticed that he was taking long walks with Nicky Valvano, and began to suspect that Carbone had gone to the police.

Jed's sister Angie couldn't figure things out. She kept vacillating. The card reader said her brother was dead, and she believed that—but, no, he was "just being Jed," he had taken off somewhere on a "kick." She thought, "Okay, then, but why did he leave his money in a bank account?" Her parents wondered the same. They had found his deposit book under his bed and had gone to Howard Savings, asking if they could withdraw the funds. They felt that Jed—"Jackie"—owed them for room and board.

Angie was nearly back to thinking he was dead when she received a very strange phone call. She could hear loud music in the background—like it was coming from some bar—and the caller sounded drunk. "Angie, this is Jackie from New York."

"Who? I don't know no Jackie from New York."

"Think about it. You know who this is. Jack from New York."

The caller was slurring his words. "If you don't stop I'll hang up," she warned. Then she realized it might be her brother. "Oh, Jackie!" she said. But the voice was growing incoherent, the music deafening. Whether or not it was Jed, she hung up.

Next a check arrived at her parents' house from the phone company. For ten cents. It was reimbursement for a coin lost in a pay phone by a person who gave his name as Jed Feldman at that address. He must be alive, her family decided. Her father had done some checking around, including a visit to Festa's restaurant, but there was no sign of the boy, and Pete, imprisoned at Leesburg, was as confused as his sister. No one had proven Pete's suspicions yet, but he knew Festa and Donnerstag were somehow in on this.

Down at the same end of the state, Special Agent Jordan had gone to Holleran and said, "Well, I guess we have a hit on our hands." It sounded like Carbone was being straight with them, Jordan said. But first the SCI checked with the Essex County Prosecutor's Office about the robberies and fencing operations Carbone had talked about, and on October 5, Martin and Son Jewelers was raided. The cops found a stolen necklace and twenty-eight thousand dollars' worth of rings and watches, part of the loot from The Bear's Bamberger score. But the main preoccupation remained the alleged murder of the Feldman boy. After reviewing Jed's arrest record, which said nothing about his incarceration at Jamesburg, just his narcotics arrest, Jordan and Rosamilia took to the pavement of Newark's North Ward. Rosamilia knew only too well that Jed was a troublemaker: he had lived on Mount Prospect Avenue himself, and his young brother-in-law had hung around Jed until he was told to stay away from him. He was also familiar with the wise guys. "We got to be careful here," he told Jordan. "I know Donnerstag. He's an *animale*."

Holleran called state police headquarters in Harrisburg, Pennsylvania, and talked with Captain James Regan of the Bureau of Criminal Investigations. "We got an informant," he said. "He's telling us a body was dumped up there—something about water. We don't know just where."

Regan nearly fell off his chair. "Holy shit," he thought. "Can this be related to the shooting case up in Troop R Barracks in Dunmore— the pond?" He grabbed for the file and reviewed the flyer they had sent out, which, in addition to the other details, described the pair of size thirty Wrangler jeans found at the shore, and speculated that the killing had taken place the December before discovery. But for now those facts were irrelevant. The key was Carbone's mentioning water. Soon Regan called the SCI director back and said, "Hell, I think our case is what you're talking about. We got one like that. It's an open case. Sounds like what your guy's saying." On the same day, October 11, 1973, Regan called the Dunmore barracks and the case was given to Lieutenant Albert Paul and Sergeant John Noel.

Noel called Jordan to find out more. They had encountered other leads that hadn't panned out. One was a false tip from a prisoner in Florida, and recently investigators had been looking at the possibility that the body was that of somebody named Ferrington.

"Look, a kid named Jed Feldman," Jordan told him. "You guys got an unsolved case up there, right?"

"We've got six or seven homicides," Noel said.

"All identified?"

Noel replied, "All but this one we've been working."

"Got a lake or pond with it, right?"

"Yeah," said Noel, but the age bothered him. Their estimates were quite a bit older.

Jordan told him not to rely too much on a coroner's guess. "A water-logged body could be any age. We may be able to identify it for you."

Paul and Noel went to Trenton for an interview with Carbone. Joe was trying to cover his nervousness with the veneer of a tough guy, trying to glamorize himself and his crimes. He would never mention that on the street some of the guys called him "Joe the Junkie." But then he didn't look like an addict; he was a smooth kid around the women in the SCI office, and had a good enough mind. And he was not hooked the same way somebody like Lombardo was.

The Pennsylvania cops got as excited as Jordan. They brought down the signet ring and a photograph of the body, which looked like globs of jelly hanging from a skeleton. Carbone had known Jed when he was dating Angie, and he felt fairly certain it was Jed from the shape of the one part of the corpse he could identify, the ears.

Jordan and Rosamilia decided to visit Jed's home at 311 Mount Prospect. They found the apartment in a disheveled state and Mr. Feldman in slippers and a dirty sweater: his wife had recently left him, and he was looking old and tired. As soon as they mentioned Jed, he asked in his broken English, "What's about this all? He's away. Two years he hasn't been here, no."

As a cover, they told him they were there with a narcotics warrant.

"Why, you see him? You hear from Jackie?" No, they said.

"Has he got any tattoos?" Jordan wanted to know. "Any false teeth?"

"Why, is Jackie dead?"

Jordan evaded an answer. He asked about the ring, which Feldman told him had originally been his. He'd had the initials changed from "AF," his own, to "JF" at Martin and Son Jewelers.

Though Feldman was polite, Jordan decided any further questioning was useless for the time being; the father was too depressed.

Feldman kept saying, "Let me call my daughter Angie. Let me call Angie." When he got her on the phone he gave Jordan the receiver.

"Did your brother have any false teeth?" Jordan inquired.

"Yeah, one tooth," she said. She sounded cold, as if she weren't interested in cooperating.

"Where did he have it done?"

"Jail," she said. "He had it made in jail, I think."

"What jail?"

"I don't know for what jail. He's been in and out of jails, always. Is he dead?"

"I don't know," said Jordan.

"He's not dead," Angie said. "We got a phone receipt here from him three months ago."

The investigators also saw Pete in prison. He was as stony as a veteran wise guy. "I don't talk to nobody," he said.

Jordan was obsessed with that tooth, the only remaining means of incontrovertible identification. He planned to interview every dentist in Newark, if need be, and he and Rosamilia got out the phone directory. They began their search with the dentists nearest Mount Prospect Avenue. The Feldman family dentist happened to be one of the first they contacted, and he was the same one Rosamilia's family used. But he didn't have much in the way of records and had no knowledge of the false tooth. And that was the key. The Pennsylvania police had brought down the partial plate removed during the autopsy: white gold wrought-iron clasps to hold an artificial central incisor in place. (It fit next to Jed's chipped tooth.)

The two SCI agents went to the Essex County Jail and grabbed a male nurse who took them to a cell filled with record boxes. Jordan went through dozens of them, finally locating Jed's file. There was no sign of dental work. In fact, the jail did none; it only removed painful teeth, didn't replace them. The investigators next happened onto a probation officer who was friendly enough to give them Jed's folder. In it Rosamilia by chance noticed a slip of yellow legal paper on which were the scrawled notation "Remanded Jamesburg" and some dates. There were no references to the reform school on the rap sheet, but they decided to try it anyway. They headed the twenty-eight miles south to the school and Jordan got hold of the warden, who told him any records would be in the medical building on the same complex as the administration offices. Again he went to see a male nurse. "Just show me the boxes," he said, "and put me in a room." He was prepared to stay late into the evening, but there was no need for that; he had his hands on Jed's file within twenty minutes. There was a chart and also a prescription stapled to an X-ray. Jed had been treated for a break in an upper tooth, which had broken in half, and there was damage to the pulp. It had been removed, and the prescription was for a replacement.

Ebullient, Jordan left in a rush, hardly noticing the neat rows of cottages around a pleasant courtyard and a gazebo. He passed under the large iron-arch entrance onto a country road that wound past farmlands and a small town before leading onto the New Jersey Turnpike. On the way back to Trenton he called Sergeant Noel in Pennsylvania. "Hey, I got the kid's records," he said. "I got the dentist's name, the guy who made up the prosthesis."

"I'll be down in the morning," Noel said.

With Noel at his side, Jordan went to see the dentist who had filled the prescription, and after looking at the plate they brought him, he confirmed that it was his work. From there they drove back to Newark to see Dr. Albert Scales, who had worked for the state home and had taken the X-ray of Jed's mouth and written the prescription. He remembered Feldman's name immediately.

There was no doubt left, and conferences were held between Lackawanna District Attorney Paul Mazzoni, the SCI, the Essex County Prosecutor's Office, the Pennsylvania police from Dunmore, and Joe Carbone, who had pegged the murder on Donnerstag, Festa, and a third accomplice he knew only as "Hank."

In the meantime, in a five-by-eight cell in the first jail Jordan and Rosamilia had visited, Donnerstag's other junkie protégé, Wally Lombardo, was falling apart. Up to now he had always seemed to get out right away by having an attorney "reach the right person"; the last time had cost only a twenty-five-hundred bribe. Now it wasn't working that way. He had made the dire mistake of having gone on the holdup of a loan company high on junk, and he had forgotten to pull up his mask. The indictment against him contained six counts—a maximum of seventy-five years—and his current attorney had told him if he didn't plead guilty the only recourse would be to "lose weight, cut your hair, and pray the witnesses don't identify you." All that fee money to be told to lose weight and pray! And no one was showing up to pay his bail.

Nor was the prospect of jail time the worst of it, not by any means. He knew he could get parole eventually, and at twenty-six that meant he could probably be back on the streets by the time he was thirty-one—plenty of time to "make the big score" that was his goal. The current problem was sheer bitterness. The summer had been miserable. He had been on a detoxification schedule aimed at getting him off fifteen months of methadone maintenance, and coming off that heroin substitute had been worse than going cold turkey from junk itself. His legs had ached, felt like lead, and every morning he awoke in a cold sweat and vomited. Two pairs of pants and a shirt, sweatshirt, and sweater could not keep him warm, and when he got off his bed, sometimes he was so dizzy that he made it to the dayroom only with the help of other inmates. Not that it mattered so much. He had cringed, got the dry heaves at the smell of food, and he had felt lucky when he could hold down tea or coffee. His only nourishment had been chocolate milk.

Through the summer he had been obsessed with doing his dope. All day he would think about how it felt to be high. He never had quite repeated the euphoria he experienced when he started at age fourteen— he never had gotten that feeling back—but he sure had searched hard enough for it, to the tune of thirty bags a day. In his cell, away from Donnerstag's copious supply, he was left with only his imagination. But what a vivid one he had! He sat for hours staring at his arms, looking for a place to shoot, wrapping his arms with a tourniquet to study which veins had collapsed, pretending he was ready to prick a juicy one with a needle. He was weak and losing weight and all he wanted was a fix, dammit. He was in the sick cell trying to get pills all the time.

Once Wally had gotten past the worst of withdrawal, however, he was able to play chess and cards with the other prisoners. Jail was like school. It had been through a previous imprisonment that he had learned all about stickups, dope connections, and how best to crack and cut a safe. (He considered himself pretty good, since he had done two bank jobs.) But his mind was always turning back to his current pinch and his hate for society at large. He felt the average person was as bad, as scummy, as he was. They complained when they were robbed, he argued, yet they bought hot merchandise. He loathed dogs, but they were better than hypocritical people, especially police and politicians; lots of times he'd seen them rubbing elbows with wise guys like Jerry the Jew. And don't mention the jailhouse doctor! He had refused to give him drugs, and so Wally planned to break both his legs "and keep moving them side to side" to compensate for the pain he felt in his own extremities. He would also "slit the doctor's stomach and with my bare hands pull his guts out," because of all the times he thought his own innards were going to come up when he was vomiting.

The best tortures would be saved for the detectives who had interrogated him. They had thrown a coat over his head and hit him with a taped baseball bat—and covered his face with a plastic bag to make him pass out. He had broken loose the sixth time he was losing consciousness and ripped the suffocating bag off, which made the cops even madder. No longer caring if they left telltale marks, the cops pummeled his stomach and testicles with the club, and there was a massive black-and-blue mark from his left upper thigh to the lower portion of his rib cage. Some day he would plant a few of Donnerstag's grenades in their fan belts and watch their cars explode, or snipe at them from a roof. Or better, he would get a bat and instead of tape he would stud it with "long, sharp spikes." He could almost hear their screams, see and smell the pouring blood.

Beneath Wally's vengeful musings was a strong undercurrent of apprehension. After all those months of ignoring him, Donnerstag had recently been sending suspicious hints about meeting his bail. For some reason Jerry the Jew wanted Wally out. Had Carbone told him about the Feldman hit, what he had said about it? Was Donnerstag still mad at the chipping of his dope?

All of a sudden, in the midst of these ruminations, Wally was getting a flurry of visitors, all kinds of cops: Essex County, SCI, Pennsylvania, DEA. They were making offers of leniency if he would cooperate with them in corroborating what Carbone was saying.

He started thinking more about his prison time—and the more he did, the longer it seemed. Jim Bradley of DEA had said, "Wally, tell me: Why does Jerry the Jew want to kill you?"

That had put a light in the junkie's eyes. Sure he knew about the murder, he told them. And he was there the day they got the newspaper.

* *

Festa was antsy. What was Hank up to? Had he just run away to be with his girl friend? How was Wally holding up? He'd heard he got quite a beating in the slammer. And where in hell was Carbone?

He tried not to think about it. He and Rose went to dinner and the movies with the Bastos and stayed away from The Jew. Donnerstag was in the hospital for a while with high blood pressure, and was preoccupied with problems on Bloomfield Avenue. The Boiardo crowd had told him to keep away; his narcotics were bringing heat.

Just out of prison, Tommy Adams said to Jerry, "What I tell ya about that bum?"

"I know, Tommy," said Festa. "How I know." He longed for the old days.

Around the time the SCI was establishing the plastic tooth as Jed's, Bruce Scrivo, the shylock for whom Festa had done some work, sent his footman Charlie Apples over to Ridge Street. Apples found Festa ready to sit down to the dinner Marie was busily cooking in the kitchen. Quartuccio was there and Charlie took Jerry aside, but Marie heard the emissary say, "I dunno what's going on, but Bruce, he tells me to come over here fast. His man"—a source in the prosecutor's office— "told him Pennsylvania's ready to come down on you and The Jew. On murder. Some kid, name of Tellman, or Feldon, or something. They got a ring and something about teeth."

Quartuccio overheard the conversation too. "Oh, Jesus Christ, Coombs!" he exclaimed. "That's it."

Festa was blank. He tried to think a while in the dining room before going over to see The Bear. Nothing much came to him except just running away. He found Basto reclining on his couch, looking somber. He had already heard. "Sit tight," he said, "and tell me something: Youse do much with Carbone in Pennsylvania? Anything?"

Festa knew he couldn't question The Bear, but it seemed certain that someone had told him Carbone was ratting. That had to be it. He had gone to the law after all. Jerry told Frank that they had done some burglaries together, but really nothing amounting to much in Scranton.

The Bear said little more except, "Don't tell The Jew nothing."

For the next three weeks Festa stayed at home as much as possible, afraid he might be followed. He left only to see Frank or to keep tabs on Donnerstag. The Jew was acting like he too had heard something; he brought up a rumor that a couple of cops were asking questions in the neighborhood. Though she was still not supposed to know anything, Donnerstag said Rose should go up to the Feldman apartment to nose around, see if anything had been said. They told her to go there and ask about his freezer. Feldman was planning to move and selling off his belongings: He had advertised the freezer recently.

Rose found the apartment almost empty. Feldman was sitting near the radiator like a meatball, frayed, looking like he'd aged ten years. In fact he was on the verge of a nervous breakdown. "Sit down awhile," he said, eager for company. She asked about the freezer, and how Pete was doing in jail, and about Angie. Then Rose got up the nerve to say, "Have you heard anything from Jed?"

He stared out at the trees near the building. "No," he said, emotionless. "I have not. And I do not expect to, no."

As Rose left, two guys came in who looked like detectives. She brushed by them and went back to the store, where her husband and Donnerstag were eagerly awaiting her reconaissance report. She screamed at them, "Don't ask me to do anything no more!"

"You were only looking to buy a freezer," Donnerstag said innocently.

She didn't care if he did find out that she knew about Jed. She'd had enough of that. "I think Mr. Feldman knows. And there were two guys come up. Looked like law."

Festa blew a fuse. "That's it, you fuck!" he yelled at Donnerstag. "We're motherfucking down the tube."

In Belleville, at Donnerstag's own apartment, another hint soon came: a phone call from Carbone. Joe was calling to feel him out, get him to say something the agents could hear. The phone call was being taped.

Donnerstag sensed as much. He acted unusually friendly. "Where you been, Joe?"

"Out of town," Carbone said.

"Well, I don't know what's wrong with you," said The Jew. "You know, so what's wrong? Why don't you come back here? No one wants to bother you. Come back home. Your grandmother's worried."

Carbone played his part too. "Jerry, I think you want me, Jerry."

"What? For what?"

"You want the shotgun back?"

"Whatta you mean, Joe, a gun? You killing somebody? You gonna kill me?"

Carbone replied, "No, Jerry. You want me."

They kept parrying. Donnerstag was fully composed. He said, "You're watching too much TV, kid. Reading too many comic books."

They hung up. Donnerstag told Festa about it. Jerry said, "Hey, well, but, ah, *he* don't know nothing about Jed, does he?"

Donnerstag said, "Oh, uh. No. Nah, no, no."

The next twist was that Feldman pleaded with the Festas to let him live with them. He was lonely, and he certainly was not thinking straight. (Indeed, he would soon be institutionalized.) Rose let him stay overnight, but then they told him he had to leave. His presence was driving Jerry crazy. He was following Festa all over the house trying to talk to him—when at the same time Festa was about to get busted for his son's murder.

Sensing that a move had to be made soon, Jerry and Rose decided to go away for a while, to Maryland. Festa had to explain the situation to Janet because the girl was beginning to piece it together for herself. "The Jew and me, we was involved in murdering Jed. He's dead," her father said. She was devastated. This man she called her dad had taken her friend's life.

At Troop R Barracks in Dunmore, Captain Nicholas Kordilla was getting nervous. Apparently tipped about the investigation, a reporter for the *Scranton Tribune* had called the coroner, William H. Sweeny, asking if the body had been identified, and if not, whether it would ever be exhumed. Sweeny told Kordilla about the call, and plans for the arrests were accelerated. The SCI met again with the Pennsylvania troopers, District Attorney Mazzoni, and Ronald Donahue, a county investigator who, as it happened, had been the one to suggest months before that Carbone might be a good source for the DEA. In coordination with the Newark Police Department, they arranged a simultaneous raid for the predawn hours of October 25. Both Donnerstag and Festa would be hit in the same sweep; at least a dozen men would be sent to each home, because Carbone had warned them that Festa had guns and Donnerstag grenades. In addition, the Dunmore troopers were familiar with Festa's past by now: their headquarters were in the same borough as Lee Mecka, the cop Jerry had burned with his lightning escapes a decade before.

On October 24, a Wednesday, Festa went about his business nervously. He had bought new tires for his car and was getting clothes together for their trip. He had several thousand dollars on hand, and The Bear gave him a few hundred more, but Rose wanted to wait for the weekend Chicken Delight receipts before they left. Just after eight Wednesday night, Festa and Basto stopped at a Pathmark supermarket in Belleville to get some meat. Festa spotted Dolly, of all people. "That's the one I told ya about," he said to The Bear. "The meatball near Park Avenue."

As usual, Dolly was poorly dressed. She was with an older man. Disheartened but not disenchanted, she was surprisingly friendly to Jerry. She asked how he was feeling and he said he had been doing fine since the "surgery." She lectured him about his health, and then, "How's my Starway Roofing?"

He said his health problems had set it back. That was too bad, she consoled him. They smiled at each other. He gave her a kiss.

Festa went home and tried to get some sleep. But he couldn't. He lay in bed watching television with Allan next to him. Joseph was in the crib. Heavily sedated, Rose was sound asleep on the floor in front of the air conditioner.

At precisely five-fifteen Jerry heard a pounding on the front door. He nudged Rose with his foot. "Rose, Rose, they're barging in the door. This must be it."

She was half asleep. "No, no. It's probably Carmen. He probably forgot his keys again."

Allan was scared. He saw his mother head downstairs and his father run out of the room. Figuring someone was after them all, he pulled the blanket over his head. As Rose got to the landing, under the stained glass that was her pride, the front door burst open and five cops rushed by her, sending her reeling sideways. Her husband had made it to the attic. He put his left foot out the window and straddled the sill. He planned to climb along the gutters and hide behind the chimney.

"Move, you son of a bitch, and I'll blow you off the roof," came a voice from below. There were two cops near the garage and three more off to the side. They had shotguns pointed at him, and they were yelling. One of them was Cyril Jordan. The other cops rushed the attic, put a gun to his head, and pulled him out of the window and back in the room. "We gotcha, motherfucker," one of them said. Jordan ran up and handcuffed the prisoner.

Janet and Marie had heard the racket and were looking out their bedroom doors. When Marie first heard the men she had peered out to the street, assuming that the DeVingos' boy, Vinnie, had gotten into a fight. She had seen all the cars out front—four of them—and as she went out to tell Jerry, the cops had come steaming up the stairs. She watched them bring Festa into his bedroom.

"Get back in your room," a detective shouted at her.

"Whose house is it?" she yelled back. "Who are you to tell me?" But she had no housecoat on, and Pinkie was about to charge into the hall. She went back inside.

Janet's dog, the German shepherd Candy, growled at them too. Janet had seen the men grabbing and pushing her father as he stumbled back to his room. Soon a chubby guy with a shotgun came up to her: "Hold that dog or I'll blow it away." She moved and he grabbed her, thinking she had a gun. She kicked him and freed herself. She could hear her father saying, "Just get me out of here quiet. You did your thing. Don't let my son see me this way."

"You should've thought about your son a long time ago," one cop remarked. Jordan did not like Festa's looks. "Scumbag," he muttered. Rose was sobbing. "Oh, no, no, no." Allan pretended to be asleep. In the background, baby Joseph was also crying.

At 675 Joralemon Avenue in Belleville, the tree-lined suburb just to the north, a similar platoon of cops, including Donahue, Paul, and Noel, encountered no such excitement. They had had Donnerstag under surveillance for several days and knew that at this hour he would probably be getting ready to head off for a construction site. Donahue pressed the downstairs doorbell in the building. Donnerstag came out of his apartment and looked down the staircase from the second floor. He casually buzzed them up. "Yeah sure," he said. "Come on in."

He was dressing, had just finished breakfast. He thought it was a standard bust—maybe burglary or drugs. They read him two documents. One was a fugitive warrant which bothered him not the least. But as the second was read, the murder warrant with the name Feldman in it, he looked shocked. But he quickly shook it off and acted unbothered again. He asked if he could call his attorney. Not before they made a phone call themselves, they said. One of the children came out of a bedroom and was sent back to bed. Shirley was upset. They calmed her and she offered them coffee. They asked if they could search the premises. "Do what you want to," Donnerstag said. At ground level, other police were going through his garage. Those in the apartment read him his rights and he began to gather up some belongings. He wouldn't need his hairpiece, he remarked—there were no women in the Essex County Jail.

Word was sent to the troops waiting outside with shotguns that the matter was proceeding without incident. The police upstairs telephoned Festa's home.

Rose answered the phone in the bedroom. A cop grabbed it from her. "Don't touch any motherfucking phones," he said. The detective got on the line and told his counterparts in the Donnerstag apartment that they too had succeeded in their arrest but needed additional men to finish the search. "We're over here in a castle," he said.

The cops searched through the dresser drawers and threw some cigarettes over to Festa. Rose looked on with swollen eyes. She was sending silent signals to her husband. Finally she mustered enough courage to say, "Jerry, what—what are these guys talking about?"

"I don't know, Rose." Festa tried to sound outraged. "They're crazy. Murder . . ."

No one bought his feeble act. The arresting officers yanked off his striped pajamas, uncuffed one hand, slipped it into a shirt, locked the cuff, unlocked the other one, until they had him dressed. "Jerry, don't worry, it'll be okay," Rose whispered. A cop grabbed the hair at the back of Festa's head and they marched him downstairs.

Marie came out again in time to see that. She had to look away. This was the man she had brought up since diapers, and he was still no gangster to her, just so *mischievous*. As they swept by her he stretched out his neck to kiss her cheek. Her own mother had once been in a similar situation with him, and she had bodily tried to stop the police from taking him off in a paddywagon. But that was for fighting in Cooper's tavern on Adams Avenue in Scranton, not for killing a kid who had not yet grown his wisdom teeth. This was so different, and it wouldn't be right to get in the way. *"Gerard!"* she said with the slight Italian inflection her mother had used. She touched him and turned away to cry.

Upstairs the two younger girls had heard their mother weeping and watched as some strange man looked into their room. Alicia thought the guy was in the Army or something. He had a rifle. She and Sophia climbed on a bed and stared out at the coming dawn, watching the police shove their father in a car and pile in with him. Alicia sobbed, "He must be stealing again."

"Finally got you," said a state cop, Alex Profka. "You're gonna get the chair." From the next block, in front of a doctor's office, ever so discreet in a parked car, Frank Basto watched the procession until Festa and the cop cars disappeared westward toward Bloomfield Avenue. They cut over to the new Essex County Courthouse, a high-rise jail with a 12-story office building where assistant prosecutors, records clerks, stenographers, detectives, probation officers, bail cashiers, deputies, and judges preside over each day's clamorous traffic. Grate lights shone down on the sterile prefab halls.

Festa's hands were cuffed behind a chair in a small, sparsely furnished interrogation room. They had to bring in the chair because Eugene M. Varzaly, a Troop R investigator who had been trying to identify Feldman's body for many months, was sitting in the only other one. It was behind a desk on which he had placed a pen, a legal pad, and a watch. Every twenty minutes he asked the same questions, made slightly modified overtures, implied the same threats. "We got you dead to rights," he told Festa. "You want to tell us about it now?"

"I don't know what you're talking about."

Each time he refused to answer, Varzaly made a note of the time and scribbled a comment next to it.

He asked who "Hank" was. Festa said he did not know.

In the Festa house detectives were still searching everywhere for secreted jewels or other evidence. They spent three hours sifting through chests, drawers, closets, linens, silver, address books, telephone bills, and shelves. As the house was turned topsy-turvy, Marie and Rose were kept downstairs, listening to the sounds coming from the attic, where box upon box was being emptied of its contents—dolls, towels, tinsel. A duffel bag of gas masks and police badges was found under an eave and tossed into the middle of the floor. Every panel was removed from the drop ceilings, and the men spent a long time in the basement looking at the receipts, invoices, and sales cards for "Starway Roofing."

When they finally left, Rose called The Bear. "Look," Basto said. "Get dressed. Get yourself together. Get down there. But don't talk with nobody. The only one you wanna talk with's your husband, follow me?" He told her to watch what she said on the phone in the jail's visiting room. "Keep your cool. We gotta find out what we can. I'll watch the house."

In the court complex, on a hill overlooking downtown Newark— the towering new Prudential Building and the rush-hour traffic of Market and High streets—Festa and Donnerstag saw each other as they were being led to an arraignment hearing. The Jew was putting on his front, acting cheerful. "Hey, what you doing here?" he said to his old partner. "Haven't seen you in a while."

"I don't know," Festa answered, just as cool. "They're talking murder."

"Murder!" said Donnerstag. "Yeah? Really? Me too!"

Because Festa's attorney was not present, the legal proceedings were postponed. Both the men refused to be extradited. "I ain't going nowhere," said Jerry the Jew, smart-alecky. "Pennsylvania? I don't even know where that's at."

They were taken to be fingerprinted and photographed—for Donnerstag, a revealing pose. Though he had maintained his amiability while the judge and detectives were around, once he was alone before the mugshot camera his features took on quite a different look—drawn, yet extraordinarily piercing, and filled with pure hate. Festa too was an unbecoming sight before the flashbulb—he looked like somebody on a chain gang, coarse and rough. But not as fierce as Donnerstag.

Rose went to the offices of the county detective force, where she was directed into a room occupied by a distinguished-looking man with gray hair. He leaned back in his chair and told her, "Your husband's charged with a very serious crime. First-degree murder." He showed her the clipping about Jed's body, which they had apparently taken from the house. (It had been hidden among her nightgowns.) "If you want to help him, tell me everything you know."

Rose refused and was sent out to a hallway bench. After waiting there for six hours she finally went home, stopping at her doctor's on the way for a shot of Valium. Shirley Donnerstag was waiting for her. "Rose," she said, "you look terrible. Go take a shower. Pull yourself together. We got a long pull in front of us. We're in it together. We got to stick together." Shirley had seen The Jew. What she said now was a barely disguised message meant to find its way back to Festa: "Don't open your mouth."

The two men had been put in cells on different tiers, but Donnerstag took care of that, "reaching out" to Vinnie Tursi, who had influence over the jail guards, and arranging it so that soon he was moved only a cell away from Jerry—the better to keep watch on him. At night Donnerstag had visitors right at his cell door, shadowy figures whom Festa quietly watched and heard whispering. One was Sergeant Ray Grill.

The house was in an uproar. Marie had spent that first day trying to protect the children from the emotional turmoil and straighten up the mess the detectives had left. Johnny Quartuccio was at his hyper best, running for the coffee urn, pushing his fingers through his curly hair. "I'm just a broken-down burglar," he kept saying. "And I'm gonna get dragged in. I know it. I know it."

Rose was able to see Jerry the next day and Shirley made sure she went with her to the jail—as she would every visiting day from then on. Outmaneuvering Festa, Donnerstag had gotten to the guards and made sure that Jerry had no visitors except when Donnerstag was also in the visiting room and sitting right next to him. The Jew was going to hear everything Rose and he had to say, in case they had any ideas about turning on him.

Rose told The Bear about this arrangement. He said, "Rose, you play your cards right, they'll be no problem. Don't talk in the house about it. They maybe bugged it. Don't talk to anyone. Don't talk to Shirley when you can get away with it. Don't show her no emotions, see. Follow? Just let me know if The Jew starts harassing him bad.

But you—you say nothing against The Jew." He drove her home from his house and hugged her as she sobbed. Then he told her to write "Joe Carbone" on a slip of paper, and cup her hands around it as she held it up against the transparent partition for her husband to see; that way Shirley and Donnerstag would not be able to read it. "Don't say nothing on those phones, like I said," The Bear counseled. "Your husband'll know what it means."

The next day, October 27, Rose did as she was told. Festa was furious when he saw Carbone's name on the paper. It meant Carbone was going all the way—and certainly *did* know about the homicide. They had no chance whatsoever now.

The third day of the worst experience Festa had ever had was notable in another way. Not that he knew or cared, but on that day a year before, Minnah Booth, the old meatball music teacher, had died in a West Orange nursing home, with no one at her side.

*   *

"So you didn't tell Carbone, huh?"

"No," said Donnerstag. "Why?"

Festa took a step toward slugging him but held on to his temper. "You dog liar," he said. Jerry the Jew shrugged it off.

Donnerstag was still getting his night visitors. One of them, Austin Castiglione, was reporting to Freda. They were trying to get to Wally Lombardo, but the junkie, for his safety, had been moved to the Bergen County Jail.

That Freda was falling in line behind Donnerstag was disconcerting and yet logical: They had supposedly done the Alvin Little hit together, Festa claimed, so Raymond could not afford to have Jerry the Jew mad at him. That was a life sentence if Donnerstag opened his mouth.

A pall had fallen over Bloomfield Avenue. The FBI was hearing rumors of plots to poison Festa in his cell. He was the new guy, most likely to talk. Though no one told him, Jerry had a hunch about that anyway. Donnerstag offered him a club sandwich sent in from the outside, telling him it was from The Bear, but he wisely declined to eat it. Whether or not that was paranoia, Donnerstag then pulled another of his inexplicable stunts, telling Festa he had two "good-bye pills"—cyanide—and they should each take one, like captured spies. Festa ignored him, and closely sniffed his rations before eating them.

Joe Paterno was silently on Jerry's side, and Andy Gerard had taken a position of neutrality, so there was no formal "contract" on Festa. His worry was not the made-men, however, but the lowly sandwich runner who might sing; Jerry had the "responsibility" for the third accomplice, known only to Pennsylvania State Police as Hank. If Ellis talked, Festa might be executed.

Frankie Bear, who shared this concern, walked Rose to the privacy of his driveway, away from any possible bugs. "Rose," he said. "I got a tracer on Hank. We should be able to find him through his license, or registration. He's gotta be roofing, so it shouldn't be too hard." He said Hank was the weak link and had to be intercepted quickly.

In this climate of fear, protecting the Festas involved other worries for The Bear. For one, Raymond Freda was taking advantage of the situation, predictably enough. He went to Rose and asked if he could borrow Jerry's Cadillac. He had to visit his mother, he said, and his own car was in the shop.

Rose let Raymond have the car, and right after he returned it Basto came by, obviously upset. He wanted to see the car. "Something bad happened in that," he said.

Rose gave him the keys and he inspected the interior. "Come here," he told her brusquely. "You see this?" On the dashboard just below the glove compartment was a wrinkle and a perfectly round burn mark, as if someone had melted through it with a cigar. He told her it was a bullet hole. And he was mad. "You don't ever give Raymond the car. This car was used for something. Don't you ever do that again." (Later, rumor would reach Festa that a dope dealer had been dumped on a highway around this time.)

While Basto was trying to keep his fingers on the leaks, SCI agent Cy Jordan, along with Tony Rosamilia and the Pennsylvania police, beat The Bear to the punch. From the state police intelligence dossiers in Dunmore they learned that in 1958 Festa had been convicted of swindling Mrs. Mary H. Kingston of Elmira in a roofing fraud that also involved Edward L. Granville and Gerald L. Walsh, both of North Washington Avenue in Scranton; Partick M. Greco, of Joseph Avenue in the same city; and Harold M. Ellis, twenty-four at the time, of 633 North Washington Avenue. Ellis's nickname was "Hank."

The state police searched for and located Hank's estranged wife Gladdie on the south side of Scranton, and her house was staked out. But she told them very little, and her relatives, the Tardoskys, had nothing to say either. The troopers were able to establish only that

Harold Ellis had been back and forth to New Jersey and that Festa was his boss.

Down Mount Prospect Avenue in Newark, Jordan and Rosamilia canvassed the neighborhood looking for Ellis, querying the Feldmans again, talking to Hank's landlady, and stopping passersby on the sidewalk. Through these labors they discovered that Ellis had gone off with a woman named Lillian a year before. "Oh yeah," said the landlady. "The Irish gal with all the kids." Were the children of school age? "Yeah," she said.

They stopped at the obvious place, nearby Saint Michael's Grammar School. The administrator was reluctant to release any students' or former students' addresses, and the agents were afraid to explain their true mission: word would too easily reach the street. But they were insistent, and they learned that two of Lillian's children had been enrolled there until just recently, when their records had been forwarded to St. Petersburg, Florida.

As pressure built in the news media ("Third Suspect Still At Large," said the *Scranton Times*), the state police wasted no time in contacting the Florida authorities. "Looks pretty good," Noel told Jordan. "The school records down there indicate the father is a carpenter. We're ready to hit the place." At four in the morning on November 1, Ellis was taken into custody by the St. Petersburg Police Department, which phoned Dunmore to say he was "ready to talk turkey." Noel and Paul boarded a plane at two the next afternoon in Avoca, a small hamlet placed squarely between Scranton and Wilkes-Barre, and after stopovers and connections in Allentown, Washington, and Atlanta, they were met at the Tampa airport by police from St. Petersburg.

At the jail Hank was matter-of-fact. "We got Festa and Donnerstag," Paul informed him. "And we know it's Jed Feldman's body." Hank nodded, showing no emotion. Would he tell them what happened? Yeah, no problem, he said. He wanted to get it off his chest. All he asked was to be tried apart from the two other accomplices.

"Okay," said Noel. "Now all we ask is for you to tell us what you know about the Jed Feldman murder, and, of course, you tell it in your own way, whatever way you want to and whatever way is easier for you to tell us, and try to remember everything, as much as you possibly can. All right? And then during the course, we may ask you some questions, but you tell us your story, now, starting at the very beginning."

They then got into the basic specifics. A cassette tape recorder was on. It was about ten o'clock.

Hank said, "Well, we were off to the country there and ah, let's see, down by the pond and Jed walked down to the water and Jerry the Jew went down and shot him in the back of the head; then he handed the gun to Festa and made him pull the trigger and then, me, I shot at the ground, but then they said there was a bullet in the back, I don't know . . ."

"Why was this done?"

"I don't remember," said Hank. "Feldman knew something."

"What were the circumstances leading up to that?"

"Well, they said something about Feldman would squeal on us or something."

"Who said that?"

"Jerry the Jew."

The murder story unfolded awkwardly, for Ellis was couching it in careful words.

"And was he [Feldman] clothed? Did he have all his clothes on?"

"I don't know if he had his clothes on or we took them off. I'm not positive."

"I don't think you'd forget anything like this, I think it's been on your mind for quite some time."

"I think the clothes were taken off," Ellis finally said.

Hank could not recall what month it was, but "the water was just starting to get cold." He thought it might have been the beginning of winter when Jed was killed.

"Is there anything else you can recall in regard to the death of Jed Feldman?"

"I guess," said Hank, "that's just about all of it."

"Have you had a good life down here?"

"Yeah."

"I'm sure, though, this must have been bothering you."

"Oh, yes," said Ellis. "It's been three years now."

"We're going to—you just told us, and, of course, we've been on tape which you consented to. Now, would you have any objection if we put this in writing, what you've told us now, all right?"

Hank said, "I guess so. Then you're gonna use it in court, right?"

"Well, certainly. Everything you've told us we have to use in court. We told you that before we got started, if you recall."

Michael Brown   182

Noel typed up a formal statement, asked a few more questions, let Ellis read the statement and make corrections. At one-thirty in the morning, Hank affixed his signature to it, and within eight hours—having bidden a somewhat tearful farewell to his girl friend—Hank flew back to Scranton with the investigators, uttering hardly another word.

Basto had no idea Hank had been busted. The state police were being unusually cautious that not a word had leaked. The Bear's attention shifted to the intrigues of Bloomfield Avenue, where every item about the murder was latched onto desperately. The wise guys feared either Festa or Donnerstag would succumb to the pressure and bring dozens of them down. Basto was not concerned that Hank could cause him any legal problems. Ellis certainly knew of his criminality, but it was hearsay evidence. He had not allowed Festa's gofer to get close. But Ellis could pound the last nail in Jerry's coffin.

The most pressing concern was Rose, who was bearing up poorly under the strain. She was nervously holding court for a constant stream of visitors—Freda, Adams, Quartuccio, Apples—who were feeling out her mood, trying to find out what her husband was saying. The phone rang day and night. Steve George came by and told her, "Anything but murder we could take care of." The cop pleaded with her never to mention his name, reminding her of his wife and kids. Others among those concerned, including Joe Paterno, were sending over unmarked envelopes of cash to sustain the family, and though she had emptied two safe-deposit boxes of nearly three hundred thousand in rare coins and jewelry, she was afraid to use this illicit wealth. To meet the lawyer's fees, already approaching ten thousand dollars, she took a second mortgage on the house.

Every night her ritual was the same. Having spent two visiting periods with Jerry—one in early afternoon, one before supper—she would walk by the DeVingos' to the corner, turn left, where Clifton Avenue crossed, and negotiate a cracked sidewalk the short distance to Delavan Avenue, where The Bear's red brick house, fronted by its sizable sun parlor and white columns, stood stately beneath tall oaks. He would take her into the living room to talk, or to the kitchen where coffee and condolences were served up by Camille. Always he began by asking how her husband looked. Nervous? Depressed? "Rose, we have to give him some glimmer of hope," he said.

But mainly he wondered about her own conduct. She did not seem to be heeding his advice about containing her feelings, which were so agitated that she was constantly popping Valium and had lost more than twenty pounds. Her neck had literally buckled under the pressure, and she was wearing a neck brace. She and her daily companion, Shirley Donnerstag, were arguing continually. She had gone up to Shirley's apartment one night and Shirley had enraged her by saying that Carbone had fingered her husband as the actual triggerman. It was a ploy to see what Rose knew, and it worked, for she began contradicting Shirley. As the debate went on, Rose heard a peculiar shuffling in Shirley's bedroom, as if someone was in there listening to them.

Then Festa's father called from Scranton with what he warned would be "real bad news." He was working as a school crossing guard and staying with Marie's younger sister, and he explained to Rose that one of Festa's half-brothers had happened across an article in the November 15 issue of the *Abington Journal,* a weekly newspaper in a town just northwest of Scranton, near where Ellis was being held. "They got Hank," he told her. "And he talked."

Rose ran to see Basto. He told her to leave for Pennsylvania immediately. "Don't tell Jerry," was the way Rose would remember this conversation. "He's behind bars. Nothing's worse than someone in jail and telling him the door's closing forever. Just bring back the newspaper."

She summoned Carmen Malavenda to drive her to Scranton, and Jerry's father handed her the paper. "Magistrate McHale Presides at Ellis Preliminary Hearing" was the front-page headline, and a subhead explained, "Scrantonian Faces Murder Charge." He had been bound over for grand jury action the previous Friday, said the news account, "after Magistrate James T. McHale ruled that the Commonwealth had established a prima facie case against him . . ." Hank had waived extradition, the article went on, noting too that he had made a confession. Though Ellis was not himself brought into public view, Noel had taken the stand to recount what Hank said, and Ellis's lawyer, a public defender, was aghast, Rose noted. "What in the world did you tell him to make him give you that statement?" he asked Noel, according to the article.

Rose spent the night at Marie's sister's and the next day brought Festa's father home with her. She took the news story to Basto's home. They went to the sun parlor, the "conference room" usually reserved for chats with Paterno, Butch Miceli, or her husband. The Bear read the article through, closely, silently. When he finished it she saw a look come over his face that he had never exhibited before. His brown eyes were no longer warm, they were Plexiglas. He hitched up his pants nervously and, to her surprise, told her she had to leave. "Don't breathe a word of this to anyone," he said. "And don't go to the jail this afternoon. I'm going. I'll tell him."

Rose walked back in a daze. Marie was at her wits' end, feeding the baby, cooking, fielding phone calls, humoring the visitors, walking Alicia and Sophia to and from school. The store was losing business because the neighborhood, caught up in the drama, was now afraid of the place. Janet had quit school to try and keep up the business. She could no longer concentrate in class anyway. She shared Marie's acute embarrassment over what the neighbors knew, and her brother Allan had come running home crying that the boy across the street was teasing him: "Your daddy's a murderer." The boy had not been told that Festa was in jail.

Thanksgiving was a disaster, an "uproar" to Marie. They had to spend it with Shirley Donnerstag, who was always coming over to leave her children with Marie. Festa had managed to tell Rose, as Basto had, not to alienate Shirley, to act like they were in it together. But otherwise they had hardly been able to communicate. Donnerstag was always there, eavesdropping.

Basto got into the visiting room without having to sign the register and without the standard pass. And for the first time, Donnerstag was kept from seating himself alongside Festa. Basto had made sure of that. "Lookit," he told Jerry. "You got a problem." He stared into Jerry's eyes and brought out the news article, holding it up to the partition. Festa struggled to remain cool as he read it. It was the end, and Basto was telling him as much. The Bear told him to keep his head, not to concede extradition, not to concede any legal points at all, and not to quarrel with Jerry the Jew. "Fight it down the line," he advised. Festa asked Basto if he had sent in a club sandwich for him a while back. The Bear said no.

Johnny Quartuccio noted that Rose hadn't gone to see Jerry that day and knew something was wrong. He woke her up that evening to find out what was happening. Eventually he too was shown the article, and instead of studying it as Basto had done, Johnny paced back and forth skimming it. "What, what, what!" he blurted as he read. "Fucking Hank! I hope he gets cancer of the tongue. Do youse know what this means? Means? And Frank told Jerry this? This is gonna crush him.

Crush him. We've had it. Hank's got diarrhea of the mouth. I thought The Bear with all his 'connections' was gonna find Hank. Hank'll say anything. Anything! 'Oh yeah, sure,' he'll say to them cops. You know the *scores* we done in Pennsylvania? Your husband'll hang, but I'll hang along with him. I'll get a hundred fifty fucking years. My rap sheet speaks for itself! I'll be an old man before I get out. I won't even see my grandchildren. *Maronna mia.* And Hank's gonna maybe give up The Bear! The Bear'll hang us! That fuckin' Jew never shoulda brought Jerry on a thing like that. He's just a broken-down burglar like me. Like me. This is gonna be an avalanche, you watch. And me and him are gonna be under it. You don't know the people we been dealing with. Freda. Wait till *he* hears this."

Angry, and more upset than ever, Rose finally asked Johnny to leave. Neither he nor Freda was her main concern right now. She had Shirley on her mind. Lately Jerry the Jew's wife had been talking about a severance of trials. They should go to court "every man for himself," she told Rose. "My Jerry has nothing to worry about. Your Jerry's in trouble. Mine's never been to Pennsylvania."

Rose lost her temper. "I was there the night of the murder!" she shouted. "I was right there." She pointed to the pantry. "I saw what went down. And I know it was *your* Jerry caused it."

Shirley left, sobbing into her handkerchief. Rose went to see The Bear again. He was irritated when she told him what she'd said. She had finally admitted she knew about the murder, and it was going to get back to Donnerstag. "You just pull yourself together fast, sister," he said coldly. The important thing now was to get "big, big money" for a lawyer who could "reach out," and he told Rose to call Jay Weisman, the fence they had dealt with, and tell him to kick in to a defense fund. With Hank talking, "the pressure really starts," he said. He told her to expect a visit from an FBI agent named Michael Wilson, who, said Basto, "got a vendetta for me." (Basto had learned about the impending visit through a clerk at the Newark office who was feeding them information.) He said Wilson would show her photographs of both him and Jerry coming out of a bar with some women—just to infuriate her into talking. These pictures were fakes, spliced shots, he said. "There'll be another agent with him who don't say nothing to ya. That guy's wired for sound."

Inside the Essex County Jail, Donnerstag was biding his time playing poker and gin rummy, and snorting cocaine smuggled in to him.

While Festa spent his incarceration in work clothes, Donnerstag was wearing his silk shirts, and he quickly assumed leadership of their section of the jail, organizing the Puerto Ricans against the blacks and making razor-blade weapons for himself and Jerry, who were the only whites for most of their stay. Another white guy had come in with them, but they feared he was an undercover DEA agent, and after some threats by Jerry the Jew, that inmate was quietly removed. There was a fourth white for a while, a kid whom Donnerstag bullied, trying to get money off him, which provoked Festa so violently that he grabbed Donnerstag and held him against a wall. "You always gotta put fear, fear, fear in people, you motherfucker," he yelled. "And motherfucker, don't get any ideas, cause I know where the fuck you're coming from. You were never in Pennsylvania, huh? Don't try that shit. I'll get them fucking phone bills from my father's house [for calls made during robbery trips with The Jew]. We go down, we're going down together."

The plots and counterplots were complicated by the fact that cops and agents were making their rounds, questioning both men. Donnerstag was taken out one day and was gone for a suspiciously long time—an hour. He came back whistling, telling Festa it was the SCI, wanting to know what he might have to say. Which was nothing. Festa was called out soon afterward and taken to the attorneys' conference room, but he left when he saw that his lawyer, Elmer Herrmann, was not there. The next time Rose visited he silently mouthed to her a message for Frank Basto. His exaggerated lip movements formed the letters "S-C-I."

Nor were Holleran and Jordan the only ones interested in what the two prisoners could give them. Attempts at turning them into informants were also made by the Treasury Department, the DEA, New Jersey State Police intelligence officers, and two Essex County detectives. But the most persistent effort was on the part of the FBI. At this particular juncture a confidential informant was working with the agency in an effort to keep the heat off himself (for the kidnaping of a banking executive in Dover, New Jersey, not long before). To throw the FBI a small bone, this squealer met with an FBI agent named Barry O'Neill in a car near his suburban home, and told him there was "a guy named Festa locked up" who could "give you guys The Bear on a silver platter." The informant was that master of convoluted treacheries, Raymond Freda.

The next time Festa was taken out for a meeting in the conference room, a guard pushed him inside and slammed the door. His lawyer wasn't here this time either. He was introduced to Special Agent Michael Wilson, a young, conservatively attired man who had arrived in Newark only two years before. Festa said virtually nothing. He only mumbled that his wife would handle such matters. He pounded on the door to be taken back to his cell.

Late that night Wilson, who had noticed Festa's sunken eyes, decided there was a chance of his cooperation, and paid a visit to Rose. He rang the doorbell and flashed his credentials. She kept him in the foyer. Quartuccio was in the kitchen. "Just a minute," she said, "I have to put the dog away."

She went to the back and told Johnny who was there. He trembled. "Don't say nothing to him," he said. "Tell 'em to leave. Don't let them stay." He scurried into the basement.

She went back to the door. Wilson was accompanied by a second agent who said nothing, just as The Bear had predicted.

"I'd like to talk with you, Mrs. Festa," said Wilson.

"About what?"

"About the trouble your husband's in," he stated.

"Look Mr. Wilson," she said coolly, "there's no doubt you showed me your credentials, who you are. But I gotta talk with my attorney first." Little else was said. The agents left politely.

Rose waited a few moments and walked over to the Bastos'. "Rose, they're gonna squeeze you like a lemon, try to tell you this one's talking or that one's talking. Don't believe it," said The Bear. "Just cause they're Feds don't mean they don't lie. If you get a call in the middle of the night to meet them, don't go. Don't put yourself in the same position as Alton Hughes."

He told her that both the FBI and the mob were surveying movements in and out of the house. But he nonetheless advised her to be polite to the agents, "like a lady."

Wilson went right back to see Festa. The Bear had made a blunder in his advice to Rose. Her behavior had only served to encourage the FBI agent. "At least she let me in the house," Wilson thought. He also sensed that Festa was the type who could be broken. At their next meeting, the agent was accompanied by Essex Detective Donahue, who was working at the moment in a special task force investigating gangland slayings, which had been especially frequent lately. Wilson told

Festa outright that his agency could not necessarily help him with the murder charge. But he would see what could be done, he said, if Jerry told him about some of his colleagues.

Donahue had been interrogating Wally Lombardo and had reviewed Festa's rap sheet. He said, "Jerry, you're no killer. To stick with a maniac like Donnerstag, it's crazy." The detective was then called out of the room to take a phone call.

Wilson said, "Look. I spoke to your wife. She told me to talk to you. In a day or two you're going to be extradited. I can tell you that much. I hope you know the danger your family's in. You're the one who put them there."

"You're after The Bear, ain't youse?" Festa asked curtly.

"That's right," Wilson said. His face turned to stone.

"I got nothing to say."

Donahue reentered the room. "We're gonna have to break this up," he told Wilson. A guard had called Rose and she had called Herrmann. The lawyer was upset that Festa was being questioned without him.

Wilson went to see Richard Gregorie, a United States attorney working with a federal-state strike force on organized crime, part of a system of law enforcement instituted years before by President Johnson to fight the Mafia. "What can I offer him?" Wilson asked, referring to Festa.

"Mike, you can't offer him anything," Gregorie said. He didn't want to grant leniency to a "killer."

Wilson was extremely insistent. "Frank the Bear's been doing this stuff for years. Nobody has laid a hand on him. We can finally get him"—and everyone else, he added.

Gregorie continued to fight against any deal, and the strike force's chief at the federal end, Jerry McGuire, backed him up. A Georgetown University graduate, Gregorie had had it with Newark crime. He was tired of seeing criminals get any breaks at all. Two FBI agents had been mugged walking in the downtown district, and he despised the city in general. There was no place to get a newspaper at night, no good restaurants as far as he could tell, no movie houses he felt safe in. It was a filthy place and the only recreation was a dark, narrow bar with a shaky jukebox that he and the staff called "The Hole." But Wilson, who was just as repelled by the city's decadence, argued hard in favor of an arrangement with Jerry "Chicken Delight" Festa. And the more he told Gregorie, the more Gregorie listened.

A couple days after Wilson's visit, Rose received a phone call from someone claiming to be Wilson and telling her to meet him late at night in Branch Brook Park. She flatly refused. She did not know whether it really was the agent or someone in the mob testing her.

Wilson again appeared at her front door. As she let him into the living room, Johnny happened by the door. She whispered to him to leave until he saw her put on the porch light, a signal that Wilson was gone. The agent sat down holding on his lap a file folder. On the side of it was written BASTO.

"I have nothing to say," she repeated.

Wilson fingered through the file. "We know you know as much about these people as your husband," he nudged her. "You want to help your husband, you talk to me." Marie listened from the stair landing. She was concerned that someone in the mob would think they were squealing, and she was not enamored of the police, especially after the way her cousin had been hauled off. She had told Camille that if they asked her any questions she planned to pretend she did not speak English. She was relieved when Rose said little more and showed Wilson out.

Donnerstag knew about the visit. "Heard your wife had company," he said. But he did not seem concerned. He spent his days doing one-arm pushups, getting himself in shape for a vacation in Florida. They would be released soon, he was convinced.

The hearing on extradition to Pennsylvania was scheduled for December 7 but postponed to December 10. Then it was delayed until the fourteenth. They were told to roll up their spare clothes and put them in a paper bag, and then they were led to the courtroom in shackles—thick hoops and braces around their waists, wrists, and ankles. They were chained together, with Donnerstag in the lead.

They went in an elevator and down a corridor, one guard behind them, one in front, and two along each side. In the hall Festa saw Rose, Marie, and Janet watching sadly. "What are they, animals?" Marie whispered angrily. Donnerstag made a joke of the shackles, which he said made them look like a railroad train. He was the locomotive: "Choo-chooo-choo. Woo-o-woo!" Festa did not see the humor. He tried to free his hand so he could hit Donnerstag.

Down the hall came Peter Feldman, who had been called to testify at the hearing. He was in handcuffs and his head was shaved bald. He looked at Rose and tears came to his sorrowful eyes. Donnerstag said, "Pete, hey, whatta ya say?"

He gave Jerry the Jew and Festa a frosty stare.

As the hearing began, Festa was fascinated by the assistant prosecutor, Joe Falcone. He was dressed in snazzy shoes and swaggered like some mob attorney. A tough-looking guy. Donnerstag told him not to worry, he knew Falcone from Keith's football team, implying that the assistant prosecutor was in his pocket.

This was quite at variance with the truth. Falcone had heard rumors that a fix was in and said, "Oh, yeah? I'll handle the extradition myself." He made a special note in his diary.

A state trooper was brought up to describe Jed Feldman's body and its discovery. But the important witness was Pete. Donnerstag and Festa thought he would be sympathetic to them when it came down to it, and word had been sent to him to testify that he had seen Jed around after the time the killing was allegedly done. Pete had been informed of the SCI's positive identification of his brother, however, and had reacted strongly to that, throwing his toiletries against the cell bars, crushing a water cup, and violently overturning his bed and everything else he could get his hands on—an outburst that led to a stay in solitary confinement. Instead of giving his old mentor Festa an alibi, Pete stood for the prosecution, leaving little doubt about who he thought was responsible for his brother's death.

The rest was perfunctory. The two defendants lost their bid to stay in Jersey and were led to a cavalcade of police cars. Festa was taken in an automobile with Pennsylvania State Police Sergeant George Owczarski, which was accompanied by a patrol car in back and front.

Donnerstag was transported in another three-car cortege. He said to Noel, "You got a lot of snow up there?"

Noel was annoyed by his flippancy. "Yeah," he retorted. "We'll show you the snow."

Every twenty minutes a patrol car waiting at prearranged roadside checkpoints picked up the caravan as a precaution against a break-out attempt by the mob. There were shotguns, automatic rifles.

"I guess you know you're gonna get killed," Owczarski said to Festa, trying to prod him. "And where's this Bob Martin at?" Festa was silent. He knew Martin had gone right back to Scranton after the bust.

They were brought to the Lackawanna County Jail in Festa's old home town. Built in 1886, the jail was constructed of huge hewn stones and short, wide towers: it had the distinct appearance of a medieval dungeon, and the walls were gray throughout the interior except for the front offices. Five locks had to be disengaged before Festa reached his destination downstairs, a wing to the left, fourth cell down. Donnerstag was across a bridge walk in a separate lockup on the right side of the coop.

Rose was operating in a trance. She could hardly pay attention to anything around her any more. But she did realize when she went to see Frank Basto that his mind was also wandering. Normally he fixed his eyes directly upon her as they talked, but now he was prone to looking away. He was anticipating what was down the road, and holding a series of "sitdowns" with Paterno. She understood his concern, and even sympathized with him. He was wanted by the FBI, and it was only her husband who could deliver him.

*   *

Extraditing two thugs was not, for Joseph A. Falcone, any extraordinary piece of business. In this case, he felt, it was simply another instance where he had to vindicate his heritage, that vowel at the end of his name. Because he was Italian, and had been raised on the corner of North Eleventh Street and Bloomfield Avenue, the son of a boxer, it was always assumed he would "take care of business" for *mafiosi* in trouble. He was tired of their games.

Soon after her husband's arrest, Shirley Donnerstag, who knew him as her son's football coach, approached Falcone to talk about her husband's case. "I can't do anything for you, or anybody," he told her sharply. A short while later, as events would have it, he was called in by the SCI for a meeting with the man who had informed on the murder and a number of thefts that interested the assistant prosecutor. There he found Joe Carbone, smiling. The kid who'd come with Jerry the Jew to the football games.

Since 1971 Falcone had been assigned to the City-County Organized Crime Strike Force; more recently he had been put in command of a small unit that would handle a special grand jury which the prosecutor, Joseph Lordi, was forming to focus on gangland murder and other organized crime matters. Perhaps because of its ambitious goals, it was treated as a joke by the other lawyers in the office. They felt it was another political ploy to impress the press and public.

Part of the inspiration for the unit derived from the rampant corruption coming to light. As the FBI and New Jersey State Police began a sweeping program of wiretapping in the late 1960s, they found an intermingling between public officials and *mafiosi* that had become shockingly blatant. Federal investigators were in fact to publicly brand the state "a racketeering playground," accusing, among others, two of the state's most powerful mayors—as well as a Hudson County congressman—of direct mob ties. In the transcription of the wiretaps, Hugh Addonizio, Newark's mayor, was often mentioned, referred to as "Hughie" by the mob. He would soon be sent to jail in an extortion case along with the son of Ritchie Boiardo. Soon too a Union County judge would be charged with attempting to bribe a prosecutor; and Newark's own police chief, Dominick Spina, would be indicted for "willfully" failing to enforce gambling statutes. When someone desired a public post, that person sought an endorsement not from a civic leader but from gangsters with City Hall connections, investigators frequently found, and so widespread were the gambling enterprises that by 1969 the mob's annual take was about equal to the state government's yearly operating budget: one billion dollars. More immediately, there were several detectives on Newark's homicide squad who were themselves reputed hitmen.

So it was not surprising that the other assistant prosecutors, hearing of new efforts to combat this organized crime, would merely chuckle. Yet Falcone was serious. He had requested the full-time services of Donahue, whose own reputation for honesty, toughness, and street-smarts were long on the way to making him as well known a cop as New Jersey ever had produced, and Ronnie was eager for the job. He knew all about Carbone, and he had been sitting for uncountable hours with Lombardo, consoling the addict, listening to him tell about the death of his father when he was young, about his home life— and finally about Donnerstag and Festa. Donahue had Lombardo talking like a mynah bird. Wally told him that Jerry the Jew and Chicken Delight ran a big robbery system consisting of "creeps and zombies," and thus gave him enough to bust Festa and Donnerstag on more than murder. The robberies were filling Donahue's ears. He went to Falcone, and Joe decided to give it all a shot. "What we need," he said, "are witnesses."

Through FBI Agent Michael Wilson, Donahue and Falcone knew the prime prospect as a government witness, a stoolie, was now languishing in Lackawanna County Jail. And it was getting to him badly. The cell in which Jerry Chicken Delight sat was cold and dim, with only a sliver of light through a narrow window. He had to duck to enter it, and it had the thinnest of mattresses and a single blanket, dusty, a world of shadows. No bail had been set, and Donnerstag, though no longer so close by, was nevertheless constantly ogling through the grates along the wing divider to monitor his movements. Rose and Shirley visited every Monday and Thursday, driving in from Newark. Festa and his wife were better able to talk here. He told her how dangerous it was getting, how every few days he would be called over the loudspeaker to go to the attorneys' room and find the state cop, George Owczarski, there, trying to finagle his cooperation. Owczarski had told Festa that, besides homicide, he would be facing burglary charges—a good number of burglary charges—that they were putting together with the help of Hank Ellis. (The newspapers reported that Hank was still in Florida, but this was of course a bluff. He had been in Lackawanna County Jail until the police received what were described as "threats" on his life, and was now being moved around under an Irish pseudonym among small jails in Susquehanna and Schuylkill counties.)

On December 21, Festa and Jerry the Jew were taken to a preliminary hearing before Justice of the Peace McHale. Because of the large crowd of cops and spectators, McHale held court not in his own office, as usual, but in the Olyphant Borough Building, just outside Scranton. Donnerstag was calmly composed as the first witnesses—a state trooper again, a pathologist, and the reform school dentist, Dr. Scales—took the stand. But during a cigarette break in the corridor, they saw that the fourth witness was Joe Carbone. He was being ushered inside by a squad of troopers. "Ah huh!" Donnerstag exclaimed.

Carbone had just appeared at an SCI hearing at which he described Freda and Donnerstag as the "Mr. Big"s of Newark narcotics and showed his audience the shotgun Donnerstag had given him; but he had appeared at that time under the name "John D.," wearing a black hood over his head. Here in Scranton he would go under his own name, using words quite outside the street vocabulary—"affluent," to describe The Jew's drug trade—and accusing Donnerstag of pulling the trigger in what had for so long been known to police only as "PSP Incident #R1-11215." He was followed by Dirardo T. "Wally" Lombardo, who said Donnerstag told him he "fired a bullet in the back of his [Jed's] head, and he even saw his hair singe." As a bonus to that, Lombardo mentioned the armed robberies they had committed, including the one that had apparently traumatized Elsie Schneider, the woman who died of heart failure.

Like Falcone and Donahue, the Pennsylvania State Police were convinced that Festa could be added to the list of state's witnesses. In their files they had noted a proclivity for talking when the odds were against him. Thirteen years before, faced with the prospect of imprisonment (for the Cecelia Myers affair), he had testified on behalf of the Commonwealth, declaring, "I had larceny in my heart"—as if he had since changed his ways. Because of this, Noel and Owczarski kept up the pressure, pulling him out of his cell time and again to ask about his crimes. By doing so they were raising Donnerstag's suspicions. "Where you been going?" Jerry the Jew was asking pointedly.

The possibility that Festa would not hold up, would not be a "stand-up guy," was also of increasing concern to Basto. He had those arsons to worry about, and the safe burglary there in Scranton. In a way, Festa was still an unclear quantity to him. On the one hand Festa seemed too emotionally attached to The Bear to turn on him, but on the other hand he might be the type who, if the stakes got high enough, would do anything to save his own hide. It was hard to trust someone who never had been totally accepted by the mob's elite and had not made his bones as a killer. But Basto had continued to counsel Rose and to maintain his seeming devotion to four-year-old Allan. He baby-sat the boy, gave him toys, candy. But around the time of the Wilson visits—late in November—The Bear had taken Allan to his house to give his "nephew" a haircut. After snipping at the boy's thick, straight hair, he led Allan to a big cabinet in his basement. "Come here," Uncle Frank said. "I got something to show you." He opened the cabinet and revealed a cache of pistols and rifles, so many that Allan would record them in his memory as being "piled up" on each other—silencers, scopes, and a "burp" gun like he saw on television.

"How do you like that?" Basto asked. The boy was thoroughly excited. Uncle Frank took him home after they spent the afternoon together, gave Rose a hearty hug and a warm kiss on the cheek, as he always did, and handed her the toy he had bought Allan that day: a shooting arcade with a gun that shot beebees. After he left, Allan told Rose about "Uncle Frank's neat guns."

She had been more perplexed than concerned about his story, and she happened to tell Jerry about it the next time she saw him.

Festa's face had dropped. Maybe it was nothing, but Basto had never shown *him* his gun cabinet, never showed it to anybody as far as he knew. And if there was a message to this, it was that Jerry should think twice before getting involved with Agent Wilson if he cherished the life of his son.

Just the same, during December Basto had scrupulously gone on watching over the Festa home, cruising by it at night to make sure they weren't being bothered, and stopping by on Christmas with toys, money, a turkey, and some imported wines. Grappling for normalcy, Rose decorated a Christmas tree and bought the children toys. If the two girls felt the strain in their home, at least Allan and little Joseph would remain oblivious. Their father was "away on business." But each time the front door opened, Allan ran to it with "Where's Daddy?"

Daddy was in that stinking dank Bastille with Donnerstag, who was in a joshing holiday mood. "Look at that bird!" he said, sauntering into the mess hall where a table had been filled with turkey and garnishes of pickles and celery. He started to sing: "Silent night, ho-oly night, All is calm, all is bright. Round yon virgin mother and child . . ."

"Motherfucker," Festa muttered. He could not remember being more depressed. He had managed a call to his children, and even Joseph took a turn on the phone, uttering some of his first words. That was uplifting, but so momentary, so fleeting. He thought about how good the odds were that he would never hold that kid again.

This was the furthest thing in the world from Christmas. Christmas was back in the old days, at Marie's mother's place, where they ate baked eels, smelts, stockfish, squid, freshly baked lasagna, bread and cakes. And where his father played a mandolin or guitar. His father. They were like brothers sometimes, fishing, partying at the Willow Club. Often he had little more on his mind than his thrice-married dad. Another obsession! He may have been hurt by how much his father wasn't around, but he loved him so much that, chrissakes, he made such a stir that time in court when his mother was trying to get him back that it made a small story in the newspaper: "Little Boy Makes Tearful Plea to Remain with 'Daddy.' " Actually made the Scranton paper! One of the last times he saw his mother, she was still sour over it. "You're no longer my son," she said. She was in that haunting dream he had last time he was doing a heavy jail gig.

He also thought about his two daughters with Dottie. His first wife was glad he was in jail because she was terrified of him. "He got it this time," she had remarked. Rose had talked with her and asked her how she was going to explain it to the two girls. Dottie had said she was going to "tell them the truth—that their father's in jail for murder, where he belongs." Mountains of shame. And here the very name "Festa" was supposed to mean "festivity": eels, smelts, lasagna . . . So it was over finally—and the journey had come full circle, to Scranton, where it all began.

Here in his home town, Jerry's name was all over the radio. On December 28 bail was set at a hundred thousand dollars, considerably less than the half a million he had been held under in New Jersey, but still the highest in Pennsylvania's history. (To put up that much money, they would have to show a legitimate income.) In January the news stories centered on what the district attorney, Paul Mazzoni, described as "the biggest burglary ring in the history of northeastern Pennsylvania." Hank and Wally were talking up a hurricane. Festa was dragged out of jail for arraignment on eight burglaries in Scranton, Dunmore, and Moscow, but this was only the beginning: there would soon be the threat of charges on more than twenty thefts, and with each burglary carrying a maximum of twenty years, Jerry was "looking at a lot of time," as one cop so subtly put it. Nor did this speak to the New Jersey crimes. To add some further pressure, the police planted an informant in the jail attempting to glean information from him.

Soon the information Ellis provided placed Bob Martin behind the same bars, and he too suspected that Jerry, his friend of twenty-five years, was going to talk. He was not off the mark. Festa met again with Agent Wilson, this time at the Dunmore barracks, where the FBI agent, along with Noel and Owczarski, mentioned a possible deal in which he would get only ten years in a women's prison (where he could be better protected) if he came clean.

"Thanks," Festa said. "But I got nothing to say." Yet he was certainly listening to their offers, and giving them snippets of encouragement once in a while. Wilson drove him back to the jail and told him that before he rejected the deal he'd better speak to his attorney. At Basto's suggestion, Festa had hired a new lawyer, a Newark man named Donald Crecca. And when his opinion was asked, Crecca said, "Jerry, they got warrants for your wife." Ellis had told the police about the Swartz score on which Rose served as a lookout—and a crime that would also drag Tommy Adams in. "As a lawyer, I'm telling you. It's bad. Real bad."

Crecca had arranged to meet with Rose on a dark Scranton street. He mentioned the possible deal and the chance—in fact, the near-certainty—that she too would be picked up for an interstate theft. Afraid that word would quickly reach Frank Basto, she did not want to talk about any cooperation. The attorney explained that the family could be hidden on a farm with round-the-clock bodyguards while Jerry was testifying, but she refused any further discussions.

She returned to Newark and went right to Basto's house to tell him about the warrants. Frankie Bear made light of it, assuring her that if she was arrested, they would have her out on bail within twenty-four hours. They wouldn't hold her because of the children, he said. "And, Rose, we'll get your uniform custom-fit," he joked. "How do you think you'll look in stripes?" Rose smiled, but she didn't like the coolness in the room. It was not like the Polish jokes. And instead of embracing her when she left, Basto didn't even get out of his chair.

Two days after Rose's session with Crecca, at eight in the evening, Camille called asking Rose to go out with her for a cup of coffee. When Camille came by in the car, Frank was in it too. Rose was suddenly afraid of him. They drove to Belleville and stopped at the pay phones outside a diner she knew was a hangout for Freda and Skins. Basto asked her to phone Eddie Powell, the Dairylea foreman who had helped him and Festa with the safe job. He knew Powell might be afraid to come to the phone if he heard The Bear was on the line. Obviously Basto was setting his ducks in a row in case her husband began to talk, trying to make sure Powell said nothing to the police. A well-dressed man who looked like an FBI agent slipped into the adjoining phone booth as Rose dialed Powell's number. The Bear waved her and Camille back to the car and hunched over the receiver to prevent any eavesdropping. After several minutes in the booth he rejoined the women. Rose asked why he wanted to talk to Powell. "I challenged him to a game of ping-pong," said Frank.

Right after that Powell arrived at Ridge Street looking terribly worried. He had to go over to Basto's house, he told Rose, and The Bear had told him on the phone that if he uttered a word about the burglary, he was dead. He was over there for two hours, and when he stopped off to say good-bye to Rose before heading back for Scranton, Eddie was putting on a cheerful act—a new man. Frank had just wanted to visit with him as a friend, Eddie now claimed. All they had done was play ping-pong in Frank's basement.

Rose did not like this at all—Powell sounded well-rehearsed. He said, "You know, Rose, what am I gonna get if I get caught? I have no record. I'll just get probation. Any time I would get I could do standing on my head. And I don't have a wife and kids. Your husband does. If Jerry wants to make a deal, you tell him it's okay with me."

Basto was gauging her reactions, and the anxiety of that caught up with her. Unable to keep the secret of a possible deal to herself any longer, she told Janet and Marie about it. Marie was shocked. And opposed. "There's no escaping these mob guys," she told Rose. "Jerry's got to take his punishment." And what would become of their business, their dogs, their house, the kids? "And what does he know about the Mafia, really?" she asked. "He wasn't in it, really."

At Basto's house the atmosphere was clammy. Butch Miceli had come by one day. Rose had seen him only once before, and Camille had been extremely uneasy while he was there. Miceli, after all, was supposedly The Bear's partner on the Paterno assassination squad, and Rose felt this visit had something to do with her own situation. Camille was hardly looking at her. She was standing at the sink absently fiddling with the dishes, and clearly upset. Miceli took a long look at Rose, a sizing-up look. He didn't say hello. He quickly went to the sun parlor with Basto.

On January 8, 1974, Assistant Prosecutor Falcone and Detective Donahue had gone to Scranton for a clandestine meeting with Festa at a Holiday Inn. Jerry had not been told why he was being taken out of his cell, and was fearful. But once he saw them there he was again interested in listening.

"I don't want any hearsay crap," Falcone began. "We got you already with what Lombardo's telling us, and we're going to come down on you."

Without much more prodding, Festa surprised them by regurgitating some interesting names. Freda, Skins, Zarro, Adams, Paterno. He was giving them the bait. But before they went much further the door burst open. Both Falcone and Festa flinched; they expected next to hear gunshots.

In came several angry-looking men in trench coats. It was the state police. They did not want Essex County talking to their—Pennsylvania's—prisoner. Behind them—as always—stood Agent Wilson.

Until the matter could be ironed out, Festa had been sent back to jail, which made him increasingly uncomfortable. Every time he came or went, Donnerstag and Martin eyed him skeptically through the partition. They kept hearing his name over the intercom, "Festa, front and center," and he pretended he was only going out for more arraignments, to face additional charges. But they were not sure what was happening, nor would they be throughout the month of January. Nevertheless, Donnerstag was preparing for the worst. He would soon arrange a long visit for Austin Castiglione and Raymond Freda.

Festa became enraged at the pressure on him. Owczarski kept calling him out for more meetings, and he felt he would get killed for it. As they tried to pull him out on yet another charge, he had struggled with the guards, fought them. They dragged him out through the snow in his T-shirt.

At the City-County Organized Crime Strike Force, Falcone, in a confidential report to Prosecutor Lordi, evaluated Festa as someone who could be extremely helpful, more so, he thought, than Carbone or Lombardo. Lordi listened to a description of the gangsters with whom Jerry had been involved and decided that as long as there were no other homicides in Festa's past, and as long as they did not have to promise him blanket immunity—only leniency—his office would participate in a three-way arrangement with the FBI and the Pennsylvania State Police. Falcone took the good news to Donahue, who had been fighting day and night to get Festa. Falcone was jubilant: "We're not going to be the laughingstock of this office any more."

Rose had saved the newspaper story about her husband being hauled to court in the cold and had called Basto and asked him to stop by her house. It was a Friday, just after a visiting day, and she needed his comfort. She was firmly against any deal—too afraid of the consequences of that—and yet she felt so terribly alone. Lately Frank and Camille were always too busy to see her.

Basto had arrived two hours later, in the early afternoon, freshly showered, clean-shaven. He had no smile for her; instead there was a stern look on his plump round face. "What's up now?" he asked. "More bad news?" He sat at the dining-room table reading the article and tapping his foot. More burglary charges . . . As he read on, his foot was tapping faster.

He pushed the article aside disgustedly. "Rose, what do you make of all this?"

"I don't know," she said. "I see Jerry facing a lot of time."

"An awful lot of time," he said. His eyes looked teary. "This is the end of Jerry. What do you think he'll do?"

"He has to do his time," she replied. "Nothing else he can do."

"Rose, let me tell you something. No man resigns himself to a lot of time." He quickly lifted himself up, pushed in the chair, hitched up his pants. He walked to the front of the house, near the columns in the foyer. Then he turned around and gave her a direct look. "Rose," he repeated sorrowfully, "no man resigns himself to a lot of time." He had draped his arms around her, under her arms—not a warm embrace, but limp—and kissed her lightly on both cheeks. There was that clammy feeling again. She felt a finality in the gesture.

He walked out and shut the door behind him, neglecting his normal practice of going with her onto the porch and waving back as he left. Instead he moved briskly to his car and never turned around.

She had run to Marie, filled with grief. "I know that had meaning to it, and it ain't good," she kept saying. She rambled through her castle aimlessly. They had just lost their best friend, and they were in danger, all of them. He was giving her a final warning.

A couple of weeks later, on the evening of February 6, while Rose was with her Scranton in-laws waiting to see Jerry, Johnny Quartuccio stopped by Ridge Street and banged on the door. Janet let him in. He was visibly upset. Not just edgy. Shaking. He sat down with her and Marie, gasping, "I was up at Freda's. He told me he got word Jerry's gonna talk. That Jerry's the 'weak link.' You get up there in Pennsylvania tomorrow and you tell him he better not. Tell him to keep his mouth shut."

The next morning, February 7—his son Joseph's second birthday—Festa arose at six, showered, and watched as the meal cart came by with cocoa, coffee, and clattering bowls of cereal. Lunch was at eleven, and Jerry the Jew had to come to that side of the jail to eat. He tried to pump Festa. But Jerry acted normally. He did the same when Martin passed by on the way to the washroom.

Over the intercom came "Festa. Front gate." Donnerstag moved to the end of his lockup nearer Festa. "Where you going, Jerry?" he asked, staring balefully. Festa said he didn't know. The Jew looked over the top of his glasses.

Heading toward Scranton, Janet felt eerie. She was on Route 80 in the company of Donnerstag's wife. Shirley was driving, and she was not her usual self. She was quiet, irritable; she would glance at Janet, then straight ahead at the sleety highway.

They picked up Rose and proceeded to the jail. There was the intimidating front gate turned by an old quarter-pound church key. A guard came out and said stupidly, "Oh. Mrs. Festa. Your husband's not here. He's over at the DA's office."

Shirley was aghast. She went immediately to use a telephone.

Rose rushed outside with Janet and they jumped into a cab, heading to the district attorney's office. It was a gloomy day, 28 degrees and overcast. When they got there the office was filled with some twenty men milling about as if they were waiting for something. There were FBI agents, lawyers, state troopers, local detectives, intelligence specialists, and assistant prosecutors from two states. Both Donahue and Falcone were there, working to finish this piece of business. They had been getting resistance from state police headquarters in Harrisburg as well as some of those in the Lackawanna County district attorney's office opposed to any deals. But the FBI was on their side, and the final points were these: If Festa testified, his family would be taken into the custody of the United States Justice Department and its deputy marshals, who would be their bodyguards. They would be given a place to stay, subsistence funds, and new identities under a federal program called WPP, the Witness Protection Program. Festa would be granted immunity only from those crimes he confessed to on his own, and he would have to cooperate with any agency that needed him. In return, the charges would be reduced to a murder conspiracy—as opposed to first-degree homicide—and, in Pennsylvania, five burglaries. The sentences on those counts would depend on the degree of his cooperation and truthfulness. Those agencies he satisfied would then go to the judge and ask for leniency, an arrangement known as a contract of adhesion.

Falcone leaned back in his chair amid the crowd. "I want you to understand something, Festa. Any time we catch you in a lie, one little lie, or anything you don't tell us, I want you to know here and now I'll prosecute the hell out of you for every crime." Donahue explained that until the federal paperwork was complete, the Festas would be placed in a hotel in the custody of Essex County.

Festa asked to be alone for a moment with Michael Sodowick, his attorney's partner. Sodowick told him this was the most he could expect. "That, or take your chances on murder." Janet went up to Festa and told him what had happened at the jail and what Quartuccio had said the night before. Freda was passing word that he was the "weak link."

Back in the room, Festa felt relieved, scared, angry. "You guys did a good job putting the squeeze in." He looked over to Falcone. Silence filled the room. "Okay," the hoodlum said. "Deal."

* *

Marie had decided she could stay behind. If Jerry turned against his "friends," she felt it was "his business." "I did nothing," she had told Rose. "If any deals are made and you gotta run for your lives, looking behind your backs forever, well, hey, I can't live that way. I'm getting too old and I'm not going to do it, much as it hurts me."

At three in the afternoon Rose had called her from the State Police barracks in Dunmore, where Festa was undergoing an exhaustive "debriefing" by Wilson and Donahue. She told Marie to prepare the children for their departure that night, and to grab a box of valuables from under Rose's bed. Festa had insisted the entire family be brought into protective custody at once. By now Shirley Donnerstag had surely gotten word to the streets.

Marie understood how bad it might be for Jerry. After all, when they got word about Carbone, and Joe testified at the preliminary hearing, Shirley had come by Ridge Street with her three-year-old son, Billy Boy, and said, "Show Aunt Rose what you're gonna do to Joe Carbone when you grow up." She took out a photograph of Carbone from her purse, along with a nail file. The boy began stabbing at the picture.

So throughout the afternoon Marie was in a state of some anguish. Donnerstag's two younger children happened right now to be in their house—she was baby-sitting them. Marie was afraid they would see her pack any suitcases. But a call came from the Essex County Prosecutor's Office telling her to be ready by six, when several detectives would be by to pick them up. She rushed up and down the stairs, trying to watch all the children (Alicia was at home sick), clean the kitchen, and put out a change of clothes for everybody. For some reason she had decided they would be gone only overnight. Her conflicting thoughts and duties overcame her, and she stopped her chores every so often to sit down and cry. She could not leave their house behind, nor her dogs, nor a lifetime of possessions. But if she stayed, on the other hand, she would lose "her" children.

Johnny Quartuccio was coming in and out, nervous as a maniac, suspicious. He heard her on the phone during one of the calls, heard her say, "I can't leave now. I got *company*." He asked who had called. Marie lied that it was Rose, and that the problem again was sickness in the family back in Pennsylvania.

"Something's wrong," said Quartuccio. "I know it. I know it."

"Grandpa just don't feel good," she tried to tell him. "We gotta go to Pennsylvania." She planned to leave for the night only because she had to watch the kids.

"Oh, no, Marie," the thief said. "It's not you. It's not the same you. What's wrong? Tell me. Tell me."

What was she going to do alone in that big house once everyone was gone? How could she let the kids go off without her? Forever?

Alicia had been cranky all day, but thank goodness Allan was play-ing quietly downstairs and baby Joseph was occupied with his wooden blocks. Sophia came home from school and saw her aunt upstairs, sitting on her bed beside a suitcase, her head down, praying. Marie looked up and told the girl, "Get in there and get some clothes for the night. Just take the things you need." Sophia began throwing night-gowns, a blouse and underwear into a carrying bag. Marie finished tossing together some clothes for herself and everyone else, dried the dishes, and fed the dogs. She took Donnerstag's children next door to stay with the DeVingos and wrote a note on the front door telling Shirley where they were.

A detective from the prosecutor's office, Charles Acocella, who was also on the task force, phoned to see if she was ready, and if who-ever was in the house had gone. Quartuccio had just left. Three cars pulled in front at about seven and she said to Alicia, "Now c'mon, get your brothers and sisters together." Joseph was sitting at the bot-tom of the stairs in his pajamas when a detective carrying a pistol came in telling them to hurry. The kids had no idea they were leaving Ridge Street forever. They just piled in the middle car with a couple of suitcases.

They were taken to the Gateway Hotel on Raymond Boulevard, near the train station downtown, where a swarm of armed guards had appropriated an entire floor for their security. One fellow stood there with an automatic shotgun near two suites of rooms they would now call home. Marie set about trying to amuse the children, and after putting them to bed and quieting them down—or trying to, for Allan was excited about all the guns around—she took out a rosary.

In Scranton, not far from where she had aimlessly roamed the streets as a teenager, Rose had been placed in a guarded hotel with Janet. They spent the night looking out the windows. Snow flurries fell. Janet held her mother as Rose wept. The thought of the following day was what petrified Rose: they would have to return to Newark with Agent Wilson.

In his small house at the center of the city, Festa's father, "Poppy," was healthy enough, and busy answering the phone. "Everything okay?" asked the first inquirer, Frank Basto, trying to find out what was happening. "Does Rose need bail or what? Where is she? Is any-thing wrong?" The next call to the old man was from Tommy Adams. "What's going on up there?" he barked. "They got Rose arrested? What the fuck's going on?"

On the trip back to Newark Rose was still worried about whether her husband had made the right move. She couldn't talk coherently to her escorts. She thought about the box upstairs she had asked Marie to take with her. Had Marie done this? It was full of expensive jewelry, and they had cash in the house. They would need that to live on.

"Do you have any stolen jewelry on your hands?" asked Wilson, as if reading her thoughts. "How about that ring?" She removed it and gave it to him. It was the least of her worries. The important problem was going back to New Jersey, where they would all be in danger now.

The Gateway, a new Hilton hotel, was nevertheless surrounded by gas tanks, old warehouses, and rusted lift bridges. Chemical plants near the Passaic River had turned this stretch into what was called "Cancer Alley," where the population had one of the highest rates in the country for malignancies of the lung, breast, and stomach; nearby, fields tainted with benzene and dioxin would be found, and soot coated the roadways. But the hotel itself was pleasant enough. A French mobile of jingling brass and copper hung from the ceiling above the long escalators, and there were mirrored columns in the lobby.

The mirrors reflected Rose's fatigue. She was moving so languidly, so dazedly, that the FBI agent was concerned. "Come, come on, Rose. Move it." He turned to Janet. "Is your mother always this way?" But the girl was preoccupied with a strange man who was reading a newspaper and giving them the eye. It was an undercover agent.

When they got up to their rooms the kids were fine. They had created a game of room service, which made them feel *"rich."* Hamburgers and chicken salad whenever they liked, served on a big glass table on a shiny silver tray. They had slept the night right alongside Marie, and they were not frightened or restless yet. Their comments were more inquiring than plaintive. Why did men with guns bring in their food, and watch the maid when she was making the beds? And why did the guards peel back the bread on their sandwiches and sniff them before they could sit down to eat? Marie said "they just have funny ways, that's all," but Alicia knew something was up: during the night she had heard her aunt's muffled sobbing.

She had managed the family's departure well—except for the box of valuables, which she forgot—but Marie was so overwrought that from now on, for some arcane reason, she would never be able to remember phone numbers. Right off, she demanded to know what would become of their possessions. "Rose," she said. "The house, the store. I wanna know: Is it being guarded? You gotta ask. You can't just stand there. Nobody ever talks to me, and we have the right to know. Are we going back or what? Why should I have to leave? Why me? And who's feeding the dogs? Those poor animals are gonna miss me right away, and they're gonna want to go outside, Rose."

Rose was nearly catatonic. Certainly too weak to ask any questions or give Marie any answers. She was worried about their getting killed at the moment, and she realized that Marie, because she did not know Jerry's associates except to say hello and leave the room, did not comprehend the dangers. "He's not in any 'Mafia,'" Marie kept saying. "What could he know?" In the room next door, Falcone, Wilson, and Donahue grilled Rose about everyone who had come into the house. She grabbed her tranquilizers each time the men came for her—double, triple the dose. She jumped up when there was a noise in the corridor, and her answers wandered.

Donahue was a cop whose brilliance was in his ability to establish rapport with most anyone, but his work was cut out for him this time. Festa's wife wouldn't discuss The Bear, and she acted as if she were walking in her sleep. The children were getting restless. Donahue went out and bought Allan a toy airplane. His boss, Captain Acocella, spent hours playing with them.

But there was no calming Marie. She had it in her head that she was going home, and she announced as much and tried to leave. "No!" Wilson said, jumping up. "She can't go back there."

Marie ran to Rose. "I didn't even really lock up the house," she said. "What's happening there? What do you mean you 'don't know'? Find out or I'm going back. I did nothing to make anyone mad at *me*."

The house would be padlocked, it was explained to them, and their possessions placed in storage until—very soon—they were settled elsewhere. It would be handled by the federal marshals. Marie was not fully buying this. She was not about to jeopardize those things she had sweated bullets for all those years in a greasy factory. And to get down to it, she was quickly growing bitter over many things that had happened since she left Lincoln Avenue in 1965. Everything—her credit line, her savings—seemed to have vanished. It was she who had provided much of the down payment on their home, she who took out a loan to purchase the Chicken Delight franchise, she who met many, many of the mortgage payments while she was still working in the factory.

"And what about the dogs? My Pinkie's gonna miss me terribly.

Rose, you tell those agents to call up the DeVingos or somebody to get those animals. Do something with my puppies. Put them in a good kennel together so we can send for them. They don't have no food." She began to scream. "My boy!" she yelled. "Nine years I've had him. It's my pet, my baby. Someone get those dogs!"

They were assured the animals had been placed in a kennel, and Rose turned to more immediate worries: how to heat Joseph's bottle (she ran hot water on it in the bathroom) and keep Alicia occupied; the little girl was growing too quiet, and she would become more of a problem over the next eight cooped-up days.

During the week they all were taken to the Federal Building on Broad Street, where bodyguards stood on the sidewalk, at the corner, and in the underground garage. They were surrounded by cops as they entered the building, and more armed men were facing them when the elevator doors opened at the floor where the strike force was. A nearby street was briefly sealed off for their arrival, and so was the law library where Rose was tape-recorded behind locked doors. The prosecutors wanted to know about a trip she had taken to sell some jewels to Jay Weisman in Florida, and she chain smoked as they told her she too would have to testify.

Rose began hallucinating again that week. This time it was Basto's face she saw, rather than Jed's. In the middle of the night, when there was quiet except for the rustling of the guards in the hallway, who occasionally peered into their suite, and the drone of television programs she was not really able to watch, she saw Frank's face staring at her from the walls and the windows—everywhere she turned, his stern hurtful face.

Janet would get out of bed to reassure her mother, looking out the windows to scan the streets far below. But she was also getting creepy vibrations, plagued by fears of Quartuccio. He had tried to do his thing with her again when her father was in jail, and she had fended him off with a butcher knife. As she now looked down at a train station and the aging rail yards, she thought about his obsessional nature. And how good he was with a rifle.

"Well, I think it's time we get you out of Newark," Wilson finally announced. The federal paperwork was done and the family was now in the care of deputy marshals, for the most part former cops or military men whose job had mainly been serving subpoenas but came to include protection of government witnesses as well. Wilson gave Rose a special number to call any time of day or night if she felt uncomfortable, and he said emphatically, "Don't tell anyone your name. You tell the marshals nothing. I'm the only one you speak to." The family would be taken to a Holiday Inn in Queens, New York, and soon they would be found a permanent home and given new documentation under an alias. (He suggested a place down on the Jersey Shore, but Janet spoke against this. That was where Johnny had hidden out after he molested her.) They left for New York in an entourage of eight cars. The federal marshals carried M-10 rifles.

Allan was no longer enamored of such exotic weaponry. In fact, as they entered the Holiday Inn, the marshals' command post #0703, he cried. He was a bright enough boy to have realized that "somebody must be after us." The deputies stood all night outside their two rooms, and as Rose surveyed their bivouac—the guards near the exit and the elevator, or napping on cots—she said to herself, "They must know something we don't." They were certainly giving them special attention.

In the middle of one night they were paid a visit by John Partington, an inspector for the entire Witness Protection Program. He had flown in from Rhode Island, which would be their next destination. Partington considered the Festas the "hottest" people in the national program, sought after by "bad, deadly, capable guys," in more danger than the sensational witness Vinnie Teresa—"a ten on a scale of one to ten." The Festas were also the largest family in the program. The visitor took notes on what was in their house and told Rose the Newark marshals were supposed to have "secured" the home and the cars. He said he was flying to Washington to expedite the issuance of their new identities, which went through the Social Security office and motor vehicle departments.

They were packed on a plane for Seekonk, Massachusetts, just outside Providence, Rhode Island, where Partington was stationed, and escorted to a Howard Johnson's motel. The kids had ice wars in the hall near the vending machines, ate more hamburgers, more chicken salad, and teased Marie as she washed what clothes they had in the bathroom sink. But they were weary. Alicia was sick of television and wanted to play in a yard. "Mommy, you get me out of here!" she screamed.

"I'm looking for a house now, babe," Rose said. "So we can get Pinkie and Candy here."

But Alicia would hear none of it. A wild look came over her face and she began banging her head against the walls and the door, holding her breath, turning red and sweating. She tried to claw her way out of the room, and Rose had to lie on top of her to keep the adrenaline-strengthened eight-year-old still. Pressed by that reaction, Rose and the marshals hastily found and rented a house in Cranston, Rhode Island, an old, too-small bungalow with a weather-beaten gray roof and a rickety porch. Something about the place felt ominous to Marie. Perhaps it was the dark, dirty attic, or the old furnace in the basement, which had been flooded in drainage water. But the house was an improvement over the hotels, and they rented some furniture for the parlor and two bedrooms. As they cleaned up the place—the roaches from the toilet, the soot from the closets—they found address books with names and numbers in them, and some erotic underwear. The last resident had been a hooker.

"There are some men who are mad at Daddy," Rose finally told the girls. "If you see any strange men, you don't go near them. If you see some of Daddy's friends, you run home. You don't trust anybody. You don't go with nobody."

"Even Uncle Frank?" Allan asked.

"Especially him," Marie chimed in.

Alicia and Sophia were escorted to and from school and taught how to write their new name: Mitchell. They were not to wander from the schoolyard, Marie told them every day; and for now they couldn't make any friends, nor tell a single classmate where they were from. Their father was being moved from jail to jail all over Pennsylvania at this time, but as far as the little boys knew, he was still on that "business trip."

*　　*

The day Festa turned, Donahue and Wilson had interrogated him for eleven hours, until three in the morning, at the Dunmore barracks; for both it was a memorable day of labor, the fulfillment of a deep-seated, long-frustrated desire to make a dent in the mob. In many ways the two men were opposites. Wilson was a strong personality and a wholly determined one—this the two men had in common—but he had come to the Newark office from the relatively calmer streets of Oakland, California, and a career first as a local police officer, next as a Naval Intelligence officer, finally as a J. Edgar man in Alabama, where he had handled reactionaries and bank robberies. He was very ambitious, strait-laced, a tight-lipped agent who worked only by the book, adhering to a secrecy that was at once impressive and unnerving to those who sought his friendship. Business was business. It was tough for anyone to get close. But he was not the type to sit at a desk all day reading the files, and he was shrewder, tougher, than just about any gangster he dealt with. Which was another thing he shared with Detective Donahue. But Ronnie was even more of a street cop. Though careful not to spill confidential data, Donahue was easier-going, and when he was not working incalculable hours in a bland office at the Essex County complex (or trying to keep up with his forty-odd incoming calls a day), he was in the bars drinking prodigious quantities of vodka and culling astoundingly candid "background"—leads and admissions—from wise guys or other sources he met, for even they respected his fairness and integrity. Donahue had been raised in the hardnosed city of Harrison, an industrial center just east of Newark, and had grown up in a neighborhood where numbers runners were as regular as the milkman—and much more sought after. There he had observed a good number of street criminals, and he had learned that however repulsive they were, to communicate with them one had to treat them as human beings, show some empathy for them, see their "side of the road"—and make sure they knew he'd throw the book at them if they let him down. He did not allow himself to be hindered by cut-and-dried legalities—he worked on instinct—and his sheer dynamism, his charisma, the way he could make people feel immediately at home, had been valuable not only in his office—where the staff gave him ironclad loyalty—but also with sad and sordid junkies like Wally Lombardo. Donahue liked people. People liked him. He knew more politicians than a state senator, more cops than the police chief, and nearly as many crooks as career wise guys. His effectiveness made him a maligned figure among men such as Raymond Freda (whom Donahue considered the most ingenious criminal he had known), but, grudgingly, they respected his candor and his toughness, when toughness was in fact necessary, and the sincere kindness—the sense of caring—he showed them if they were cooperative. In their different styles both Donahue and Wilson were capable of masterful work.

Donahue had thrown out to Festa a whole list of "ballplayers," criminals he was interested in, and both he and Wilson were joyous over what the hoodlum knew. Jerry Chicken Delight was like no other criminal they had worked with up to that point: he had a side of him that nearly wanted to do right, and he trusted both cops immediately, immensely.

After the eleven-hour interview Festa was taken back for a final night in Lackawanna County Jail, and in the morning, when he saw Donnerstag and Martin, he tried to tell them he had been away on a theft charge, this one from up in New York State. After Festa gave them his alibi, Bob just stared at the floor. "He's a fucking rat," he mumbled. Both he and Donnerstag had their stony faces on; by now they knew the truth. As he was taken out of the jail (where there were rumors of another plot to poison him) and given the alias "Tony Binardi," a "parole violator from New York," Martin glanced up at him, first with a hurt look, then a withering one. It was the last time the two old buddies would speak to each other.

* *

Once they were settled, Rose and Janet began making occasional furtive trips to Newark, trying to find out what had happened to their belongings. At first Wilson and the other FBI agents wouldn't let them go to Ridge Street, fearing, with reason, that the house might be booby-trapped with a bomb. Wilson went there on his own at first, and when he returned he was nearly speechless. The movers must have made a mistake taking the stuff to storage, he said. All he could find of any value in the house, as far as clothes went, was not quite enough to fill a plastic laundry basket he held. One of the few items he returned with looked to Janet like a message from Quartuccio: in the basket was a nude beheaded doll.

Festa was in Newark to appear before a grand jury, and the FBI agent took him aside. "I think I know the answer, but I want it from you. The only furniture left there really was the dining-room table, with one chair at the head of it."

Festa thought it was a piece of Basto symbolism. It was the chair Jerry always sat in during their meals and discussions, and "it means my last supper," he said.

At the U.S. marshals' office in Providence, Rose demanded to know where their clothes, their cars, their furniture were. No one knew just where the stuff had gone. And because the matter fell in the jurisdiction of the marshals, the FBI was not allowed to become formally involved. The marshals in Rhode Island could not say exactly where the stuff had supposedly been taken, and the Newark deputies were oddly evasive when they were asked about the house. Hysterical, Rose stormed out of the office to calm herself in a nearby coffee shop. She thought of just boarding a bus and going off by herself somewhere across the country. She could hardly bear to tell Marie that no one seemed to know a thing about the dogs. Finally she went back to the house with the bad news. "Well, God!" Marie shouted. "Who's feeding those animals?"

"They say they're in a kennel somewhere," said Rose. "Supposed to be sending them. But the furniture—I don't know what to do." Since she could not get in touch with her husband—Wilson relayed messages from him occasionally—she telephoned the FBI man, distraught.

"Rose, I told you not to call on the phone," Wilson said. "This is dangerous."

"Fuck you, Mr. Wilson," she yelled. "I got word from the marshals that they don't know where nothing is. I'm getting the impression we're just scum, and we're supposed to be lucky where we are. Well, I think when I see Jerry I'm gonna tell him if he testifies the kids and me are leaving."

Wilson made his point bluntly. "Jerry will go back to jail, then, and stay there."

Rose was too angry to continue the argument. "Fine with me," she said.

The agent did not actually know all that was going on, and his agency at times seemed at war, or at least in competition, with the Marshals' Service. First the Festas had been told the house was pad-locked and their belongings were in storage, then that no one was certain where these belongings were stored—if they were stored at all. In reality the mob, with the help of certain Newark marshals, had ripped the place off.

But the Festas maintained a slim hope that there was more left in the house than Wilson had had the chance to see, and late in April, two weeks after Janet's seventeenth birthday, the Rhode Island marshals decided that she, rather than her mother, who was emotionally overwrought, and still suffering from a respiratory ailment, would be taken back to the house to survey the premises for herself and recover whatever else might be there. The marshals gave her plane tickets to New York City, but when she arrived there were no bodyguards to greet her. Afraid she was being set up, and spotting a man who looked like a Newark gangster, the teenager hid in the baggage room until she gathered enough nerve to call the marshals' office.

An hour and a half later the chief Newark deputy arrived, a short, rude man named Angelo Bove. Bove was uneasy, as well he might have been. Along with at least one other deputy marshal, Bove had been in communication with the Basto regiment, and it was he who had allowed—indeed, helped—the mob ransack the house. Janet did not know this just yet, but she distrusted him at once. She insisted that they stop at the Newark Federal Building so the FBI would know where she was before they went to the house.

"Hurry up," Bove said when they got to Ridge Street. "We can't stay here long." To appease the Festas, the marshals had ordered a moving van to stand by out front, as if there was anything to move. Janet boldly went next door to the DeVingos', thinking they might have a set of keys to the front door. She knocked, and Josephine answered. Once such a close friend of the family's, Mrs. DeVingo now shut the door in her face and called to Carmen Malavenda, who had been staying with the DeVingos since Festa turned. Carmen came to the vestibule and reached out the door with the keys, hardly showing his face. He was an enemy too, and all of them were in cahoots with what had happened next door.

"Jesus Christ, hurry up," Bove insisted. "We got to get out of here." Janet tried the front door, but it was boarded shut from inside. They went around the side of the house and forced their way in another barricaded entrance.

Feeling as if she were entering the home of someone who had recently died, Janet went into the dining room. Now even the table was gone, and the sun coming through the bare dusty windows shone only upon litter lining the baseboards. She went into the kitchen, and as she did so her feet felt as if they were scraping against sand. A deluge of water had warped the tiles, for someone had broken the faucets—rip-and-tear Johnny?—and poured salt all over the place. The kitchen table was still there, but the new refrigerator was gone.

Next, to the empty pantries and living room. The couches, the chairs, the rugs, the end tables and television set—all were gone. The walls and doors were smudged and scraped where the "movers" had hurriedly bumped their way out with the Festas' belongings. Janet looked in the foyer and in the closets on the first floor. All were empty.

Janet decided to go upstairs, even though she feared someone might be lurking there waiting for her. "You don't have to go up there," Bove fidgeted. "You can see everything from here." But she was becoming more angry than frightened, and she ran to the attic first, to check the crawl space where valuables had been kept. It was empty, and so was the next room she inspected, her parents' bedroom.

All her father's leather jackets, boots, and shirts were gone, and so was her mother's great pride: the mink-cuffed seal coat. The sliding compartment concealed in her parents' room and the jewel box which had been built into the wall were empty.

"Come on, damn it," said Bove, visibly shaking. "Hurry up!"

In Marie's room, all that seemed left were a few trampled clothes and some old ripped-up pay stubs from her days at the factory. A new black dress Marie never had the chance to wear had vanished. As in the rest of the house, photographs and other decorations had been stolen.

Janet held her breath before going into her own bedroom. There was still a faint hope that this room might have survived, and she had brought along a suitcase in case there was anything left. But there would be no need for it. She halted at the entranceway, crushed, feeling deeply violated. It was not her room any more—no longer the place where she could retire in comfort and be quietly alone. The stereo she had listened to as a kid with the Basto girls, the records she and Jed had enjoyed together, were smashed or gone. Instead of clothing there were just some shredded knits and balls of fuzz. All the furniture had been hauled off somewhere, and on the floor was her Barbie doll collection with the heads chopped off. In the other kids' rooms, someone had broken all the toys.

She descended the stairs past the stained-glass windows and past the cubbyhole which had once contained the nubby loveseats. Looking around the first floor one last time, she noted that tar had been poured onto it. She fruitlessly searched for a new pair of knit pants, a collection of stuffed animals, and Marie's religious souvenirs, but all she had found were school papers which had been set afire and two pairs of eyeglasses smashed on a floor. Air-conditioners, silver sets, an antique desk, a breakfront—everything was gone. Bove pressed her again to leave. She dashed into the basement. Soggy papers were strewn on the floor. A damaged washer and freezer, and a clothes press which had been hammered at, were the only appliances. The storage boxes there all had been pilfered.

They went outside, and Bove hurriedly walked over to the De-Vingos' to return the keys. Janet stood in front of the house, stunned, staring. The neighbor on the other side of the house came out and hugged her.

"They took all our furniture!" Janet said, trying not to cry.

The woman whispered, "I can't say anything, but those guys were around here picking the stuff up." The woman nodded over at Deputy Bove.

Janet noticed her father's roofing truck in the driveway and looked to see if any tools were inside. Carmen and the DeVingos were coldly staring at her from windows in the kitchen and an upstairs bedroom.

Janet got back into the car and for some reason Bove made a U-turn instead of safely heading back in the direction they had come, driving right past The Bear's house on the corner. Then he took her to the airport.

What hurt most was the destruction of her Barbie dolls. They had come a long way with her, had been a comfort back in those days when she felt abandoned in Scranton, when she was staying with her mother's "friend" Fran while Rose and Jerry were hiding on Lincoln Avenue. She hadn't told them right away, but Fran had been sadistic, beating her, threatening her with a knife, making her kneel for hours at a time on a floor which the woman, as a punishment for any tiny infraction, had coated with raw rice that scarred the girl's knees. Fran would lock her in a closet sometimes, and she told the child that her mother had abandoned her, even though Rose had been sending money for her. In those days, when Janet felt alone in the world, motherless and friendless, it had been the Barbie dolls she cried to.

Now she had to face the one woman who had always been good to her, who had made her feel welcome when she first came to Ridge Street, and she had to tell Marie as well as her mother that those articles of pride in their lives were in ruins. On the plane back to Rhode Island, Janet thought about her aunt, and about her own dog, Candy, which she loved nearly as much as Marie loved Pinkie. *That night when they came to arrest her father, and the cop had yelled at her growling dog, she had screamed back, "You blow her away and consider yourself dead too." But actually she had tried to remain aloof from dogs ever since the terrible hurt in Scranton when Fran discovered a stray dog she had been secretly caring for and put the poor animal out to be run over by a car.*

But Marie and Pinkie: that was another matter. The dog had been a good chunk of her aunt's life. It had been that way since the dog weighed only a pound and Marie could carry him around in her coat pocket. What a puppy! Marie had warmed food on the stove for the dog, fed him eggs, and after all those years of good cooking Pinkie looked like a short, fat sausage. Which is not to suggest the other dogs who at one time or another were in the house—Thunder and Hoss besides Candy—were not also part of Marie's life. Marie was a Pied Piper when it came to animals, and they all padded behind her up the stairs when she went to bed, fighting for a place next to her. It was just that of the pets they had, Pinkie was the clear favorite, and he could always make her laugh. He terrorized the neighborhood with his nipping and barking and growled jealously when Marie's attention was distracted. She would look at the little black-and-white-spotted terrier and say gleefully, "Mommy's naughty baby bad little doggie." That was a dog with moxie: unafraid of other dogs four times, five times its size. Pinkie had gotten lost once, clear across town, but he had found his way home in a hurry.

How was Janet to explain that Pinkie was not in a kennel, she discovered, nor had he been adopted—as one agent told her—by a sweet older couple who would care for him? How to tell Marie that Pinkie and Candy had been sent off to the pound, and that both of the dogs had been gassed?

*   *

"Rumors started going around that Festa was cooperating with the police but no one really knew for sure," says Raymond Freda, looking back, in correspondence with a journalist, at the day Festa turned. "When Frankie Bear, John Quartuccio and myself, along with many others in Newark, found out he was cooperating with the feds, everyone had gotten very scared as they all knew that Festa could send everyone away for a very long time. Jerry the Jew was already sewed up with the murder case in Pennsylvania.

"I remember the night I was sitting at home looking at TV. It was very late at night, and my phone started ringing. I went over and picked up the phone. It was Bear calling. He said, 'Ray, I can't talk on the phone, but it's very important that I see you.' I told him, couldn't it wait until morning? He told me it could, 'but I think you should come down to my house.' I told him to give me a couple of hours and I would be there. When I got into the house we went down to the basement to talk.

"At the house that night was Bear, Johnny, and myself. Frankie told me that he had found out from a New Jersey marshal, Angelo Bove, that Festa was cooperating with the feds and Essex County, that he had given up Jerry the Jew on the murder case, and that he had given up at least fifty people in Newark, and that I was one of them. I knew that if he sang I would go away for a long time. Bear told me we shouldn't take any chances with it. If he went bad, he went bad on everyone. And he was right about that.

"We had known that Festa was in the hands of the Newark marshals, so Bear had known he could find out where he was being held at, if the right marshals had moved him to and from Newark. Johnny said he knew where Jerry Festa's family had lived in Pennsylvania, and he was pretty sure that was where he was hiding out. They wanted to make the trip out there and stake the place out. They said the sooner we take care of this, the better all of us would be, and I did have to agree with them. We had decided to go to Pennsylvania that day after we met. Frankie also said that the U.S. marshal may have some more information for him, as he didn't know at that time just where he was being held. We got into the jail to see Donnerstag after giving a guard a hundred dollars. Jerry the Jew told me that he knew Jerry Festa had told everything he knew, and that we were all in trouble.

"At first Bear found out that they had Festa in a county jail but there was no way that he could have gotten in. Everyone was to try and get him in Newark, as everyone knew the city and different ways to get away without having many problems. And most of all you could buy off most of the police except for the Essex County Prosecutor's Office, as they had a cop named Ronnie Donahue you couldn't buy, and they had that new crime task force working jointly with the FBI."

So had begun the efforts of the mob's own task force to execute Jerry Chicken Delight by any means available. Though Freda neglects to mention him, the initial search-and-destroy missions also included his quiet, trusted brother-in-law, Austin Castiglione. As Basto had an inkling, Festa was indeed being shuttled between county lockups in Pennsylvania, hiding, for the most part, in places throughout the northeastern part of the state: in Wayne County, to the northeast of Scranton; in Susquehanna, near the New York State border; in Schuylkill, some sixty-three miles southwest of the Dunmore barracks (where Hank too had been sheltered); and fifty-five miles to the northwest of Scranton, in Towanda, where the tiny quarrystone jail had twenty cells for overnight stays by the town's pot smokers and drunks.

Festa had no illusions about his safety, and he realized that he had to watch out for "bad cops" who might give Basto and Freda information. Already, on another trip his family made from Rhode Island, an incident had occurred which demonstrated to him that Basto had inside information. Rose, Janet, and his son Allan, who desperately wanted to see his father, had pulled up in a car at the federal offices in Newark, and there, standing on the curb, was Uncle Frank—an arm's reach from the automobile. This was no hallucination: they all saw him, and Rose and Janet dived for the floor, screaming at the marshal to get out of there. They yanked Allan beneath them as the shocked deputy swerved away from the curb, and they immediately went to Wilson, telling him The Bear had somehow found out their precise time of arrival, and had been there sneering. Wilson ran to the street, but Basto was gone.

Wilson knew the pressure would get worse. In his private thoughts he figured The Bear would eventually get Festa. During the preliminary interviews Festa had mentioned not fifty people, as Freda estimated, but a hundred and twenty-two gangland names. His propensity for talking at great length was backed up by his truly phenomenal ability to remember where a house was, how many rooms it had, what colors the walls were, what time of day the burglary was, what everyone said, the position of each piece of furniture, who the victims were, how much the crew got from the score, what carat the jewels were, who reported to whom, how old everyone was, what their facial expressions were like, what clothes they were wearing, whom the gangsters slept with, whom the killers killed. Along with the standard information of an informer—how loan sharks and crap games operated, who the biggest fences were—he added little surprises: A state senator had helped set up that "School Mistress" burglary, he alleged, and he named at least seven crooked cops. One, he told them, had caused two murders, and another, Ray Grill, provided him and Donnerstag with their gear.

"So [Sergeant] Ray Grill gave you walkie-talkies, right?"

"Yeah," Festa answered.

"Did he ever give you or Jerry the Jew any weapons?"

"I don't know if Ray Grill gave the weapon, but we had a hand grenade that we were suppose to put on Sporty McNair's [a dope dealer's] car."

"Sport McNair?"

"McNair, the guy that was testing."

"What kind of grenade?"

"What kind? Army."

Michael Brown 218

In these interviews with Wilson and Donahue, Festa talked about the dispute with Nicky Boy Valvano that had occurred just before Jerry's murder bust. Indeed, when the cops came in that October night, he had not been sure whether it was the police barging in or mob hitmen outraged that he had backed off the antique robbery after he had been told the plans.

"This is when Moose and Nicky Valvano would come to my house. They wanted to talk to me out in the car. Now they told me they had a job down in Lakewood for me to meet a man. Gave me the license number, the color of the car, and just all I'd have to do is go to the door, knock on the door, because being I was a roofer and I solicited my own work, they figured that I had a better mouth . . . but I was afraid. It didn't sound right. It looked like I was being set up for a hit. I refused. Johnny Moose blew his stack."

"What did he say?"

"He said, I'll fucking wrap your head with a baseball bat. I says, Johnny, I says, I can't go. I'm up with Raymond Freda. I got to be up there tomorrow. I used that for an excuse. So they let it slide but in the meantime Nicky went in my house and called Raymond and Raymond said, well, no, I need him tomorrow. So when Raymond seen me he asked me what it was all about and I told him. He said, well you just tell them no, you don't have to go on the score. I said, but Moose won't take 'no.' "

"What did Raymond say?"

"Raymond said fuck him, let me get a hold of Nicky Boy. Meantime that next night they came again. This is when Nicky Boy comes in my house when I refused outside. I refused to go out to the car. Moose got mad as all hell. He burned rubber away from my car and Nicky came in the house. He called me everything in the sun."

"Nicky did?"

"Nicky Boy, Nicky Valvano."

"Okay . . ."

"He says, motherfucker, get a gun, carry it with you, because I'm gonna blow your fucking brains out."

"That was over this job?"

"Over this job. He says, you blow this fucking million-dollar score on me. My sister and wife," Festa continued, "were standing on the stairs."

"They heard it?"

"They heard everything. This is why my sister [actually, cousin Marie] is so terrified to go around with us now."

As Wilson listened intently, Festa described Frank Basto as "a very, very, very precise man . . . you're never gonna catch him with his pants down because he don't keep nothing around."

"Well, where does he, does he keep some of the stuff at his house?"

"Some of the stuff is around," Festa said.

"Where does he keep it, in his house?"

"The tools for safes are in a bag in the cellar where the boiler is. It's in a regular bag."

"Big overnight bags?"

"Right."

"How about blow-bars?"

Festa said, "Yeah, but now I wanna know since this problem came down: Just before I got arrested, I know he got rid of the . . . he got rid of the gas masks, he got rid of gas, tear gas, grenades, and a coupla of . . ."

"Smoke bombs?"

"No, ah . . ."

"Hand grenades?"

"Hand grenades he had. He said he was gonna bury 'em."

"What . . . does he have in the [way of] radio equipment?"

"He has one right in his cupboard. That's for the City of Newark there."

"In his cupboard?"

"It's attached right there. In other words, he picks up the first, second, third—all your precincts, he got the buttons for 'em."

"Okay, what about melting equipment for jewelry?"

"He has," said Jerry, "a melter that you plug in. Works right off your own plug here that you plug in. Works right off your own plug here that you just take the jewelry as soon as you get it. Throw it in there and within seconds . . ."

"It melts the . . ."

"Right, yeah."

"All right. How about a tranquilizer gun for animals?"

"Yeah."

"He has one of those?"

"He had a guy come in from Boston, had a coupla horses in Monmouth with plastic right through the—he used the [racing] program.

One shot into the horse, the favorite, it went down. The favorite went down. We're at the railing. As the horses start coming down, he [the guy from Boston] has the program rolled up and this plastic vial, whatever the hell it was, was in there and as the horses start walking by—two horses had already gone by—he hit the fourth horse, and all that happened was the horse's tail went up a little bit and that's all, and he did a little prance but nothing . . . It didn't show nothing or nothing. But the horse went down. He didn't come in. He came in fifth or sixth, I forget," he went on, "no speed. No nothing."

At especially useful points in Festa's revelations, Wilson would jump up and run to the phone to call his FBI office. He wanted to keep Jerry on tap full time, but first the Pennsylvania State Police were allowed their time with him, and for the first few weeks Festa rode around incognito with Owczarski, Varzaly, and Noel, pointing out houses he and his crew had robbed (among them the home of his family doctor, Dr. James Skeoch). He explained to the detectives how he found out who had what jewels from businessman Jay Weisman, and then would steal it and sell it to Weisman. Jay would resell it to a customer and tell Festa who had it now so it could be stolen again for resale.

Jerry was dishing out burglaries to the troopers like a luncheonette chef at the steam counter: scores in Dunmore, Scranton, Moscow, and Clarks Summit that had baffled them for years. In two weeks' time he gave the troopers and a city detective, Bill Walsh, twenty-four cases. Up at Rowlands, in the Poconos, he took them to the scrap yard owned by "Black Bear" Cardinale, slumping to the floor of the car when they spotted the obese gangster coming out of a bar. (The cops themselves were disguised as fishermen.) Though unable to locate the pond where Basto had stood discussing a hit, he found the dirt road leading up to the hilltop dump, and the large inn where wanted murderers and other crooks—including Valvano—had hidden out. On February 12, 1974, he signed a murder statement on the Feldman hit for District Justice Michael S. Polizzi, substantiating what Ellis had admitted.

By February 20 Hank too was being debriefed by Donahue, Wilson, and FBI agent Barry O'Neill. Ellis was not quite as helpful as Jerry; he had not had as much contact with the higher-ups and had problems remembering the surnames even of people like Quartuccio, who had lived at the house with him.

But Jerry filled the gaps. The state police too were amazed at

Festa's memory; they compared his recollections with the original burglary reports and found they matched almost perfectly. But the more valuable he became, the more they worried about his safety. They shifted him around constantly, because only a week or two in a new jail was time enough for the locals to begin spreading rumors about a "big *mafioso* called Chicken Delight" being kept in their very own Main Street jail. His name had been on television, and among the long-haired dope peddlers and raw rural motorcyclists, his attire—patent-leather shoes and black slacks, which had been brought from the house before it was pillaged—tended to single him out, and in one jail he was able to stay only two hours before the state police took him to another obscure location.

Though the police were not fully aware of it at the time, and considered some of his fears paranoid (a phobia about being near any buildings with flattop roofs, for instance), they learned later that Freda, Basto, Quartuccio, Castiglione, and other hitmen were making a concerted, persistent attempt to find Festa. As Freda was eventually to explain, their first guess—his father's house in Scranton—did not pan out:

"John and Bear had made many trips up there. Two days later [after their initial conference] we got into a car, Johnny, Bear, and myself; we headed for Pennsylvania. It was a long ride and Jerry Festa's family lived in a little town. After spending the day up there Johnny had found out that Jerry Festa was not around there, as Johnny had known some people there in Pennsylvania. Bear had said that he had to be killed, as he [Festa] had done a great deal for a captain [Joe Paterno]. He said Joe had put a price tag on his head. Bear said that he would get back to me in a few days, that he would try to find out when Festa would be appearing in court or before a grand jury. He could be gotten going into the courthouse or coming out, or either catch him on the road . . . as the marshals were taking him back and forth." Quartuccio was brought along, says Freda, because of his expertise with guns, especially rifles: they would try to hit Festa at a distance—from any available rooftop.

At the beginning of March Festa was flown back to Newark. (At the airport in Pennsylvania he had to hide in the baggage room, as Janet had done in New York.) In New Jersey, where he was to appear soon before a federal grand jury, he was met by two federal deputy marshals from the Newark office, which was under the supervision of

Angelo Bove. Instead of taking him directly to downtown Newark for a meeting at Wilson's office, these marshals headed their station wagon in the opposite direction.

They were moving south, to Somerset County, when Festa demanded, "Where we going?"

"Don't worry," a marshal said. "Bove told us where to take you."

Festa was alarmed, and he would have been more so had he recognized the name "Bove" as the man he had seen on occasion with the hoods at Jimo's. But he did realize he was supposed to be heading directly to the offices of the federal strike force, and not to the Somerset County Jail, where Riviello and Adams had always told him they had "good connections."

In Newark, Wilson was also apprehensive. He had accepted the first hour of delay, knowing that planes were often late and that traffic near the Newark International Airport was heavy, with more than a hundred thousand vehicles passing each day. But by the second hour he had begun making rather pressing phone calls trying to find out where his principal was, and soon, it seemed, the whole strike force was frantically inquiring about his whereabouts. Wilson was concerned that Chicken Delight was being set up for a hit.

Peculiarly enough, Festa was introduced to the guards at the holding pen in Somerset not under his code name (Tony Binardi) but as "Gerard Chicken Delight Festa, 566 Ridge Street." He was taken into a room where, again without explanation, six photographs were taken of him in street clothes.

"Get on the phone!" he screamed. "Call the FBI. Get me the fuck out of here! Take me back to Scranton."

He caused enough of a ruckus so that he finally was driven into Newark, but again the marshals' actions were disconcerting. They did not slip him into the Federal Building through the underground garage, as prudence and protocol dictated, but parked in a lot across the street near a post office and walked him down and across the busy street in plain view of the ghetto rooftops. The two deputies did not walk immediately at his side, as in normal procedure, but six or so feet in front of him, out of the way of stray bullets should a sniper find the range.

When Festa reached Wilson's office and told him what had happened, the FBI agent was furious. Technically the agency had no control over the marshals, but Wilson quickly arranged to take Festa out of the Newark marshals' hands and get him to another office a safer distance from Basto's influence—in Brooklyn. The deputies there took him to spend the night at a jail in Nassau County, on Long Island, but here also Festa was justifiably afraid. He recognized a guard there as one who had gambled with him and Basto at Aqueduct, and this man said, "Jerry. What happened? You went bad?" (Fortunately the Brooklyn marshals, Sandy Fox and Paul Haney, overheard the conversation and rushed him out of there to the Federal Building in downtown Brooklyn, where he spent the night under their guard in the infirmary.)

He was returned to Newark the following day, and members of the strike force offered him whisky—which he refused—to soothe his nerves. Then he went to the Essex Courthouse to meet with Joe Falcone and testify for several hours before the special grand jury, escorted not by the Newark marshals but by bodyguards Wilson insisted be brought in from outside offices.

Donahue and Falcone were delighted with Festa's performance: he somehow managed to remain calm in front of the jurors, relating with his usual detail his experiences with the Gambino mob and promising to "go down the line with you" if "you people give me your backing." They gave him a standing ovation.

From there he went back to the Federal Building for another grand jury appearance, this one in regard to the key federal offense, interstate transportation of stolen property. Rose was in the office, disguised in a blond wig, and Wilson told her, "Your husband was great at grand jury. Falcone told me he had those people eating out of his hands. We have it made."

"Maybe *you* have it made," she said bitterly.

Wilson was more aware of Festa's terrible predicament than Rose would have guessed. He took Jerry aside. "Look, I want you to know, you got to be careful. As of right now they put a fifty-thousand contract on your head. Tell the marshals *nothing*."

Festa was next driven under heavy guard to the little jail in Towanda, Pennsylvania, to complete his work with the state police. At Tardosky's pond he went with them down the path where Jed was slaughtered and threw two Pepsi bottles into the water, indicating as best he could where the guns had been tossed.

When he returned to Towanda, he was told that two men outfitted in hunting gear had stopped by to inquire about the jailhouse kitchen.

They said they were guards from Nassau County and were simply interested in how prisoners in another state, at a smaller jail, were fed.

Festa wanted out of there! And within a few days the authorities agreed with him that holding him as a prisoner anywhere made him a sitting duck. A bail hearing was hastily arranged, and he was released to the custody of the federal government on a greatly reduced bond of twenty-five thousand dollars, which was raised by sneaking Marie from Cranston into Scranton, where she put up, as security, a house her mother had left her and her sister.

Festa was kept under strict guard at Dunmore until these proceedings were over. Then he was escorted by six cars to the Avoca airport, where marshals from Rhode Island accompanied him and his sister back to the house in Cranston. Soon he would learn that, along with his house, the business too had been vandalized. Someone slashed across the storefront (with yellow spray paint) a new name for the store: "Canary Delight."

*   *

While Basto and Freda were the point men, working together after an estrangement of four years, the task of eliminating Jerry Festa was not theirs alone. No faction of the Newark syndicate was free of concern, and if Festa "hit the stand," as Donnerstag put it, prison sentences awaited members and associates of the Gambino, Genovese, and Bruno fraternities. The time had come to move.

Of those others who wanted Festa dead, FBI agents were most concerned about the "Silver Lake Crew" from Belleville: Skins, Zarro, and Robert Emilio Bisaccia, the enforcer known as "Cabert." Cabert was a gutsy young man associated with all the major organized-crime factions in Essex and Passaic counties, and his exploits were appreciated by Freda himself. A softball pitcher in his younger days, Cabert was said to have once held up a store in his cleats and uniform after a game, and he had a penchant for shooting up a tavern if he got mad at a patron. He was a short, handsome man with a coppery complexion, jet-black hair, and an irascibility—a festering anger—quite reminiscent of Jerry the Jew. Though the stories about him, as about many other hoods, may have been the product of ornamentation, if not outright myths, a substantial number of cynical cops told them in all seriousness. A typical one was about Cabert's crew having forced the bare breast of a robbery victim onto a hot stove. He was "serious as a heart attack," according to Raymond Freda, and Basto had always warned Festa to stay clear of him (another piece of advice which Jerry did not fully heed). Cabert was in the same category as Nicky Valvano and also a strikingly clean-cut construction worker who was closely associated with them, Gerald Sperduto.

Added to these reputed killers were of course Tommy Adams and his son Jackie; the notorious Campisi clan of South Orange Avenue (whose lieutenant, Biaggio, had been a gambling partner of Festa's); Vinnie Tursi, who, Festa told Wilson, had recently killed a man named Richie Tyson in a car; James "Jimo" Calabrese, a Boiardo associate who operated their favorite hangout; high-echelon mobsters such as Scrivo, Paterno, and Demus Covello (who could command help from any region of the country); and, at the other end of the spectrum, the lower-level freelancers—Malavenda, Quartuccio, and Martin—who were also facing prison time.

"Any one of thirty-five guys would have killed him," Freda says. "Guys were looking for Festa, driving around, different towns, going to Pennsylvania: a lot of time was put in." Freda says Paterno personally raised the ante: there was soon a hundred-thousand bounty on Chicken Delight's head.

The main responsibility, however, fell squarely on the shoulders of The Bear. "Everyone was mad at Basto," says Freda, "for bringing Festa around . . . We knew Festa had New York marshals now. It was a little while longer before I seen Bear again. He told me he would have some better information in a few days, as the [Newark] marshals had told him they found out Jerry Festa was now in Rhode Island, and they were keeping him hid out there. They told Bear that in a few days they would get the address of the place Jerry Festa was hiding out.

"Bear called me up one night and told me to come and see him. 'Santa Claus' had come through. I knew by that he had some good news as to where Jerry Festa was at. I told him I would be right down there, as I lived in Boonton Township. I was making a great deal of money in the narcotics business, and I sure didn't want to go to jail. I went to Bear's house and Johnny had been there. Bear told me that the U. S. marshals had told him that Jerry Festa was staying in a safe-house in Smithfield, Rhode Island. Bear had the address. He said the marshals had told him there was a river on the other side of the fence, and that they go fishing back there. If we had a person that was a good shot, Jerry would be easy pickings. As the place was surrounded with woods. I told Bear that it sounded real good. We would take a ride out there the next day.

"That morning we got into the car. We had no guns with us as we wanted to see the place. It took us about five hours to drive there and find the house, as none of us knew what we were looking for.

"After we found the house, it was in a woods. There was a small paved road going in front of it. In the yard there were two green cars. You know what fed cars look like. Sure enough the marshals were there, and we seen some men moving about. It looked as though there was some movement in the back of the house. It was really a broken-down house. One would never look for anyone out there. It had a very high fence all around it. We seen niggers and white men there. We didn't know one from the other. There were too many men there just to be guarding Festa. I told Bear we just better check it out, then come back with a car with Rhode Island plates on it, as our Jersey plates stuck out too much. We were looking for Jerry's kids to be in the yard, or his wife, but never did see that day anyone but men and never spotted Jerry yet. There was a sign on the fence that read, 'Government Property— Keep Out.'

"We seen a guy down the road a little bit and asked him about the property price around there. We said we were from out of state and wanted to invest in some property. After talking to the guy awhile, I asked him what that house was, with the big fence around it. He said that it belonged to the government, and he believed that's where they took training. Bear's face lit up, as he knew if Jerry jogged on that road, it was his last jog. We then went home. We discussed how easy it would be to hit Jerry on that road, but the problem was getting away, as you were way out in the woods. Bear said he would meet with two marshals and find out a little more about it. There was no doubt in my mind, Jerry was there, as you couldn't pick that place out if you didn't know where it was. It was too far out in the woods. But all the men there had me wondering why so many people were guarding his house. Jerry must have really been singing.

"When we got home we went to Bear's house. He told me to come down to his house the next night, as he had to meet with a few more guys to see what we would do. As by this time there were [all kinds of] people looking to make a hit of Festa.

"Bear called me a couple days later, he told me that he found out from the marshals why there were so many men at that house. Only four of them were marshals. They lived right there with Jerry, and that the other men were to be witnesses against other members of organized crime. He only told us about Jerry. He could not tell us which men were marshals as they all dressed alike at times at the house. The marshals didn't just wear suits. Bear said that he was going into New York to get a couple of guys to make the hit, and that we would split up money and give them fifty thousand dollars to make the move on Festa. Bear said he had the guys. One was named Jackie. I know they were going back and forth and staying up there at Rhode Island, trying to hit Festa, but one time they had gotten stopped, and they had a driver's-license check, so that blew the complete deal, as they asked the guys what they were doing riding around that area so much. Bear told me they told them they were looking for some property . . ."

The assassins had been given the wrong address—the Festas were still in Cranston—and Festa had not yet arrived there when they made the trips to Smithfield. There were only Marie, Rose, Janet, and the four bewildered children, none of whom was having an especially pleasant time, though at least they had a yard to play in now. Alicia was suffering fevers so high she had to be taken to the hospital, and Joseph had developed an infantile hernia. The illnesses aggravated the household tension. Rose and Marie—who, besides her heartache over Pinkie, complained sourly that no buses ran by their place, that they had to walk in plain sight to get to the grocery store, and that no church was nearby—began to argue with each other. "Who cleaned out our house?" Marie kept asking. "Rose, it's impossible. Our home, all that stuff, and all they can get from it is a laundry basket with my winter coat in it?" Rose became so upset with Marie that they discussed her going back to Scranton to hide out with her sister. But that was too dangerous, and so was Marie's proposition that she be allowed to go with a guard back to Ridge Street, so she could see for herself. Rose told her to forget about it, and to stop mourning the dogs. "Oh, no," Marie said. "When you love something you just don't forget about it." She was constantly crying.

It was something of a relief to put the kids back in school, even if Marie and Rose were nervous until they were home safely each afternoon. At first Sophia kept forgetting to sign their new name on her class papers and a confused teacher called Rose to ask why a girl registered as "Mitchell" was insisting that "Festa" was her name. Rose made up a story about having just been divorced to explain the discrepancy in surnames. Alicia also subconsciously resisted the idea of "Mitchell," but as the older of the two, she was more careful to obey Rose and keep her distance from the other students; when Sophia began to be too friendly with a girl in her class, Alicia dutifully mentioned this to Rose, and Sophia—in a storm of tears—was ordered to tell the girl they could not be friends. The only excuse she could think up was that she "didn't like the girl no more."

At the end of April, Festa joined his family. His face was emaciated, and he weighed a mere hundred and fifty-five pounds (compared to periods when Marie's pasta had ballooned him to more than two fifty). But after a six-month absence, his reappearance, however gaunt, and however tense, was dramatic to the children (though baby Joseph did not recognize him at first).

Marie cooked up spaghetti and meatballs, but everyone was too excited to eat much. It was Christmas, Thanksgiving, and the Easter they had missed rolled into one.

Festa was also too emotional for sleep. That night he spent hours with a note pad on which he scratched criminal names and characterizations for cops, agents, and prosecutors. "Teddy Riviello: Tommy DeMarco [owner of the diner] is Andy Gerard's man. Teddy has to have an OK. Teddy's connection for guns in Maine [is] the gun shop. Dr. G———. Very close to Joe P. and Bear. Teddy did things for him in '67. Herky: used to be Teddy's partner . . ."

The next morning he walked Sophia and Alicia to school so he could acquaint himself with the landscape, and after that he spent most of the day inside with the shades drawn.

On his second day in Rhode Island he met with John Partington of the Witness Protection Program, who had asked him to list those who might be after him. "It could be anyone," Festa told him.

Partington had been with the alias program since its very inception, and his involvement in concealing the identities of government witnesses (which would number some five hundred before he left the program) dated back to the crime-busting era of Robert Kennedy. He told Festa flatly that no one was ever in more danger than he. "You," he said, "are the hottest potato going." He warned Festa to limit his contacts with any local police.

Festa was irritated at the atmosphere of the Cranston house. The rented furniture looked to him like it belonged in a trailer, and eight people were crammed into two bedrooms and on a pull-out sofa. But a feeling of normality had been filtering into their modest, government-subsidized homestead. Rose had purchased towels, linens, dishes, and kitchen utensils, and a work uniform for her husband (the dark shirt he had on looked like he was ready for a score). As if in further celebration, Rose extracted from their monthly stipend of $1,080 enough to stock the freezer and prepare a turkey dinner for his third day home.

After the feast he decided to walk Allan to a drugstore in a small plaza down the street where he could get the kids some book covers for their school texts. It was just a couple of doors up and a left at the corner, where there was a bank. On the way he passed a Dunkin Donuts in the plaza, noticing, amusedly, that a patrolman was in there with a girl on his lap. At the drugstore he bought the school supplies and some candy for the kids. It was nearly dusk. He and Allan headed home.

As he passed the doughnut shop, Festa noticed a police van pull up and a sergeant get out—trouble, he figured, for the amorous patrolman. As he watched that small drama he also happened to glance across the street and caught sight of four men talking in front of a tavern, Kathy's Den. Three of the men had their backs to him. The fourth he recognized at once. It was Cabert's associate, Gerald Sperduto.

Festa grabbed Allan and dodged behind the pillars at the bank. He waited there for about two minutes until Sperduto turned away. Then he walked quickly down the side street, saying to his son, "Don't look. Don't talk." Once they were in front of their house he hoisted Allan over the bushes—threw him, really. "Get in the house," he whispered urgently.

Too panicked to think, Festa at first hurried on past the house and down the street, figuring it would be best not to go inside. Then he realized the senselessness of that: If hitmen were just around the corner, the mob already must have his exact address. It was not as if they were up there randomly searching for him.

He headed back to the house.

Marie was in the bathroom, Rose and Janet watching television. The girls were getting ready for bed.

Janet had heard Allan's commotion in the shrubbery and, looking out the window, had seen her father briskly walk past the yard. Allan had run inside crying, "Dad just said get in the house. He's afraid." A moment later Festa burst in breathlessly, moved a coffee table against the front door and shoved the handle of a lawn mower under the latch of the rear one. "Rose, they're here," he said. "It's a meet. They're on the corner."

She said, "Jerry, how could they find out where we are? We been here for months."

"You only seen these people one way," he barked back. "I know how they operate. It's a meet. I seen them. They're here and the only reason is for me."

"Are you sure?" she asked again.

"Sure," he said, scurrying around the house, and trying to pump thoughts into his own head. "Sure as I see you there."

He telephoned Partington. "Do you have a partner?" Partington asked, meaning a gun.

"Fuck no," said Jerry, anguished. "Fuck no. I just been gotten out of jail, chrissakes." Partington was skeptical about such calls. In his long experience he had heard too many witnesses cry wolf. When one's life was in jeopardy it was easy to act without rationality; he remembered that the most celebrated of all informers, Joe Valachi, had murdered a fellow prisoner he mistakenly took to be a killer.

Partington told Festa to get hold of Wilson in Newark. Rose helped him dial—his fingers were clumsy with excitement. They managed to catch Wilson through the emergency number, and the agent said he would check right away.

There were maddening phone calls back and forth. It was getting dark. That was what the hitmen—if they were hitmen—would be waiting for. Jerry screamed on the phone to Partington, who had not yet received official permission to take action—he was awaiting word from Newark.

"C'mon," Festa shouted. "This ain't no party. They ain't gonna bust in here at your convenience."

In their room, Sophia and Alicia were sitting rigidly on their bed with Joseph, listening to the tumult in the other room. It was not unlike the night of the bust. Alicia said, "Someone's after Dad again."

Janet had spent nearly three months practicing what she would do if just such a thing happened, if one of the kids, coming home from school, happened to spot Uncle Frank. Outwardly she was remarkably composed. Actually her heart pounded in the wash of fear.

She went with Marie into the bedroom to see that the windows were securely fastened shut. Marie told her nieces to get up and dress, and to help put some clothes on little Joseph. "We're leaving," Janet solemnly announced. The girls watched as Marie once again threw underwear, nightgowns, and a change of clothing into a small suitcase and brown-paper bags. Then she took the children up to the dark attic.

In fact the whole house was dark now except for the porch light.

Time was dragging as they awaited the phone's next ring. Dan Williamson, a federal attorney, called. His voice was cracking. "Sit tight, Jerry," he said. "They're going to pick you up. Don't move. Don't run. Lock the doors."

Festa could hardly hear the words. He was nearly screaming—*was* screaming—at all of them. Wilson had sent an informant out to the streets—to the night spots where Festa's colleagues hung out—and this confidential source had quickly established the situation. "Look, Jerry," Wilson said. "We got the word. They got you spotted."

Virtually certain now that an assassination attempt was imminent, Partington set about organizing a detail of police to accompany him to Cranston, and arranged for a substitute place to take the Festas. Approximately two hours elapsed from the time Festa sighted Sperduto to the time when sufficient clearances had been made, and information culled, and details ordered, for action.

Fearing that in the commotion one of the hitmen might sneak through a back window or into a bedroom and try to kidnap one of the kids, Festa and Janet huddled the children together on the floor of the living room, where they clung to Marie. "Just be quiet," Marie calmed them. "Don't say *anything*."

Janet peered from a side window, then watched the front. As she did this she heard a rustling around the house, bushes moving. She had planned to throw the children out the back way if gunmen rushed the house, but now it seemed to her as if someone might be ready to attack from there also.

Maybe it was just her imagination, those sounds. She didn't scare, at least didn't panic, easily. Not for nothing had she gone through those similarly harrowing times when she thought Fran was going to actually slice her with that cleaver, or dump her back in the closet. She had kept her cool then. She would keep it now too.

The girl looked over at her father, who was watching the street from the front-door window, off to the side, so they could not see his face from the road. Jerry and Janet kept looking back and forth at each other. Rose was watching them from the couch.

They saw a green station wagon pull up in front of the house, directly in front of it, and halt there. Janet glanced back at her mother. Somehow Rose knew. She had a look of horror on her face. She had been watching their reactions, knew something, someone, was out there.

Festa thought it was the marshals coming to get them. The horn sounded. Two beeps. "Let's get the kids and go," he said, reaching for the door knob.

"No!" Rose and Marie shouted simultaneously. Marie said, "Are you crazy? Don't go out there! It may not be them. It could be the other people."

"That's not the way the marshals work, Jerry," Rose said frantically, breaking out of her paralysis of terror.

Then she nearly began to be resigned to what might happen next. Which was no longer unusual, not for her. God knew how many times she had nearly been killed before, riding around with those drunken hoods. And if not death by accident, well, hadn't there been times—in the house of detention, or when her stepfather was on top of her, groaning—that she contemplated suicide?

The next minute passed with paranormal slowness. As Janet stared at the vehicle, she counted five men in it, and she could tell they were looking directly at the house, waiting for some cue. She was also convinced by now that the silhouettes, the thick silhouettes, belonged to some wise guys she had seen before, and her heart slammed against her ribcage. This was an indescribable moment for her—eight years later she would still be haunted by it, still unable to find the appropriate words. But she mustered strength enough to look up at Jerry and see that his face was grave and the color of plaster. She tried to give him a sign, a gesture of encouragement, forming her hand into an upraised, clenched fist, as if saying to him, "We're in it together, Dad. We're with you." As they waited for the car doors to open she was absolutely certain she and her family would soon be dead.

Festa's eyes were wild with fear. This was some homecoming gift for his young family. Thoughts flashed through his mind about how they would do it: front through the window; no, just barge right in; no, through the side; no, through the back and front together. He expected them to rush the house soon.

Certainly he was already lucky to have lived as long as he had. Forty-four was not such a bad age to go—he had lived a dozen lives. Maybe Marie was right when she said that there must be Irish angels looking down kindly upon him. Like the time he came out basically unscathed when his baby pajamas caught fire as he was sitting in a high chair, and when he walked away from totaling a car, or up in the hills, when Donnerstag didn't turn his gun on him. He always got out of everything.

But maybe there were dark angels too, and maybe it had come to be their turn.

Just after the car beeped, something made Festa switch off the porch light. The people in the station wagon seemed to react to that. The wagon began to move, then bolted up the street. Perhaps it was because the men had seen cars coming up behind them. Marshals, cops. It was Partington and four police cars, quickly sealing off the street.

Partington went up to the house. He knew something had happened. They were barricaded in there. He rushed them into the cars and back to the Howard Johnson's in Seekonk, where they would spend the night. Alicia was sick at her stomach. Rose took enough Valium to pass out. And Janet tried to comfort her father. His hands were trembling. He broke down.

They had to be shipped off somewhere in a hurry, somewhere far away. Neither Wilson nor Partington knew what to expect next. It seemed as if there were columns of cavalrymen out there trying to find their man. And the WPP bureaucracy was not moving fast enough, seemed always to jam. Partington decided to put the family in the hands of a western deputy marshal, Bud Warren, an Indian "who could shoot the eyes out of a frog at fifty feet."

The next day, in the afternoon, they would be flown through Boston to Chicago and would change planes for a destination, a state, Festa had never even heard of before. Their new home, he was told, would have to be Fargo, North Dakota.

* *

Donahue's desk was a mess. It was jumbled with folders, mugshots, rap sheets, a calendar, manila envelopes, and green message slips—a dozen of those. He wore a white short-sleeved shirt, freedom for arms which were always reaching, waving. He was a study in perpetual motion, that was the least that could be said: working the phones while answering questions for an assistant prosecutor while introducing to the staff a criminal he was ready to interview while coordinating some warrants or wiretaps. Neat paperwork, scheduled appointments—that was for lawyers. Donahue had a big room's worth of file cabinets in his head.

The special grand jury unit had moved into a conference room on the third floor and an office that had shredders, specially locked files, and a sink and stove for snacks and hangover remedies—it was the intelligence room, but Ronnie called it the Kitchen. There were dull gray cabinets, a graceless drop ceiling, and, in the background, always in the background, the shouted complaints or catcalls or whistles from the adjacent Essex County Jail.

This was where Ronald Donahue somehow worked his miracles. This was where criminal confessions and cooperation poured forth. He played "straight down the middle" with the thugs, did not manufacture evidence against them, did not promise what he could not deliver: "Hey, look, you did something wrong, now you're gonna have to even the score and do something for me. And if you do something for me, we got a game plan." That simple, that direct.

Or was it? There was of course more to it than that, and whatever it was had helped him, in his career, turn around a number of improbable cases, solve some especially baffling and grisly murders. This was because, beyond his words, he had the same energy of attraction Festa did. But Ronnie's was a higher power.

Where there were a great number of Jersey cops who had profited by cooperating with the wise guys—and had large automobiles and new suburban homes—Donahue was an unpretentious man who wore scuffed loafers and lived modestly with his wife and four children and a huge, lumbering mastiff called Sir. There was something gratifying about "doing the right thing," fulfilling "a piece of what I'm here for," and when his children asked why he didn't make as much money as the neighbors, he said, "I'm a cop. That's it. That's what I gotta go with." Cracking a case gave him a push, a "rush," that could not be purchased with a bribe. Once, Donahue was working the bizarre case of a wealthy woman and her daughter found hanged in their home in Upper Montclair. The case obsessed him to the point of taking to the streets at ungodly hours, coming home just long enough to talk to his wife about it over a hurried meal, meditating on it while he was taking a bath. He solved that and other cases in this fashion. The answers didn't come sitting behind a tidy desk.

He had first seen Festa when he was coming out of the interrogation room after the murder arrest, and while many of the cops and prosecutors considered Jerry fierce, or at least intimidating, Donahue figured him for a "big country boy" who was in over his head. Ronnie knew Festa was not like Donnerstag, a "stone killer," and he sensed immediately that Festa was in desperate need of reassurance and guidance. He spent hours talking to him and Rose, and many more than that soothing him on the phone. For here was a man who now was totally friendless.

There was a suffocating amount of work to be done, and though

Festa's life was in serious danger, all the more reason why the cases had to be pulled together fast. Donahue and his partner, Joe Martino, the tenacious detective who had followed Freda around, began compiling burglary and arson reports, checking back in murder files, and, with four guards in an undercover van, taking Festa to the Newark streets so here too he could point out the places his crew had robbed.

What Agent Wilson had set in motion was quickly evolving into perhaps the biggest case in the county's recent history—in terms of both the kind and number of crimes. Donahue knew the turf pretty well, but Festa was turning him on to an "unbelievable crew of guys," and though he bore them no personal grudge, he and Wilson were going to come down on every criminal they could, putting them where they belonged and should have been long ago: in prison.

If the maneuvering by both Wilson and Donahue was a study in superior police work, so was the prosecuting end, that length of rope held by Falcone. Though, as an attorney, he was more orderly about what sat on his desk, Falcone (the name means "falcon") too was a rugged operator, certainly a vigorous operator, a weight lifter, a guy who had played stickball with soon-to-be wise guys in the Newark streets. From his neighborhood Falcone knew of Freda, Cabert, and Vinnie Tursi, and one of his closest boyhood friends would do prison time as a bookmaker. Falcone was not a Boy Scout. By the age of twelve he was necking with the girls in the movie houses and getting into schoolyard scraps and hanging out with a gang called the Condors and sneaking off to the halls to jitterbug—not learning how to tie a square knot. But he did not drink cough medicine or sniff glue to get high, and he was not especially impressed by the sharpies who wore ostentatious hats and ran the numbers. His idols were Mickey Mantle and his own father, a Sicilian tile contractor who had drilled into him the necessity of school. His dad just might raise a hand to him if he didn't come home with an arm-aching stack of books. At the same time, Falcone Senior would not tolerate his son's taking any guff from the bullies. He made him go back—as Joe did—and finish the fight.

That influence had propelled Falcone past high school (where his average was 99.4, and he was sports editor of the paper) into college (at Rutgers, where he majored first in premed, next psychology) and (changing gears) through Rutgers Law School in Camden, from which he graduated to a clerkship for a state supreme court justice and soon into the prosecutor's office, in 1969. He met Donahue that year, and he too was taken by the homicide detective's warmth. At the Christmas party, Donahue noticed that Falcone hardly knew anybody, and so he took the young lawyer and introduced him around.

The rapport Donahue and Falcone established with Wilson nearly equaled their own compatibility. Instead of creating a climate of competition between the state and federal agencies, the FBI agent exhaustively sought to tie up every loose end of what Festa told him, whether it was a federal or a local case. Ronnie might get mad at him sometimes ("Hey, you're from *California*"), but both men were experts when it came to informants, and they had the deepest mutual respect.

Because most of the crimes Festa "gave up" were state cases, as opposed to federal ones, much of the burden in actual case making fell on the Essex County Prosecutor and, to a lesser extent, the Lackawanna County District Attorney. All three men were convinced that, despite the pressure of uprooting his family and trying to stay ahead of pursuing killers, Festa would be an unprecedented witness. "We could tell," says Donahue, "that he was giving us everything. That he was giving us a hundred percent, a fair shake." He could recall the minutiae of the burglaries so well that to Donahue it was "like he had written the original police reports." Everyone had an anecdote about Festa's memory: that besides how much they stole, and precisely how it went down, he could recall the color of walls, or the number of second-story steps. Despite a disorderly, rambling way of recounting a story, and a poor recollection of chronology—for he had not worked by a calendar schedule—it was fair on the whole to say that Jerry Festa's memory was eidetic, an astonishing camera into the past.

As Festa's questioners continued to compile incident records and dossiers, cataloguing them and preparing the basic information needed for an indictment, it became clear a major bust was in the offing, one that in real importance and in the degree of criminality involved would substantially exceed previous breakthroughs such as the 1969 roundup of gamblers, or the much-publicized 1960s wiretaps on Sam DeCavalcante and Gyp DeCarlo. The taps may have revealed more direct information about the top echelons of the mob, but before Festa was through, according to the FBI, his testimony and information would lead to at least two hundred and thirty-three indictment cases, twenty-five of them federal and two hundred and eight New Jersey and Pennsylvania state cases. (And at that, the FBI's records may not be complete; for one thing, they do not include certain local spin-off cases whose records have been scattered.) It can similarly be estimated that between one hundred and two hundred law enforcement personnel would have some form of involvement in the case, whether simply to arrest a suspect, deliver a burglary report on him, guard him, or spend hours interviewing him with a recorder. Though Festa's rise in the ranks had been modest, he had forgotten virtually nothing and nobody.

Frazzled by what appeared to be efforts to set him up by some of the Newark marshals, Festa would arrive at Donahue's office by way of a locked fire stairwell and through the rear of the building. The shiny dark exterior reflected the scurrying bodyguards. He would grab the rail and pound hurriedly up the echoing steps in the gray stairwell, entering a hall only after marshals had thoroughly scanned it. In the interview room, near the stairs, any unexpected noise—a knock on the door, or a file falling—made his heart constrict. He hid behind an office door when anyone came into the room, and kept his head bent low as he ran with his bodyguards in and out of their vehicles.

Meetings on how to get him were being held all over town, but nowhere was the congregation more harried than at one of his favorite hangouts, DeMarco's diner on Bloomfield Avenue, where Adams, De-Marco, Gerard, and The Bear met often (and within range of a police bug) in the back kitchen. They brought in Quartuccio for some of the discussions, and Carmen Malavenda (who arrived at one such session wearing a suit of Festa's). One conversation went something like this:

"Oh my God, I'm done, I'm done," said Quartuccio.

DeMarco asked, "How much did you tell him about me?"

"I didn't say nothing," insisted Johnny. "Nothing. I don't know. I took two busts with him—honest. No, no, never said a word. He probably—an undercover all along, son of a bitch. I can't run. Where am I gonna go? I'm a broken-down burglar. I got nothing."

"Who you bullshitting? Get to your [safe-deposit] boxes."

"I don't got nothing. My car—it don't even run. Held with wire. I'm destroyed. I'm destroyed." Johnny's voice was high, whimpering.

"Well, maybe Chicken Delight's gonna get some fucking of his feather's plucked," said an unrecognizable voice.

DeMarco commented, "That no-good cocksucker. You brought him around!"

Johnny: "I'm dead, I'm dead. Pennsylvania. Here. I got everything on me."

"You better make sure he don't hit the stand," said a voice.

"What about Paterno?" Quartuccio asked.

"Don't worry about that," said Gerard.

DeMarco: "We got people working. We'll see where he's at."

"What about his family, his kids?" asked Gerard.

Johnny replied, "I don't know. The fucking government's got 'em."

"The guy was so quiet," said Andy. "How could he know so much?"

Johnny: "He knows everything. Been all around everybody. Ray's going crazy. I got a meet with him tonight."

"Yeah," said DeMarco. "The Bear's coming in. We got a meet with Valvano . . ."

"Honest, honest, on my life, I didn't know," pleaded Johnny, who was himself soon to offer the cops intelligence information in return for clemency. "It's because The Jew—the fucking big-mouth motherfucker fucking bastard. Andy, I'm dead. What does Biagg [Campisi] have to say?"

"Say?" said DeMarco. "Out of his mind. All of 'em."

Johnny: "Oh Jesus Christ!"

In Pennsylvania, Jerry Donnerstag had spent these months impressing the Scranton jail with his melodramatic show as the big-time gangster, looking solemn, talking only briefly, pointedly, causing every inmate to fear him profoundly. He was also the Good Samaritan. Put in charge of the canteen, he saw to it that all the stealing stopped, and he helped save the life of a kid who hanged himself with a belt. To the guards and the assistant warden, who would vividly remember him many years from now, Donnerstag was a smooth operator who talked about what a good "family man" he was (his listed hobbies were fishing and playing with children), and he expressed shock and dismay over the number of young guys who were brought to the jailhouse. He couldn't understand their using drugs. ("I can't see their sticking that stuff in their arms," he said.) He was cool, clean-shaven, "knew how to do his time well," as the assistant warden would remember. But he was rarely without a Lucky Strike dangling from his lips, and he had stomach pains that placed him in the infirmary. On March 29 his mother had flown up from Florida and managed to raise fifty thousand in cash and fifty thousand by bond to bail him out. Donahue was quite aware of his impending release, and had him under surveillance as he left Pennsylvania on a snowy night and entered New Jersey only to find the detective waiting, at ten minutes to seven, to arrest him on a new charge: the slaying of dope dealer Tony Garcia, whose body Ronnie had seen on July 5, 1971, on the banks of the Passaic River in Livingston, hidden in a clump of bushes with a quilted jacket pulled over his head.

"Ah, c'mon Ronnie," Donnerstag said.

"Sorry," said Donahue. "Come on. Let's go."

Working with the greatest dispatch, Falcone and his unit, which included another assistant named Michael Steiber, organized the indictments that were coming out of the grand jury, and, working with some sixty police officers, arranged for a large, sweeping bust. On May 16, a mere three months after Festa began to talk, these policemen were sectioned into teams of four or five men each and provided with a package of papers describing whom they were to pick up, the number of their car licenses, where they lived, where they worked, where they played; and they set out with Falcone's warrants. That was a Thursday, and by the weekend about thirty men had been arrested for charges by the state and federal governments, among them Tommy Adams, who, because of his reputation, was picked up by Donahue himself.

Adams just shook his head. "I got problems."

"You sure do," Donahue said.

The Bear was in a bathrobe when Wilson went for him, and Quartuccio was apprehended entering Freda's construction offices in Morris County. Johnny was indignant. "Why you bothering me? You can't believe that lying motherfucker, he's getting off with murder. I'm a broken-down burglar. Why you bothering me over this? Over this?" Also detained was Sergeant Ray Grill. He was again suspended from the force.

There was one hitch: No one could find Raymond Freda. But the gangster telephoned Donahue, saying, "Hey, Ronnie, how ya doing?"

"Well," said Donahue, "I got a warrant for your arrest."

"Ah, that's bullshit," said Raymond. "Tell the judge I'll be in Monday morning. I got a house I'm working on. Half the side is torn off, and it might rain this weekend."

"I can't do that, Ray," Ronnie said, knowing that Freda was simply waiting to see what the bail would be, so he would not have to stay in a holding cell. "I'll find that house if I have to."

"Well, then I'm not coming in," Freda said. (Indeed, he would not appear until the following Monday, after his bail was set. He had slipped out a window when the cops came to get him.)

On Bloomfield Avenue, crap games were being moved or postponed as the mobsters tried to guess who would be next. The Pennsylvania authorities were also bringing charges against The Bear, and coming down with a vengeance on Bob Martin, whose wife, Shirley, dragged into her husband's crimes as Rose had been, now had a federal charge against her. As he had so accurately predicted, Quartuccio found himself under an "avalanche"; in Pennsylvania, thirty-one indictment counts were returned against the thief.

If Festa's life on the streets had been a hectic one, on the other side of the law, as a witness, he was even busier. Though it was being postponed because of a change-of-venue ruling (transferred from Scranton to Wilkes-Barre), the Donnerstag murder trial nevertheless was gearing up, and Festa would be occupied for months at dozens of preliminary hearings in Dunmore, where, by another order of the court, all the other cases in Pennsylvania had been consolidated for reasons of both convenience and security. (These hearings were to establish prima facie evidence against the defendants before each case was presented to a grand jury and the Court of Common Pleas.)

The magistrate to whom the task of hearing all these cases fell was Michael J. Polizzi, who ran his court behind a glass-and-brick office front on Blakely Street, a hilly avenue of gas stations and fast-food enterprises. Among the prosecuting officers, ironically, was Lee Mecka. He had apparently forgiven Festa and his escape through the woods, for he was so friendly he brought pitchers of water to the star witness. Marshals and troopers swarmed around the tiny office. They guarded the arrival-cars so no bombs could be planted, and mounted the roof of an Arco gas station across the way with rifles and binoculars.

The depth of hatred for Festa was expressed succinctly by Martin, who, at a July 15 hearing, screamed, "You may be going to run a kangaroo court here, but I don't have to sit here and listen to it." He tried to leave the room but encountered a wall of police in the adjoining chamber, struggled with them a few moments, and returned handcuffed to his chair. When mention was made of a contract to kill Festa, he shouted at the court, "A hundred thousand? I'll do it myself for free."

Festa was being hidden in a motel in nearby Clarks Summit, or in a two-bedroom apartment at the Tobyhanna Army Depot, an hour's drive east. The caravans transporting him back and forth to the hearings took circuitous routes so they could not be followed, and as certain plots against the informer found their way to the FBI's attention, he was moved time and again. Partington himself had flown in to survey

Polizzi's office, along with the Scranton marshal in whose hands Festa now was, Edward Scheu. Neither Partington nor Scheu (an experienced bodyguard once assigned to Joe Valachi) liked the location of Polizzi's office: precisely one hundred and one steps up the street was an old and decrepit white apartment house, within clear sight of the office and four stories tall. Later it would be alleged that Freda and Quartuccio were perched there on occasion with a high-power scope rifle, and in fact had gotten the Festa entourage in its sights, only to be discouraged by how well Jerry was shielded by his guards. Another deputy, Richard Callaghan, spotted suspicious onlookers from one apartment window, and during the hearings at Polizzi's word was sent that the mob was ready to make a move by throwing a pipe bomb or a grenade through the front window. Court was stopped, and the guards rushed Festa out an old back door of the office by prying off a wall panel and breaking the lock. The door led into a beer distributorship in a connecting building, where Festa was snuck past twenty-foot-tall stacks of Heineken, Ballantine, and Moosehead beer cases to another set of cars (a "gun car," a "principal's car," and a "follow car") waiting for him at the side.

There were other ominous signs during these and subsequent hearings. A car with New Jersey tags was parked for days at the downtown Holiday Inn in Scranton, and, with the local police, Scheu walked about ten miles around and through the city looking for other suspect cars. At Festa's father's house, the next-door neighbor heard a prowler at two o'clock one morning and, looking outside, watched as two men (one quite heavy-set and in his forties) slipped through her back yard and up to the window of an annex in which Jerry's father kept his tools. "These were not your normal burglars," she later commented. "They stayed for only a moment, peering in there, and both were wearing suits."

At the other end of town, Rose's stepmother received a strange phone call. A sweet-talking woman said she was a friend of Rose's and urgently needed to get in touch with her. Rose's stepmother did not buy the ploy, and her stepsister, a feisty woman named Margaret, got on and began to tell the caller off. Soon a male voice came through the receiver: "We know where they're at. We know they been in touch with you."

"Who's this?" the stepsister demanded. "Who is this?"

The voice said, "You'll find out, lady." With that these two women were also taken into protective custody for the night, and armed guards were posted at Jerry's father's house.

But Festa, through his own wits and the efforts of Special Agent Michael Wilson, was surviving; and in the Federal Strike Force office in Newark, the names of additional mobsters were attached like targets to a chart on the wall. The rapport between Festa and the authorities was not always easy: Festa was livid over the loss of his house and business, and let both Wilson and Donahue know it. "Forget it, I quit," Jerry would yell. "I ain't testifying. Fuck youse."

Wilson screamed back in the emotional atmosphere, and after the same kind of heated exchange with Festa, Donahue laid it out: "Fuck you too. You don't wanna do it, don't do it. We'll just go to the judge and you can go back to jail."

Festa continued to cooperate, however, not only as a duty now, but almost as a mission. On June 27, 1974, at his second appearance before the special Essex Grand Jury, he had sounded evangelical. "[Before] I wouldn't talk to nobody," he told the jurors. "I finally met two [sic] people . . . Joe Falcone . . . Mike Wilson from FBI, and Ronnie Donahue. I wanted to get out [of organized crime] a long time ago. I couldn't. Only one way out: in a box. Once you're in you're not getting out . . . And believe me . . . watch your grocer, watch your milkman, watch your meter man," he said, referring to those from whom he had gotten information. He told the jurors it was "all in your hands . . . and there are gonna be a lot of badges to get tarnished." He further spurred them on by explaining the power of Gambino and Paterno: "If you keep them on the street, Newark is done." The strike forces, he emphasized—and his own role as a turncoat—had caused the city's gangsters to begin distrusting one another. "You're breaking them. They're running scared."

Who could dispute the last remark? More busts would be coming down: On September 13, a Friday, a second major arrest sweep would ensnare twenty-seven criminals on more charges. Festa appeared as a surprise witness in the trial of Donnerstag's vicious assistants, Joe Zelinski and Joey Bontempo, helping Lombardo convict the duo of robbery, kidnaping, and, in Zelinski's case, two murders.

Nor had the chieftains been totally untouchable. Early on, the SCI had subpoenaed Capo Joe Paterno to appear before its commissioners. And faced with that, Paterno, in March, had permanently fled town.

III. Under the Hoodoo Star

FAR FROM THE STILL backwaters of the Atlantic, balls of thistle moved on the sorrel prairie like litter down a Newark street. There were no sirens to be heard in the distant nearness, however. Only the lowing of cattle.

The North Dakota hideout had seemed a welcome reprieve from the horror that visited them in Rhode Island, but the very first evening they had settled in for the night, in Fargo, the sky turned violet and an odd calmness descended on the fields of barley. Out in front of the hotel, farmers were pointing up at a funnel cloud. The cloud had never formed into a tornado (which occurred so frequently here that until recently not all of them were even reported), but it had sent Rose hiding in the bathroom and the children under the beds.

Fargo was a small agricultural city of sixty thousand citizens, and the decision to move the Festas here was based on the indisputable conclusion that the East was too hot, and was getting hotter. The FBI was preparing for the first federal trial of Jerry's former buddies—interstate theft charges against Quartuccio, Martin, and Jay Weisman—and both the mob and the FBI gauged it as the test case: if the prosecution was successful, in a trial based entirely on testimony from the Festas, then all the other hoodlums would fall.

If this was going to be the way of life from now on, Marie almost wished her cousin would stop talking. She and the children were in their own sort of prison because of it. In fact, on the urgent flight from Rhode Island, Marie had hurriedly put on a blue denim shirt jacket Jerry had worn while he was in custody. It was so long on her that it hung past her knees.

The deputy marshal in charge of the family in North Dakota, Bud Warren, was unsympathetic to their plight. He was of no mind to cater to a criminal. "I'll get you a job as a cab driver," he told Festa. "But I'll have to tell them you're a murderer." Jerry came close to punching him in the mouth.

After a week in the hotel, where once again the children were getting claustrophobic, Warren took them to a little old house, completely unfurnished, which the WPP rented for them. There was virtually no money left from their last monthly stipend to set up housekeeping—they had of course had to leave behind their food stores, heating oil, and utensils—and Warren brusquely told them there wasn't any place to rent a bed or sofa. That put Marie into a frenzy. Jerry and Rose had flown off to New York for the legal work, and she was left as the steward of a situation she did not fully comprehend. She was, more and more, realizing the immense dangers facing them. Before, her mind had rejected the notion that all those men she had served coffee and dinner to would think of harming her or the children. She "hadn't known them that way."

And how could she side with the cops? She had seen them at her dinner table too, one of them in uniform; and as she understood it, they were lookouts on the scores. Nobody had ever explained to her the real doings of guys like Basto. She hardly knew them, and they would not even remember her name.

But she had learned a lot that hideous night in Rhode Island, and no longer did Frank Basto seem like a "gentleman." She too had been sure he or his cohorts were going to break in on them; she too had been ready to die. Yet she'd found it in herself to keep the children tranquil, talking to them as if everything were normal, and she attributed such strength to the Blessed Mother and Saint Anthony. Anthony had been her favorite patron since childhood. Her mother always told her he was the one to pray to if you lost something dear to you, and when, as a schoolgirl, she misplaced a new spring coat, she took her mother's advice, and sure enough she found it in the unlikeliest place: a box in the basement. Later on some lost rings and earrings were found by the same method. So Saint Anthony was her guiding force, and that was why on Allan's second birthday she was angry when Donnerstag—trying to curry favor with the family and show that, despite what had happened to Jed, he possessed higher thoughts—had given the child a Saint Anthony medallion.

But Saint Anthony would be hard-pressed to come up with all she had now lost. The house was one thing, her insurance and her pension, another. Still, what really got to her, what she could not erase from her thoughts here in North Dakota, were the material possessions of sentimental value: the knickknacks, silver, and wine glasses handed down from her mother and indeed her grandmother; the good pots and pans her mother had slaved for; the fancy tablecloths, crocheted bedspreads, dresser scarfs; and the doll collection—hundreds of dolls from around the world which she had accumulated since her early days in Scranton. The collection was going to be her great gift to Alicia and Sophia, what they would remember her by when she passed on.

There would be no place, *could* be no place, to remind Marie of her losses more powerfully than North Dakota. Their house had no beds, no chairs, no tables, no curtains, no pictures, no radio, no television, no books, no plants, no dresses, no dishes, no pots, no silver—nothing in the way of utensils. While the days were warm enough, at night the air of the Red River Valley dipped into the thirties, and there wasn't a blanket in the house. The refrigerator did not function, and there were no toothbrushes, no toilet tissue, no glasses, no towels. And no phone.

All they had at first was a shag rug, and that in itself was a problem. The previous residents had kept a bunch of cats in the house, and so the floor on which they slept (huddled tightly together to keep warm), and on which they were forced to sit all day and eat their baloney sandwiches, was heavily infested by fleas. Alicia was naturally the first to encounter them—red blotches on her legs, and little lumps. At first they figured it was another of her allergies, but then everyone got itchy and red and they had to spend food money for some sheets and insecticide to cover the floor. (Years later, both Alicia and Janet would bear reminder scars on their legs.)

Except for Janet, the children still had little idea of why they had been thrown into such an upheaval. They didn't know what Daddy had done. Before he left for pretrial conferences, Festa had sat Alicia and Sophia down and explained that they were in "trouble" but that "it ain't gonna last long." Alicia kept to her theory that it had something to do with thievery—those jewels she had peeked at on the dining-room table. But that did little to explain the "weird" places they had been, or why their mother and Marie had been so ardently repeating to them that they must watch out for strangers, that they should respond to no one who wanted to give them a ride. Marie didn't let them play in the yard now, unless she herself was out there hanging what little laundry they had, and boredom set in, those many days of merely sitting in a nearly barren house on an itchy floor. They had a few coloring books, but those were quickly completed and the crayons worn to their nubs. Hide-and-seek would have been fun, but since that "scary" night when the station wagon pulled up, and they were all pushed into cars with motors racing, straying anywhere out of sight was against Marie's rules; and in the house itself, of course, there was little to hide behind.

What Sophia wanted to know was why, for the second time in just three months, she and Alicia had to practice writing a new signature. Back when they were in school in Newark, it had been enough of an achievement learning how to spell their real name. Then suddenly their name was "Mitchell"—was it two "ls" or two "ts"?—and when they got to Fargo, the "guy with the guns," their deputy marshal, told them their name would be "Newton." That sounded weird to her, and at the motel registry the clerk had looked up funny at Daddy's strong long Italian features when they told him their new name.

Sophia was a dark-haired girl, and like Alicia she was tall for her age, and thin. She was the least prone to depression and in a quiet way possessed the best sense of humor. It was Alicia everyone had to worry about. She threw those fits occasionally, and was always sickly, like her mother. Asthma had strained her respiratory tract, and a cold soon developed into pneumonia. Where Sophia could slough off the pressures and confusion, adjusting to whatever needed adjusting to, Alicia was preoccupied by how strange her family had become, how Marie was no longer carefree and happy. She was cursing now, and crying at night over Pinkie.

But it was their aunt who was holding them together, she who in many ways had come to be almost their mother. It was Marie who kept them from succumbing to the stark tedium, making up fairy tales, telling them ghost stories. At night on the floor of the dining room they all listened for imagined bears and wolves in the woods, pretending they were huddled near a wood fire.

Janet could not sleep. She was plagued by headaches that had turned her morose, puffy-eyed, and, being the eldest child, she felt the family's security rested on her frail shoulders. Hour after hour she sat on the screened porch taking note of every passing automobile. Periodically she ventured out a few blocks to call Agent Wilson and make sure nothing had happened to her parents. Before Rose left, Janet had also gone with her mother to find a general store, and there, with what money Rose had saved from expense funds, they had purchased a few essentials: tissue, blankets, plastic forks and spoons. They had stocked up on lunch meats and bought the small boxes of cereal which could function as bowls.

Janet did not like it when Allan wrestled too hard with Joseph. She was leery of any loud sounds. One day she was sitting against the wall napping and there was a sudden banging against the windows which sounded like gunshots; luckily it turned out to be another example of the strange weather of the prairie: fifty-mile-an-hour winds and half-inch hail.

"That's all we need," she thought. It was dark enough without a storm. Most of the light fixtures did not work, and in the whole house, there were only two incandescent bulbs.

She needed no one to explain the dangers. Johnny might have been a comical character to some people, but then they didn't know really all he had done to her. *It had not been just once that he had molested her, she claimed, not just some drunken rush of juices; no, it had been an ongoing thing, a cold, well-planned pattern. He had approached her the first time in the bathroom and Marie's room, where she was getting Sophia (then only three) ready for bed. He had rubbed against her funny and she complained, "You're weird. Don't touch me." That night he snuck into her room and knelt next to the bed, then leaned over her. "If you don't do what I say I'll kill you." She tried feigning sleep as he did his thing but it was hard not to notice, especially those times he held a gun to her head and ripped her from her vagina to her anus. Glamorous gangster he was. She let him do this for months before her father discovered it, and then when he was back on the scene later, and her father in Lackawanna County Jail, he would gesture at her lewdly as he was leaving the house and make "perverted" phone calls, like "I miss being next to your pure white body." He would circle the Chicken Delight while she was working and just stare at her, and then call her from a pay phone near the Pathmark.*

Somehow Janet's traumas did not make her resent her adopted Dad. He was warm to her—certainly warmer than Fran—and she looked upon him not as a criminal who robbed people (just as others now had robbed them), but as a "good provider." As far as "fathers" went, he was all she had known, and in North Dakota she kept imagining a phone ringing, and picking it up only to find that he was dead. She also feared for her mother, who was acting different lately, like "someone who belonged in an asylum."

So she wondered, "How's Dad? Where's Mom?"

Rose was in a hospital in Boston. She had been sent there by the Federal Strike Force as soon as she finished a grand jury appearance in Newark, for they saw that she was shaking like a leaf, and that she was down to a hundred and twenty pounds (where normally she weighed over a hundred and forty). And she was absent-minded, forgetting nearly everything they told her.

Festa had complained about her condition to Wilson and Dan Williamson, the strike force attorney, and, upon seeing her, they sat her down to ask how she felt. She could not talk; she was choked with tears.

The government hospital was an old, dreary place, but Rose was content there, thankful to be away from the urgent problems. She could have stayed for a month in a lightless closet. She just wanted to be by herself.

She was worried that she had her mother's genes, and that like her she would lose her sanity. Something inside her was failing. She was too weak to walk far, and often she couldn't move once she lay down. For long periods of time she made her mind go completely blank—no images, no internal dialogue. If anything, she imagined she was on vacation somewhere very distant. Nothing had happened. Nothing was wrong.

She was more miserable than her husband about turning on guys like Frank. Jerry realized he could hold nothing back, but Rose felt he talked too much. That, she said, had substantially increased their danger. The clincher now was that she was being sucked into the federal case, and Wilson had brought her under heavy guard down to Rich's Pawn Shop on Broad Street where she had identified a number of stolen items. Despite the FBI's security efforts (she had been surrounded by every available agent), the experience had badly rattled her: in one box was a pair of gold earrings hocked there by the man whom she considered the most sinister—Freda.

Yet she knew it was only right that she testify. Had she not benefited from the crimes? Loved the jewelry? And could she not have made it easier on herself by disregarding her fear of Jerry and listening to Marie, refusing to help with the scores? She'd known it was wrong, but hadn't seen, hadn't wanted to look at their victims' side. Now that her own family had lost all their worldly belongings, look how destroyed they felt.

Not since Feldman's murder had she felt so dark. This time violence was being done against her own children. She wondered if she or Jerry could ever forgive themselves. Were the kids safe out there? Were they eating? Warm? Crying for her?

She put them out of her mind. The guilt was maddening. When she thought about them she would sweat and shake, and in the night, if one of her kids' faces popped into her head, she called a nurse for more Valium.

She didn't want to talk with anybody. She rolled on her side and stared listlessly out of the window when the doctor was trying to tell her something. Only twice did she call the strike force, and they told her what she wanted to believe but did not: that everything was all right. Fine. The doctor, feeling something was seriously wrong, wanted her to take a breathing workup. But at this point the results were hardly a concern to her. She wanted to run off again somewhere, and she gave some thought to killing herself.

She thought back to her rape as a child, her stepfather coming into her room with Noxema on his face, ready for bed, but wanting to get rid of some urges first, and looking like he had a Halloween mask on his face. That ghoul! In retrospect, there would never be anyone she hated more, nor feared more, than he. He was the very worst memory she possessed, the most difficult to extract, worse than thinking about the murder or Rhode Island. Worse than seeing her mother with the bowl-headed nuts in the asylum. Quite some life she'd had. Had anything not *been crazy? . . . But she'd had some small revenge on her stepfather when he got sick with tuberculosis and was in the sanitarium. He was sixty-four and a shriveled-up sight and she had visited only out of respect for her stepmother. She told him off. He had once made her consider suicide, and now she suggested—right there at his bedside—that he end his own life. He was trying to get her pity. She had none to give. "If you really love mom you'll take a pair of scissors [and kill yourself] so mom can have a life of her own." Then she said, "The next time I'll see you you'll be in a casket." Which damn well was nearly the truth. He died a few months later from internal bleeding.*

Michael Brown 250

She was at the hospital at the time, and she went behind the curtain when she saw he was taking a turn for the worse. She wanted him to die alone.

As she herself headed toward the brink, into that abyss her mother knew, Rose began to fight hard against the tug of insanity. Every time she felt herself near it she let the kids back into her mind, cried, then wiped them out again. Another week of nothingness would pass. She did not read, talked to virtually no other patients. She only pecked at the hospital meals, drifting under the surface, losing more weight, down to a size nine from thirteen. Jerry arranged a clandestine visit, but she wanted to hear nothing about what he was doing. She only wanted to evaporate.

Rose had recurrent stomach ulcers, fibrosis of the lungs, unfocused eyes, and her arms and legs felt heavy all the time. Here she was a woman of thirty-six and she could not walk more than a couple of blocks. And there was a mass in one of her lungs. A doctor there suggested further medical observation, but Rose was shocked to learn that she had already been in the hospital for two months. She had to rejoin the children (who had been moved, she learned, to Texas). They would settle in Houston, in a better home in an urban setting, the government decided. They also had been given choices of Virginia or California, but Texas seemed the safest spot for permanent housekeeping.

Before that move could be accomplished, however, there was the legal business at hand. More indictments needed to be put together, and there was also the federal trial.

*   *

"Festa was hid out well," laments Freda, who was charged with burglary and armed robbery. "We couldn't find him. It's hard to find a guy out of state. Bear had told me after several meetings that the only chance we had was getting Festa in Newark . . . [There] we could buy our way out of most anything, except for the new strike force. They were tough, and they meant to convict people. It was the first time the feds and [county] really worked together in something, as the FBI never did trust the Newark police—they would do scores with you, set people up for a hit. Very few [of those] cops had a good word for Detective Donahue. He was a rotten bastard to them. You couldn't buy him, and he would send anyone to jail that committed a crime.

"Bear had found out that they were bringing Jerry Festa in from the back of the courthouse through a stairway. But the [deputy] marshal told him they had to be very careful, as the Newark task force and FBI were there to meet them. They had to call ahead to say they were coming. At the door where Festa was being brought in there were some old houses back there, but it was risky, as there was only one way out. If you took the other route, it went around the jail, and there were so many guards from the jail around, and the prosecutor's detectives, that you were bound to get caught. Bear checked it out a few times. He said there could never be a hit made that way. At that time I told Bear that the only way [it] could be done was with a rifle."

At the Holiday Inn near Kennedy Airport in New York City, where he was staying, Festa's nervousness had caused a bare spot to appear on his head and jowls. He was quaffing Maalox and complaining of chest pains. He could not eat. He felt the presence of his enemies everywhere. Near a restaurant he recognized a guy whom he knew to be the son of a New York button-man, and after spotting Festa and his entourage this man dashed for a pay phone inside. The deputies chased him down the street away from Jerry.

He kept thinking about Johnny Quartuccio and his rifles. The time Johnny went on that rampage against his wife, he had killed her Pekingese dog with a single dead-eye shot from the window. And dogs like that were small. No one would tell Festa why, but suddenly he would be surrounded by twelve FBI agents as he went into a hearing, and two of them went with him to the john.

Wilson was moving like a besieged field commander, trying to keep his vital witness alive. He had heard much about Basto even before Jerry turned, and the craftiness of The Bear's crimes convinced him again that the gangster would find a way of getting Festa. The young agent kept in contact with his secret sources, consulted Donahue and Falcone on an almost daily basis, and heard rumors from honest deputy marshals or others who had an inside ear. And he was always on the phone to other agents. As an added precaution, Festa was often debriefed at the Gateway, where the FBI had rented offices, instead of at the task force offices on Broad Street. At times the whole process seemed disorganized, but such glitches were not due to any incompetence on Wilson's part. Rather, they stemmed from the complex, chaotic nature of Festa's former colleagues and his criminal life. Jerry breathed turmoil, and it was difficult to separate imagined dangers from those that were undeniably real. Though he did not say much about it, as the trial date approached, Wilson, on occasion, was himself being followed.

During the first week of September both Rose and Janet were flown in from Texas to join Jerry for the big trial. After the burglary of a doctor's home on July 7 of the previous year, the two had been sent by Festa, Quartuccio, and Martin to Tampa, Florida, where Weisman paid handsomely for the take. "If we win this, everything else will be easy," Wilson told Rose. "You *have* to win this trial."

But for a long time she was adamant about not squealing on Basto. She said she would talk about anyone but Frank—an insistence that infuriated the agent. He threw down his briefcase and shook her out of her stupor. "This is a man," he shouted, "who plans to kill your son."

As September 11, 1974, approached—the first full day of his actual testimony—Festa paced all night practicing his ability to remember. He understood the importance of winning only too well: a jail sentence still hung over his head, and the authorities would not be so likely to influence the sentencing judge unless their cases had been successful. And it was not going to be easy. Weisman had hired an excellent attorney, Arnold Levine, a former federal prosecutor, and he had filed a flurry of pretrial motions to suppress evidence, seeking inspection rights on just about everything Festa had done in the past and what he was doing now, even the records of his phone calls since he had been in protective custody. The trial began with United States Attorney Daniel Williamson's remarks about his key witness. "Mr. Festa is a professional thief," he told the jury in a packed courtroom. "He is going to tell you that. Mr. Festa has been burglarizing and committing these crimes for quite some time." No one was pretending he was a nice man, Williamson was saying.

As Festa entered the courtroom through a side door, in a wave of marshals and FBI agents, he spotted his peers at the defense table. Martin had his head down, but Johnny was looking up at him anxiously, for any sign at this final moment that his friend might recant. At the courtroom entrance a metal detector like that used in airports was in place and everyone was searched for weaponry.

"GERARD CHARLES FESTA, called by the Government, sworn."

"Sir," said Williamson. "Will you please state your full name and former address, please, for the jury."

Festa mumbled the answer. "Speak up so they can hear you at the end of the box," said the judge, Curtis Meanor, an outdoorsman with straight white hair and a tan.

"Do you know the defendant John Quartuccio?" asked Williamson.

"Yes, sir."

"How long have you known him?"

"About seven years."

"Is Mr. Quartuccio in the courtroom?"

"Yes, sir."

"Could you point him out, please?"

"Standing right there, standing up."

"Do you know Robert William Martin?"

"Yes, sir."

"How long have you known him?"

"A number of years."

As the preliminary rituals went on, the door in the courtroom opened, and all eyes fell on Frank Basto, who was making a show of his entrance, settling himself in the most obvious of locations: directly within sight of Festa in a seat near the front.

Festa looked at him nervously. Basto gave him that cute smirk. A smile. He formed his right hand to look like a handgun and motioned as if pulling a trigger. It was difficult for Jerry to regain his composure, but he did.

"Mr. Festa, how did you come to burglarize Dr. Grossbard's house?" asked the prosecuting attorney.

"In the middle of June, around the middle of June, I was with Frank Basto, myself, Johnny Quartuccio, and Robert Martin up in Hackensack, New Jersey, at Garden State Coin Company. The owner at that time was John Sarapucciello."

"Is Mr. Basto in the courtroom today?"

"Yes."

"Would you point him out?"

"Sitting right there."

The defense attorney, Levine, interrupted. "Is he a defendant? I don't understand who he is pointing out."

Judge Meanor said, "I don't know what the purpose of it is."

"I object to this kind of display," complained Levine.

"Is Mr. Basto here?" inquired the judge.

The Bear said, "Yes, Your Honor."

"Stand up," said Judge Meanor.

"I am a spectator," said Basto.

"For some reason," said Judge Meanor, "counsel wants the witness to identify you. He has done it. Please sit down."

Basto was displeased. "He's got his point across," he said.

Now Williamson: "You testified that Mr. Basto, yourself, Mr. Quartuccio, and Mr. Martin went to Hackensack, New Jersey?"

"Yes, sir," said Festa.

"What happened there?"

"Frank Basto and myself was in talking with Garden State John, as I know him, and through the conversation Garden State John had told us about this Dr. Grossbard; that he had sold him quite a lot of coins and it would be a good house to burglarize."

The judge asked, "Who is Garden State John?"

"John Sarapucciello, sir. He gave us the address and we left. Went out to my car."

Jerry next explained how he, Quartuccio, and Martin cased the house, learning it was not alarmed. Before he got to the details of the actual entry, a lunch break was declared, and Festa waited for the jury box to empty before he was ushered to a side room by the phalanx of bodyguards. (This was done so the jury would not become prejudiced against the defendants because of the security Festa needed.) He was then transferred to a secret location and returned to the courtroom at two-thirty. By this time it was obvious he was going to be a significant witness, perhaps a superb one—steady, sincere, and his memory coming up to speed. In the spectator rows, watchful gangsters were ever more apprehensive. Austin Castiglione rolled his eyes and wrinkled his nose menacingly.

In the afternoon Festa continued: "At that time we then came down around by the garage where they had the car parked. And then we seen the car was not no Buick, no Mercedes, and it didn't belong to the Grossbards' residence, where the doctor and his wife lived."

"Was anything said at that time?" asked Williamson.

"They were going to go back again a second time."

"Who said that?"

"Johnny Quartuccio."

"What did he say?"

"He said, 'We will go back in. I just found something.' They claimed that it was locked, and this was why he wanted to go back in for a second time."

"Did Mr. Martin and Mr. Quartuccio return to Dr. Grossbard's home?"

"Yes, sir. I drove down, dropped them off at the house before Dr.

Grossbard's. They got out and proceeded in again. I then proceeded down, made a U-turn, came back around, and parked at the same spot where I approximately was before, where I could keep the house under surveillance."

"At this time that you're doing the surveillance, are you alone in your car?"

"No, sir. My wife was with me."

"And what happened at that point?"

"Approximately about fifteen or twenty minutes later the porch light went on in the rear. A lady came out, stood on the porch about a second, walked off the porch and walked to the curb of the street, and it seemed like she was waiting for the law. I felt possibly maybe they had made some noise in there and she had called the police. I again blew the horn three times, again, and pulled down, turned around and started to come up, and at the time I was coming up Robert Martin was crossing the street going down towards Johnny Quartuccio's car. I then made a left, went down towards Johnny's car to find out where Johnny was. He said he was in the bush. I told him a lady had come out and was standing by the curb, and it looked like she was waiting for the law. He started the car up and pulled up ahead of me to go and pick up Johnny Quartuccio. I noticed the same lady and man talking with a police car. I believe it was a police car.

"Bob then went and made his turn, picked Johnny up, and I went down past the garage. I think there is a driveway down there. I pulled in, backed up, and came back up. That's when we proceeded back to my home at Ridge Street . . ."

Stepping in for a vigorous cross-examination, Levine grilled Festa on the deal he made with the prosecutors. He wanted to know how the gangster had prepared for the case, and what documents he had seen beforehand. Soon enough it turned into a sparring match, with Levine complaining that "the witness seems to have a proclivity for answering questions that don't exist." At a sidebar conference, an assistant prosecutor working the case, Jim Deichert, told the judge that Levine was raising his voice to "get to the jury." Levine was hitting again and again at how Festa had been granted leniency for what he was saying. The previous Monday, murder charges against Jerry had been dropped.

"Did you understand that you could not come up for sentencing in Pennsylvania [for other crimes] until they were satisfied that you had fully satisfied your deal, that they were going to hold off as long as they could?" Levine asked.

"As long as they could, yes," answered the witness. "But how long that would be, I was never told whether it would be after I'm finished or not." And on this went.

The judge: "It is four o'clock, adjournment time. Please be back in your jury room in time to resume at nine o'clock tomorrow morning. I wish you a pleasant evening."

For Festa it would hardly be that. As the marshals began the journey back to New York and the Holiday Inn, they spotted a Newark city patrol car tailing them. The cops stopped near the city line, and as the cavalcade of three federal cars proceeded east, another tail, this time an unmarked automobile, picked up where the police car had left off.

Someone was trying to find out where they were going. To ditch the tail, the marshals spent two hours on back roads and opposite-way highways before taking Festa to the hotel. At eleven that night, Festa, his wife, and Janet were rushed out of the hotel to a motor lodge in Hempstead, Long Island. A bomb threat had been made against the hotel.

Freda would remember it this way: "Festa was being followed from the back of the courthouse to New York. He was kept in a Holiday Inn in New York, but after careful checking out the hotel, it was taken notice that U.S. marshals had the complete floor of the Holiday Inn, just as told to us by U.S. Marshal Bove. The marshals had the first room and they had the floor pretty well guarded. They also took their witnesses to eat with them, when they didn't eat right in the Holiday Inn. You just can't lurk around the Holiday Inn parking lot. While checking the lot out he [The Bear] had noticed many U.S. marshals' and government cars parked at the hotel."

So they wanted to pry Jerry out of there, get him somewhere else. And in addition to the Newark marshals, they were being helped by somebody in the city's police department.

All night Festa walked back and forth. He chatted with the deputies at their command post in the hall, wanting to be near their guns. Exhausted, Rose tried to fall off to sleep, but her husband kept coming in to talk. "Now they know I'm a scumbag," he told her, pushing his hands through his hair. "They know I'm gonna go through with it."

They were picked up at six in the morning, leaving time for a quick breakfast (or in their case a few gulps of coffee) and a long, circuitous trip to Newark. Levine hammered away at the close relationship Festa had with the FBI, tripped him up on a few dates, grilled him on the FBI interviews. He launched into an elaborate litany of the crimes currently known to have been committed by Festa—including, unsurprisingly, the Feldman homicide—and focused on those that were most embarrassing.

"Do you have an outstanding charge relating to a breaking and entry February 11, 1972, of South Catholic High School?"

"I don't know."

"You don't know?"

"I don't know. I really don't know."

"Let me make a note of the things you are not sure of," Levine said sarcastically.

But Festa was remarkably candid in admitting guilt to his other crimes and was learning some courtroom finesse himself, turning the tables on Levine.

Levine: "And do you know any other outstanding charges other than the twenty-two or so I read here with the Commonwealth of Pennsylvania that are outstanding against you?"

"Yes, sir."

"I can't hear the witness," said Levine.

Judge Meanor looked at the defense lawyer and said, "You better approach the bench." Whereupon, at a sidebar conference, the judge told Levine that Festa had "leaned over to me and indicated to me that there are others, and that Mr. Weisman is involved in them . . . So be careful."

Levine grew outright hostile. In eliciting one answer, he said, "I'm not asking you to do anything. I'm telling you."

"Yes you are," Festa bellowed back. When Levine attempted to pin him on the time and location of meetings with the federal agents—hoping, obviously, to give the jurors the impression that Jerry had been schooled as to what he should say—Festa grew indignant. "Mr. Levine, it's none of your business where I was at that time. It's not to be told where I was at that time." He felt Levine was trying to find out his hidden location.

Further along in the questioning, which would consume the entire morning, and run into the afternoon, Festa explained that although Weisman paid eighty-three hundred for the haul, he and Rose had told Quartuccio and Martin that Weisman had paid only twenty-five hundred dollars, neglecting to include a diamond ring which had fallen off the dining-room table as they had dumped the pillowcases of jewelry there. In other words, everybody was trying to cheat everybody else.

Michael Brown 258

Rose had picked up the ring and slipped it in her pocket, and then all of them had lied to Basto about the true value of the rest of the score.

Levine said, "So all of you stole from the doctor?"

"All of us stole from each other," Festa said.

"Well, let us take it in steps. I want to make sure that is correct. "All of you stole from the doctor?"

"Yes."

"And [the] three of you stole from Basto?"

"Yes."

"And then you and your wife stole from Martin and Quartuccio, is that right?"

Festa said, "And Quartuccio stole from us."

The jury had been retired at ten forty-five for an hour, and as the trial resumed, Deichert complained at the sidebar that Basto, who had come back into the court not long before, was again trying to psych out the witness. "It has been brought to my attention that Mr. Basto was sitting in the front row and repeatedly made gestures such as putting his finger across his throat, holding his hand as if it was a gun to Mr. Festa while he was on the stand," Deichert said. (To prevent further histrionics, an FBI agent named John Thurston took a seat next to the gangster, telling him not to use his hands for anything. "If you got to blow your nose," said the agent, "let me know. I'll get the handkerchief.")

Martin's attorney, a public defender, next took a shot at cross-examination, but his assault was brief and clumsy. He confused the two other defendants, twice referring to his client as "Robert Quartuccio." He attacked Festa's claim that Janet was really his daughter, saying that she had been fathered by Martin, and he rehashed the burglary, eliciting the fact that Festa and Quartuccio had entered the premises several times previously before pulling the actual score. Responding to the queries, Festa described the home in careful detail: "It is on a corner, on the main drag. It is a white house. The windows are taped on the first floor. You go in the front door, open the front door, it goes into an alcove. This door leads to a porch. This is a side door, where the key is for the alarm. The next door over it has a little window. It heads upstairs to the doctor's apartment. There is a little table right on top . . ."

Levine repeated his questions about Festa's arrangement with the government and his criminal past. There was constant concern among the agents that if Levine knocked Festa down here, all the wise guys would go to trial instead of copping pleas, and perhaps successfully repeat Levine's defense. No one could be sure how a jury would take to relying on a former hoodlum. But Festa was getting more impressive as the hours—the long hours, with the roar of landing jets in the background—wore on. He learned quickly what was admissible and what he could not say, and called for his own sidebar conferences with Judge Meanor.

Milling around in the corridors, the gangsters talked about his coolness on the stand. They were surprised. And irked. After the first day of trial, the Essex County Prosecutor's Office had taken advantage of the mob's congregation to issue many of them additional indictments—part of the second bust—as they left the building. "You're not gonna win," one of the hoods told Wilson. "He ain't gonna last. It's just a matter of time."

Some of these comments found their way back to Festa, and though he had contained himself on the stand, Basto's attempts to intimidate him in court pushed Jerry over the edge. Leaving court with his bodyguards, he turned to face Basto straight on, and pointed at The Bear's face. "You," he shouted to Frank, "you're fucking done!"

When the time came for Rose to testify, she was so upset, and so full of sedatives, that she seriously feared she would not be able to speak. Coming into the hall with her ten bodyguards, she spotted her former neighbors, J. B. and Josephine DeVingo. They had their heads down as she approached. Festa's first wife, Dottie, was also there, to testify for the defense. Rose stopped. The deputies had to push her forward. The first person she saw inside the courtroom was Frank Basto, and she froze again, as if in shock. They got her to the witness chair. Johnny craned his neck to stare at her, and in the audience she saw Martin's wife, Shirley, who had been a close friend back in Pennsylvania.

Preoccupied with avoiding The Bear's eyes, Rose raised her left arm instead of her right one as the oath was read, and spoke so low and haltingly that she was nearly inaudible. First she was asked to describe the Festa household and who had lived with them. As she began what would be many hours before the jury, she noticed that Agent Wilson, whom the defense had not allowed to be present in the courtroom, was peering in through the glass panel of a door, tiptoeing high enough so that she could see him and giving her a clenched fist—making sure she knew he was there, rooting for her. She tried to concentrate on his help-ful cheerleading as Williamson took her through the mechanics of the crime:

"They drive down a few doors and let me off. I walk up to the doc-tor's home. I entered the front door, which is open, and I knock on the door to the right of me. After a few minutes a man appears at the top of the stairs, picks up what appears to me like a key case, and comes downstairs, opens the door, and I ask him the directions to a certain street. He tells me he can't help me. I thank him and leave."

That was why she was brought along—a woman was not so suspi-cious, and she acted lost, like she needed directions, allowing them to see who was at the targeted home. She grew shakier as the day wore on. "Take your time," Williamson said. "Take your time. Relax. If you need some time to stop and think or relax for a second . . ."

Levine interrupted. "Mrs. Festa has not indicated she has a prob-lem."

Williamson said, "She gives the appearance . . ."

"She doesn't give me any appearance," Levine snapped back.

Rose continued. "We went right into our home and proceeded right to the dining room."

"And when you got to the dining room what did you do?"

"John Quartuccio and Bob Martin started emptying the pillowcases onto the dining room table. My husband was standing there. I walked around to the side of the table. As I was going to sit down to look at the items with them, I spotted an article on the floor. I bent down to pick it up, and as I was picking it up I noticed it was a diamond ring." She "sat down for a few minutes, then I excused myself to go into the kitchen where my daughter was sitting. She had been making coffee for them. I handed her the ring." They separated the jewelry and "I went into the kitchen after that to get another cup of coffee, and I asked my daughter had she put the ring away and she told me yes. Then I went back into the dining room, sat down. At this point there was a knock on the door and my husband went to answer it and Mr. Frank Basto walked in, and with him was the man I only know as Pete."

"When they entered," asked Williamson, "what did you do?"

"I immediately went upstairs."

"When you got upstairs, what did you do?"

"My daughter came into my bedroom and I asked her where the ring was. She got it for me. I asked her to get me the jewelry cleaner and I started cleaning it up and trying to decide if it was really a diamond."

When they decided to send Rose to Florida so Basto would not know the real amount of the take, she was terrified—not only because of the crime involved but because she was afraid of airplanes. So they had Janet go along to comfort her. Weisman's office was above a bank, and she was surprised by the beautiful antiques and the Oriental rug adorning it, and impressed that Weisman had a Western Union ticker tape providing information to wholesale coin collectors and jewelers, as well as a high-powered scope to investigate a diamond's quality.

In her second day in front of the jury Rose was still fighting to maintain her composure and to ignore the dangers swirling about them. During their nights in hotel rooms Festa had begun explaining to her more about the violence his cohorts were capable of. Somehow, she told him, she still didn't feel they would harm the children.

"You're in that fantasy world of yours," her husband said.

Levine pounded at her unmercifully. He reviewed again her dealings with the prosecution and her life in crime. To refresh her own memory Rose had made notes on a slip of paper she had in her purse, and Levine caught her off guard when he asked if she had ever written out the facts of the case. She was speechless for a long moment. Did he somehow know about the notes in her pocketbook? And was that improper? Would it blow this whole case? Finally she said yes, she did have some, but she "ripped them up and threw them away."

"And how long had you been living off these burglaries and larcenies and robberies committed by your husband?" Levine asked.

Six years, she said, and began to cry. The judge gave her a handkerchief. That notwithstanding, she managed to tell a cogent, credible account of taking the goods to Tampa, and how the ring she had found on the floor had fascinated Weisman, who cajoled her into selling it for fifty-eight hundred. It was a circular diamond, and it had no black spots—carbon residue—among its molecules. Weisman had seen that through his magnifier. It was perfect, he said.

The trial ran into evening before recessing for the weekend. Wilson praised Rose for her testimony, and she explained that she had been helped along by a man in the audience who kept raising his fist in the air and shaking it, urging her on. Wilson gave her an alarmed look. Urging her on? "What did he look like?" he asked. She described the spectator, and how he had run a finger along the side of his nose and above his lips before shaking that fist of his, and had also bitten a knuckle.

This was no gesture of encouragement from an idle court watcher, the agent immediately realized. He was a hitman. And what he was doing was giving Rose the Sicilian death sign.

Wilson hurried her over to the sixth-floor window of the strike force, which overlooked the court exit. "Point out who he is," he told her as they watched the crowd empty onto the streets. She spotted the spectator, an aging, thick-necked man, heading for a station wagon with Basto and Tommy Adams.

Moving from one hotel to another, Rose, Jerry, and Janet spent the weekend worrying over what awaited them before the trial's end. They were brought their food only by marshals Festa trusted, or whom Wilson had okayed, and they made sure not to leave anything in the room when they left it—certainly not prescription medicine bottles, which had their names on them, or any clothes with labels. If they had to go outside, the marshals first secured the corridors and parking lot, wielding machine guns as the Festas ran past startled maids and room-service staff out the employees' door.

In Newark, meanwhile, Deputy Dick Callaghan was writing a confidential memorandum saying that a New York thug named "Whitey" had been recruited to help get Chicken Delight. With the aid of New York Police Department mugshots and intelligence files, which were shown to Jerry and Rose on Sunday (and a description garnered from FBI agents O'Neill and Thurston, who had also seen the man leaving the courthouse), Callaghan wrote that "an unknown subject made Italian death sign to principal's wife, Rose, as she was testifying," and quickly went on to identify the man as Michael P. Altimari, a *mafioso* from Puritan Avenue in the Bronx who was connected with the Genovese family and Tony "Bender" Strollo. It was also noted that Altimari was closely allied with a Genovese henchman who had been a suspect in the attempted murder of Frank Costello in 1957. Altimari had a record of narcotics and homicide arrests and had an indirect association with a jewelry store on West Forty-seventh Street in Manhattan, where Festa and Basto had gone. In an earlier memorandum, at the start of the trial, Callaghan had written to John Brophy, chief inspector of the witness program, advising him that "a contract to hit subject witness had been given to a made member of the New York family." He recommended continuous changes in Festa's hideouts and protective custody for Festa's father and Marie's sister Josephine, both still in Scranton.

When the trial resumed the following week, Janet took the stand. Though she too was tense—she would see Basto outside the courthouse, stern-faced, the smile gone—the girl appeared remarkably serene. She sat on her hands so no one would notice if they started shaking.

"Do you know Quartuccio?"

"Yes, sir."

"How long have you known him?"

"For about five or six years."

"Is he in the courtroom today?"

"Yes sir."

"Could you point him out, please?"

"Man over there in white shirt, blue jacket." She was steady, unhalting. She testified about the night they came in with the pillowcases, how she was making coffee for them and heard them in the dining room. She corroborated her mother's account of the Florida journey.

At eleven forty-five on the morning of September 20, the jury foreman wrote a right-slanted "G" in each of thirteen slots on the verdict sheet. Guilty as charged.

But there was no time to savor the victory. In two weeks the Donnerstag trial would begin, and before that Festa and his wife wanted to visit the children in Texas. The FBI took them to Kennedy Airport, where a plane was instructed to taxi out to the runway. Then a cortege of agents drove Jerry and Rose right to the plane. The stairway was dropped for their special boarding, and they rushed up the steps, safely out of sniper range.

*   *

Marie had cried when she saw Rose. So had the children. When she rejoined them at The Roadrunner, a motor lodge outside Houston, after her hospital stay, their mother looked like a walking cadaver. But at least they were all together again, which had not seemed likely when they set out from North Dakota. The deputy marshal there had told Marie he could not get a plane ticket for her and she had screamed at him, "What do you mean I can't go with them? I'm not leaving without the children, or letting them go alone. Tell me: How the hell did I get here to begin with? And how did I get to Rhode Island?"

Janet had made a hurried phone call to the FBI, but right until the last day, the Fargo marshal was going to leave her aunt there, penniless, in the empty house.

The problem was that officially Marie was not in the alias program. The government had hesitated to include her because she did not want to change her name to Newton: "Festa" was the name she had been baptized under, one she felt obligated to carry forth, and the thought of relinquishing her heritage repelled her. If she formally joined this program she feared she would never be able to go to Scranton again, and that meant more than the loss of whatever name she might own. She would lose her uncle, cousins, and sister.

Wilson had gotten them out of Fargo after more vociferous complaints from Jerry. "No one ever said it was going to be easy," Mike tried to tell him, but Festa was incensed. He pounded his fists against filing cabinets, cursing about how someone among the Newark marshals had allowed his house to be destroyed and were trying to help those who were after him.

Unsure of what was happening to their parents, and seeing—despite her attempts to conceal her feelings—that Marie was constantly upset, the children began to show physical signs of the psychological burden. Janet's whole head was a switchboard for streaks of throbbing, dizzying pain. A doctor told her the problem stemmed from tension and asked her what it was. "I guess just moving," she fibbed.

Alicia was flailing her arms again, and wheezing, and now wetting the bed. During her fits she felt high, her brain too big for her head; she felt like cutting off the top of her skull. But then the top would start to grow, grow right up to the ceiling, past it, like she was leaving her body. She always imagined someone was behind her. Her eyes were blurry, and she was dizzy. When someone tried to talk to her, their lips were in slow-motion, and she couldn't hear their words, only sirens or "television static" ringing in her mind, making her nearly want to strangle someone.

Yet Marie found ways to control her and the others, even to amuse them. In Houston she encouraged them to play "Blindman's Buff," or to write letters to relatives like their aunt in Scranton, even if they could never be mailed and were in fact thrown away before the motel maid cleaned their room. Away from the terror in Rhode Island, and the awful house in Fargo, Marie again found it hard to believe that Frank Basto—Allan's Uncle Frank—would hurt them, or that it could be so dangerous back home. But an FBI agent was authority enough for her, and Wilson said she could never return to New Jersey.

Along with Donahue and a flock of other detectives and attorneys, Joe Falcone, working seven-day weeks late into the night, was arranging the quickest possible disposition of the cases Festa was giving them. For the most part these charges would be handled by Judge Ralph L. Fusco, another former military intelligence officer who in one wide stroke had scheduled trial dates for thirty-nine of the defendants—including Basto and Freda—in November and December of 1974, and the first two months of 1975. Motions for severances and dismissals began in earnest from the phalange of defense attorneys.

As they prepared for the major prosecution (with the help of Wally Lombardo, who himself caused twenty indictments), the dangers increased proportionately. On October 2, Falcone sent a secret memorandum to the court urging "that at the forthcoming trials before Judge Fusco, extraordinary security measures be taken." Seven of the witnesses (including Joe Carbone) would be "in jeopardy," he emphasized. "Information provided by the FBI indicates that a 'contract' for fifty thousand has been made for the assassination of Mr. Festa. This figure has been increased to two hundred and fifty thousand since Festa's testimony in Federal court led to the convictions of all defendants as to all charges."

With the bounty on his life at a quarter of a million, Festa was understandably skeptical about his own prospects—and hardly able to follow the plight of his own family members, who were beginning to look like war refugees. Marie had only the clothes she wore on the plane from Fargo—slacks, an old blouse—and they were forced to accept poor-box clothing from some friendly local nuns.

Soon after Rose and Jerry arrived in Texas, the family moved into an apartment project near Hempstead Highway in Houston proper. It was a part of the city consisting of body shops, freight distribution centers, and industrial storage facilities—in short, a modern rendition of Newark. Geared to those of lower income, such as immigrant Mexicans, the complex looked like a narrow warehouse, but there were handsome town houses across the street, and their own complex had car ports in the back. On the whole the quarters were satisfactory: furniture at least, and three bedrooms spread over two floors. A sense of serenity again began to flow from these surroundings, and Alicia, Sophia, and Allan were soon enrolled at Saint Jerome's Church Grammar School, which, to Marie's delight, was located just next door.

This had also lifted Rose's spirits, but she was still popping pills and drinking coffee instead of eating, and she often spent the day without saying a word, sitting stonily on a chair in her nightgown. She needed sleep every few hours, and was in no mood to talk with her husband, who, she felt, had neglected their welfare in favor of the legal tasks before him. And she hardly responded to the children. All she could think about were the trials still to come.

And though certainly an improvement on Fargo, their apartment in Texas could not compare with "home." There were the normal complaints about the unfamiliar locale: Texas-size cockroaches, and the sweltering heat. But these were only aggravating factors. Far more dismaying was the reclusive style of life they had brought upon themselves: having always to stay behind locked doors and shaded windows; living in fear of any car sounds in the parking lot; and observing a head of household who, when he was there, would not venture even to a laundromat fifty feet away. Festa had a sawed-off shotgun now, and he got Janet a pearl-handled thirty-five-caliber pistol small enough not to cause a bulge in her purse.

The children were good about not asking too many questions of their preoccupied father. They kept their thoughts to themselves, a repression that triggered more ailments. Allan, who was just beginning kindergarten, had managed a surprising degree of tranquillity for his age, but now the tension was causing him to go into spells of silence like his mother's, and at night he would wake up in a cold sweat, screaming. Or he would be playing in the yard and suddenly run in the house, breathless, red-faced, looking as if he were having a heart attack. He was taken to see a specialist who said there was no organic malady: the boy was suffering from "some potent fright." Usually a pillar of calm, Sophia was finding it difficult to cope in class, and would be made to repeat the second grade. That humiliation was compounded by the dreams she was starting to have: gunmen trapping her and her father along a road and telling him, "Shut your mouth or you'll all get it." She and Alicia were careful about staying away from the road when too many cars were around, and they were allowed outside only at certain times, under the strictest supervision.

On her trips to a public health clinic, where she went for her continuing respiratory distress, Rose disguised herself in sun glasses and avoided crowded avenues, while Janet dyed her blond hair brown and slept overnight at the hospital if her mother was being kept for observation. They took early-morning buses to the clinic and ate breakfast in a Woolworth's, with their eyes trained on the door. Together the family trooped more than a mile for their groceries, pushing the carts along a highway at dusk when the dimness was enough to conceal their identities, nomads at the desert's edge.

During the day Janet remained at home posted by the window. Her father seemed always to be in Newark working with the lawyers, and she did not want to leave Joseph, Marie, and Rose alone. She could not have attended school anyhow: her records had not been transferred. Neither she nor anyone in the house had a full legal identity. At certain times her father would call in coded signals so as not to leave any records of their phone number; he placed person-to-person calls to a fictitious "Dr. Schwartz," which Janet of course would not accept, pretending she was the medical secretary and that the doctor wasn't in. This way she knew Jerry was alive, however.

Donnerstag was next to go on trial, but Marie did not want to think about him. She distracted herself and the children by telling ghost stories from her childhood. One was about an old uncle of hers who had once seen hooded apparitions in the farmlands where downtown Scranton would soon erupt, genuflecting spookily near an abandoned barn. But the most spine-tingling stories had come from her grandfather, who had lived in a house where something kept yanking off his quilt as he slept, and the neighbors told him a young girl had been killed there. That was why it happened, Marie said. There had also been a time when, as a youngster in Italy, walking down a country road, he had heard a baby crying. It was dark, naturally, and he was passing a graveyard when he spotted a bundle of blankets on a flat tombstone. He figured someone had abandoned an infant there, but as he went to pick up the child, it just disappeared. There was a sound like air rushing by. *Swoosh.*

"Could it be that's what's after us?" Allan asked seriously.

"No. Spirits can protect you," she said. And she put no little stock in such tales. Her religious feeling was the all-encompassing sort, venturing beyond religion into the occult. Telepathy, the hereafter, future-telling—all these she found readily believable, and no matter what she told the kids, there were times she viewed their current situation in terms of the supernatural. Jerry was alive not only through the guidance of those Irish angels, she thought, but because of his ESP, knowing what would happen next. Perhaps it was an instant karma that had zapped them since the Feldman boy died. Or spirits like the hooded creatures her uncle saw.

They were being tested, she felt, and if she had taken to profanity since her house and dog had been stolen from her, that was not to say she had stopped saying her prayers, or that she didn't feel grateful that at least they were all alive, had survived so long. It was just that they all had become nonpersons, without a real home, without birth certificates, licenses, school records, insurance, or even a real name. "We exist, yet we don't exist," she said sadly. "This is no life for the kids."

Nor was it a beneficence dealt by entities from a supernormal sphere. If fate was tied to the whirl of constellations, the position of planets, theirs was not the luck of any Irish angels, but fortunes brewed under a hoodoo star.

*   *

The Bear went up to Ray Freda's place in Rockaway. He hardly ever did that. It was a measure of his desperation. He told Ray they had only one major chance left—the Donnerstag case. After Donnerstag, they would be next. They were going to have to make another run to Pennsylvania. And they would have to play it by ear. Bear's contact at the marshals' said he would not know how Festa was transported until the day of the trial. "They would get back to The Bear to let him know how the move was being made," Freda says.

Three weeks before the trial was to open, Ed Scheu, chief of the Scranton deputies and a man with law enforcement experience in New York City, began elaborate preparations for Festa's security, the most elaborate arrangements so far. He held seminars with the local, state, and federal cops whose job it would be to secure the courthouse in Wilkes-Barre. The trial would be held before Judge Arthur Dalessandro. He too would be under guard.

Unconfirmed rumors wildly flourished everywhere: that certain killers planned to bomb the entire courthouse floor, if necessary, or spray Festa's whole entourage with automatic fire. They were ready to go "cowboy-style."

Tightening the noose of security, Partington and Scheu stopped using the local airport in Avoca; for his flights to Texas the marshals drove Festa to Pittsburgh instead. Jerry took to lying on the car floor during the car rides to and from court. But there was little that could be done about his outstanding height. Or the cars. In Dunmore someone had been seen taking down all the license plates of government automobiles.

The state police had a similar (if less intense) concern about Ellis, who would be the second major murder witness. But Hank seemed almost oblivious to such matters. When he caught Festa's eye during one hearing, in Dunmore, he waved at his former boss and gave him a sheepish look. "Hi, Jerry," he said.

On Sunday, October 20, Festa was taken into downtown Scranton for a meeting with Ed Miller, a Lackawanna County detective who had spent many fruitless months investigating the Feldman killing. They had discussed the murder with Jerry many times during the robbery hearings, but both the district attorney and the state police were interested in the one vital piece of evidence that was still missing: the gun. After the discovery of Jed's body, and again when Ellis gave them his statement, there had been several unsuccessful attempts at locating the weapon with a metal detector and industrial magnets lowered into the muck by rope. Frustrated, Sergeant Noel had inquired about draining the pond, but he had been told that it would disrupt the water table of the surrounding corn fields. So at the last moment they made a final effort by showing Jerry an enlarged aerial photograph of the pond and islet. He pointed to where he remembered Donnerstag throwing his pistol. They had already searched that general vicinity, they said, but Scheu spoke up. "Well," he said, "why don't you try a junk-yard magnet?"

The district attorney's office contacted a scrap recycler, John C. Bauman of Carbondale, and by Monday his men were at the spot Festa had indicated, with a crane operator named Lorenzo Beam. At the end of the crane's boom was a one-ton electromagnet powerful enough to lift a car, and mine filings were used to fill in the marshy shoreline and construct a road for the twenty-five-ton crane.

The trial was beginning that very morning. In the heavily guarded courthouse, jury selection had commenced, and to keep the prospective panelists away from any attempts at bribery or coercion, Judge Dalessandro made all the candidates remain in the same room as each was interviewed by the judge and attorneys. There were initially fifty-two potential jurors, with ten more added on Tuesday, but the number was quickly whittled down to thirty, and by Wednesday the final selection was announced: four men and eight women.

Through this all Donnerstag strove to maintain a polite and unflappable image. He had shaved his prison beard and tried in every other way to pretend he had nothing to hide. ("Take my picture any time," he said to news photographers.) As the trial began, Jerry the Jew scanned the room with no show of emotion, calmly watching the guards who had surrounded the place with automatic rifles. The host of undercover agents planted in the crowd to listen for any suspicious conversation were identifiable to each other by small fraternity insignia pinned to their lapels.

At the same hour the jurors were seated, Bauman's crane began making semicircular sweeps into the water, starting from the shore and progressing outward three feet at a time, then swinging back to land eleven times to release metal debris—beer cans, sash weights, fishing gear, a meat hook—which had accumulated on the bottom. There were problems at the end of the ninety-foot boom: the magnet was getting caught in the reeds and lily pads. But Beam handled the controls with delicate precision, clearing it each time, and on the twelfth arc—only fifty minutes after they began—the searchers hit paydirt. Among the litter clinging to the magnet was a partly rusted Ivor Johnson pistol. It was dumped in a bucket of water to deter rapid oxidation and rushed by helicopter to the state police ballistics laboratory in Harrisburg.

Actual testimony began at two-twenty on Wednesday afternoon. After all the spectators had been searched with a metal detector, Ernest Preate, the young assistant district attorney, opened on behalf of the Commonwealth of Pennsylvania, describing the crime as "a case of a hit" which "the Commonwealth intends to prove [was] first-degree murder." Donnerstag's representative, Thomas Livingston, a distinguished-looking lawyer from Pittsburgh, objected to the term "hit" but declined to make an opening statement.

The trial had been moved to Wilkes-Barre because of all the publicity in Scranton over Donnerstag's second charge, murdering Tony Garcia. The move seemed pointless—since Wilkes-Barre and Scranton were so close they shared many of the same television and radio stations—but it afforded the trial an especially majestic courthouse. Set on the shores of the Susquehanna, the cruciform building had a marble dome and a terra-cotta roof. Only two years before, the river had overflowed its banks and destroyed much of the city's business district, filling the courthouse's lower floors with floodwater. But the structure had risen from the deluge with no loss of grandeur: the gold-leaf molding, the mosaics, the bronze and mahogany were left intact; and the courtroom itself, Number One, had silk velour draperies and a mural over the judge's bench: an Indian maiden in a placid sunlit valley. It was entitled, "Prosperity Under the Law."

Though by nature an objective and deliberate man, Judge Dalessandro was bothered by many aspects of the case. For one, he had never heard of a more "cold-blooded murder," and he was fully cognizant of the need for extraordinary security. He himself was given a photograph of Frank Basto, so he would know The Bear if he saw him, and bodyguards were provided for Dalessandro's ten-year-old son. But he found Donnerstag more intriguing than frightening. The hitman just sat there as if getting caught was "an occupational hazard," the judge said, and didn't seem the type to carry a grudge. But Dalessandro was not deceived by such an appearance. He made sure the door near the jury box was locked.

The first witness was sworn. Eugene Telep, who had discovered the body. He was followed by Troopers Gunster and Zanin. They routinely established the location and condition of the corpse, and the original pathologist, Dr. Skovira, somewhat unsettled the prosecution when, under Livingston's cross-examination, he admitted that clinically there was no pure proof whether the bullet wounds had been inflicted before or after the actual time of death. But Dr. Anthony J. Cummings, county coroner at the time of the murder, quickly dismissed such scientific rhetoric, saying that the cause of death could hardly have been from drowning or a coronary, "not with four bullet wounds in him."

His successor as coroner, William Sweeny, then described a second autopsy that had been performed the previous January. The county had hired two New York City medical examiners, Doctors Lowell J. Levine and John Devlin, so the examination would be as thorough as possible. By then the body had been under the earth in a gray metal coffin for nearly three years; skin, cartilage, and muscle tissues had completely disintegrated, and the nose was undiscernible. The flesh sloughed off the skeleton like pudding. And there was a ghastly odor, the smell of gangrene—or "a thousand dead mice," as Sweeny put it. The doctors had to rub Noxema on their surgical masks and even then it was difficult to remain in the room. Though they were down in a basement morgue at Scranton State General Hospital, the stench pervaded the floors above the autopsy room, forcing maintenance personnel to spend three work days spraying aerosol deodorizers as high up as the sixth floor. Sweeny had to destroy his socks, shirt, pants, and Hush-Puppy shoes because of the clinging odors. But after four hours the examiners had found what they were looking for: three additional bullet wounds in the body, which was consistent with the Ellis and Festa accounts of having shot into the dead boy.

Jed's younger sister, Ramona, was brought before the jurors to identify a photograph of the corpse, and she cast further doubt on the desperate defense notion that Jed might have drowned before he was shot by describing her brother as "an excellent swimmer" who "used to swim across a lake" and right back again. She remembered that from a few camping trips the family had taken. Dr. Devlin added wryly, "It's more reasonable to assume that he was shot and thrown in the water than that he was in the water and shot."

As the trial moved into its fourth day, Thursday, it was time for Harold M. Ellis to appear. He was surprisingly good on the stand, except for one suspicious lapse of memory.

"At that table," asked Preate, "what did [Donnerstag] say to you?"

"He said that he had to find a place where we could get rid of the body at," said Ellis, "and I don't remember if I mentioned the place or not."

Hank recalled how he had "turned around and went back towards the road and just as we got to the road, Jerry Festa said that Jerry [Donnerstag] don't like the pond. He don't think he's gonna do it. Just as we said that we heard a shot, turned around real fast and Jerry Donnerstag had his two hands on the gun, just like that [clasping his hands] and he was shooting and you could see the flashes of the gun."

"Do you know where the gun was pointing?"

"At Jed Feldman," Ellis said.

He explained how Donnerstag had ripped up Jed's license "and threw it out the window and his wallet and then started laughing. He said it's the cheapest hit he ever had, just six dollars out of Jed's wallet." The murder, he added, caused friction between him and his boss: "Festa was telling me I wasn't doing things the way I should be doing them."

Before court was closed for the day, and the witnesses and jury sequestered, testimony was also taken from Carbone and Lombardo. Wally's candor made points with the jury, which was amused at the direct examination.

"Are you employed at the moment?" asked District Attorney Paul Mazzoni.

"No, I'm not," Lombardo said.

"What was your occupation?"

"I was a thief."

He went on to describe how he had come to learn about the killing. "I had a conversation with Mr. Donnerstag and in the course of the conversation I asked him if I would be with Jed Feldman [on future scores] and Donnerstag told me that Jed Feldman went away and then he gave me a real arrogant smile, a grin—you know, the kind like the cat that ate the canary . . ."

However, Wally's was hearsay evidence. Hank was the only eye-witness thus far, and the prosecution needed corroboration—someone more detailed, more impressive than poor pudgy Ellis. So, as Ray Freda remembers, "the day had come for Festa to take the stand. Bear had found out that they would be taking Festa to Pennsylvania in a U.S. mail truck. They said that would be the way he would get into the courthouse. Bear and Johnny had made the trip up there just where the court was at, and how they would be taking Festa in there. They had made the run two or three times before Festa was to take the stand." Once they had learned precisely how Jerry would arrive, The Bear's crew staked out the site from every angle—on an overlooking hill, from an avenue alongside that connected with a bridge—looking at the flow of traffic and planting their getaway vehicles in running distance from the scene, with drivers ready. If a gun fight erupted with the police, that would just have to be faced. It was that or concede defeat and go off again to Lewisburg to be caged like an animal.

At six o'clock Friday morning, Scheu and a detail of three Plymouth Furies picked up Festa on the grounds of the Tobyhanna Army Depot, speeding bumper-to-bumper the twenty-two miles into Wilkes-Barre. Check-point cars in radio contact with Scheu watched all along the route, and around the courthouse itself, five blocks were closed to public traffic and lined with state, county, and city patrolmen and detectives, who made these avenues look as if a holiday parade were on the way. Thus Basto was not going to be able to make a run at Festa in the middle of camouflaging traffic, and Scheu further confused the hitmen by sending out a decoy, a brawny marshal in sunglasses and flashy clothes who resembled Jerry. He allowed no deputies except the driver of the car carrying Festa to know beforehand which courthouse door would be used, and he radioed ahead just before reaching downtown Wilkes-Barre, screeching up to a door leading into a basement records room.

Surrounded by a dozen bodyguards, Jerry ducked his head and ran in, followed by his exhausted wife. There were cops everywhere, and each floor was sealed by handcuffs locked onto the door handles. Jerry was jammed into an elevator with agents carrying Uzi submachine guns, then locked into the jury room until nine-thirty, when he entered the courtroom itself. He looked at Donnerstag, who was wearing a col-legiate sweater. Donnerstag squinted and turned his head in the opposite direction. At the bench, Judge Dalessandro leaned to the side of his platform furthest from Festa. The marshals had warned him that anything could happen—even right there, during the proceedings—and that it "would be the most dangerous case I would ever have." The judge had little doubt about that. At the windows, deputies scanned a parking lot on a hill across the street for snipers; others stood facing the rows of spectators or lining the walls.

Wilson, Falcone, and Donahue came in from Newark as a token of support. But Festa was already prepared to convict Donnerstag with a vengeance. He began by describing the last time he saw Feldman and gave the date. Mazzoni asked how he remembered it specifically, and Festa replied, "I could never forget that date."

"Why?" the district attorney asked.

"Because a man was killed," he said.

Festa explained how the Glen Ridge holdup had caused the homicide, and the defense, sensing a strong tide on the rise, moved quickly for a mistrial on the grounds that, by mentioning a second crime, Jerry had prejudiced the jury. The motion was denied. Festa told about the detective who said Jed was an informer, and how they had lured Feldman into Pennsylvania. "[Donnerstag] called him over to the car, he says, 'Come up to Jerry's house in twenty minutes to half an hour. We got a big score in Pennsylvania.' When I say 'score' that meant a burglary or whatever it would be." As Hank had the previous day, Festa recreated the brutal slaying: "I turned around to Hank. I says, 'Why did you find this place' and at that time I heard a shot and we turned fast and it was rapid, a few more shots, boom, boom, boom. All I could see was Mr. Feldman's body going down like in slow motion and he [Donnerstag] spun around, he turned around and put the gun on Hank Ellis and that's when I pulled the thirty-two and I says, 'No, Jerry.'"

The judge took off his glasses and rubbed them with a handkerchief. Just a young kid, he thought. He watched and listened as Festa climbed from the witness box so he could indicate on a photograph where the body was dumped, and discussed the news articles which had been mailed to his house.

Mazzoni then led him through a detailed description of the firearm. "It's about that big and it was about like that," said Festa, spreading his gnarled hands apart.

"Could you indicate for the record the approximate measurements?" asked the judge.

"I would say it would be approximately six inches, seven inches.

The grips were like rubber or plastic with two designs and a design on each side of the grip. Also it broke open."

"The weapon broke open?" asked Mazzoni.

"Yes, sir."

"Was it a cylinder or a noncylinder type of weapon?"

"Cylinder, sir."

"Do you know how many bullets that particular weapon held?"

"Five."

"Whether or not—well, go ahead—you describe the rest of it if you can."

Festa said, "I remember when he was trying to clean it, he couldn't close it, bring the barrel back up, because whether it was warped or the bullets or something, he had to fool around with it before he could get it closed." It was a hammerless type of handgun, he told the jury, "dark, like black."

A courtroom door opened and through it came Sergeant James Deffley, a ballistics expert from the Harrisburg testing laboratory. He walked to the prosecution table and took a weapon out of his briefcase, holding it gingerly in a handkerchief.

Mazzoni strode toward the witness stand. "I show you, Mr. Festa, what has been marked for identification as Exhibit Number Sixteen for the Commonwealth. Please take a careful look at that particular exhibit, sir, and [I] ask whether or not you can make identification after you've had the opportunity to look at it."

"Am I allowed to handle it, sir?" Festa inquired.

"Yes, you may, sir," said the judge.

"That's it," Festa announced.

There was a shuffling among the crowded rows of spectators. Reporters and broadcasters headed to the phones.

Donnerstag rested his chin on his right palm. His mother, among the spectators, looked as if she were ready to collapse. A deputy marshal left for the anteroom to tell Rose the news. "They got the gun. Donnerstag's had it," he said.

But Jerry the Jew's attorney sprang into action.

"Mr. Festa, is this the first time you ever killed a man?"

Jerry was cold and angry. "Sir?"

"Is this the first time you ever killed a man?"

Mazzoni objected. Sustained. Livingston modified his query. "Is this the first time you ever participated in the shooting of a human?"

"You may answer, sir," said Dalessandro.

"Yes, sir," Festa said.

Asked if his testimony was based on the promise of a light sentence, Festa again explained that he would not know how many years he would have to spend in prison until he appeared before a federal judge. Livingston shifted to the issue of Jerry's own feelings toward his former partner, reminding Festa that the previous Friday, when Livingston tried to interview him, Jerry had obstinately refused to answer.

"Do you recall on that occasion indicating to me any hostility toward Jerry Donnerstag?"

"Pertaining to what happened to my house?" He was referring to the way it had been ransacked.

"No," said Livingston. "The question is did you on that occasion indicate to me that you were hostile to Jerry Donnerstag?"

"All I told you at that [time], Mr. Livingston, was whatever I had to say I would say on the stand, and also about my house, a twelve-room house, ripped off of everything . . . furniture—eight people, all their clothes, everything . . ."

Falcone grinned as he saw how expertly Festa was fielding the questions, turning them to his own advantage—how he was learning the intricacies of criminal law. He watched as Jerry called a sidebar conference with Judge Dalessandro to warn that Livingston was leading into organized-crime matters, which could result in a mistrial. Livingston tried to rattle him by asking Jerry to put on the signet ring found on Jed's finger, but this did not seem to bother Festa, and when the lawyer asked if he had ever observed Feldman with a gun, Festa took the opening. "The day Jerry the Jew gave him the gun to pull the Glen Ridge job," he said pointedly.

After three hours of examination Festa was raced onto Route 81 in a diversionary direction from the depot. Near a gas station at an exit, three other cars with Georgia and Alabama license plates were waiting. The trio of additional government vehicles headed in the opposite direction as a decoy while Festa and his ten guards switched into the new set of wheels and sped back to Tobyhanna.

Court was recessed for the weekend. Behind the courthouse, The Bear and Johnny saw a mail truck pull into the drive. But they had been tricked. Festa was not being transported in that, as they mistakenly thought. It was only another decoy.

*   *

The jury foreman was John Burns. In his thirties, he was the youngest member of the panel. He wasn't the shy type, but neither was he overly aggressive, just a guy who worked quietly on a refinishing crew (at the Tobyhanna depot, of all places), and lived in a tiny place called Inkerman. That was near Pittston, a pizza-and-draft-beer miners' town where there was a good deal of Newark-style corruption. Ballot boxes were stuffed on voting day and the names of dead people turned up on nominating petitions. But as far as John Burns knew, Pittston had nobody like the seemingly "meek and humble" defendant in this case. It was extraordinarily difficult for Burns to believe some of the testimony about that man. He was such a well-behaved person, Burns thought. He could not take his eyes off Donnerstag.

The Friday session had ended with Beam pointing on a photograph to the precise spot Festa had shown the investigators on Sunday, and telling the jury that was where his huge magnet had yanked out the gun. Though Sergeant Deffley was not able to prove scientifically that the bullets from Jed's body were from this specific weapon (he had fired it into a test tank, but owing to barrel corrosion the scratch marks did not quite match those on the murder bullets), the Commonwealth's presentation, including as it had four criminals who had worked with Jerry the Jew, seemed open-and-shut.

On Monday, however, as the defense began to present its key witnesses, some of the jurors began to have second thoughts. The focus was the credibility of Festa, who became the target of an *ad hominem* attack.

Festa had known it was coming. Word was that the defense was going to have Darlene and Denise, his two daughters by Dottie, testify against him. Their own father! But really it was not so surprising. They felt he had abandoned them, and Dottie was making the most of this opportunity to strike back.

Livingston first brought to the stand a tavern owner who had seen Festa "numerous times," carrying a shoulder holster. He was followed by James R. Martin, a patron of that tavern, and currently a resident of the county jail—in fact of the same cellblock as Jerry the Jew. In a bizarre turn to the trial, Martin claimed to have seen Festa carrying both a thirty-two *and* a thirty-eight, and said Festa had boasted about killing someone.

"Did you have any discussion with Festa concerning the reason that he killed the man?" the question went.

"Yes," said the inmate. "He had to wipe out a debt in New Jersey. He owed a favor for the big boys in Jersey, he said."

But Martin soon enough alienated the jurors by an exchange with Assistant District Attorney Preate. When asked why he had not reported the conversation to the police, Martin replied, "It was none of my business. I don't care who's killed. I don't care if you're killed."

Much more effective was the testimony elicited from Darlene, who, along with her sister, claimed to have seen a "gun room" at Jerry's house in Newark when they visited. And after them came Dottie.

"How long have you known him?" Livingston asked in his direct examination.

"Approximately twenty-seven years," she said. "I was married to him about seventeen and divorced [after] about nine years. So about twenty-six years I've known him."

There was a sidebar conference at which the prosecution tried to stop the testimony from focusing on Festa's character. But Livingston plowed on. "Mrs. Festa, did you ever observe your husband carrying weapons in Lackawanna County?"

"He came to my house when I lived at 1201 Vine Street and he had two weapons with him, I believe more than once," Dottie said.

She was about to tell the jurors that her husband was not a truthful man, but the district attorney objected and his motion was sustained. Beginning the cross-examination, Preate asked, "With respect to a fight that he may have had with you, did he ever fight with you?"

She said, "We had numerous fights."

"Was one of those fights over another man?"

"It was more than one fight," she said. "He beat me."

Preate was an inexperienced attorney, and the questioning was getting away from him. "Okay, he beat you. Why did he beat you—over this other man?"

"He assumed that we had had a relationship and it was not true," she answered.

"He assumed that you and this man had a relationship?"

"Yes."

"An adulterous relationship?"

"I don't know if you would call it an adulterous [one]," she said deftly. "He assumed, and he took me out and he beat and threw me on the highway naked."

Jed's sister Angie was next, and she too was hazardous for the district attorney. Her relationship with Jerry the Jew had continued even after her brother's murder, and she had been cold toward the prosecution. She was still confused, not convinced that the autopsy photographs were of her brother. Donnerstag, when she visited him in jail, had assured her that he did not murder Jed. ("You have to believe me. This is a frameup.") And during the trial she had a dream in which she saw "Jackie," who told her, "Don't worry, everything's all right." What that meant was not clear, but somehow it had raised doubts in her mind. Anyway, she was not going to hurt Jerry Donnerstag. She got on the stand and said he had been "friendly" to her brother while Festa had been "hostile."

Angie's sister, who the previous week had served the prosecution well, was now appearing a second time—for Livingston—and the district attorney was apprehensive. During a recess he had overheard Ramona being prodded to return as a witness by a private investigator Donnerstag had hired. They were nearly shouting at each other, and she seemed scared. If she was, there was no telling what she would say as a defense witness.

On the stand Ramona confirmed that Donnerstag had treated Jed "very well" and alleged that Festa had "started beating up [Jed] at the house and he ran out, he ran to the park and he hid in the park for a while and Jerry came in a car and started shooting at him and he finally made his way home." She had not brought this out at her previous appearance, she claimed, because the district attorney had told her not to volunteer any information.

Aware that these witnesses were entangled in hopelessly conflicting relationships, the jury was surely more influenced by Dr. Cyril H. Wecht, billed by the defense as a distinguished pathologist from Pittsburgh. Dr. Wecht criticized the initial autopsy report on Feldman (failing as it did to reveal all the bullet wounds), and cast grave doubt that the murder could have happened quite as Ellis and Festa described it.

Were the head wounds consistent with bullets being fired into a free-standing individual?

"Absolutely not," Dr. Wecht said.

"Why?"

"There's no way that a human being, free-standing, would be struck with a thirty-eight-caliber bullet behind the right ear and remain erect so that the second bullet would enter in about the same area, move in the same fashion, and the third bullet would enter in the same area and move in the same fashion and the fourth bullet would enter in the same area and in the same fashion. In no way can this happen with a living human being who is standing in any kind of an unfixed position unless he is wedged and his head is also wedged. There is a tremendous amount of force of a thirty-eight-caliber bullet and you've got four bullet holes located in a relatively close area and you've got the direction of fire about the same, apparently."

Donnerstag was beginning to look sure of himself. This was what he had paid a highfalutin attorney for: to bring in a witness like Wecht. The prosecution raised the possibility that Jed's muscles had locked at the moment of impact, allowing him to remain upright, and that the hair trigger of the gun would allow such rapid fire, but under a second round of questioning by Livingston, the doctor held his stance, saying that the murder, as it was described by the eyewitnesses, was "biologically impossible."

The defense was further bolstered by the position of the bullets found in the recovered gun. The unspent cartridges were on the side of the cylinder away from the trigger, which was inconsistent with Ellis's and Festa's accounts of how the shots were fired. But the major surprise of the afternoon would be the correct-looking man whose life was now on the line.

"What is your name?" Livingston asked of his next witness.

"Gerald Donnerstag."

"And how old are you, Mr. Donnerstag?"

"I was forty-one on October 7."

"Now, do you understand, sir, that you need not take the stand in your own defense in this case?" his lawyer asked.

"Yes. But I want to."

"Did you serve in the military?"

"Yes, I did."

"What branch?"

"The Navy."

"Did you ever receive a commendation?"

"Yes."

"For what, sir?"

"For saving a man's life."

"Do you know, sir, that you are charged with the murder of Jed Feldman?"

Donnerstag's voice cracked. "Yes."

"Did you, sir, murder Jed Feldman?"

Looking on from the jury box, Burns was sure Jerry the Jew was going to bawl. "No," he croaked.

Livingston turned his client over to the prosecution for questioning. There was consternation at the district attorney's desk. Mazzoni called for a short recess and he and Preate argued about what they should do. Normally they would have dreamed about just such an opportunity; now if they didn't seize it and question Donnerstag, it might look to the jury as if they had something to hide. And Jerry the Jew would seem like a man able to withstand any scrutiny.

But on the other hand there were rumors that he had prepared an alibi. Rose had told them that before her husband began cooperating with the government, she had heard talk about Donnerstag and Jerry obtaining bogus airline tickets showing them to be in Florida or Puerto Rico at the time of the killing.

Mazzoni stood up as court resumed. "I have no questions, Your Honor." More shuffling about. The newsmen, and deputies.

Before Judge Dalessandro dismissed the jury for the day, Mazzoni began rebutting the defense witnesses. He brought up Trooper Eugene Varzaly, who described the Feldman sisters as having been "most reluctant" to testify because of their fear of Donnerstag and because Angie told the cop she was "carrying on an affair with him [Jerry the Jew]—course she used a four-letter word." The district attorney's counterattack stretched into the next day, Tuesday, the trial's seventh. Dr. Cummings reappeared in a rejoinder to the defense pathologist, stating his belief that Jed certainly could have remained in a standing position as the shots were unloaded. And this contention was buttressed by Sergeant Deffley, who explained how quickly the trigger may have been pulled: "I discharged two shots in sequence on two occasions and it was within a fraction of a second of one another." He also offered a possible explanation for why the revolver's cylinder seemed to be in the wrong position: it could have been moved that way if the breach had been broken or as the result of someone very lightly pulling on the trigger, unleashing the lock, then manually spinning it so that the bullets were out of position. The obvious implication was that Donnerstag had done precisely that before throwing the guns into the pond. Festa had already testified how Jerry the Jew took his gun and wrapped his shirt around it as if cleaning it. And as for Festa's having a "gun room," Newark Detective Louis P. Maiorano, who had searched the Festa's house after his arrest, said there was no truth to the allegation.

At ten fifty-three that morning, court was recessed so Donnerstag and his lawyer could hear the tape cassette of Ellis's murder statement, which Livingston ardently demanded. In the judge's chambers Donnerstag politely volunteered to plug the recording machine in an outlet.

"Watch you don't get a shock," someone warned him.

"What's the difference," he joked, "if I get electrocuted now or later?" He felt the waves coming against him again, sensed that his defense was faltering. Noticing how thin he appeared, Judge Dalessandro asked after his health—if anything was wrong. "No, nothing," Donnerstag responded. "Except that I'm scared."

As the trial neared its conclusive moments, Livingston began a last-ditch effort to squeeze his client out of his predicament, moving for a mistrial on the basis of a quote in the *Wyoming Observer* by someone in the district attorney's office who had called the recovery of the murder weapon "an act of God." The motion was denied. Livingston also asked to have the jurors interrogated about the effect publicity had had on them, but this time he simply withdrew the motion.

In his closing statement to the jury, Livingston recapped the testimony of his witnesses and advanced the theory that Hank and Jerry "took the victim for a ride, dumped his body in a pond, made up a story" in collusion with each other, and put the blame on his mild-mannered client.

The district attorney's statement lasted about the same length of time: an hour. He asked for a conviction "at all costs, if we are to preserve law and order in the community." Livingston strenuously objected to such rhetoric. Court was adjourned until the next morning. But there was going to be no mistrial. The judge turned to the jury: "Now, ladies and gentlemen, I have given you preliminary instructions . . . The defendant is presumed to be innocent and the burden is upon the Commonwealth to prove the defendant's guilt beyond a reasonable doubt. If, after consideration of all the testimony, there is a reasonable doubt of the defendant's guilt, that doubt belongs to him and should work to his acquittal . . ."

At about four o'clock the jury retired to the fourth floor—where security was better—for its deliberations. It was not a cut-and-dried case. If someone dissented from the majority's opinion, they had a hung jury; Donnerstag would have to be tried again. Burns was surprised at how difficult the decision was. Some people wondered about the technicality of charging Donnerstag with "first-degree" murder.

They wanted a full explanation from the judge on what that meant. Premeditation. Was it premeditated? Well, finally, yes; he did sit there cleaning his guns at Festa's house. But according to whom? Ellis and Festa said that. And the judge had told them to take their word with "caution and care," calling them "a corrupt and polluted source." But, then, there were the two other polluted witnesses: Carbone and Lombardo. And Festa seemed so accurate, and straight, somewhat upset by the murder, trying to clear his conscience. He had made no bones about his criminal past. Plus there was the gun. That was impressive. Festa had described it precisely before it was dramatically brought before their own eyes.

They sent out for sandwiches. The judge said no matter how late, they were going to stay there until a verdict was reached. This case was too touchy for them to be dismissed for the night. In the courtroom Donnerstag's wife and mother sat waiting with Ramona and Angie. Jerry and Rose had spent the week holed up at Tobyhanna, worrying, waiting for news.

At five after nine the jury returned to the room. The judge was summoned; so were the attorneys and the defendant, who was brought in by prison guards. He eyed the jury carefully, looking for sympathy.

The minute clerk said, "Members of the jury, please rise. Members of the jury, have you agreed upon a verdict."

Foreman Burns said, "Yes."

"The foreman will read the verdict," said Dalessandro.

Burns was a guy with two kids of his own, a boy and a girl—young children whom he wanted safe from such criminals. He did not dislike Donnerstag at a personal level, but he said, "We the jury in the above-entitled case find the defendant guilty of first-degree murder." He looked over at Donnerstag and was "astounded." Donnerstag took a slow, deep breath "and became a different person. I couldn't believe it. He had been so humbled and meek all through the trial. After the verdict was read, he got very cocky, swaggered, you know. I went home frightened."

Donnerstag's mother fainted into Shirley's arms and a doctor was called to administer oxygen. In the commotion, someone in that row dropped a purse, and envelopes of cash spilled onto the floor. FBI Agent Michael Wilson went to a phone and called Tobyhanna to tell Festa the verdict. Jerry closed his eyes tightly, squeezed the ridge of his nose with his fingers, and handed the phone to Rose. She got off quickly and two marshals went with her for a long night walk among the elms in the hilly yard.

*　　*

Finally The Bear lost his patience. He could not hope to wait for another shot at getting Festa. It was February 6, 1975, and after what had happened to Donnerstag, Basto had started copping pleas, admitting guilt to arson, burglary conspiracy, and interstate transportation of stolen property. Neither he nor many of the others charged with felony offenses wanted to face Jerry at trial. Standing before Superior Court Judge Ralph Fusco in the Essex court, The Bear was told to pay six thousand to a Newark couple who had furs and jewelry stolen from their home, and was given a seven-year term for torching the Foodtown supermarket in Hoboken. Basto took that calmly, and remained unmoved as Judge Fusco sentenced him to three years for the b-and-e. But his equanimity vanished when the judge—a judge who could not be intimidated—ordered him to pay another three thousand in fines. And the beefy gangster became enraged, fit to be shackled, when Fusco told him he must make a $241,338 restitution to the fire insurance firms concerned.

"You, Your Honor, you're Italian!" he yelled. He looked at Falcone. "And the prosecutor is Italian. You should be ashamed of yourselves. You're a disgrace to the Italians. The Irish are laughing!"

Donahue, Wilson, and Barry O'Neill watched from the rear of the courtroom as Judge Fusco revoked The Bear's bail for this uncharacteristic outburst. As he was ushered out of the courtroom and to the Essex jail, Basto was so angry that he decided to testify the same day as a defense witness in another case Fusco was trying, against Jackie "Adams" DiNorscia, Gerald Cohen, and John Sarapucciello, the latter a millionaire commodities trader and coin dealer who had fenced property for them.

Festa was the main witness in the trial, and the defense was vehement, claiming Jerry had a sexual relationship with his daughter Janet. This allegation came from Festa's daughter Darlene, who had been staying at Tommy Adams's house. And Festa was nearly killed when Jackie and his father learned what time he was arriving at Newark International Airport for this trial, and that the marshals would not be there to meet him. He was saved from this setup because a businessman named Pat Kelly, who worked with Adams, was also cooperating secretly with the state police and the FBI—and ran for a phone to alert them. The marshals again appeared to be part of the plans.

The defense attorney in this case, Jack Gold, called Basto to the stand. The Bear claimed that neither DiNorscia nor Cohen had participated in the crime, and said the same about the fence, Sarapucciello. Then came cross-examination by the assistant prosecutor Michael Steiber.

"Mr. Basto, are you known by any other names?" asked Steiber.

"Yes."

"What name?"

"The Bear."

"How long have you been known as 'The Bear'?"

"Oh, since I was about ten years old."

"You testified that you pleaded guilty in Federal Court [on another charge for which he was sentenced] to a case involving some stolen property?"

"Yeah, transportation of it, yeah. You see, there are so many counts in the indictment, I don't know exactly what count I pleaded guilty to."

Steiber referred to the burglary charge he had been sentenced on that morning. "Are you upset about that?" he asked.

"Would you be upset?" said The Bear.

"Are you upset?"

"Would you be upset?"

Steiber persisted. "Are you upset, sir?"

Basto lowered his voice. "To a degree, yeah."

Despite his guilty plea before Judge Fusco, Basto now maintained his innocence. Steiber asked how that could be.

"Okay," said Frankie Bear, "I pleaded guilty because of the plea-bargaining system, because I didn't have the proper money for a big organized-crime figure like you made me, that I wasn't, and lawyers ask a lot of money when you say that." He went on to say that "youse try to frame people."

But Steiber asked, "Isn't it a fact that Jerry Festa was your man?"

"Was he?" said Basto.

"Isn't it a fact?"

"Of course not. Jerry Festa was the kingpin of the whole thing. Are you kidding?" If Steiber wanted any more information, he should "ask Festa—he'll give you the answer you want."

Steiber said, "Isn't it a fact that you told me right outside this courtroom that if I called you as a witness, you would hurt me?"

"No, I didn't," said The Bear.

When Basto left the stand a dispute erupted about just where he should sit.

"Move his seat next to the prosecutor," said Judge Fusco.

Basto refused. "I don't want to sit by them."

"Mr. Gold doesn't want you to sit by him," said the judge, referring to a defense motion.

Basto insisted, "I don't want to move there."

A sheriff's bailiff spoke up. "Did you hear what the judge said?"

Gold was leery of Basto. "Judge, I withdraw my objection."

"Sit right there," said Fusco

Basto gave the bailiff a vicious look. "You're a piece of shit, you."

Another witness, Georgie Pifer, walked to the stand, and Basto shouted, "Make sure he knows me. He never knew me before today."

"Sit down, Mr. Basto," said Judge Fusco. "And thank you."

"Make sure he knows me!"

Defense attorney Gold said, "For the record, I would like [it] to reflect Mr. Basto is seated right in front of both counsel. On prominent display in front of the jury."

"Put me on a chandelier," Basto remarked. But his histrionics were pointless.

After several other outbursts, each one much out of character for Basto, The Bear ended the day shouting that Pifer (who was related to one defendant) was "a lying bastard." On the way out, The Bear turned and spat at Joe Falcone. Unfazed, Falcone returned to his office to conduct more pretrial interviews, then joined Detective Donahue for dinner at the Vesuvius Restaurant on Bloomfield Avenue.

The prospect for easy sentences or a timely payoff had disappeared when it had been announced that these cases had been assigned to Judge Fusco. At sixty-three he was a spry man who jogged and pole-vaulted for exercise, and his approach to the bench was equally athletic. He was a crusader, a "hanging judge," and he had cleared the calendar for most of 1975, sending letters to other judges advising them that many local attorneys would be tied up in his Superior Court hearings through much of the year. He scheduled as many as eleven defendants for preliminary motions on a single date, determined that these hoods were not going to get away because of legal delaying tactics. He denied motion after defense motion.

Born in Perth Amboy, Fusco had graduated from Rutgers and been on the staff of the World War Two command that planned an invasion of Tokyo before the atom bomb instead brought the conflict to a halt; and after that had been a military intelligence officer in Korea. In civilian life he had been a mortgage attorney, a criminal lawyer, and then a special prosecutor in Bergen and Passaic counties (in the latter locale hiring an assistant named Brendan Byrne, who would one day become governor). He had also been the state's Public Utilities Commission president. A flamboyant man with a bulbous nose and bushy eyebrows, he operated in an audacious but disciplined manner. For two years during the Festa case Fusco and his wife had round-the-clock bodyguards, but it was difficult to frighten a man who had been ready to face a million Japanese troops.

"He was a *real* tough judge," says Ray Freda. "We all called him The Madman. He wasn't gonna let any attorneys bullshit him with postponements. He had all the lawyers make their motions. All were denied. They had me for possession of stolen goods. A pair of earrings! The trial lasted about four days. I was found guilty. After the verdict the judge told me my bond was lifted. And told the court bailiff to arrest me. Then he told my attorney to be ready for my next trial on Monday. I knew we didn't have a chance with him hearing our case. I tried to get into a different court. Our motion was denied. I went on trial for my next case. It was a break-and-entry. It lasted four more days. Jerry Festa was the witness again. The jury went out to reach its verdict. While they were out, Judge Fusco said that he would use the courtroom next door to the one he was in and start picking the jury for the *next* case. All the others that were to go on trial were worried. As they knew there was no chance of a win in Judge Fusco's court. He meant business. March 6, 1975, was my date to be sentenced. He told me the prosecutor had filed papers for me to be tried on the other two cases as a fourth offender. That would mean a life sentence in prison . . ."

Fusco's court, Room 506 (utilitarian and small, with slivers of glass for windows and a black-enamel witness booth), was swept for explosives each morning, and the restrooms were placed under guard. Festa's driver, Deputy Callaghan, imagined that any day a panel truck would pull alongside them on a highway and open up automatic fire from its rear door as it passed. Whenever he feared a tail, Callaghan pinched off his headlights, ran traffic lights, sped the wrong way up one-way streets, or drove up on the sidewalk hugging the courthouse.

Having gone through more months of preliminary hearings, and a major scare (when a suspicious man just happened to find his way to

Festa's hotel floor), Jerry was buckling physically. His arms and legs wouldn't obey his orders, his lungs were hard up for air. After one day when he spent nine hours on the stand in court, he suffered a stomach hemorrhage and was taken to a Pennsylvania clinic. His mind was reeling, trying to remember the vital legal facts as well as which security men he could trust, which he could not. There would be a time or two when a news camera would catch a glimpse of him as he rushed into a building, and, relishing the publicity, he would quickly wave and grin. But he knew the prosecution had to move as fast as possible and, much to his dismay, there was no time for Valachi-style celebrity.

Festa was also aware of Basto's enormous anger. After pleading guilty to some additional charges in Scranton, Basto had said to Ernest Preate, "You tell your fucking friend Festa he's too ugly. He can't hide the rest of his life." In February, Falcone had sent a memorandum to Judge Fusco warning that the "contract" to execute Jerry "is still in full force and effect" and "could be as high as $500,000." Festa's father had been sent to Houston to hide with the rest of the family after two men grabbed one of Jerry's cousins, known as Uncle Charlie, thinking he was the elder Festa, demanding to know "where that fucking stoolie is" and putting a gun to his head before they discovered (by looking through his wallet) that they had the wrong guy. They threw him on the hood of his car. At the courthouse in Newark, Tommy Adams was seen hanging around for a suspiciously long time near the doorway (an internal report on this was made on May 19 to the sheriff's department), and, in December of the following year, Basto would be heard in an elevator saying, "We'll take away Judge Fusco. We'll get him later."

Before they were sentenced, The Bear and Freda devised their most brazen, most outrageous plot. "Bear said there would only be one plan left to do," says Freda. "The best was to try and get Jerry right in the courtroom. [Basto] had a guy that was getting him some strychnine. We learned that Festa drank the water from the judge's pitcher, and that was brought out to the judge by a bailiff that took the judge to court and home. And it was brought and taken away as the judge sat on the bench, so we decided against that. [Bear] said he believed that if it [the poison] made contact with [Festa's] hands and he were to touch his mouth, it would kill him on the spot. It was supposed to be a nerve poison. I told him he had a good idea if we were able to get it on top of the ledge in the witness stand."

Though Freda gives Basto all the credit for these and the other murder plots, it is safe to assume he played an equal role in originating the far-fetched ideas, and that it was he who perched with Quartuccio on rooftops, waiting to spot Festa leaving the courthouse. By his own admission it was Freda who surveyed the courtroom to see if the poison could be introduced, and backed off because he saw that the place was guarded even at night. Unable to get to Festa there, Freda displayed his frustration during one of his trials. "Festa, your wife's a whore," he screamed.

"Come on, Raymond," Festa shouted back from the witness stand, fists raised. "Come on. You don't have a gun now and my name ain't Alton Hughes."

Freda's eyes bulged at the mention of the Hughes murder—which had never come out in court—but he wisely brought his anger under control and called for a meeting with the detectives. He was beginning to think of cutting a deal himself. Watched by marshals and detectives, Freda and Festa briefly spoke to each other in a downstairs conference room. "Jerry," Raymond said reproachfully, "What are you doing to me?"

The day of The Bear's outburst in court, Johnny Relief Quartuccio was in Scranton before Federal Judge Richard P. Conaboy, Jr. Instead of spewing anger, he tried to win the judge's sympathy. He had "lost twenty-five pounds in the last ten months," Johnny said, "and that's—that's easy: My wife is half-dead. All this pressure nearly killed her." All he asked, said Johnny, was that he be given a chance to start a new life. "I know it's late, but maybe with the grace of that guy upstairs, somewhere along the line, someplace, something will work out for me." Though Quartuccio's attorney tried to make the point that no one had been seriously injured in Johnny's burglaries, Judge Conaboy brushed that aside and gave Johnny ten years for the crimes in Pennsylvania.

Though trials and retrials would proceed for nearly three more years, this spring and summer of 1975 were most noteworthy, for the county-federal task force during this time turned Bloomfield Avenue into a mob graveyard. Aside from the flood of guilty pleas (which made formal jury presentation unnecessary), and the trials in Scranton and in federal court (where the setting was much more lavish than the Essex facilities, with stone pillars and statues), Festa and Lombardo would help the state win eighteen of the first twenty trials, a percentage that would remain intact throughout future dispositions.

Festa was a witness in three murder trials in addition to the Feldman verdict, and every week seemed to see the end of one trial and the beginning of another. Nicky Skins, Sperduto, and Cabert went down on a burglary rap, and the FBI, eager to grab every possible prosecutorial opportunity, was able to charge Cabert and Skins with a civil rights case that had been lost earlier because of a bribed juror. The two men were retried and found guilty of brutally assaulting a black man, Robert Chavers, whose presence in Ed's Diner had so offended the hoods that they had repeatedly smashed his head against the floor.

Among the others taken into custody on a fine variety of charges were old names—Peter Feldman, Brady, Malavenda, Herky—and new ones—Tosi, Corsaro, Piperato. Tommy Adams was sentenced to three years in prison, and the burglary fences and sandwich runners all fell together.

Of all the victories, none was more significant than Falcone's skillful conviction of the police sergeant, Ray Grill. His was not merely a case of shaking down bookies and drug dealers—the offense most often found among dishonest cops—but of engineering the armed robbery of Sidney and Helen Osterweil of West Orange. Grill had operated as a full partner of Jerry the Jew (who, despite an incurable optimism, had no chance of ever being free again; there were forty-six charges against him). In yet another case, tried by an able assistant prosecutor named Glenn Goldberg, Festa alleged an involvement higher than Grill's. This went back to his first contact with Donnerstag, the stealing of the "School Mistress" portrait, which, he said, had been fingered by the city councilman. The councilman, Anthony Imperiale, who had become a rather well known state senator, running as an anticrime crusader, was never convicted of the crime.

But the time had also come for Jerry Festa to be sentenced, because his agreement with the authorities included immunity only for those crimes he had volunteered to the detectives, not from the burglaries Ellis, Carbone, and Lombardo had cited—and he had already pleaded guilty to five of them. While the murder charge was out of the way, and he had been granted clemency in Federal and Superior courts in New Jersey, he still had to face Federal Judge Conaboy in Scranton, and he fully expected to get ten years.

Conaboy wanted to give him twenty. He felt that organized-crime associates, more than the average criminal, had consciously made a choice in their life styles, and it seemed to him that "a guy like Festa" could "squeal without giving up much in the bargain." As far as he was concerned, Festa's presence at the Feldman murder scene made him as guilty as Donnerstag. Conaboy was the type of judge who had come to believe in the death penalty, and as for burglary, it was in his rating a "seven" on a scale of one to ten.

As they had promised the day Festa turned, Wilson and Falcone set out to soften Judge Conaboy's viewpoint. Though both men found Jerry's former activities despicable, cowardly, and foolish, and were unconvinced that his decision to cooperate was based primarily upon his concern for his family's welfare (which was what he often claimed), they nonetheless considered him a most surprising hoodlum, tough and weak at the same time, emotional, hard, loyal, disloyal—a misguided person full of contradictions, and yet with a side not totally bad. He did seem deeply guilt-ridden over some of those harmed by his selfishness, and he was watchful and worried over his relatives when he was not immersed in court. He was prone to cry over the Feldman death in a way that was wholly different from the emotional acts he had put on to get sympathy and money from the meatballs, and he had been sincere with the prosecution, standing up to vicious cross-examinations in addition to a level of danger they had never before encountered. Also, he had volunteered reams of intelligence information on the mob's local structure and actions. If the caring, warm side of Jerry had fallen into a gap in his conscience, still, they were convinced, chances were reasonable that he would never be a criminal again.

But Judge Conaboy was obstinate. To him Festa was simply another of those who cared about no one but himself—think of those old ladies who had been beaten and robbed!—and would do so as long as it brought him an income he could not have obtained in a normal, law-abiding life. He had to play unfair to get his hands on big dollars, Conaboy rationalized, and then, after taking from someone's honest savings, he would go to the crap or monte games and piss it away.

Wilson and Falcone went to Scranton for a session with the judge, pleading against a prison term. No witness had ever been so cooperative with them, so candid and accurate, so memorable on the stand. If he went to jail, insisted Wilson, the mob would find him, kill him, torture him first. Any confinement, no matter how far away from Newark, would amount to the death penalty.

Sentencing was scheduled for July 15 in Court Number Three, a red-carpeted room in the turreted and rustic Scranton courthouse. Two days before, Conaboy called Judge Fusco in New Jersey. He was unable to make a final decision and still quite inclined to mete out some stiff prison time. Fusco was against Festa's serving a jail term. He urged Conaboy to let him off.

"But I'm letting this guy get away with murder," Conaboy protested.

"We're giving him hell as it is," argued Fusco. "You can be assured that if he so much as spits on a sidewalk the rest of his life, any sentence suspended can be picked back up. There will be people everywhere wanting to see him incarcerated."

Although impressed by that exchange, Conaboy remained reluctant to follow such advice, and he would remain so right up until it was time to walk across Washington Avenue from his office to the court bench. Festa was brought in for sentencing under security arrangements even more stringent than those at the murder trial. Though the ringleaders were in jail, many others were worried about what Festa might say next, and, with the Newark crew disabled, hitmen had been brought in from Florida and New York.

At the Tobyhanna depot, before he left, Festa turned to Chief Deputy Marshal Scheu and cried. "If I get sent away, you gotta watch Rose for me." Scheu did not and would not believe that this display was simply melodramata. He transported Festa in a twelve-car caravan that, in another diversion, split off in three different directions, converging—red lights flashing, sirens wailing—before quietly separating again. Three government cars had been stationed at the courthouse the previous night as decoys, and though the court was in the very heart of Scranton's commercial zone, all streets around it were sealed off. Deputies and members of a SWAT team toted binoculars and automatic scope rifles onto the roofs of the surrounding buildings: the Scranton Life Building, a hotel, and the clock tower of the courthouse itself. Festa was sped the wrong way down a one-way street, a central avenue called Spruce Street, and into the building. On each floor an agent stood next to the elevator, making sure no one tried to get in; and once again, no one was allowed to walk into the hallways.

Conaboy was annoyed. As a Democratic county chairman years before, he had been along on the final day of campaigning for John F. Kennedy, who swung through Pennsylvania on the way home, and the security on that occasion had not been quite as thorough as this. All for a minor hood. And all the machine guns bothered him. He wondered if one might accidentally go off.

Festa literally burst into the courtroom, running with his bodyguards. The judge winced. Hank Ellis was also there, but Hank had been just a servant to Festa, someone Conaboy could feel a bit more sympathy for, and in fact Ellis was to leave that day for a tiny mountain town in northern Pennsylvania, where he would spend the following years in a ramshackle house.

Assistant prosecutor Preate, who had tried the Feldman murder, spoke first. He told Conaboy that Festa had given him "the fullest cooperation," and that because of it he had "left himself open for many kinds of extreme danger, great amounts of extreme danger," which hung like "a Sword of Damocles over his head." He pleaded that Jerry be given probation.

Conaboy asked to see the indictments. Festa's anxiety rose. He glanced around the courtroom and saw a few guys he had gambled with, drunk with, fought with at places like Cooper's. It had been a long road since those wild times when, during the brawling, he would sometimes sneak behind a bar and run off with the cash register.

After certain legalities were concluded, Judge Conaboy heard from James G. McDonough, a local attorney assigned to Jerry for his Scranton appearances. "I think it's fair to represent—it has been represented to me by the federal and state officials, the strike force, and special prosecutor of the strike force in the state that he [Festa] has become the most significant and important testimony in the dissolution of organized crime in certainly the state of New Jersey and possibly the United States," said McDonough. "Jerry Festa did this knowing what it meant. It meant that he no longer could live a life as he normally lived. He did it, basically, I believe, for his family. As a result of his testimony, he has been wiped out. His business was sold by organized crime. His home was wrecked . . . If he is in jail for one day, it is death. When he decided to testify on behalf of the government and the law enforcement officials, Jerry Festa, in essence, sentenced himself to life imprisonment, whether it's in custody or out of custody. He can never again lead the type of life that a free man can lead. They have promised that they will get him, that he will not live. For Jerry Festa, he will always have to look twice before he goes anywhere. He possibly has sentenced himself to death."

Dan Williamson, the federal attorney from Newark, also spoke on Festa's behalf, saying that Jerry had been totally reliable; and Falcone then rehashed the murder plots against the witness, repeating that "he never lied to us." Conaboy was affected by Falcone. The young man

Michael Brown 294

had worked awfully hard putting the cases together, and the judge was convinced that if he gave Festa a stiff sentence, it might ruin things for Falcone—the witness would stop talking. The judge was upset, as upset as he could remember being. Viscerally he wanted to levy a seven-to-twenty-year term. Anything less than that didn't smell right. Festa deserved little sympathy, he felt. His business? His home? But what had he done to other people? What had he brought upon his own family? Whose fault was that?

Conaboy looked at Falcone and felt sorry for him. He was a judicious man, the judge figured. If he had cut this deal, Conaboy was convinced, it must be a fair one. Falcone was not the sort to pander to criminals who see the light only when they are faced with the bars of a jail cell.

"All right," Conaboy began. "I suppose in this type of a case, Mr. Festa, anything that I might say would certainly be an anticlimax to a startling career, to say the least. Usually when I impose a sentence, I try my best to explain to the defendant and his counsel and the prosecutors and anyone else interested and for the public record as to why I impose a sentence. I think that's a very important thing to do in any case, much less yours. I fully realize the extensive cooperation that you have given to the police officials and the investigation and prosecution officials, and I'm aware to a large measure of the success that they have had in prosecuting others involved in these matters. Forgotten many times in these cases are the victims of these things. As I told you, while I am appreciative, as much as any human being can be, of another's unhappiness like you have subjected yourself to, I, too, am aware that many other people have been sentenced to a similar type of life sentence because of the fear that has been imposed upon them by having their homes burglarized. As I indicated to you, there's nothing worse to me than the fear that a person lives with for the rest of their lives when they have had their home burglarized . . . However, the people who have spoken here this morning have placed on the record all of the reasons why any judge would impose a sentence. I'm going to impose a probation sentence in your case, and I don't want to create any further tension or surprise or anything in this case. I'm going to impose a jail sentence and I'm going to suspend it."

Jerry turned hastily to Ellis. "Just watch yourself, Hank. That's all I can tell ya." Tears streamed down Festa's cheeks as he ran out with the deputies.

Several spectators tried to shake his hand. Outside, a lunchtime crowd of nearly three hundred people had gathered to see him, but the security route was too diversionary for that. No one caught a glimpse of the tall local boy who had caused such a city-stopping commotion.

*　　*

The past Christmas had been nearly a festive season. The Festas bought a small artificial tree and set it on a pail so it fairly towered over the children. Each played with a toy Rose bought by saving a dollar here and there from their stipend: Joseph his first bike, Allan little figurines designed after the warriors in *Planet of the Apes,* Sophia a doll that she nursed with a bottle of water. They cuddled on the floor with the warmest present of all, the gift Marie could appreciate most: a German shepherd puppy that Rose snuck in under an overcoat so the kids couldn't see it. It had a bright red ribbon around its neck, and not without purpose, they named the animal "Faith."

They also had some clothes Marie had scrounged from a local Goodwill drop. Embarrassed to keep asking for handouts from the Houston nuns, she would poke her head into the drop door at night and look for something that would fit the kids. It was dark in there. She was afraid a cockroach or a rat would leap at her face any moment.

Then in August a call came to Saint Jerome's. The voice was female, asking if an Alicia, Sophia, and Allan were registered there. The Mother Superior was by now in their confidence. She called the marshals, who in turn went to see Marie and Jerry. Festa was visiting Rose at Spring Branch Memorial Hospital, where she was being treated for more lung trouble. Without telling Rose why, he and Janet went home and helped Marie put what they could in some boxes that two deputies brought over. They waited at a hotel for Rose to be released. The doctor said she needed a respirator. She would have to do without. The next day they flew to Baltimore.

The caller had claimed to represent a bill collector searching for payment of some back bills, but under their new name it seemed improbable that a collection agency could have located them. A great fear set in. Perhaps it was a crank call somehow originating in Houston: a disgruntled deputy marshal who wanted the Festas out of his hair, or someone else in one of the marshals' service offices.

Either that or it was the mob.

In Maryland, the motor lodge was on Security Boulevard, just west of Baltimore, at a highway crossroads known as Woodlawn. They would remain there for nearly two months before beginning another leg of their hegira. During the next five years they would settle into four homes. Jerry switched back and forth between various aliases.

"When we going home?" Allan kept asking. His parents avoided the answer. Instead he was lectured about not straying from their room. There was a witch who would get him, they said.

Back to washing their clothes in a sink. Back to sitting on the bed eating hamburgers. Marie's culinary skills had to make do with a coffee pot and a grill plate. What few belongings they had acquired in Texas were in storage for the time being. They wore T-shirts every day, and when the snow came the kids had to plow through it in worn sneakers. The only untroubled child was Joseph, who was preoccupied with learning how to talk. The rest were grateful that at least here they were allowed to roam out on a balcony.

Rose stayed in bed. The Boston diagnosis of pulmonary fibrosis had been confirmed in Texas. Yet she could not quit smoking. There were days when she was dizzy and her hands swelled, but she still went through three packs of smokes. A cooler climate had been suggested by her Texas physician; now she at least had that. And they felt closer to "home." Marie appreciated the East. She never had liked it when people said, "Y'all."

They began to tell the two younger girls more about what was happening. They had a "rough time" ahead, Rose told Sophia, explaining that "people Dad was with don't like him no more," and adding that they could never go back to Ridge Street. As Sophia understood it, her father had "killed someone," and she disliked him for that until the adults convinced her he had not actually done it. Alicia was not as depressed as she was "real mad." She almost wanted to hit some of those big guys from the government who made them stay in all these rented rooms and kept moving them around. And she was sick of bread and butter and bean soup. All this, she thought, because of some stolen necklaces or something. She thought back to their house and how she and Sophia would wrestle with Pete and Jed and pretend their dogs were ponies. In Texas she at least had been taken to a horse stable, and they had flown kites a few times and even gone to a carnival once—though her father would not go near any crowds. When Sophia had a hard time sleeping, Rose taught the child to get her mind off it by writing, "government, government, government" dozens of times. That was because it was the "government" who let everybody steal their belongings, she said, and who told "daddy's friends" they were hiding in Rhode Island.

Both girls still remembered their Barbie doll house, and their new bikes back in Newark—that basement seemed filled with their toys. So now Alicia complained and banged on the motel walls some more, in tirades. Rose finally told them if they didn't stay where they were, and be quiet about it, "some men" might find them "and we might be killed."

An alert boy who had shown considerable promise before he was so confusingly yanked out of Saint Jerome's, Allan caught on fast. He knew it was big trouble because Marie kept lecturing him about not going with anybody who might come by in a car, "even our friends back home." He could not get Uncle Frank out of his young head for the longest while: every time they went somewhere in a car, it seemed, he would ask, "Are we going to Uncle Frank's house?" But in Maryland that stopped, and he started having nightmares. He overheard enough talk to know gangsters were after them, and soon he was having dreams about it. The guys in his nightmares had on pin-striped suits and white ties, like in a movie, and one had curly hair; another sounded strikingly like Nicky Valvano. In the dreams Allan would be sitting in a kitchen and a car would drive up and slow down. Next thing he knows Uncle Frank comes up and gives him a hug. ("How you doing?" Uncle Frank asks. The boy says, "Okay. Until now, though." "You wanna come with us or get shot?" "Shoot me." "Have it your way.") Allan is shot in the head, blood comes down his shirt, he wakes up. Or he is on a bus with his parents and everyone starts screaming: here comes Uncle Frank with a submachine gun. He blows everybody away. Or guys are dragging his father to a van. Allan thought about the neat games, especially the shooting gallery, Basto had given him. He wished it was here to play with. He had spent long hours shooting bee-bees at the plastic men with that blue gun, so it was difficult to understand why he had to fear someone so nice. But he was afraid, and Rose would find him sitting on his bed in the middle of the night, trembling badly.

As the cold weather moved in from Chesapeake Bay, WPP officials relocated the family in a bungalow near the program's headquarters in Falls Church, Virginia. There were weeds halfway up to the house, and the septic tank overflowed; a sizable nest of garter snakes slithered through the marshy yard. Some of their possessions arrived from Houston, but Rose felt more than ever the pain of losing their house.

Most disillusioning of all was the bureaucratic disarray prevalent in the security program. Created by the Crime Control Act on October 15, 1970, and originally known as the Witness Security Program (as opposed to the WPP), it was growing too fast for its facilities and was run on a nearly random basis; few of the deputy marshals had any experience in assisting and counseling relocated families, or for that matter guarding them against professional assassins. They were men whose previous experience in security had come only from occasionally guarding a judge, and many of them were resentful that the government was providing food, transportation, and medical costs to criminals who had never contributed their fair share of taxes. The marshals' ineptitude was aggravated by the number of witnesses pouring into the young program, which was supposed to establish these outcasts in new locales. Although not every witness had to change his identity, and few approached the level of danger encountered by the Festas, in 1975 there were 659 witnesses in the program and a budget of $2.7 million. By 1978 there would be a total of 2,436 witnesses and approximately thirty-five hundred of their family members who had been in the program, at one time or another, and by 1982 the budget would balloon to $28.7 million. Yet there was no central system of coordination; only two full-time people were assigned to provide witnesses with driving licenses and Social Security cards if their names had been changed. Witnesses were not given the depth of documentation they felt was essential for starting a new life: birth and baptismal certificates, marriage licenses, school records, and medical histories were missing, more often than not. The understaffing allowed corruption to flourish unseen, and delays in moving furniture opened the opportunity for vandalism by the vengeful mob. Worse, no one person had complete authority over the program. It was run by the Marshals' Service, a division of the Justice Department, and was overseen by a director appointed by the Attorney General. But each district marshal was chosen by presidential appointment, and these marshals often chose to ignore the program's director. Burdened with other responsibilities as well, the local marshals and their deputies were frequently too busy to spend all their time protecting witnesses.

This lack of coordinated manpower was aggravated by the stubborn psychology of those being protected. Like others in the program, the Festas had not been adequately briefed as to what the government could do for them; the system was not designed to fabricate credit references, buy homes, or give the families a false family "legend."

When the deputies made an effort to find jobs for criminals, the latter often spurned the employment for which they were qualified—manual labor, clerks' jobs, and assembly-line work—because it not only involved honest hard work but also paid far less than their former illegal enterprises. There was no way to solve that dilemma—the witnesses had all but unmarketable skills—and regulations stated that subsistence payments (the maximum was $1,080 a month) for food, clothes, rent and miscellaneous expenses would be terminated one hundred and twenty days after entry or sixty days after the witness's last court appearance, whichever came first.

Janet and Rose complained that they never knew what was coming next and were getting contradictory answers depending on which marshal they spoke to. They were unable to comprehend that the federal government could not simply wave a wand and magically bring them what they needed, and they were endlessly bitter about the loss of their belongings. "Maybe we should of just taken our chances alone," Rose said. By this time their business was completely gone; when they defaulted on the rent, the lawyers sold off the equipment in the store—fryers, freezers, soda and cigarette machines. Rose wrote a letter to the authorities in February of 1976 saying that "we have asked everyone who has been in charge of us to get started again. No one would give us any answer to why our home was left standing with all our personal items and furniture so long. It may have not been important to anyone but it left us with no hope for a future. It has affected us very bad." She explained that in Texas Janet "became friendly with the nuns and told them all we owned was lost in a fire. They gave her clothes for the children. This helped us a lot but we had to move again. The clothes given to us was for that climate which was eighty or ninety degrees ten months of the year. So now we are back in four seasons and faced with the same problem . . . What has been the biggest blow to us is the way it happened. We had so much faith and trust in the Marshals Service and they never took the time to get our furniture and personal items, even our two dogs . . . We are not normal people. We will never be."

Though he again threatened not to testify unless his family was better treated, Festa commuted to Newark under the guard of different deputies to continue participating in the trials presided over by Judge Fusco. Many more indictments had been handed up the previous April, and he was beginning to almost enjoy the legal proceedings, for he had become sort of a Wunderkind of jurisprudence. He felt entirely loyal to Wilson and Donahue; and together they headed for more victories in court. Feeling that he was part of the strike force staff, Festa, though still sensibly afraid of his former buddies, had begun testifying as a means of retaliation. On the stand, looking directly at the jurors, he revealed every detail he could remember, thinking of how the mob was trying to hurt him and his family. On the opposite side of the law, at the defense table, Donnerstag was looking bored. Having been in so many proceedings now, he too was an experienced hand, and he was prone to soliloquies.

THE COURT: Mr. Donnerstag, is there anything that you want to say in mitigation of your punishment, sir?

THE DEFENDANT: Well, yes, Your Honor. I don't know how to go about starting. I'm not as eloquent as Mr. Falcone, so I'll have to go about it in my own way. Your Honor, it's a small word with a huge meaning. What I'm trying to get at is that we are a new nation, very new, and it seems 'honor' is something a lot of people don't have, and some do. Maybe some people would say I'm a hawk or a dove, whatever you want to call me, so be it. I guess it's the simplest way, the easiest and fastest, that I think honor is the most important thing to me personally, only to me . . . If I was to stand up here and be anything but a man, in my sense of the word, and I tell you, I wouldn't feel as a man, so honor to me is very, very important. I could have pleaded to any of these charges, simple. Mr. Falcone came to see me, other people, my attorney came to see me with deals, as you call them here, or plea-bargaining. One man's life for another man's life. That's what the deals were . . . I already wrote to you what I had to say about that, the homicide, which will come up, and I know that you will see where the honor lies, who was telling the truth and who wasn't. I'm not willing to sacrifice what they want—a loss of honor—for the lies that they want me to tell. I just won't do that."

When that did not work—he was convicted with detectives Costa and Cuff for bribery, and also stood trial for the armed robberies—Donnerstag tried to turn his case into a question of anti-Semitism. Despite his own promotion of his nickname when he was on the streets, Donnerstag now took umbrage at being referred to as "Jerry the Jew." "That's what [Festa] wants to call me, let him call me that. I'm a Jew, my name is Jerry . . . Jerry the Jew. If I was black, would you allow him to call me Jerry the Nigger? . . . I'm an avid reader and in 1952 six million Jews, five hundred Russians, three million gypsies, two million Poles—they all went to the ovens because other people told different stories about them . . ."

In the privacy of the legal conference room at Rahway State Prison, where he had been sent after extradition for the Jersey charges, Donnerstag was more his old self, referring to Festa as "The Scumbag" and vowing that however long it took, Jerry Chicken Delight would pay for this grief. He tried to convince himself that the Feldman verdict would be reversed, and relished grapevine talk of how Festa was about to face Cabert and Skins again in court. Perhaps they would get him after all.

Regrouping in the aftermath of Paterno's departure (on the unrelated SCI subpoena), and the imprisonment of Basto and Freda, Paterno's assistants Jimmy Higgins and Butch Miceli were assigned by Gambino to run the Newark turf. Around this time, according to room bugs and wiretaps, Carlo Gambino told Higgins, "Here's my phone number. Not to bother Joe [Paterno]. Call me directly." Butch Miceli, at a meeting in his basement with Basto and an informant, said, "Chicken Delight's a good name for him, the prick. But they oughta take the 'Delight' off. Just 'Chicken.' " Higgins complained about the new hierarchy: "I told Joe this was gonna happen . . . The First Ward is coming down and there is no one left on Bloomfield Avenue . . . Newark ain't the same as other places, who's in Arizona, who's in Florida. If there is no one around there is no one around. The only thing we will have left is the [Y-Ki] restaurant." There were more attempts to find Festa, and wise guys such as Tursi and Demus Covello were, coincidentally or not, spotted near where he happened to be.

But Festa was now turning his energies to the marshals themselves, or rather to the crooked ones who had given up his whereabouts. The marshals had protected him well in most cases—he was living testimony to that—but the Newark office, with a few exceptions, was a den of corruption. Soon it was all he talked about. Looking back, he remembered a three-thousand bribe he had once given a deputy marshal on Tommy Adams's orders years before, and the indictment documents Donnerstag had been able to get before they were even signed, courtesy of a crooked deputy. The FBI began to investigate these and other charges, and to protect Festa with still more marshal details from other parts of the country.

As the investigation progressed, the Federal Marshals Service took a sudden interest in the family's problems, especially the loss of their clothes and furniture and the fast-food equipment. It asked him to list what had been in the house, and he and Rose did so immediately, filling twenty-four hand-written pages. Five cars were gone, and the empty house had been sold by their attorneys to pay off debts, including the fees owed the lawyers and for mortgage payments. The dangers had been too great for the Festas to try to sell the property themselves, or get a rent release from the store. Their main complaint was the disappearance of property from the house after the Newark deputies, led by Angelo Bove and the marshal himself, Carl E. Hirshman, failed to guard it.

Called to a meeting at the WPP's headquarters, Festa found Bove in the group of marshals. Jerry ran to attack him: "You motherfucker, you tried to have me killed, you sonuvabitch! You motherfucker, we go back a long ways, Bove. You fucking tried to set me up in Somerset jail. You blew my house." Several others jumped between them, pulling Festa off. Soon afterward, in May, the service agreed to give Jerry twenty-four thousand dollars in what he mistakenly considered a partial payment for his property losses. The money was presented in cash, stashed in a briefcase, and placed in a safe-deposit box until he took it out to buy clothes, furniture, a 1976 Chevrolet, and set his family up in an old but bigger house near Arlington. With the payment was a release form freeing the Marshals Service "from any and all claims, demands, damage, costs, expenses, loss of services, actions and causes of action arising from any and all . . . property damage, loss or damage of any kind . . ." Needing the cash, Festa signed the agreement. Within a year's time the money was gone.

The trials had slowed down, but Festa was still understandably jittery. If Rose was five minutes late coming home from the grocery store he would become almost hysterical, and for a month at a time he would not so much as walk out into the yard. Finally, when Rose pleaded with him to at least take a trip to a shopping mall near their first house, sure enough somebody yelled, "Hey, Jerry!" It was an old Scranton gambling acquaintance who had also relocated. (Festa shook his hand and said he was just passing through. Afraid the man had seen him come in from the lot, however, they sold the car and got different license plates.)

Back in school, the children were still discouraged from making friends. If anyone asked what their father did, they said he was a retired construction worker. They could tell no one where they were from, of course, and without some personal history to talk about, it was difficult to make friends anyway. Janet stayed out of school to help Marie, but she was also far from well. Her blood count was unbalanced, her hormones out of kilter. She listened to her father while he obsessively watched television and talked about how he only hoped if the mob found him they would not torture him for long.

In January, Festa appeared before a secret grand jury investigating the Newark marshals, disguised in gray hair, a beard, and a mustache. Wearing a bullet-proof vest, he was spirited in through an underground garage once again. He claimed a loss of four hundred thousand dollars and, along with others in the program, alleged direct mob ties to the marshals' office. Among other things, Festa charged that several deputies had vacationed at Teddy Riviello's lodge in Maine, and another witness portrayed the Newark marshals as "errand boys" for Bayonne Joe Zicarelli and DeCarlo. Others described jailhouse bribes sent through a deputy named Leonard Stacey to Bove so that mob prisoners could remain at the Metropolitan Correctional Center in New York instead of being transferred to distant institutions, and they also recounted how marshals had actually held a party in a cell for Adams's old crony Tony Bananas. Soon it was to be charged that when Deputy Marshal Callaghan tried to expose the malpractices, his car tires had been punctured with an icepick so that they blew up at high speed. Stacey, who turned into a witness himself, went beyond that: "Bove called me in to set Callaghan up for a murder." He said he had been told to shoot Callaghan during the raid of a pimp wanted on a federal warrant.

None of these charges led to formal convictions, but there was a flurry of resignations, including that of Hirshman. Between March 20 and April 14 of 1978, a subcommittee of the Senate Judiciary Committee would hold hearings on the WPP in Washington. Festa, too full of anger to worry about his own safety, appeared before a special closed session.

Rose was frustrated. Festa's testimony had caused trouble enough for the family, she felt; now he was going against the very people who gave them their monthly subsistence and were technically charged with their protection. (In fact, Festa was soon attacking the new WPP director, Howard Safir.) In the midst of the hearings, Festa was offered help in relocating his family to Ossineke, Michigan. He and Rose traveled there to look at a new five-bedroom brick house on forty acres of land

and a small diner nearby which they could build into a business. The Marshals' Service said it would help them arrange credit for the purchase and advance them two thousand dollars for a security deposit.

For the first time in four years, Rose felt optimistic. She and her husband returned with pictures to show Marie, and Marie adored the whole idea. Rose was almost as pleased as when they first moved into Ridge Street. The payments would be difficult at first, but the diner had good potential if they were willing to work it. They could renovate the interior as they had done with Chicken Delight, and Jerry would construct a takeout window at the driveway. They felt the move might calm Alicia: there was plenty of room for a horse stable.

Rose had set her mind on a straight life. She knew that in many ways their punishment had been just, but she wanted a new start as ordinary people. Unfortunately they were not going to get that chance this time. Once the Senate hearings were over, the Michigan offer mysteriously evaporated, and with it many of her hopes. Jerry took to the phone and screamed uncontrollably, convinced that the offer of help in Michigan was only a temporary ploy to appease him as he testified about the marshals, and was withdrawn as a reprisal for rocking the WPP boat.

Rose was up to twenty-one cups of coffee a day, and she was wheezing badly again. If they had been moved to Michigan she might have been able to visit a relative she had up that way; without that possibility she felt totally cut off forever from her past. Through the years she had developed a special relationship with her stepmother and stepsister; despite what had happened with the stepfather, she loved the two women and missed them terribly.

Soon her stepmother died, and to protect Rose, who insisted on going to the funeral and would have been in great danger if it had been public, the death was never announced, not even to the rest of the family. Rose was among the handful of those allowed to attend, and because so few relatives were present, two marshals had to help carry the casket.

It had been more difficult a year earlier, when Rose's stepsister Margaret died. An obituary notice somehow got into the Scranton newspaper, and that made it too dangerous for Rose to go to the wake or the funeral. Determined nonetheless to pay her respects in some fashion, Rose persuaded Jerry to drive her near the site of mourning. As they sat in their parked car across the highway from the funeral home, a blackout swept the street. "My sister's mad I can't go in," she said, crying. "She's mad at what's happened."

Then they had secretly followed the funeral procession to the grave-yard and climbed a hill that overlooked it. From behind a clump of trees, Rose watched through binoculars as the casket was lowered.

BOOK THREE

UNTIL THE LIGHT COMES

Children of yesterday, heirs of tomorrow,
What are you weaving? Labor and sorrow?
Look to your looms again; faster and faster
Fly the great shuttles prepared by the master.
                              —Mary Artemisia Lathbury

O N APRIL 10, 1978, at two-sixteen in the afternoon, Officer Earl Johnson rushed up to a small gathering of inmates in the exercise yard of Rahway State Prison. Lying there, thrashing about, was Gerald Donnerstag, Inmate 56946. Johnson blew his whistle for a sergeant.

Donnerstag had been jogging. He tried to do a mile. He was in no shape for it. Recently he had complained of shortness of breath. He was smoking a lot of cigarettes, and blowing marijuana.

He had stopped to rest and lost consciousness when he tried to stand up again. He came to slightly. An inmate had propped a spoon in his mouth so he would not swallow his tongue. Dr. Howard Gross arrived, administered oxygen and attempted cardiopulmonary resuscitation. Donnerstag's pupils were fixed and dilated. The doctor pumped him with Adrenaline. To no avail.

In his final days Donnerstag had joined a program at Rahway called the Lifers' Program (or "Scared Straight"). The name was appropriate. He was about to serve a life sentence plus a few decades or so, and the goal of the program was for "lifers" to talk young delinquents into going straight: that meant cursing, screaming, scaring them. The most hardened kids were so intimidated they would begin to cry. Television crews filmed the sessions. Donnerstag became the star.

He was popular at this prison also. No one messed with him, but at the same time he was a likable guy and rarely lost his temper. If Shirley sent in a package of food or smokes, he shared it gladly. He read books and attended special classes at Mercer County College, and was president of the social club. So he was judged to be quite scholarly. And lately he was beginning to look it. Horn-rim spectacles had replaced his aviator glasses. Only a few times did he mention Festa ("I hope a brick building falls on the scumbag"), and never the murder of Jed. He pretended he was innocent and told his social worker, "I'm going to beat these cases. You can make book on it." He didn't really believe that, though. He told other people that when he got out it would be only as a corpse. Immediately next to the prison was a small pond, and a narrow service road which ran past the pond to the twenty-eight-foot cement walls. It was near this pond—and an islet of reeds—that Jerry the Jew fulfilled his own prophecy.

Street sources suspected that Donnerstag had been murdered. According to a young killer who had helped him on a few homicides, Jerry had passed a note shortly before his death asking to cooperate with prosecutors. And in prison he had become friendly with the Campisis, who would have worried about what he knew. They were suspected of having murdered Ira Pecznic, an informer who had been in the Witness Protection Program. But this all seemed unlikely. In all probability Gerald Donnerstag died of what the doctor said: a heart attack.

Word of Donnerstag's death was quickly passed to those fearing his vengeance: Lombardo, who was in a Delaware jail (and would also die soon of heart failure), and Joseph Carbone, who was in Virginia. Donahue told Festa about it, and when Jerry got off the phone he said, "How do ya like that, Rose? The Jew's gone."

Rose was indifferent. She had enough problems herself. Maybe her own heart was bad. She could hardly walk the length of the living room. And their finances were plummeting. Because Festa was almost through in court, the government subsidy would be terminated soon, and it was not easy for him to find a job. He was afraid of wandering out-of-doors, and he had no capital to buy a restaurant. Their refrigerator was absolutely bare, and Rose "thought we were gonna have to pitch a tent on the street." At the last moment Festa slipped in a two-day trip to Texas, where there was an attorney he knew from the Newark task force, Roy Beene, who temporarily stopped the termination.

Rose also understood that Donnerstag's death did little to improve their security. Though not all of them got jail terms, at least seventy-two people had been indicted as a result of her husband's testimony or that of other criminals who turned informants in his wake. That was far more than Valachi, who, though a more significant stool pigeon because of his higher rank, and the intelligence he provided, had actually convicted only two people, in a hijacking case. And Jerry had done it in Newark, where Vinnie Teresa, a fleeting celebrity as a witness in the early 1970s, had balked at entering the courtroom. Teresa was fearful of Paterno's assassination squad and openly said so. Newark was the "last place" he wanted to testify; it was "like walking into a lion's den," he wrote, "and daring the lion to bite."

What made it worse was that the hatred directed against Festa was not only professional but deeply personal as well. Though the made-*mafiosi* inspired his greatest fears, those at the bottom were also in a killing mood. He had betrayed them emotionally. They had stayed in his home. He had called them his "cousins" or "brothers." In the end, he made meatballs of them.

Bob Martin, who was released from prison in 1979, says "words cannot describe" how it was sitting behind bars knowing Jerry got off free. Martin had also done a term at Rahway (with Johnny Quartuccio), and in confinement he had suffered four heart attacks. His wife fantasizes about getting everyone Festa sent away into a circle with Jerry in the middle of it, and letting each do whatever he chooses. Her husband knows what he would do: "Strip his skin off from his neck to his toes." There is "no punishment good enough for him," says Martin. "Tell him never mind the big Mafia guys. If he walked in that door"—to Martin's trailer home, near Scranton—"he's dead."

Carmen Malavenda once kicked a television set to pieces when Festa's name was mentioned, but his sense of betrayal does not match that of Jed's brother. Pete Feldman loved Rose dearly, loved her more than his own family, it seems safe to say, and after the murder trial he realized Festa had not murdered his brother. (Later, happening upon them in the Essex County Courthouse, he begged the Festas to take him into hiding with them: "Rose, I can't survive without youse. I'll end up a stone junkie.") But the years have soured him. He has taken busts for malicious damage and atrocious assault, and he feels the Festas abandoned him. He is increasingly sorrowful over the murder. ("Jed was just a kid. You know? Just a kid.") He has come to blame Festa for letting it happen. If he ran across Jerry, he would kill him "in a minute," he says, "and hang his balls from a tree."

None of which is to discount the danger from those more accomplished criminals with a formal La Cosa Nostra membership card. The "experts" are divided on what they will do. Some say Festa cannot be allowed to get away with it, or more stoolies will follow. Others believe the button-men are much too preoccupied with current business (and new worries about jail) to spend their time hunting down Festa. It is certainly hard to imagine any massive search currently underway—and there is no recent evidence of one, since the mob lost its initial bids at killing him. But Nicky Skins, for one, is still furious—violently so. In 1982 he was overheard to say that he has his own recurrent dream: "Chopping Jerry Chicken Delight into little tiny pieces, slowly."

Basto spent five years in jail, much of it in Lewisburg. It is no country club. Inmates there do "hard time." And the experience, says his wife, has been extremely draining. ("What they put us through!") His children watched him dragged from the house on several occasions as new warrants arrived for his arrest. After prison he moved his family out of Newark to the suburb of Belleville. Responding to an inquirer's attempt to hear his side of the matter, The Bear was cautious and critical. "They let go by far the worse criminals with the Witness Protection Program," says Frank Basto. "They're given false identities [to] go out and commit crimes again—let loose on society. Right? They beat the wheel.

"All they had were a bunch of penny ante thieves they made big cases on. What happened was that they let Festa go on a series of serious crimes and put others away for less serious crimes, you know what I mean? He went home and slept for two, three years that this body was in the pond. It didn't bother him a bit. He encouraged Jerry the Jew to kill Feldman. He never figured Jerry the Jew would go through with it. His [Festa's] main thing was swindling old people, home-improvement with roofing and all; his main *schtick* was robbing people's houses. Wouldn't you say he's a dangerous man? If there were a hundred crimes in all, he was in on all of them. He done them. I was in maybe four, another guy three."

The Bear is bitter about a hijacking for which he was charged. He did not do it, he says. And at one point he too faced a possible life term. The FBI "was looking to bury me." He claims Festa "is a bad hombre who knows how to turn everything to his advantage." He believes Jerry was given "hundreds of thousands" by the government. "Festa was marketed by the agents." Asked if Festa was a murderer, Basto says, "Nah. He's a bum, an asshole. He was nothing."

But Bear Basto asserts that he is uninterested in meting out any punishment to Festa. His jail time, his monetary losses, the harm to his standing with his cronies for bringing Jerry Chicken Delight around— he says none of these have embittered him. "When I say there's no bitterness—he's not my *friend*. But I mean we're not bitter where I'm gonna go out and kill him, or I'm gonna go out and look for him. It's in the past, it's forgotten about. I done my time. Nobody's gonna do all those things. That's all hyped-up bullshit. I felt that—I didn't feel bitter with him. I felt I was paying for my sins."

Basto does admit irritation that the federal government also cut a deal with Freda to obtain his cooperation—Raymond squeezed out of a life sentence by testifying against Joe Paterno and Demus Covello in a case the prosecution lost. Some believe Freda intentionally "threw" the trials in which he was called to the stand, winking at the defendants and alienating the jury; others say in the Paterno case there were problems among the jury itself, which, for reasons one can only guess, looked sympathetically upon the suave Paterno. Whatever the facts, Raymond Freda, as a government-protected witness, was sorely disappointing, leading to few major convictions and treating the matter as if it were a game. In the bargain, Basto argues, the prosecution unleashed "about the most dangerous criminal in the United States. With Freda, for the people they put away, which was hardly anybody, what they let go was ridiculous. With Festa they got so much mileage he was worth his weight in gold. Freda's a whole different bag of worms [from Festa]. Any field ya wanna get into. [Freda] was into everything. Dope. Counterfeit. Where ya gonna find a guy who robbed twenty-five banks? That's unheard of. Here's a guy who killed seven people—and maybe a few more they don't know about. You know what I mean? They let go of John Dillinger and put away Mickey Mouse."

Freda had the lives of a cat and the prowess of a cougar. There seemed no way for him to avoid a lifetime at a place such as Rahway— until he finagled his way into the deal. Up in the task force office with the detectives—who were understandably anxious to have him as a witness, since he knew about a long list of gangland slayings—Freda regaled them with the details of his night-deposit box, and told Paul Smith, an investigator on Donahue's squad, how the eyes of a shooting victim tended to roll back at the instant of death. The smaller-caliber bullets, Freda said, would ricochet around for a while in a target's brain.

Having testified in Newark, Freda was relocated to Houston, Texas, under the alias "Raymond Conti." Seeing that he had gained a free ride on the alias, law enforcement officials described him as a "triple agent," deceiving other gangsters at the same time he was deceiving the police. Freda! Though he arrived in Houston with only seventeen thousand dollars and the 1976 Monte Carlo he drove, within three years he owned real estate, a jewelry store, and a carpet-cleaning firm that specialized in bank maintenance. On his land he built a chain of massage parlors: Cuddles' Den, Gentleman's Spa-Hot Tub, the Foxy Lady. He was also suspected of operating a huge burglary ring, and whether or not that was true, there were new Cadillacs in the driveway of a beautiful brick house (with barred windows and doors) he built in a fashionable suburb. When fires broke out at competing massage parlors, and the owner of one of them was bound in a chair and shot point blank, not a few eyes turned toward Raymond Conti-Freda.

On April 2, 1980, Freda was convicted of ordering a Texas crew he had organized to burn down the Golden Stein, an expensive Houston eatery. They attempted this with another invention of his, a home-made time bomb consisting of toilet tissue, lacquer thinner, and a lighted cigarette, which, as it burned to its butt, would ignite a pack of matches and the solvent-drenched tissue. Agents of the Federal Alcohol, Tobacco, and Firearms Bureau caught these men in the act, however, and Freda, with eight felony convictions already behind him, was suspected of having two hitmen attempt to kill the key witness, a hairdresser named Peter Kalfas, just a week before the trial. But the assassins too were apprehended (as they rolled up to Kalfas's office in a car, armed with a revolver and a sawed-off shotgun), and Freda was sentenced by Judge I. D. McMaster to life imprisonment under the habitual-criminal statute.

At the sprawling state penitentiary near Lovelady, Texas, Freda managed permission to keep his patent-leather shoes instead of institutional footwear, but clearly he got caught in the wrong state. He received some favors earlier, too—using a phone to call his massage parlors while in the county jailhouse—but otherwise the Texans mean business. Fields of cotton surround the high-security prison and inmates have to work in them.

He is desperate to get out. He has his lawyers working every angle.

He is a caged, pacing cougar. "These fucking Texans are crazy," he says. "And hot? In August they fucking fry eggs on the sidewalk." All of it started with Jerry Festa. "He was my big downfall," he says.

Ray Freda is a frightening presence. His eyes—eerie, frozen, protruding—are not done justice in his mugshots. In matter-of-fact language he describes murder as "something that has to be done, and that's it, like going to work in the morning, or slapping your wife in the mouth when she needs it." Homicide is "part of surviving, the easiest thing in the world to get away with."

"I should've been the last guy Festa got," he complains. "I saved him from getting clipped once [during the Valvano dispute]." Festa is alive, he says, because the mob needs connections in the motor vehicle department near his hideout (to find his precise address) and must nurture a relationship with the local marshals there before they can make their final move. They do not know what his current alias is, or in which region of the country he is hiding. "Once he's out of Jersey, it ain't easy." But Freda is not pessimistic about the outcome, and disagrees heartily with Frankie Bear on the issue of revenge—though he too claims no personal hard feelings. "Sumbitch, everyone was mad at Bear for bringing him around. They'll kill Festa instantly, they will. The buttons want him, the captains want him. If they find him he's dead.

"But me, I'm not mad. Jerry's a nice guy. I hope he lives forever."

*   *

"If it has to happen I hope it's fast and furious, that he wouldn't even know what hit him," says Marie. "And not any taking him alive. Because then they would torture him as long as they could. I wouldn't want that to happen to anyone."

Jerry Festa is a partly broken man. He spends entire days on the worn, sunken sofa reliving events of the past. The sound of a car door invariably causes him to head for the shaded window and peek out. If he is in a chair across the room, watching the soap operas, he can still see through a split in the curtains and observe movements at quite a distance down the road. At fifty-four Jerry Festa still has his extraordinary eyesight.

He scarcely sleeps. He watches his fading, fuzzy television until three or four in the morning. Even when he appears to be asleep, breathing heavily, small sounds make his eyes flash open. Years of such fitful sleep have greatly darkened his raccoon's mask, the circles surrounding his eyes. He is a hypochondriac, but he continues to chain-smoke despite a touch of emphysema. He is prone to terrific swings of mood, confident one day, free enough to engage neighbors in conversation, then suddenly apprehensive. He no longer owns shiny boots or a closetful of silk shirts and leather jackets. He has his family near him but is abysmally lonely, reaching out for any new friends. He is obsessed with his past, proud to have been a part of the mob, discussing it all the time. He speaks contemptuously of the great majority of people he has ever met. Adverse events, minor or major, imagined or real, are inflated into major crises.

He is a friendly man, easy to speak with, difficult to pity. Like others of his lot, his central need is filling the void in his own self-esteem, and to this end he sought exposure in the media. He denies involvement in certain deeds that others say he had a hand in—such as a burglary in which a dog was shot—and since he has proven to be more truthful than his former colleagues, one more willingly accepts his side of the story. Whatever the case, he is not a hero. He says he knows this. He rides a gray, stumbling old mare—not a white horse. But he is a survivor. Before long he would manage a new television, another car. Then, just as suddenly, he is stone-broke again, unable to put food in the refrigerator.

But he is free when he could have spent the rest of his life incarcerated. He is alive when he could easily have been killed.

Though much too late to do any good, he has developed a stronger sense of guilt. He cries with a regularity that is surprising in a man whose appearance is so rough. Perhaps he is disgusted with himself. The household is in a state of perpetual tension, and much of it arises from his personality—forceful and self-possessed. "I know these guys," he says, referring to his mob partners. "I broke bread with them. I lived with them. The agents didn't. They know only what they're told. I know what I seen. Ain't no way they're gonna leave me live."

Certain images are lasting. He vividly recalls the junk yard owned by Black Bear in the Poconos, where he was told they burned bodies, and the pond where Basto stood. His wish is that he could find a way of shortening his legs so he wouldn't be such an undisguisable fugitive—and target. Along with the mounds of pepper he pours onto Marie's spaghetti, the pressures long ago caused him to have an ulcer operation in which a good portion of his stomach was extracted too. *Tell your fucking friend Festa he's too ugly to hide forever.* "The Bear's got the patience of a saint," he says. "He'll wait ten or fifteen years if he has to."

Contrary to popular lore, the henchmen of La Cosa Nostra are neither as organized nor as powerful as the law enforcement community. They are not omniscient, and they have not infiltrated every organ of society (except perhaps in the state of New Jersey). Nor do they regularly hold mass conclaves at which all their pertinent business is discussed. When the day comes—if ever it does—there will be no large conference of fifty criminals at which a *capo* takes out maps and charts and briefs them on how they will execute Chicken Delight. More likely a small faction or a single individual with a searing grudge will decide it is finally safe to tie up this loose end of business, and in this vein Festa worries the most about Quartuccio. Johnny is an emotional man who never forgets a personal slight, let alone the betrayal, by his closest friend, which led to a prison term. And he is sneaky. The Bear always told Jerry that Quartuccio was "the one you gotta watch," and now, in hiding, he remembers that advice. Several times he has heard unidentifiable noises in his yard and has become almost hysterical about them, blasting warning shots into the quiet air from the rifle kept under his couch.

*   *

Because of Johnny, it was a long time before Janet could make herself go out and get a job: she was afraid he would waylay her on the road. Finally she has begun work in a country store as a clerk at the register. In her middle twenties she has lost most of her youth and has no boy friends, goes to no parties. On the way home from work she carefully varies her routes, and watches her rear-view mirror constantly. Janet has been severely damaged by the tension of their existence; she is still unable to get relief from her headaches, and is constipated for weeks at a time. She talks very little and her only recreation is listening to rock records on a tape deck she recently purchased. Often she spends whole days alone in her room, thinking, staring. She hears everything around her. In the dead of night she will bolt out of bed at the sound of a car idling near the house they moved to just recently.

"My life is destroyed and it always will be." Janet says that straightforwardly, not in a mood of self-pity. A supreme cynic, she trusts hardly anyone she has met since the flight from Newark, and she resents memories of the mobsters her adopted father knew; they were "crude pigs." Watching for any sign of them, she memorizes the faces and names of everyone who comes into the store, looking outside to check their license plates if something about a customer is suspicious. Occasionally a local farmer, mechanic, or fisherman tries to start a conversation, but meeting anyone new makes her more anxious and brings on another headache. She wants nothing to do with the neighbors. "We can't afford to stay in the same place," she says. "People talk. They wonder." She is fanatically loyal to her stepfather.

Her dream of becoming a doctor or a medical technician has been shattered. A steady and reliable worker, she is convinced she will have to move from job to job for the rest of her life. She says her life will be clouded whether Jerry is killed or not: "Johnny will still try something out of self-satisfaction." She is the one who will back up her father if they come for him, "which I know they will." She has a gun in her tiny bedroom. It is not far from her Jordache jeans.

* *

Rose is not as afraid as her daughter. Her fear of death greatly diminished in the spring of 1979, when she was in the solarium of a hospital and a doctor said, "Rose, can I speak to you in your room?" Tests had come back. In her left lung was a cancerous tumor. They told her she had a choice of chemotherapy or having the lung removed surgically, a dangerous procedure but her best gamble, the doctor said. At first she just wanted to die and get it over with, but then she stared out the window as she had the night Janet was born, and she chastised herself for being a coward. If she died, the kids would be more alone. So the next day she chose the operation. Afterward she woke up in the intensive-care unit in critical condition, with tubes jammed up her nostrils and Janet trying to feed her. But it hurt too much to eat, and she drifted in and out of consciousness as her fever rose. "I was approaching a seizure," she recalls. "I must've passed out. I was in a long black thing, like the inside of a tornado, just black all over, and I saw a light and my [dead] stepsister was standing at the end of it with the most beautiful smile. It was a blinding light. I was looking—here I am looking to say hello to her and I heard like kind of a pop. I opened my eyes and saw the nurse trying to take my temperature. I heard her say, 'Her fever's broken.' " It was another hallucination, but one that made her think about her life and how it was finally time to fight. She made a personal vow that if she was allowed to live she would make sure her children "had a correct path in life" and that Allan and Joseph would somehow receive their First Holy Communion rites. During 1982, in a secret ceremony, the two boys were taken to a chapel after all the masses were over and were made bona fide members of the Catholic Church.

* *

A big boy at the age of thirteen, nearly six feet and a hundred and eighty pounds, Allan still reacts physically to the stresses. When he heard about his mother's tumor he pounded at the refrigerator, the bathroom wall, his pillow. School has become difficult for him. Once he wanted to be a doctor, lawyer, or an astronomer. Now, a professional football player. "I'll make good money and buy my folks a house we can stay at." His adolescence has brought with it a steep decline in grades (especially history and language arts) and he gets into a lot of fights. His heart comes up his throat when some kid slams a hallway locker.

Like the other children, Allan has learned what precautions they must take. If the phone rings, which it does infrequently, he makes sure the voice at the other end is familiar: one of the few agents who maintain contact with Jerry, or his mother's doctor. "Who's this?" he asks immediately, before acknowledging whether the caller has reached the correct number.

If the phone is answered and someone hangs up at the other end, that creates chaos in the household. The Festas have changed their unlisted number about ten times since they left Texas, each time after a suspicious wrong number. His father has a new first name now, too, so there would be a panic if someone called asking for "Jerry."

Allan, Sophia, and Alicia are also adept at watching the road for cars that slow down near their house or have out-of-town plates. About once a month they spot some vehicle they don't like, and they memorize the plate number. If a strange noise is heard in the yard, they all know to gather in the room furthest from the sound, and none of them are allowed to leave the house alone. Their departures and arrivals on schooldays are strictly noted. (Once Joseph went home from school with a classmate and panic swept his family.)

The scares, legitimate or not, are constant no matter where the Festas live. They have been terrified by a drunk who came to their door by mistake, by a door-to-door salesman, by a costumed adult chaperoning kids on Halloween. (Johnny might one day be behind a mask, they feel.) "You're always afraid the bubble's gonna burst," says Rose. "It's something you can't cope with. You know sooner or later you're gonna be brought back down. If you happen to meet a neighbor, you wonder, 'What would happen if they find out?' You don't want to get close to anyone. You know sooner or later you'll have to leave them and never be back. You feel different from them. Even if we had money"—they are currently on welfare and food stamps—"we couldn't be normal people. You see people buying things, or painting their house, planting shrubbery, and you don't wanna do that because you'll be leaving that too. You got to keep the windows closed even when it's summer out. And the porch light on. You don't know what to expect. You know the bubble's gonna burst."

Their last home was a case in point. Festa spotted someone at the airport who looked like Basto. The agents were called in, and the Festas planned to move again.

"It's always the same," says Allan of the nightmares such events provoke. "People are coming after my dad. The one I always see has a machine gun. I see flashlights in some woods and I see strangers in shadows. I feel scared. Makes me shake and sweat a lot. I go to my aunt because Mom's sick. I don't want to worry her. My aunt [Marie] tells me it's only a bad dream. We pray together, ask God to clear everything up. Sometimes I fall back to sleep. Sometimes I just lay there until the light comes."

With the girls it's a fear of going upstairs alone. Alicia and Sophia share a bed and give each other strength in the dark. If the mob arrives, they might try to make it out the window, or scurry up to the attic. "I think there's a good chance Dad's going to be killed," Sophia says, lowering her voice. Both she and her sister get spooky feelings in their bedroom: sudden chills, or hearing a sound like a rubber band snapping in the air. Alicia's tongue swells, and she feels as if someone is grabbing her.

The two girls remember their cross-country flights only in bits and pieces: the strange cars near the Baltimore motor lodge that caused yet more hysterics. Sophia and Alicia are both attractive, deeply loyal and affectionate, deeply sincere. They are not allowed to participate in most of the normal teenage fun—there are no weekends when they can hang out with their classmates at a pizza parlor, and they didn't see a movie for five years. Little events mean much to them. They look forward, for days, to a shopping trip, or being allowed to play basketball in the yard behind Allan's school. But for the most part they are restricted to the fields behind their home, where they make a game of running their dogs: the shepherd called Faith and an antsy young Doberman Pinscher.

The dogs are also Marie's recreation, of course. They stay near her in the small kitchen waiting for handouts from the hamburgers or soup she is cooking. They are big dogs, and she is always tripping over them. They encircle her at the table, fighting for her attention. She loves these animals; she takes them outside and watches them through the day. But she cannot help herself: There will never be another Pinkie.

And there are haunting money problems that may never go away. The springs are poking out of the couch Festa sleeps on; and their present house, a two-story structure with four bedrooms and a tiny dining area, needs painting and landscaping. Because they are in a rural part of the Atlantic shoreline (where maple trees are tapped for their syrup, and corn is grown), the land nearby turns marshy in the springtime and an occasional rat finds its way inside to gnaw noisily on the plaster. From odd jobs such as housecleaning or baby-sitting in the neighborhood, the kids have saved for small but significant improvements: blue-flowered paper for the kitchen walls, a radio, a new set of dishes. If the house is not as expensively furnished as Ridge Street was, Rose and Jerry are not as destitute as many others who are on public assistance. They have saved enough to get a stereo for the kids and to buy Joseph a ten-gallon fish tank. They celebrate birthdays well, and if the kids frown at the potato soup that is often served, on Thanksgiving they have pasta and turkey like any other Italian-American family. And Festa's luck can still get hot. One dreary time he took a few dollars Rose had stashed away and snuck out to hit a long shot at a track. He brought home enough to make their Christmas.

But at other times the bills mount to the point where they are penniless. On the very coldest day of 1982, at the other side of their luck, they ran out of heating oil and had to huddle in winter coats and blankets. A thin glaze of ice began to develop in Joseph's aquarium. At times like this, Festa, filled with anger, has threatened to "go back to the streets," pull off a score. But as far as anyone can tell, he has not done so, and after nine years of basically staying straight, the prospects are not farfetched that he will keep on doing so. Knowing his old friends are finishing up their prison terms has increased his fearfulness, and he wonders aloud what they might do to him. Hang him? Castrate him? Maybe they will be quick—as Marie so fondly hopes—and merely shoot him. But there are other times when Jerry acts as if nothing at all is wrong. Sometimes he is paranoid, sometimes remarkably lax. He has attended a few social functions in his vicinity, played poker, let slip a few hints of who he is. There is currently a trend toward making their existence more normal.

A key concern is that the mob may get to him by kidnaping one of his children. For this reason Janet drives them to and from school when she can, or he does. Joseph is too young to understand their "problem" and they would rather he did not know. But he is eleven now and has heard enough conversations to have his own nightmares: "I'm walking down a road and I'm little and it was real dark and then I don't know who they are but somebody—two people—and they grabbed me and threw me in a car." It is a country road, he says, in a voice that turns to sobs. And the men have "things over their heads, just like pantyhose." He has gotten to the root of the truth, but he has suffered far less than his brother and sisters. Certainly he is a long way from the psychological disturbances of Alicia, who has attempted suicide. She did that when her head "started getting high again" and every color seemed pale to her. She had a knife hidden under her bed for a while, and has thought about razors and pills.

Festa himself has considered ending it all, but Rose emphasizes the effect it would have on the kids. Marie has belittled the idea of suicide. ("What? After all we been through you're gonna politely leave like that?") As for Rose, her will to live is perhaps the strongest it has ever been. The hospital scans have shown no sign of the cancer spreading or recurring, and she says, "We can make it. We made it this far." Laughter sometimes enters the household but always there is something to bring up the past. In 1979, on the way to a clinic near Baltimore, on the left side of the Jones Falls Expressway, Rose and Jerry saw a faded green water tower with an advertisement—for a radio station?—that made them change their route. The letters facing them were "J-E-D."

*   *

There is a strong daily pattern in the hideout-home, and it begins like this: Marie rises with the two younger girls at five to give them breakfast (if they will eat it) and see them off to school. They might remain in bed if their aunt did not get up. They don't like school. Probably because it's the sixth school in as many years. They're tired of being the new kids on the block. Marie gives them yet another lecture about the importance of an education and complains that they are drinking Coke so early in the morning and smoking, besides. Hearing their exchange, Festa cracks open his eyes there on the living-room couch—he has had his couple of hours' sleep—and immediately reaches for a cigarette. The girls labor for a full thirty minutes over their long, thick hair, bending it all the way around their curler-brushes, holding it, flipping it; then they dab on some eye makeup. Janet comes down to take them to school, and they follow her reluctantly.

Joseph has awakened about now. He has fed his fish and is teasing Marie by crumpling up the food wrappers and making jump-shots toward the garbage pail, leaving his missed throws as a trail of litter. He leaves for a different school later in the morning, so he sits watching the early talk shows with his father and is soon joined by his older brother. Festa scolds Allan. The boy is slumped in a chair, trying to avoid getting ready for class. There is an absenteeism problem with him—he stays home "sick" a lot—and both of the past two years he has been in danger of failing. Finally the two boys are gone and Janet off to work or errands. Festa, in gray sweat pants, remains on his sofa, legs up, coughing hard. He watches the Phil Donahue Show and asks Marie to bring him a bowl of asparagus and onions. He has odd tastes in food these days.

The day holds only small events. As Marie moves swiftly about, making beds and picking up dirty laundry, Rose slowly, tiredly, descends the steps in her red robe. She takes a Librium, washing it down with coffee, and blankly watches television. Later she too will do some housework if she's not too fatigued. And despite her husband's admonitions that it is hazardous, she has taken to cleaning a neighbor's house once a week for the extra thirty dollars. She is no longer obsessed with jewelry, and not only because she can't afford it. "You become greedy," she philosophizes about her past. "Your morals turn around, snowball-like. You don't even realize it's happening." If nothing good is on television, her husband stares at the curving road waiting for the next car to pass. Normally there is a five-minute lapse between vehicles along the main road that connects to their less-traveled street. The cars are driven by farmers off to a small hamlet near the ocean or an occasional commuter on the way to a city more than an hour's drive away. Jerry can recognize the faces in the cars at an incredible distance, and by watching them every day—what time they pass, who they have as passengers—he has learned a good deal about the neighbors. "Mr. ———'s heading to the office," he says. "And he looks fucking pissed. I'll make book he lost another client." Gossip passes the time, and he also culls it from what the children hear at school, or a brief chat with a neighbor. "Look at the tires on ———'s car," he says suddenly. "Down to nothing. To the rims." Misery loves company: his own car needs a new front end.

As always, Alicia and Sophia, being only a grade apart (and their own best friends), come home from school together in mid-afternoon;

today they have bummed a ride with a neighbor. They make a few cracks about some of the kids at school, but their faces are drawn and tired. They head straight for Marie's lair, the kitchen, and plop their books on the table. Sophia rests her head on her texts and closes her eyes. Headaches again, always at this point in the day, and she does not feel like cleaning her room (as Marie insists) nor is she up to doing homework. She is often the optimistic one, but not when her head hurts. When that happens she says her life is "too screwed up" for any thought of the future, and says she will never get married because she would be too embarrassed, or afraid, to tell a boy friend about her family. She looks as if she could have any boy friend she wanted, but, like the rest of the family, she is outside society, and she feels inferior.

Dinner is at six. Marie has cooked it and she eats it in the kitchen with Sophia and Alicia, when they are in a mood for eating. The rest are in the dining room, which is too small to accommodate the whole family. Festa pours pepper all over his meat loaf and takes his plate back to the couch to watch the news. Janet arrives home from work and serves a plate for herself. She too will eat in the living room. She is in no mood to talk; her head is throbbing.

The children sit around the kitchen table for the remainder of the evening. They dabble at homework, talk excitedly about a fist fight at school or—in the case of the two girls—about somebody in class who has a "*good*-looking" new boy friend. Joseph sneaks behind Alicia and makes quite a joke about putting a matchbox on her fluffy, meticulously arranged hair without her noticing it. When she discovers it she jumps up and gives him a good whack on the arm. It stings. Her knuckles are heavy like her father's. But Joseph has not learned his lesson. He covers his mouth, giggling.

Music constantly blares from a black plastic cassette player on the table, which is battered from their horseplay. A chunk is missing from one corner. Allan is the disc jockey, and despite complaints from his sisters, who prefer Rick James, he always puts on the Beatles. Sometimes he taps the table in time with the songs, mouthing the words he knows by heart, or accompanies the songs, and does it well, on a guitar his parents recently bought him. As often as not the album he has on is "Abbey Road." At the very end of the second side is a lilting dirge that begins with the words, "Once there was a way / to get back home . . ." But he prefers the faster song earlier on the same side:

"She Came in Through the Bathroom Window." He turns the volume higher. His dad's booming voice comes from the living room. "Turn that down or I'm gonna whack ya."

The children savor visits from anyone new who is allowed in the house. It is an event for them, another of the little and few-and-far-between things they look forward to. Joseph is full of energy and yanks on the arms of a visitor he knows is allowed to take them for car rides. "C'mon, man," he keeps saying. "You promised we could go into town and get them clams." Finally, one by one, they file up to bed according to what hour in the morning each has to rise. (If it's a weekend night they play Monopoly past midnight. They all aim for the major realty: Park Place and Boardwalk.)

Days such as these are repeated with minor variations for months on end. The Festas were permanently terminated from the WPP in 1979—after Festa's testimony was complete—and he is fanatically preoccupied with how curtly they were treated. "The Bear coulda got me documents overnight better than what it takes the government forever to do," he charges, complaining about the long periods his family has gone without a full identity. "I don't legally exist. Who am I? And who buries me?"

In May of 1979 he filed an *in absentia* lawsuit against the government, but it was dismissed before it came to trial. Speaking about the marshals brings out the violence in him, and there are two holes in the living-room wall attesting that age has not robbed his fists of their strength. The anger has also spurred him, on two occasions, to be filmed at clandestine locations (wearing a ghoulish black hood) by television networks investigating the WPP. However dangerous this may be (his children's names have to be disguised for journalists, to prevent neighbors from knowing), he basks in the limelight (missing the action of his former years), and he maintains contact whenever possible with those who are still loyal.

He is thankful he met the law enforcement people he did. Wilson saved his life, Donahue stayed in touch, and Judge Fusco: "Your Honor," he wrote to Fusco in 1976, "I am writing this letter to you for I feel I just have to let you know what an honor it was and will always be to know that there are men like you who cannot be bought or intimidated by the people I was involved with. In a way, Your Honor, you have placed your life on the line the same as I have. There were times when I appeared at trials and some of the lawyers I went against

I had known from before. At first this ate away at me to see them making my life an open dirty book. But now I pity them for they do not own their own life. They are obligated to these people for the rest of their lives just as I was. I know Your Honor that in your own mind you know what they are up to but your hands are tied the same as mine. My whole outlook on life has changed. I only pray it is not too late. I know the power of organized crime. I know they have me marked to die."

Having been raised in that Newark neighborhood, Falcone, now the prosecutor of Passaic County, and another person Festa keeps in contact with, says, "It's a matter of time before the mob gets to him." Wilson, Donahue, and Falcone hear his problems, and so does a former federal agent who stops by to check on the household but who cannot be named here.

Over and over again, in calls to congressional investigators, agents, attorneys, and journalists, he has pounded out his complaints against the program, viewing the marshals now as more of an enemy than the mobsters. In his lawsuit, filed in the United States Court of Claims, he alleged that the government reneged on its oral promise to find "a new business opportunity . . . identification and redocumentation in support of all of the aforegoing, medical care, tax free subsistence payments pending the relocation of his family, as well as counseling to assist the family in its transition toward a new identity." He asked for $4.5 million in damages, claiming he was "terminated without cause or justification and in breach of all its previously stated promises and assurances" before his family was permanently settled (he believes they still are not) and given yet another new name. Though the family does indeed have a new identity of sorts, the absence of birth certificates has, for example, prevented the girls from getting drivers' licenses.

Festa's case was thrown out of court when a judge ruled that it was not in the court's jurisdiction and cited a precedent established by another lawsuit against the WPP in which it was decided that "nowhere does a statute or regulation expressly or by implication establish a right that plaintiffs be paid anything." Instead, said the previous ruling, "benefits to be afforded those who are permitted to participate [in the WPP] are a completely discretionary function . . ." Officials of the WPP have asserted that Festa belongs to a small minority of disgruntled witnesses, was uncooperative with the marshals, and breached his own security—though they also claim he is no longer in danger. In Washington the WPP spokesman, William Dempsey, argues that while there were problems early in the program's existence, these have been ironed out, for the most part. He says there are more people working at job placement and redocumentation, and more inspectors who are trained to specialize in witness security. He claims that there are fewer complaints from witnesses against a program that has been widely described as the most important tool in history against organized crime.

Rose tries not to dwell on the past, but sometimes she can't help it. She still wonders about the Ridge Street house (it is now owned by an immigrant Italian couple named Collorafi) and about their food shop (now a bodega). She worried for years about whether her real mother was still alive in the asylum before being told that she had died of cancer at the Laurel Hill Nursing Home in 1978. She recently brought herself to ask where Jed is buried: The unmarked, overgrown grave is at the bottom of a knoll at the Archibald Protestant Cemetery, near Scranton.

"Hash, rehash, and hash again," Marie complains. "Hey, we gotta start living for the future." The tedium has gotten to her. There are no sidewalks, no place she can walk here, no bagels like they had on Broad Street, no magazine racks. Even if the environment is far better than Newark, the local accent here irks her too, and she is filled with cynical humor. She can't get over how "bar" is "bah," "tour" is "tur." Only after months of acquaintance does she show her deeper feelings to a visitor, and sobbing—sour, choking sobbing—is the result. Though such grief pours most freely when she reminisces about Pinkie, her other greatest sorrows are the vanished religious articles and the pension she lost. She feels worse over a gold-framed picture of Christ crucified which she had hanging over the Ridge Street fireplace (it had taken *years* to save for that frame) and her twenty-one-inch statue of the infant Jesus. She went everywhere to find a crown to fit the Infant and several outfits of clothes (which some nuns finally made for her), and she says vengefully, "Whoever has my Infant will never, never have any luck."

Then she adds quickly, "Hey, I'm sorry, but I can't help it. This all ruined me. It made me a different person. I was developing a hatred toward everyone. I nearly lost my faith. I did. But I found a prayer that helped. I memorized it. Just a short little prayer, how to heal the hurt—not to be bitter. I don't know how we'll survive this. I don't know how we *have* survived, but I have to say it's prayer . . . Nobody knows. Only I know. I know. I worked for everything, there was nothing illegal I had. But me, I never spoke up. I fell right into it, and, hey, it was wrong. And I'll never get over it. Never. If my mother was alive, she would never have let this happen to me, would never have seen this. She would have taken me home. She was stronger. Now I can't even feel comfortable going back to Scranton. She must be rolling in her grave . . . My friends won't know when I die. What—am I supposed to visit them? In Jersey? Hey, everything was serene when I first moved to Newark, and believe me when I tell you I'm not the same person."

Still, she loves Jerry. In spite of all he has done, he was there wrapping his arms around her when she had hardly anyone else in the world to love, and he is affectionate to her. They're blood. She does not believe Basto when Frank says he will not hurt her cousin, and she figures Jerry's chances to be "about fifty-fifty." "Just please God make it fast," she repeats. Then she says again, almost in a whisper, "And please don't let any of the kids be in the way."

* *

Marie is staring out a side window—why she doesn't know. She makes a joke about it: it's as if she is waiting for a friend to arrive. But of course no one comes. Outside it is overcast, as it often is here in a northeastern rain belt. It is the dead of August; the sun is not as hot as in Texas, but the humidity does compare with Newark's. As the afternoon wears on, a cool breeze from Canada starts to relieve the mugginess. Six miles down the road, however, a haze still hangs over the open ocean, and the swelling waves pound against the jagged shore.

AFTERWORD

This book is based in large part on interviews and consultations with more than a hundred people in addition to members of the Festa family, with whom I spent four months. These talks were with law enforcement officers, other criminals, businessmen, lawyers, judges, clerks, prison inmates, and bystanders of all sorts. I spent many days at the Essex County Prosecutor's Office in the company of Special Investigator Ronald Donahue, one of the most generous men I have ever known. Prosecutor Joseph Falcone of Passaic County was also extremely patient and kind, as were members of the New Jersey State Commission of Investigation, the New Jersey State Police, and the Federal Bureau of Investigation. My good friend from Harrisburg— who will see himself identified below—was the spark who set this effort in motion.

Additional information was culled from court records, confidential memoranda, criminal-history sheets, transcripts of wiretaps and room bugs, private notes, diaries, newspaper articles, medical records, intelligence dossiers, and other historical records. Many interviews were conducted by phone or mail as a matter of prudence. The conversations repeated in this book are as they were remembered by one or more participants who were asked specifically to recreate such dialogue to the best of their ability. Where there were discrepancies in details, I used my own judgment on which to choose. Most of the key scenes—including the murder at Tardosky's pond—are described on the basis of my visits to the actual locales. At times this involved undercover rides with detectives, reconnaissance of mob hangouts, living in Pennsylvania in an apartment owned by an organized-crime figure, and a car trip with an active criminal reputed to be a hitman who worked with Donnerstag.

I owe thanks to: FBI agents Michael Wilson, Barry O'Neill, and John Thurston; FBI Director William Webster and his assistants Roger S. Young and Ernest Porter, for efficiently organizing interviews; Cyril Jordan and John Davies of the SCI; Robert Buccino of the New Jersey State Police; Essex Prosecutor George Schneider and his assistants Glenn Goldberg and John Matthews; Essex detectives Paul Smith, Joe Martino, and Mike Reheis, and their chief, Charles Acocella; Mary O'Brien, who keeps their paperwork in order; Judge Ralph Fusco; Judge Richard Conaboy; Judge Arthur Dalessandro; and, from the Pennsylvania patrol, Captain James Regan, Captain Nicholas Kordilla, Albert Paul, Eugene Varzaly, Homer Jones, Russell Thomas, Mike Chaplin, and John Noel. Others who have my appreciation include Dick Gregorie, Mike Steiber, Jack Farley, Tony Rosamilia, Mike D'Alessio, Mike Filo, John Partington, Paul Mazzoni, Ernest Preate, Joseph Delaney, Ralph Salerno, William Walsh (in Scranton) and William Walsh (in Newark), Robert Delaney, Roy Beene, William Christensen, William Sweeny, Todd O'Malley, Jim Bradley, Jack Liddy, Joseph Lordi, Michael Polizzi, Lee Mecka, and some other agents (from the FBI, the Secret Service, and the Pennsylvania State Police) whom I do not here identify.

I was greatly assisted in the Pennsylvania aspect of research by William Gallagher, who drove thousands of miles with me; Donna Wood, who capably conducted some of the interviews; and Steve Craig. For logistical support during the research I thank WNEP-TV of the Scranton–Wilkes-Barre area; Kevin McLaughlin; Natalie Pinzotti; Vee Donahue; and those four friends of mine whom I will call "BR," "Big Red," "Guido," and "Agent S." I also owe a great debt of gratitude to J. R. Freeman (who helped with the arrangement of this work), Donald Warsaw, Rick Nelson, and Bruce Laughlin. Also: Eugene Telep, Robert Tardosky, the Edwards family, the Collorafis, Sue Wilson, Donald McNeil, and Suzanne Daley.

Much vital information was gleaned from those who will know themselves as "The Three Ds"; "Del" and "G"; "Babe"; "The Three

Bakers"; "Raymond Conti"; "John D"; "Rudy"; "Hugo"; "Hong's Chum"; "RM"; "SM"; "A"; "Natalie"; and "Mister C." Aside from shielding the names of a few non-criminals, I have also slightly fudged several minor details pertaining to locations.

Background material was provided by the Herbert Lehman Library at Columbia University; the Newark Historical Society; the Newark Public Library; the New York Public Library; and the Lackawanna County Public Library. I thank the patient (and even impatient) clerks at Luzerne County Courthouse; Lackawanna County's records room; the Federal Archives in Bayonne, New Jersey; the state law library in Trenton (and the federal records room in the same city); the Pennsylvania Crime Commission; WDAU-TV in Scranton; the *Star-Ledger* of Newark; the *Abington Journal;* the *Scranton Times;* and the *New York Times*. Also helpful were the following books: *To Drop a Dime* by Paul Hoffman and Ira Pecznick, *Brothers in Blood,* by David Leon Chandler, and *My Life in the Mafia,* by Thomas Renner and Vinnie Teresa. I am also grateful to my friend "RC" for allowing me to use his unpublished memoirs. Former Deputy Attorney General Ed Stier gave me valuable consultation.

And I thank those friends of mine who listened to me in times of anxiety and jubilation.

I might add that there were a number of touching personal moments during the writing of this book: explaining to Festa's children by his first marriage how their father (whom they have not seen in nine years) is living now; telling Festa he now has a grandchild; explaining to his youngest son what had happened to the family (he had never been formally told); and telling Rose of her mother's death. I was also able to recover for them an album of family photographs. I hope the future bodes well for the children, who have become dear to me. I hope to see them again.

ABOUT THE AUTHOR

Michael Brown, thirty-one, is a freelance writer whose work has appeared in many newspapers and national publications, including the *Atlantic Monthly*, the *New York Times Magazine*, *Saturday Review*, *New York*, *New West*, *Penthouse*, and *Reader's Digest*. He is the author of *Laying Waste: The Poisoning of America by Toxic Chemicals*.